54.50

60B

I0850259

Dealing with inequality

The question of 'equality' between the sexes has been of long-standing interest among anthropologists, yet remains intransigent. This volume sets out not to dispose of the question, but rather to examine how to debate it. It recognises that inequality as a theoretical and practical concern is rooted in Western ideas and concepts, but also that there are palpable differences in power relations existing between men and women in non-Western societies, that are otherwise, in world terms 'egalitarian', and that these need to be accounted for.

The volume comprises ten essays by anthropologists who discuss the nature of social inequality between the sexes in societies they know through first-hand fieldwork, mostly, though not exclusively, in Melanesia. This regional focus gives an important coherence to the volume, and highlights the different analytical strategies that the contributors employ for accounting for gender inequality. Running through the essays is a commentary on the cultural bias of the observer, and the extent to which this influences Westerners' judgements about equality and inequality among non-Western peoples. By exploring indigenous concepts of 'agency', the contributors challenge the way in which Western observers commonly identify individual and collective action, and the power people claim for themselves, and, surprisingly, show that inequality is not reducible to relations of domination and subordination.

The volume as a whole will be provocative reading for anthropologists concerned with gender studies and the Pacific, and will be an invaluable resource for anyone who would turn to anthropology for cross-cultural insight into gender relations.

Dealing with inequality
Analysing gender relations in Melanesia and beyond

Essays by members of the 1983/1984 Anthropological
Research Group at the Research School of
Pacific Studies, The Australian National University

EDITED BY MARILYN STRATHERN

Professor of Social Anthropology
University of Manchester

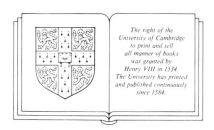

The right of the
University of Cambridge
to print and sell
all manner of books
was granted by
Henry VIII in 1534.
The University has printed
and published continuously
since 1584.

Cambridge University Press

Cambridge
New York   New Rochelle   Melbourne   Sydney

Published by the Press Syndicate of the University of Cambridge
The Pitt Building, Trumpington Street, Cambridge, CB2 1RP
32 East 57th Street, New York, NY 10022, USA
10 Stamford Road, Oakleigh, Melbourne 3166, Australia

First published 1987

Printed in Great Britain by Bath Press, Bath, Avon.

British Library cataloguing in publication data

Dealing with inequality : analysing gender relations in Melanesia and beyond.
1. Women-Melanesia-Social conditions
I. Australian National University.
Anthropological Research Group
II. Strathern, Marilyn
305.4'2'0993   GN668

Library of Congress cataloguing in publication data

Dealing with inequality
Bibliography: p.
Includes index
1. Ethnology – Melanesia. 2. Sex role – Melanesia.
3. Equality – Melanesia. 4. Melanesians – Social life and customs. I. Strathern,
Marilyn. II. Australian National University. Anthropological Research Group.
GN668.D42   1987   305'.0993   86-32737

ISBN 0 521 33378 4 hard covers
ISBN 0 521 33652 X paperback

Contents

Notes on contributors

DIANE BELL, Professor, Australian Studies, Deakin University, Victoria, 3216, Australia. Diane Bell began her working life as a teacher. After the birth of her two children, she returned to study, completing a BA at Monash University and a PhD at The Australian National University. She has undertaken extensive research and consultancy work in the areas of Aboriginal land rights, law reform and resource management. The changing role of Aboriginal women in central and northern Australia is the subject of *Daughters of the Dreaming* (1983). She is also co-editor of *Religion in Aboriginal Australia* (1984) and co-author of *Law: the Old and the New* (1980).

ANN CHOWNING, Professor of Anthropology, Victoria University of Wellington, Private Bag, Wellington, New Zealand. A graduate of Bryn Mawr College, she took her MA and PhD at the University of Pennsylvania. She held a Senior Research Fellowship at The Australian National University, and has taught at Bryn Mawr College, Barnard College (Columbia University) and the University of Papua New Guinea. Ann Chowning has been carrying out long-term research in Papua New Guinea since 1954, working in four different societies. Her publications include *An Introduction to the Peoples and Cultures of Melanesia* (1973, 1977).

LESLIE DEVEREAUX, Lecturer, Department of Prehistory and Anthropology, Faculty of Arts, The Australian National University, G.P.O. Box 4, Canberra, ACT, 2601 Australia. Leslie Devereaux holds degrees in both Anthropology and Sociology from Harvard University. Research over fifteen years has spanned a study of women's lives in Zinacantan, Mexico, and an ethnographic history of the Hopevale Aboriginal community (North Queensland). *The Women of Zinacantan* (in preparation) will be a monograph on the labour of femininity in a changing Maya world.

FREDERICK ERRINGTON, Associate Professor of Anthropology, Keene State College, New Hampshire, 03431, USA. Recent fieldwork among the Chambri adds to that on Karavar (Duke of York Islands, Papua New Guinea), as well as Minangkabau (West Sumatra) and Rock Creek (Montana). His BA is from Wesleyan University; PhD from Cornell University. *Karavar: Masks and Power in a Melanesian Ritual* was published in 1974; *Manners and Meaning in West Sumatra* in 1984; and *Cultural Alternatives and a Feminist Anthropology: An Analysis of Culturally Constructed Gender Interests in Papua New Guinea* (with Deborah Gewertz) in 1987.

DEBORAH GEWERTZ, Associate Professor, Amherst College, Massachusetts, 01002, USA. Deborah Gewertz's first degrees were in English Literature at Queens College, City University of New York and at Princeton University, her PhD in Anthropology from The Graduate School of City University. Author of numerous articles about the Chambri and of *Sepik River Societies: A Historical Ethnography of the Chambri and their Neighbors* (1983), her most recent work is *Cultural Alternatives and a Feminist Anthropology: An Analysis of Culturally Constructed Gender Interests in Papua New Guinea* in 1987, co-authored with Frederick Errington, which they began at The Australian National University.

JANET HOSKINS, Assistant Professor of Anthropology, University of Southern California, University Park, Los Angeles, California 90089, USA. Educated at the University of Paris, Pomona College, Claremont, California and the University of Lund, Sweden, Janet took her MA and PhD at Harvard University. Two and a half years of fieldwork in Sumba, Eastern Indonesia provided the materials for her dissertation and a monograph on spirit worship and feasting (currently in preparation).

ROGER M. KEESING, Professor of Anthropology, Research School of Pacific Studies, The Australian National University, G.P.O. Box 4, Canberra, ACT, 2601, Australia. Roger Keesing began work on Malaita in 1962, and his extensive publications on the Solomon Islands include *'Elota's Story: The Life and Times of a Kwaio Big Man* (1978), *Kwaio Religion: The Living and the Dead in a Solomon Island Society* (1982) and (co-authored) *Lightning Meets the West Wind: The Malaita Massacre* (1980), as well as a Kwaio dictionary. He has since embarked on fieldwork in North India. Before becoming head of the Department of Anthropology in Canberra, he taught at the University of California, Santa Cruz.

MARTHA MACINTYRE, Lecturer in Social Anthropology, La Trobe University, Bundoora, Victoria, 3083 Australia. Compiling a bibliography on *The Kula* (1983) inducted Martha Macintyre into the ethnography of the Massim area, Papua New Guinea. A teacher and a historian before she turned to anthropology, she was educated at the Universities of Melbourne and Cambridge, and received her PhD from The Australian National University. She has also held a research post at Monash University.

JILL NASH, Professor of Anthropology, State University College of New York at Buffalo, 1300 Elmwood Avenue, Buffalo, NY 14222, USA. Jill Nash took her PhD from Harvard University. She maintains a dual interest in problems of matrilineal organisation and social change, as reflected in the title of her monograph on the Nagovisi of South Bougainville, *Matriliny and Modernisation* (1974).

MARILYN STRATHERN, Professor of Social Anthropology, Manchester University, Brunswick Street, Manchester, M13 9PL, England. She was formerly a Research Fellow with the New Guinea Research Unit of The Australian National University; a Fellow of Girton College, Cambridge, where she obtained her MA and PhD, and then Fellow of Trinity College. Publications on the Papua New Guinea Highlands include New Guinea Research Bulletins on legal change (1972) and migration (1975), *Women in Between* (1972); and the co-authored *Self-Decoration in Mount Hagen* (1971), co-edited *Nature, Culture and Gender* (1980). Her year at The Australian National University provided the basis for a more general work, *The Gender of the Gift* (in press).

JAMES F. WEINER, Lecturer, Department of Prehistory and Anthropology, Faculty of Arts, The Australian National University, G.P.O. Box 4, Canberra, ACT, 2601, Australia. Educated at Northwestern and Chicago Universities, James Weiner completed his PhD at The Australian National University on fieldwork in the Southern Highlands of Papua New Guinea. His monograph, *The Heart of the Pearl-Shell: The Mythological Dimension of Foi Sociality*, is in press.

MICHAEL W. YOUNG, Senior Fellow in Anthropology, Research School of Pacific Studies, The Australian National University, G.P.O. Box 4, ACT,

2601, Australia. Michael Young's account of ceremonial exchange on Goodenough Island in the Massim, *Fighting with Food* (1971), has been followed by an interpretation of mythical and biographical narrative, *Magicians of Manumanua: Living Myth in Kalauna* (1983). He came to The Australian National University from London and Cambridge (where he taught) and has worked in Indonesia as well as Melanesia.

Editor's preface

Anthropologists, who place so much value on long periods of fieldwork, are rarely able to enjoy lengthy contact with colleagues from nearby field areas. The Research School of Pacific Studies at The Australian National University provided just such an opportunity over the two years 1983-1984.

'Gender Relations in the Southwestern Pacific: Ideology, Politics, and Production' was the title of a Research Group organised by Roger Keesing, Marie Reay and Michael Young in the School's Department of Anthropology. It attracted participants with fieldwork experience of Aboriginal Australia, Indonesia and Melanesia, though one of the contributors (Devereaux) to this volume has chosen to present comparisons drawn from fieldwork she had also undertaken elsewhere. Throughout the two years Melanesianists were in the majority, and Melanesian preoccupations dominate these essays. The preoccupations were perhaps saved from becoming obsessions by the salutary and valuable presence of the non-Melanesianists.

Theoretical interests among the Group's members certainly cross-cut their regional specialisms, as is reflected in the organisation of this collection. Other volumes arising from the Group's activities are in the process of preparation: Margaret Jolly and Martha Macintyre are editing the proceedings of a conference on Christianity, Colonialism and Transformations of Family and Household in the South Pacific held in 1983, at the end of the Group's first year, and Deborah Gewertz those of a conference at the end of the second year on Myths of Matriarchy. Individual members have also been productive on their own account. I speak for us all in collective acknowledgement of the generosity with which The Australian National University has made this work possible. The present book is not itself, however, a collective undertaking in the accepted sense of the term. On the contrary, as the Introduction makes clear, we have endeavoured to preserve the differences between us as well as our common ground.

Several of the Group enjoyed a year or more of contact with their colleagues; others came for shorter periods of two to six months. Overlapping participation, as well as overlapping interests, has meant that not all the members are represented here even though they contributed substantially through debate and criticism: they include Michael Allen, Margaret Jolly, Mervyn Meggitt, Douglas Lewis, Kerry James and Nicholas Modjeska. In addition to her general contributions, Marie Reay commented helpfully on a number of the chapters. We would also thank Terence Hays for his participation while these chapters were in their final stages, and for the critical scrutiny he gave them.

The Group has profited from the congenial company of other members of the Department of Anthropology (R.S.Pac.S.) and its sister department in the Department of Prehistory and Anthropology in the Faculties. Among those who participated in the discussions which led to essays presented here were Gregory Acciaioli, Patsy Asch, Shirley Campbell, Nerida Cook, Christine Helliwell, Simon Harrison, Robin Hide, Maureen Mackenzie, Caroline Ifeka, Cecilia Ng, Kalpana Ram and Nicholas Thomas, and from outside Anthropology, Suzanne Dixon and Evelyn Hogan. Several visitors gave us the benefit of seminars and working papers. In connection with the specific themes of these chapters, mention should be made of Amy Burce, Gillian Gillison, Rena Lederman, Diane Losche and Jean-Marc Philibert.

The support, skill and patience of Ann Buller, Helen Collins, Ita Pead, Judith Wilson and Ria van de Zandt are tremendously appreciated. The map was prepared by the Cartography Department in the Research School of Pacific Studies.

*   *   *

There is often an imbalance in a work of this kind between the scrupulous naming of those who have helped in its production and all those who were in fact the cause of it. I mean here the people whose lives and societies we have taken the liberty of describing. The imbalance reflects of course the quite different orders of magnitude involved. All of us are conscious of a considerable debt to our various hosts. But it is not to be discharged through an easy word of thanks. The gratitude I record here can do no more than simply acknowledge the fact of debt itself.

*   *   *

The question of 'equality' between the sexes has fuelled attention to gender issues within anthropology since the early 1970s. It remains intransigent. Indeed, because the debate over equality and inequality speaks so closely to concerns of our own in the 'Western' world, the question is never disposed of, and we do not propose to dispose of it here. Rather we propose something both novel and realistic: to take the debate as a debate, and thus locate its inspiration in specific concerns without thereby performing a vanishing trick. We may deal with equality as a Western concept; that still leaves us having to deal with the nature of the palpable differences in power relations between the sexes for non-Western societies.

The contributors enquire into how effective social action is conceived and implemented, how men and women differ or compare in their effect on others, how we may regard them as significant social agents. In this region as a whole, such considerations lead into wealth transactions, ritual and cult participation, and control over speech making. That these are societies whose polities are, in world terms, 'egalitarian' gives the analysis of agency a particular interest.

MARILYN STRATHERN
Canberra, August 1984
Manchester, March 1986

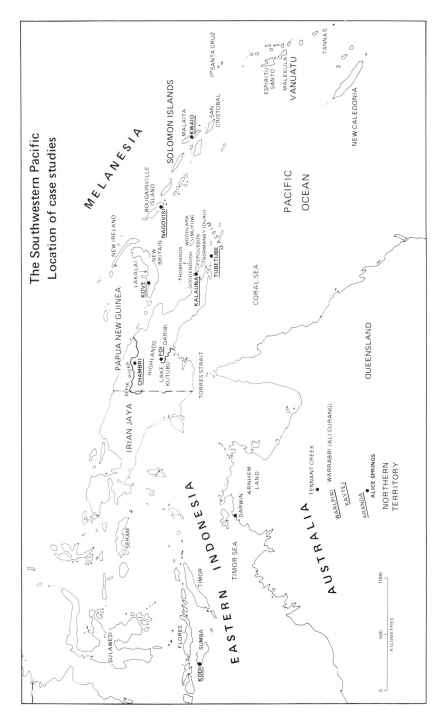

The Southwestern Pacific
Location of case studies

Introduction

MARILYN STRATHERN

Whether phrased as an interest in sex roles (Schlegel 1977; Sanday 1981), gender constructs (Ortner and Whitehead 1981) or feminist anthropology (Rapp 1979; Atkinson 1982), the question of inequality has dominated recent anthropological approaches to the study of male–female relations. It has dominated by dividing. Time and again writers recreate a split, as for instance between

> those that consider inequality to be conditioned by relations of production or distribution that arise historically...and those that trace it ultimately to fundamental biological differences between the sexes, and thereby are universal. (Schlegel 1977:10)

Universal inequality is not always related to biological causes; it is also possible to talk of cultural or social universals (Ortner 1974; Rosaldo 1974;1980a). The split thus appears to be generally between evolutionists and universalists (Bell 1983:245). We have here a debate, then, in which explicit positions are taken in relation to inequalities between the sexes. The significant issue becomes whether such inequalities 'exist' everywhere. Anthropology is drawn into this project for its cross-cultural expertise.

By way of example one may cite Schlegel's comparative approach to a theory of sexual stratification. She differentiates various dimensions of stratification (rewards, prestige and power) in order to assess both the relative status of the sexes within a given society, and the variables which determine that relative sexual status – 'the factors that shape equality or inequality' (1977:17). Although she concludes that explanations must be directed to the problems which arise for each society 'in terms of the forces to which it is responsive' (1977:356), Schlegel's cross-cultural project is echoed in Sanday's exploration of why cultures select different styles of interaction between the sexes 'Why is there sexual symmetry in some instances and asymmetry in others?' (1981:4). Male dominance, Sanday asserts, is not universal. Rather,

male dominance and female power are consequences of the way in which peoples come to terms with their historical and natural environments ... Power is accorded to whichever sex is thought to embody or to be in touch with the forces upon which people depend for their perceived needs. Conceiving power in this way, one can say that in some societies women have more power, or men have more, or both sexes have an approximately equal amount. (1981:11)

Sanday's models for measuring female power and male dominance allow her to adjudicate in particular instances about the equal or unequal possession of power by one or other sex.

The present volume makes a contribution to this debate from another vantage point. It is non-adjudicatory in character, non-exclusive in method. Rather than foreshadowing a conclusion about the prevalence of sexual inequality (for instance 'universalist' or not) or following dominant theoretical suppositions (whether or not it espouses 'a cultural- ist' approach), it draws attention to problems in anthropological prac- tice. To regard ourselves as dealing with inequality is to make an explicit stand in relation to the analytical activity which here defines us: how we make known to ourselves that inequalities exist.

Dealing with inequality

It is helpful to the construction of such a vantage point that the cases it presents are drawn from a single region – the islands of the Southwestern Pacific – though we have taken advantage of setting off this material against two studies which lie culturally beyond them. Most chapters deal with societies from Melanesia. These, and the one eastern Indonesian society, share many cultural features, and some speak related languages. The peoples of this region are characterisable as 'egalitarian' in world terms: horticulturalists, whose local organisations are small scale, and whose cultural efflorescence is to be found in institutions based on wealth exchanges and life cycle events. Big men and institutionalised ranking flourish to a lesser or greater degree, but nowhere is property ownership in land or the alienability of labour a systematic basis for social discrimination between men.

Yet egalitarianism stops short of relations between men and women. Sexual inequality strikes the outside observer; Leacock, for instance, argues that male dominance emerges in parts of this area (specifically the New Guinea Highlands) as a consequence of men's competition with women for control of what women produce (1981:294). Much of the observed asymmetry concerns overt differentials in the distribution of rewards and prestige to men and women, in their participation in public ceremonial, and in their effectiveness as managers of events. And it is no new observation to note that where inequalities are structured between men, it is most dramatically through their relations with or via women (Forge 1972; Rubin 1975; and see Chowning 1977:57). 'Sexual antagonism' (as between spouses) has been an organising metaphor for gender studies in large areas of Papua New Guinea (e.g. Herdt and Poole 1982); while for the Pacific in general adjudications have been made about the degree of 'complementarity' between the sexes in sibling relations (e.g. Marshall 1983).

By contrast with the Polynesian systems reviewed by Ortner (1981) or central Indonesian societies (for one pertinent discussion, see Millar 1983), hierarchical relations are most visibly constituted on the basis of gender itself.[1] Thus asymmetries appear to turn on unequal relations created by kin ties reckoned through women, or on the unequal allocation of power to the sexes, or most dramatically on the necessity for one sex to withdraw from the other and elaborate its own internal distinctions in exclusive cult practice. In other words, inequalities between men and women seem to be 'about' themselves. Gender symbolism turns in on itself: it appears to organise relations between the sexes, and it appears that these relations comprise the principal locus of social inequality.

Devereaux's chapter on Mexico underscores the interest of the Pacific vantage point. The very different egalitarianism of Zinacanteco ideology is contextualised by a particular ethnic position. The manner in which members of this Mayan community categorise men's and women's behaviour, as a matter of manifested cultural form, speaks to ethnicity as much as it does to gender. Internal equality is set against what Devereaux calls the pressures of external economic and political hegemony. Significantly, such inequality as exists within the community also turns on differential access to economic and political resources.

For the Pacific systems reported upon here, however, what happens to the sexes cannot be taken as a reflection of other orders of inequality. The symbolised relations between them do not simply 'represent' or 'express' the colonial encounter, or class struggle or ethnic stratification. Relations between men and women themselves appear as both chief cause and chief result of inequality. A similar conflation is the starting point for Collier and Rosaldo's (1981) examination of simple societies. They are concerned largely with the same kind of context as Bell's (Chapter 4): systems based on hunting and gathering where relationships are organised through interpersonal claims to services. The Melanesianists in this volume, on the other hand, are dealing with systems where wealth items move between persons and stand for the claims which link them. Relationships become mediated through such transactions. Indeed, the emphasis which Melanesian societies put on wealth exchange emerges as their single most distinctive feature. This is crucial to several of the analyses which follow. Men's and women's differential participation in public wealth transactions is examined as a principal locus of the difference between them.

It is clear that if the major organisational divide in these societies concerns that between the sexes themselves, the manner in which we might explain this phenomenon becomes highly circumscribed. We certainly cannot excise discrete variables nor extract explanatory principles out of its constituent parts, out of the mode of descent organisation, cult activity or beliefs about the respective powers of the sexes (cf. Lederman 1983), for these are elements of the phenomenon to be explained.

Normal social science explanations often function ecologically, that is, relate disparate data such that one grounds or contextualises the other, as Sanday does in referring sex segregation to societal or environmental stress. Establishing the irreducibility of certain elements in order that others may be marshalled as 'variables' is one of the most important projects of cross-cultural analysis. Agreed-upon definitions have to be sustained (cf. Southwold 1978), insofar as these irreducible elements – measures of power and domination, for instance – are used as bridges which the anthropological exercise throws across societies. The elements considered here pose a special problem, therefore. If inequalities appear to be located significantly in relations between the sexes, then there are only the ramifications of these inequalities to deal with. We cannot relate sexual inequality as a set of variables to some other set of unequal social characteristics which lie outside it. This conundrum forces us away from explanation in this conventional sense.

It also forces us away from conventional cross-cultural analysis. The contributors to this volume have not agreed upon a definition of inequality, nor collaborated in developing a common approach to these societies, nor even focused on the same structural elements in their different instances. On the face of it, not many bridges. And this is because there is that other boundary to cross. As Atkinson put it for gender studies in general: 'the anthropology of women does what cultural anthropologists do best – namely, it heads full tilt at culture-bound assumptions in our own thinking' (1982:238). However adept we are at making bridges, we are also adept at pulling them up after us. This of course can become a different ecological refuge, cultural relativism.

Yet the essays presented here are not really in search of such a refuge.

The chief comparative advantage of cultural relativism lies in the reflexivity which the analyser brings to his or her materials. Certainly the contributors here are forced to be explicit about how they propose to utilise concepts such as 'dominance' or 'complementarity'. Some of the chapters deal with this more squarely than others; none of them takes the concept of inequality for granted. At the same time none is content merely with local interpretive exercises. Together they address the central problem of comparative analysis: how to create (anthropological) concepts of value. These have to be concepts dually constructed: transactable between societies in order to elicit comparison, yet also retaining an intrinsic connection with social realities as they are differently lived. The essays which follow allow a reflexive scrutiny of the concepts which motivate them. But they also offer substantive approaches to sexual inequality as a societal phenomenon.

Dealing with inequality can be taken as an organising metaphor for the volume. Questions about inequality have to deal with the place which the concept holds in anthropological analysis and in those parts of Western cosmology to which such analysis claims to speak.[2] For instance, formulations of inequality as they enter anthropological discussion rest on certain systemic peculiarities in Western constructions of difference, a matter to which I return in the Conclusion. Simply put, difference is often taken to culminate in conversions, that is, an evaluation of a relationship or context in favour of one set of relations at the expense of the other. Various anthropological models of society evince this tenet, as in the supposition that a problem facing 'individuals' is having to cope with the constraints of 'social structure'. Social relations in turn are seen as designed to cope with (say) the exigencies of stress. Coping with inequality in this sense makes inequality itself a cultural exigency which bears on people's lives. This leads to other kinds of dealings with which these essays are concerned. 'Dealing' can also refer to distribution, allocation. Not 'coping with' (constraints) but 'dealing out' (items) or 'dealing in' (values) as an instrumental activity. For cultural arrangements are also instruments. They may be instrumental to the pursuit of particular personal or social interests, even though these interests can never be independently defined. They are certainly instrumental in respect of any analytic interests one might have in the issue of agency – that is, accounting for the sources of people's actions and for their being perceived as actors.

As far as the Pacific societies are concerned, we are not just dealing with various institutions, arrangements, structures, and images, which show the factors and effects of 'inequality'. If the problem were of this nature, then investigation would indeed have to be adjudicatory.[3] We would want to know how to weigh and measure this or that index of inequality. The resultant assessment would necessarily participate in the adjudications of those we have under study. Are women everywhere excluded from public life; what does that exclusion mean; what does it entail? Whether using exogenous indices or indigenous ones, the questions would collude in the modelling of society that (in this instance) puts emphasis on exclusion. Yet, since we cannot apparently explain sexual inequality except by tautologous reference to other parts of the same complex of relationships, we are left with something else to explain: the construction of inequality through sexual difference. Thus enquiry shifts – from the nature of inequality between the sexes, to the construction of inequality through sexual difference.

Such a shift of emphasis admits the extent to which, for these societies, inequality is played out in a gender idiom; in this sense sexual inequality is irreducible.[4] And it is this perspective which enables one to see beyond the sexual relations themselves. For one should not be misled by appearance and imagery. If gender differences are instrumental in the structuring of unequal relations, this may include the concealing of other inequalities. They do not express these other differentiations but, as Bloch (1977) might say, hide them. Thus material inequalities between men may be hidden by an indigenous emphasis on inequality between men and women (Josephides 1982). Where sexually constructed inequality emerges as an important instrument of all kinds of social differentiation, then these differentiations are mediated through but are not, as it turns out, necessarily reducible to differences between men and women. I return to this observation later.

In the meanwhile we do not have to decide, on behalf of the peoples referred to in this book, whether men or women 'have' power. Rather, it is helpful to describe how they make known to themselves that this or that category is powerful, that these persons are unequal, and so on. This gives some insight into how people construct relations.

The peoples of this part of the world lack the rhetoric of a Judaeo-Christian past (cf. Burridge 1973:ch.1) or the yearnings of a Rousseauesque present (Bloch and Bloch 1980). They do not have the conceptual tools of stratified state systems which project fantasies of a common humanity or unitise the citizen-isolate (Lawrence 1984:163), nor indeed of a capitalist economy which commoditises 'sex' (Illich 1982). Many of them, however, do seem to have a vested interest in maintaining internal relations among themselves through exchanges of all kinds which simultaneously preserve differences between categories of persons and enable them to enter into relations with one another. They live as it were the cross-cultural problem: how to transact with items which retain value by reference to their origins (in the activities of persons) and yet can move between persons and thus have value to that extent detachable from persons.[5] One solution to this constructional issue in the building of relationships requires that things/persons also be conceptualised as standing for things/persons they are not. What is striking about many of the systems described in this book is not the immutability of gender, but its transactability. Contrasts between men and women become a vehicle for the creation of value: *for evaluating one set of powers by reference to another*.[6]

Preserving the debate

The differences between the members of the Research Group are instructive. This section touches on how we dealt with them, in the context of debate deliberately kept open; but some general observations must be made first. These stem from the charge that dichotomous theorising in the specific debate over sexual inequality echoes the posturings of a morality play (Losche 1984).

As soon as one becomes aware of such dichotomous thinking, the temptation is to generate a third term. History may so intervene. Thus the universalists and evolutionists may be brought together, as Rosaldo indicated (and cf. James 1983), by turning attention to the specific historical embeddedness of social inequality.

Gender in all human groups must ... be understood in political and social terms, with reference not to biological constraints but instead to local and specific forms of social relationship and, in particular, of social inequality. (Rosaldo 1980a:400)

Recent comparative attempts to treat the issue of sexual inequality in the context of other inequalities have been made for the Melanesian region. Allen's (1981, 1984) survey of political systems in island Melanesia and the essays in A. Strathern (1982) on the Papua New Guinea Highlands both have a historical cast. Allen's work is considered in the Conclusion; here I briefly make mention of the latter collection.

From a historical concern with the manner in which systems of domination (male/female and male/male) have developed, Godelier and Modjeska analyse relations of production. Control over persons and control over resources are related to one another in the disposition of labour. Given the marked sexual divide in the division of labour, it is inevitable that the kind of value put on female labour should be seen as crucial to relations between the sexes. This perspective opens up an avenue for speculation into the evolution of different labour-using technologies among Highlands horticulturalists, as Lindenbaum (1982; and see Tsing and Yanagisako 1983:514) envisages. It would be narrow minded to set the present endeavour against such analytical interests. Rather, a comparative political economy of the kind Modjeska (1982:50) promises is needed before one can begin to assess the significance of labour in the 'history' of these societies. Gregory (1982) offers as much in his investigation of present-day Melanesian exchange systems in terms of the objectification and personification of values. Meanwhile it is worth noting the emphasis which Modjeska, Godelier and A. Strathern all place on the contemporary manner in which human values (the values of certain relationships) are or are not mediated by items commonly described as wealth objects.

Lederman (1983) writes that divorced from the contexts and politics of their use, gender constructs yield ambiguous information about men and women as such. She is alluding to the Highlands, but the point is generally taken. The contradictory idioms and perceptions which inform gender thinking arise from cross-sex and intra-sex differences and combinations being used as the terms for discriminations which may be about relations other than those between the sexes. This is the sense in which Biersack refers to gender as a master code, a source of self-reflective activity: out of the sameness and difference of the sexes comes an indigenous conceptual vocabulary, 'a very simple discursive device for talking about diversity and variability' (1984:134). In order to sustain systematic discriminations, discourse must display some internal consistency; it would be a naive (and archaic) historicity which drew us away from analysing the structural interrelationships between peoples' ideas.

However Losche (1984; n.d.; cf. Dwyer 1978:227) has properly castigated those such as myself who proffer bland assumptions that cultural categories are shared representations. Thus she would argue that contradictions in gender thinking are not to be sorted out in relation to different social contexts of usage as Lederman suggested and as some of the chapters also suggest, nor as Biersack (and others of the contributions indicate) to be resolved in terms of their functioning as a code addressed to issues of diversity in social life. Rather, they should be taken as speaking to irresolvable differences of interest.[7] The ideological status of certain sets of ideas means that they work in the interests of some and not others. In effect Losche (1984) is criticising oversystematised accounts of other cultures. She argues that 'oppositions form, not a hegemony of categories, but the subject of debate and questioning in other societies as well as "our own"'. Of course; but it remains the case that claims to hegemony frequently have recourse to systematisation in the promotion of an inevitable world view, and must enter our subject of study as such. Furthermore, the contributors to this volume question the kinds of interests which gender ideologies may serve, since it is by no means to be automatically assumed for other societies as perhaps it is for our own that men and women will be always divided by social interest.

In also referring to 'our own' I commit that other culturalist error of appearing to assume 'we' inhabit a homogeneous world with recognisable attributes. It is necessary therefore to be explicit about the differences between the chapters which follow. They deliberately keep open several vantage points, which have diverse and heterogeneous origins. 'We' as collected-together contributors do not share a single world view; indeed perhaps some of the social differences between us – our histories and politics – are replicated here as intellectual difference. One can agree with Losche that there are important reasons for keeping debates as debates. Third terms, which attempt to transcend or collapse difference may also displace and mystify the grounds for difference. There is no attempt, then, to homogenise the contributions to this volume; on the contrary, we have tried to preserve a sense of debate. Unity of purpose has its place in social life; but we are not I think required to take it as the only model of collective action.

The point can be underlined in relation to the innovative collection edited by Ortner and Whitehead (1981).[8] Their intention ('This is a book about the ways in which gender and sexuality are conceptualized in various cultures' 1981:ix) is placed in a specific theoretical field, symbolic anthropology. At the same time, they locate the essays within two broadly contrasting methodological frames, roughly corresponding to 'culturalist' and 'sociological' emphases. And they clearly feel the need to relate further differences between their contributors to different traditional orientations (Marx, Durkheim and Weber are all mentioned). Simultaneously, given that the essays are rich and subtle ethnographies, the editors of *Sexual Meanings* are also able to show that the papers – sometimes singly, certainly collectively – transcend these theoretical dichotomies. Thus 'even the more sociologically oriented studies are committed to a symbolic (or "cultural") view of gender, and that even the more culturally oriented papers have important sociological underpinnings' (1981:2).

Transcendence requires that the sources of difference lie beyond the project in hand. This is one version of the Western culture/nature dichotomy: through culture Westerners deliberately collectivise their activities, against a nature innately differentiated. Nature in this particular instance is the set of assumptions and precepts by which its practitioners were socialised into varieties of anthropology. It is noteworthy that the *contemporary* fragmentation of anthropology sometimes causes concern. People feel they should be contributing to the same enterprise, where they might be quite comfortable with the idea that the dead giants were radically different from one another. Marx, Durkheim, Weber do not have to be assimilated to one another; on the contrary they are the precursors for the 'natural' differences which exist today in the subject and which one strives to overcome. *Sexual Meanings* opened, then, with a strongly idealistic statement on the unity of endeavour, indexed in its common name (symbolic anthropology).

As a historical fact, the members of the ANU Research Group had come together with different theoretical interests and antecedents. Moreover the experience of sustaining discussions, over as much as a year for many of them, did not lead to the submergence of these interests, as a briefer interaction might have done. Precisely in so far as we were involved as whole persons, such a submergence was not even desirable. Although participating in a provisional agreement that we were all 'doing anthropology', it is clear that we each had different versions of what that subject entailed. Indeed, to have constructed a unitary subject matter would have instantly thrown up the problem of what to do with our differences.

Yet given their regional focus, one might expect that at least for this part of the world a small group of anthropologists could agree what they wanted to mean by 'gender' or 'inequality'. That is, they would establish conventions through collectivisation. For many anthropological tasks it is desirable to establish definitional conventions. However, if one actually looks at past debates of theoretical interest, it is an intriguing fact that debates usually subside not through unanimity but exhaustion. The fervent arguments two or three decades ago – do primitive societies have 'law'? What is the character of 'descent'? – are over, not because in the end there was agreement as to what 'law' or 'descent' meant, but because of a quite different reason. In the effort to deal with law or descent, anthropologists at the time brought to the discussion their complete tool kit of theoretical issues and considerations, and this was their achievement. The questions mobilised and thus displayed all the discipline's going theoretical resources. Consequently the resurrection of old debates always looks odd, insofar as it is impossible to recapture the contemporary significance of that display. Issues of gender currently hold anthropologists in dispute, as a similarly important arena for the display of disciplinary expertise.

There are in addition ethical reasons for preserving the sense of debate. For it is not just the case that we can allocate the theoretical differences between ourselves to different positions among different ancestral giants.

It is also the case that we came together with a contemporary range of personal philosophies and politics. As is most notably true for Bell's Aboriginal colleagues (see Chapter 4), to deal with gender inevitably places our concerns in contexts also shaped by other interests. Current anthropological studies in the field have been fuelled by the academic branch of the women's movement and by the growing and self-conscious body of feminist theory. This is not to be ignored. Implicitly or explicitly, whatever we do enters into some kind of relation with feminist endeavour, even including the argued position that its theories are irrelevant.[9] For the quality of the relationship established with the material objectifies our own interests. This is particularly important for scholars whose work speaks to overt politicised concerns. Here the participatory aspects of the present endeavour have roots not only in the routinised reflexivity of cross-cultural analysis, but in the kinds of commitment other anthropologists with an interest in feminism have declared in their works (e.g. Rosaldo and Lamphere 1974; Rosaldo 1974:42; Leacock 1981; Reiter 1975:11,19). Bourque and Warren (1981:43) make a general plea for self-consciousness 'about the impact of social values on research'. In so far as intellectual positions have consequences for the perception of different social interests, they comprise vehicles through which such differences continue to be recognised.[10] A homogenised world view that merely stresses 'variety' is not enough. By their nature interests may be in irreducible conflict. The motivations anthropologists bring to bear in studying gender should not, then, require unification. We should, nonetheless, be aware of the grounding of our differences.

To follow the course of settling on conventions would have opened up differences in the group in a manner subsequently requiring deliberate submergence. The original intention of the Research Group programme was to consider:

> the political and economic foundations of gender ideology, production and social reproduction, as well as the symbolic constructions of gender ... This focus of the Research Group does not imply a commitment to any particular framework of explanation, other than the attempt to view cultural systems as ideological as well as symbolic, and to explore how they operate to reproduce systems of social relations.

If the contributors to this volume have implemented that goal, it has been through an academic practice which has sought to homogenise neither its presuppositions nor its end product. Instead it is oriented towards a particular engagement with ethnographic factuality. And does so through a device which anthropologists have used for a long time – that of displaced focus. Young refers to it in his metaphor of indirect gaze, looking just to one side of a distant clock tower to make it yield its message.

In setting out to do one particular thing, one also does other things, minimally the grounding and contextualisation of that task. I do not mean simply that one starts a Malinowskian enquiry about land tenure and concludes with a disquisition about magic. But much more precisely: that any directed activity has to assume a context. To address the notion of inequality, for instance, implies fashioning the ethnographic context for the application of the concept.

One problematic aspect of the task which the Research Group set themselves was the conceptualisation of gender relations as such. It was necessary to displace that focus on to issues which would not only select out a range of data, but would in turn display the utility of gender as a concept. Thus the issue of gender as ideology is not posed directly, whereas that of sexual inequality is. We test our own responses by looking over the shoulder to enquire: in addressing this second topic did we in fact have resort to the first, to analysing gender constructs as ideology; to making the notion of ideology relevant; and what indeed has been the status of 'gender' as a concept in our arguments about inequalities in these societies? Perhaps looking over one's shoulder in this way is the nearest that social science approaches to an experimental situation – being able to be surprised by its own results. If one subject matter of these essays is the character of gender relations in a particular part of the world, then to focus on ideas of inequality as they affect men and women will tell us a great deal about what we assume gender relations to mean. It will be of interest to ask after the event what material was marshalled to expound particular points. Yet to be so self-conscious, so exegetic, about practice is to summon the spectre of an infinite regression of knowledge, that at each penetration of the recesses of our endeavour we confront ourselves, like Baktaman boys through their initiation rituals, with the proposition that what was thought to be subject matter is to be displaced by further 'real' subject matter.

In truth, anthropological endeavour has a grounding whose reality is not shifted by such regression. We do not create other societies and cultures; we merely recreate them in the ethnographic record. If the major problem of cross-cultural comparison is to retain something of the lived authenticity of what ethnography merely recreates, then what must be created is a position which will be open to surprises. Displacing focus away from the ethnographic record to concepts explicitly of exogenous devising, such as inequality, enables one to stand back a little. For the ethnographic data marshalled to elucidate these concepts in turn yields information about both. This is not a comment on the factuality of facts, but a comment on descriptive procedure (cf. Anderson & Sharrock 1982).

In thinking about inequality, the contributors have gathered together data on the division of labour (Devereaux, Nash); ritual, magic and cult activity (Hoskins, Macintyre, Weiner) and kinship ceremonies (Chowning); myth (Young) and narratives (Keesing); decision-making processes (Bell, Errington and Gewertz); and so on. All the Melanesian cases (Chowning, Errington and Gewertz, Keesing, Macintyre, Nash, Weiner, Young) and the eastern Indonesian example (Hoskins) draw predictably on the significance of prestige and wealth exchanges, as had been part of our plan. One intention was to make conceptual discoveries; in concentrating on conceptual issues, we have also made ethnographic discoveries. It was not deliberately planned, for instance, that the accounts would refer to mortuary rituals, yet in certain cases equations between women and the dead emerged as highly relevant to the analysis of gender concepts. This specific association demands comment, and I return to it in the Conclusion.

The contributors also differ in their systematic emphasis, and thus in where they locate the relations they analyse. For some it is a question of an overview of interactions between men and women, in terms of particular episodes (Errington and Gewertz); demeanour and the conduct of daily life (Devereaux); or through the way women talk about themselves (Keesing). The ethnographer's job is to make the data trans-culturally intelligible. Others are more concerned with following through the systemic implications of social arrangements – as with descent and residence (Chowning) or the domaining of ritual and politics (Bell, Nash) – which leads to formulations about relations between men's and women's social roles. Four chapters (Hoskins, Macintyre, Weiner, Young) deal explicitly with gender as an instrument of conceptual differentiation and with relations as though they were elements of a code. All the chapters were, however, approached with the concept of 'agency' as well as 'inequality' in mind. The relationship between the two terms must be stated.

Inequality

If one were to enlarge the inclusive we of this book to its readership, there is no way, I think, in which, we, could agree about what to mean by inequality. Indeed this makes it a good concept to think with. For it is impossible to utilise the word without being self-conscious of the fact that 'visions of equality, like those of hierarchy, are themselves Western historical constructs' (Atkinson 1982:240).[11]

The rhetoric of egalitarianism provides an entry into academic questions which stem from practical ones; thus some feminist enquiry turns to anthropology for answers to questions about universalisms in dominance and subordination. The Western notion of equality has explicit legal and political roots, and decisions about the grounds on which people are or are not equal are also the observer's decisions about where authority and power lies. These concerns inform how we might choose to describe whole societies – in this vast sense the notion of equality could take on the whole of anthropology. It is illuminating, then, to approach it through what appears a single issue, namely equality between men and women. Gender relations thus become themselves an instrument of enquiry. In sorting out issues to do with equality between the sexes we may find ourselves in a better position to know what to intend by applying 'egalitarian' to whole 'societies'. Debates about sexual inequality will thus problematise the idea of inequality in general. Collier and Rosaldo's (1981) argument, for instance, that however egalitarian certain systems appear to be, fundamental inequalities are invariably constructed through marriage arrangements, clearly raise the question of whether one can usefully stretch the concept of equality to cover both same-sex and cross-sex relations. In this volume, Bell treats aspects of Australian Aboriginal society which Collier and Rosaldo's account addresses directly. Yet their point can be taken more widely, and at the other end of the politico-economic spectrum, Devereaux is explicitly concerned with similar issues in the context of a peasant economy.

For the Melanesian cases it is worth noting a set of comments made by Josephides (apropos the collection of essays on inequality in New Guinea Highlands societies mentioned in the previous section). Josephides writes of the 'dynamic relationship between the ideology of male equality and female subordination' (1984:41) which emerges from these studies.

This is an inference I made in 1978 while reviewing material from Mt Hagen. I argued then (Josephides 1982) that whereas antagonisms and inequalities among men were suppressed, between men and women inequalities were overt and differences exaggerated. Male solidarity demanded the wholesale subordination of women as a scapegoat class (which also disguised, or sometimes justified, inequalities among men), as well as in their capacity as producers and reproducers. Andrew Strathern (1979) has suggested that men tolerate a certain inequality among themselves in order to maintain a common front against women, while ... Modjeska reverses this proposition: inequality among men must be contained lest it lead to a breakdown of the solidarity which is necessary for the group's security. (1984:41)

To focus on gender, then, is not to ignore the manner in which inequality conceptualised as sexual difference conceals inequalities among members of the same sex. On the contrary, in so far as gender is constitutive of the way inequality is perceived, differences between men and women may well refer to differences between men (or between women where this is an issue), and vice versa. But, as I noted earlier, they do not stand in an 'expressive' relationship to non-gendered differences between categories such as class or ethnic group. The point is that the structural alternatives present themselves as *either* cross-sex *or* else intra-sex (same-sex) comparisons. It is this which creates the conundrum that sexual inequality in this region appears to be only about itself.

Godelier's reference to the 'double hierarchy' (see note 1) is a reminder of inequalities among men. For the patrilineal case he presents, differentiation is established through the ranks of male initiation, and through competition among men (1982:15-16). The categorical domination of all women by all men, by comparison with the variety of differentiations among men, recalls analyses of Vanuatu society. Here men differentiate themselves through ranked grades while women may be excluded from all grades (e.g. Jolly 1981; Rubinstein 1981). It therefore looks as though we might be able to provide explanations in terms of the relationship between male/female inequalities and inequalities among men. The analyses cited by Josephides attribute a causal role to certain male interests, especially that of solidarity. Yet this is of course an artefact of exegesis: male solidarity is not an independent variable in the construction of social differentiation. Lineage solidarity built on the combination of male and female efficacy (as found for instance in the matrilineal systems to be described) suggests an important qualification to assuming the apparent autonomy of male interests.

Indeed these latter cases present examples of institutionalised (ranked) inequalities between lineages conceptualised as the joint products of male and female endeavour. This combination (cf. Damon 1983) of gendered contributions is an outcome of separations very differently managed from the intra-sex differentiation of (say) Highlands men. I always run the danger myself of giving a Highlands-centric view. The contributions which follow must speak for themselves.

They do not explicitly theorise the nature of equality. Debate lies between them. Of interest, I have suggested, are the kinds of other concepts which the authors have marshalled to write about inequality: in so far as the concept is very specifically placed within Western thought, it can have no simple counterpart in the conceptual schemes of those under study, and narrative frameworks have to be established for its use. Thus Errington and Gewertz, as well as Chowning, have put the issue of inequality into the context of dominance relations – the extent to which actors impinge and depend upon one another – and indigenous notions of autonomy – the degree to which people are able to follow their own desires. Bell considers the context of effective public action, the nature of local politics, and separate space as a necessary requisite for one's voice to be heard, a set of issues also considered by Devereaux from an economic point of view, in terms of access to resources. Similarly, Keesing, Hoskins and Macintyre observe the limits on the extent to which the sexes are seen to act differently from one another; Macintyre refers to the inseparability of male and female interests in lineage affairs, but the overt relation between these differences may appear to be one of complementarity, in the sense that the activities of one sex 'completes' those of the other. In this vein Nash explicitly addresses constructions of sameness and difference, posing questions that people themselves would not necessarily ask. Weiner and Young describe differentiation as a specific cultural activity, men being depicted as active agents in deploying valuables, and in Weiner's example maintaining difference between social categories. Several theoretical[12] positions are thus represented here. The authors are creating the contexts in which to write about inequality. These contexts in turn reveal some of their assumptions about the subject matter of anthropology.[13] The chapters thus fall into separate theoretical sets which cross-cut their regional orientations. They can be grouped as follows:

(1) **The interpretation of experience.** One set of contributions, drawn from three disparate geographical areas, displays inequality through the perspective of subjective experience. They deal openly with the question of making an overall assessment of the nature of inequality through a grasp of what it is like to be a woman or man in these societies. The interpretation of subjective experience in turn requires the counter-interpretation of how personal goals are constituted.

Keesing (Chapter 1) attends to the manner in which Kwaio women from the Solomon Islands perceive their goals, in implicit antithesis with men's accounts of themselves. The notion of a well-ordered life is enshrined in women's attitudes towards their own responsibilities and powers. Indeed they regard themselves as active keepers of rules, and as transmitters of them. Here we have the voices of several people, talking about how they view the world. Keesing makes it clear that self-accounts are partial accounts. But the perspective on which they rest depends on a range of cultural precepts; unless one understands these imperatives, one cannot interpret the extent to which men and women agree or disagree over the quality of their lives.

From the Sepik river of Papua New Guinea, Errington and Gewertz (Chapter 2) also invite us to think about the way a life is led: what makes a good life to a Chambri man or Chambri woman. Any adjudication about the quality of Chambri lives leads inevitably, as they point out, into the issue of false consciousness: into assessing how people achieve their goals and assessing how good a representation of reality those goals are. That is crucial to men's and women's differing perspectives. As a yardstick, the authors offer a general definition of 'dominance' whose applicability in each case turns on specific, as they say cultural, definitions of persons of worth. The sociology of, and Chambri concepts of, indebtedness between kin and the nature of political tactics enters their argument at strategic junctures to illuminate the predicaments in which people find themselves. It reveals values critical to the authors' final evaluation as to whether one category of persons is dominated by another. The question is made relevant to a particular course of events, so that the unfolding of a single case history displays Chambri social structure. This strategy constructs, as one central subject for discussion, just how individuals see themselves to be at an advantage or disadvantage in relation to others.

There are no individual voices in Chapter 3, but Devereaux's account of daily life achieves what a case history does for Errington and Gewertz and biographies do for Keesing: it provides an insight into the small details of existence which together add up to what it is like being a woman rather than a man. The ethnographic reason for this emphasis renders the Mexican material illuminating as a foil to several of the other chapters. Daily life is significant because, as a matter of outward form, it is forever on show. Externally, this is a facet of Zinacanteco ethnicity; internally, assessment of behaviour speaks to the concept of work. Work defines the person, and the division of labour within the community is inseparable from gender difference. The domestic complementarity of men's and women's labours is replicated in the interdependence of the sexes in public and ritual work. Devereaux observes, however, that the ideological value put on interdependence should not prevent one from analysing very real inequalities between the sexes, in terms of access to resources held to be essential to personal well-being. These inequalities lie in relations beyond the (complementary) asymmetry and difference imagined in explicit Zinacanteco gender ideology. They stem from the character of the material forces of production, and of public space, which the sexes do not control to the same degree. Her chapter thus looks forward to the next set.

(2) **Domains of action.** Bell, Chowning and Nash investigate the character of political and economic organisation which delimits certain

arenas of action. Enquiry into equality between the sexes must refer to the effectiveness of participation in these arenas, and to the relationship between them, that is, their structure. This type of analysis thus requires an understanding of relations between domains of action. What women do in their daily lives becomes a background for the analytical decision of how to weight exclusion from or participation in this or that activity.

Bell's data (Chapter 4) is again drawn from outside Melanesia, and concerns conditions in colonial and post-colonial Aboriginal Australia. She shows that analysis of women's power must rest on a structural appreciation of the given relationship between women's and men's domains. The point is a general one, but crucial to her case. Aboriginal men and women are similarly locked within separate domains of action. This constitutes a formal relationship of interdependence. What men and women do, and alone can do in their own spheres, contributes separately to the prospering of 'country'. Aboriginal politics rests, then, on the categorical autonomy which each sex claims, and in the central Australian case makes it possible for there to be a collective women's voice as well as a collective men's voice. In a commentary very similar to Devereaux's, Bell further shows how external factors have introduced an asymmetry into otherwise complementary relations. However, and although men appear to have seized on the advantage, these factors she regards as largely foreign to the possibilities inherent in Aboriginal social organisation as such.

Chapter 5 deals with a society, the patrilineal Kove of New Britain, where on the face of it male and female domains of action are kept apart to the denigration of women. Women's mats and food products are considered unimportant by men when compared to the shell wealth on which they base their prestige, and one might think this applies to the roles of women and men also. But Chowning makes it clear that without understanding the relationship between men's and women's participation in exchange one cannot understand the considerable influence women exercise over men. This is most marked in respect of what men prize most: access to wealth. The extent to which men value women is intimately bound up with their significance as sisters and wives. A woman is valued by her brothers (and father) as an avenue to wealth, and by her husband as someone who will help create wealth for him. The extent to which women themselves have access to valuables, or even conceptualise what may be to their own benefit, leads to an analysis of women's interests vis-à-vis men's interests in the management of affinal relations. Women's roles as suppliers of food and feeders of men creates another arena of dependency, both for men who are nothing without the support of (several) women and for women who are nothing if they do not carry out their duties. Yet because each woman can feed herself and care for men by herself, Kove women, like Chambri women (Chapter 2), secure a reputation for themselves with a greater degree of autonomy than men are able to exercise. Men's reputation, of course, rests on their manipulation of a range of social others, and they would not want to be like women in this regard. Chowning offers the chapter as a cautionary tale against any simple correlation between institutional form (in this case, patriliny) and the freedoms and powers exercised by the sexes.

For the matrilineal Nagovisi of Bougainville, neither life in the lineage nor life in the household can exist independently of the other, a domaining not between male and female spheres but between two arenas of action in both of which the sexes play a part. Nash demonstrates this simultaneity in the internal structuring of Nagovisi sexual attributes (Chapter 6). Nagovisi construct two sets of differences, between husbands and wives and between brothers and sisters. The differences turn on that between talk and strength, the distribution of these qualities between one pair reversing itself in the other. The question of equality/ inequality is thus broached through understanding the dynamics of a categorical relationship. The relationship is one of pairing. One can thus analyse these Nagovisi attributes (talk, strength) separately from their sexual connotation. Although talk and strength are specific to one sex or the other in particular social contexts, as the contexts change so does the association. Either men or women may be associated with either attribute in being distinguished from their opposite spouse or opposite sex sibling. There is no overarching context which encompasses both, and which would then offer a standard by which, in Nagovisi terms, to measure equality between men and women.

(3) **Reflexive commentary.** The first two chapters in this theoretical set are also concerned to elucidate categorical relationships, but emphasis has shifted from assessment of social contexts to the nature of the categories themselves. Social context becomes background information rather than the foreground problem. Indeed the last two chapters invite us to share neither the experiences nor social milieu of men's and women's lives but their imaginations. Three of the four accounts here are, like Kwaio (Chapter 1) and Kove (Chapter 5), drawn from Austronesian-speaking cultures, though the Kodi of Sumba in eastern Indonesia (Chapter 7) are geographically distant from Tubetube (Chapter 8) and Kalauna (Chapter 9) both situated in the Massim area, off the eastern tip of Papua New Guinea.[14] Chapter 10 deals with an interior Papuan society, of a quite different linguistic ancestry.

Hoskins (Chapter 7) approaches inequality through gender symbolism evinced in mortuary ceremony, a focus of Kodi public life. This symbolism employs the difference between the sexes as a vehicle for organising other differences. Thus, for instance, the dramatically feminised corpse can be the corpse of a man or a woman, but it is put into a 'female' state in order to be detached from the living. Hoskins discusses Kodi notions of what constitutes the contrast between a female and a male state – as between attributes of passivity and activity. Complementarity is conceptually required, for neither state has meaning without reference to the other. It becomes a separate analytical point, as other contributors have also argued, whether or not this conceptual complementarity is translated into an equal evaluation of men and women as social actors. Men and women, it turns out, are differently circumscribed by the requirements of having to act as 'male' and 'female'. As Devereaux shows in Chapter 3, the material characteristics of the attributes may introduce an inevitable asymmetry in men's and women's ability to act, in Hoskin's phrase, on the world.

Chapter 8, however, presents a different case. There is a developed symmetry between the capabilities of the sexes on Tubetube in the Massim. But rather than resulting in male and female domains of action, the differences can be subsumed under the matrilineage as aspects of its own capacity for being an effective presence in the world. Supernatural power, available to both sexes, manifests itself differently in women and men as a matter of inherent and acquired ability (indeed gender associations serve to some extent to differentiate the powers themselves). Irreducible difference, Macintyre argues, is manifest between spouses. Between lineage siblings the matter is more complex. Men's and women's acts imply or refer to distinct types of power and influence; nevertheless, brothers and sisters, sorcerers and witches, work together in cooperation. Either sex can use their powers to positive or negative effect. Although within the lineage, then, the forms of men's and women's respective power are radically differentiated, the lineage itself provides them with a common cause to act. Thus the manner in which Tubetube people regard them as necessarily combining does not discriminate between their social importance. It is not on the basis of sex (but for example on kin loyalties) that interests are opposed.

Young (Chapter 9) addresses himself to a corpus of mythology. His subject here is the manner in which people craft gender associations: which bits they fix to which. The myths he has chosen are about disembowelling things of value. What in the narratives emerge as persons extracting parts from one another, in the exegesis is an understanding of how different peoples in the Massim represent to themselves the relationship between sources of value and how value is to be transacted. In so far as persons are seen to have power over the body parts of the other sex

– chopping up penises or excising pectoral shells – the ownership of attributes becomes ambiguous, though one might argue that in the end the myths specify what can and what cannot be detached from the persons. But from the point of view of the observer, it is clear that to some extent gender floats, that is, the points at which a difference between male and female becomes crucial are not predictable. Young's subject is thus also how people make gender associations plausible to themselves. The crafting of imagery in a narrative mode is itself interesting; the myths create concepts of both transactable and self-generating power, with no ultimate resolution in favour of one sex or the other.

Chapter 10 is concerned with a similar process, in the Southern Highlands of Papua New Guinea, revealed through ritual and cult activity rather than mythology. Weiner's subject matter is the manner in which the concept of difference is fashioned. Gender difference, like that between categories of kin and between the living and the dead, has to be constantly sustained: indeed Foi men distinguish themselves from women by taking responsibility for differentiation. The difference between the sexes is thus an activity rather than a state, which an outsider learns about through what men do (here in their cults). Men see themselves as establishing the social identity of both sexes and Weiner's account is offered as a description of how Foi men, rather than women, must maintain gender differentiation. The distinction between them is thus first and foremost a question of the effectiveness with which persons act, and to what ends. Gender difference itself is taken by Foi as evidence of the effectiveness of one sex rather than the other.

Whether men's and women's interests are directed towards the same or separate ends, one way and another the chapters all deal with the question of goals individually experienced. For any Western-derived discussion of social inequality is bound to lead into that of choice and intentionality.

Agency

'Agency' holds a different status from 'inequality' in these accounts. It is provocative in an opposite way – not as the focus of explicit controversy but rather because its range of meanings tend to be taken for granted [15] and thus present the contributor with freedom to employ it in novel ways. At the same time, the term is beginning to insert itself in analyses of all kinds.[16] Alongside the anthropological development of gender studies has emerged a parallel concern with constructions of personhood so-called. Thus, at the 1982 Wenner-Gren feminism and kinship conference (Tsing and Yanagisako 1983) conceptualisations of personhood was regarded as a major area in which participants acknowledged a substantial contribution from feminist-inspired sources. The concept of agency certainly has a specific contribution to make here, provided that agents are not simply taken as doers of things done. Let me expand that.

Ortner importantly brings the term prominence in her overview of the last two decades of anthropology. She writes:

> For the past several years, there has been growing interest in analysis focused through one or another of a bundle of interrelated terms: practice, praxis, action, interaction, activity, experience, performance. A second, and closely related, bundle of terms focuses on the doer of all that doing: agent, actor person, self, individual, subject. (1984:144)

She reminds her readers that it was Giddens who dubbed 'the relationship between structure and "agency" one of the central problems of modern social theory' (1984:145).[17] Ortner herself proposes that agents, persons, selves etc. *do* praxis, interaction etc. In the following pages this becomes the methodological problem raised by the extent to which 'the system' determines human actions. She writes (1984:148): 'modern practice theory seeks to explain the relationship that obtains between human action, on the one hand, and some global entity which we may call the "system", on the other'. Although her paper is also a critique of modernist theory, she clearly sees it as addressing the relationship between individual actors and society or culture. This leads to the formulae of how the system shapes practice, how practice shapes the system (1984:152,154). Ortner criticises the essential individualism of some current forms of practice theory, but only to say that we must recognise the cultural origins of individual motivation. This still leaves the individual actor as one who knows his/her interests [18] as also the subject of theoretical interest. One might recall that Sahlins' (1981:68) discussion of the sign as an interest had it placed in 'an oriented scheme of means and ends' as the reflex of 'the actor's experience'.

However, references to agency in this volume do not only address that individual:society matrix. There are other connotations of 'agency' – for instance, one Ortner herself uses when she refers to Sahlins' (1981) work as revealing Hawaiian women as 'agents of the spirit of capitalism' (1984:157), that is, agent in the sense of working on behalf of someone else, a source of independent action but not necessarily with independently conceived aims in mind. People act, but the interests in terms of which they act may be ambiguous. One does not act necessarily *for* the self, any more than the self is necessarily the source of the act's effectiveness.

Put simply, we could do worse than to enquire into what constitutes effective action. That is, how are people seen to impinge upon one another; how are they affected by others? Are persons the authors of their own acts? Or do they derive their efficacy from others? If power relations are in Western terms to do with effective action, then what in these non-Western societies counts as evidence of it – what is seen as the origin of particular events, outcomes, sets of behaviour? The concept of agency is a shorthand for these questions. It refers to the manner in which people allocate causality or responsibility to one another, and thus sources of influence and directions of power. To ask about the exercise of agency is also to ask about how people make known to themselves that ability to act. Instead of asking how we know whether women are oppressed by men, rather there is a question as to how *they* know: that is, how do they make known how men and women affect one another? We would not be dealing in the first place then with individual motivation, but rather with the more general issue of how social effects are registered.

Actors' interests thus become significant as a *particular*, not a definitive, source of efficacy. Of course, it seems sensible to ask what mechanisms people have at their own disposal for persuading, influencing, overriding others, and if same-sex opportunities differ from cross-sex opportunities. Indeed much Melanesian politics turns on the critical assessment of other people's mental intentions, as revealed by their actions, in the context of a general unwillingness to presume what is in their minds. This is one way in which the impact or efficacy of a whole range of acts (a theft, say, or a sharing of food) is registered: through what people compute to be the intentions behind it. Acts originating from the mind are also registered on the minds of others. Yet acts originating from either mental or bodily states may equally well be registered in the bodies of others (Biersack 1982; Gillison 1980), or in landscape and memorials (Rubinstein 1981; Battaglia 1983), or in the flow of wealth which regenerates social identities (A. Weiner 1976;1982). People's 'minds' are not necessarily at issue. People's 'persons' may well be.

The concept of agency does not simply set up the question of whether people can know or determine interests for themselves, and thus whether individual wills are crushed, bent or expanded. It demands explicit attention to the contexts in which will is relevant to action; and thus to how will as such is defined. The idea that persons are accountable for their actions might come to typify particular social categories under particular circumstances. But people can, as I have asserted, have an effect on one another not registered through their minds at all.

From this perspective, an interest in agents is not to be confused with an interest in subjectivity or in inter-subjective meaning. The problematic is not how individuals construct and spin meanings out of situations, but how social and cultural systems allocate responsibility (in Gluckman's legalistic phrase) or capability (Giddens 1984:9). The usefulness of Giddens' term here is that it displaces the concept of intentionality with an encompassing definition of the ability to act. Yet Giddens' discussion is also firmly located in a conceptualisation of the individual as a source of action. With such individualism, one can only get away from (conscious) intentionality by envisaging complex layers of the 'mind', the 'regularized consequences' of aggregated repetitive activities (1984:14), or else 'structural properties' of 'social systems' which are for the individual enabling as well as constraining (e.g. 1984:177). In this approach, 'agent' and 'structure' comprise a duality: the sociologist's problem predictably turns back to whether individuals know in their minds what they are doing.

Turning instead to how causative action is registered may encounter quite different indigenous concerns. The point has already been made that 'minds' are not necessarily regarded as either the author or the register of acts. Moreover the particularised individual (body, person) may be more plausibly the locus of effect than of cause. Thus the enactment of certain *relationships*, through transactions or flows of substance, may be held to have consequences for the health of an individual person. The cause is to be found in the conduct of the interaction, which may not be open to manoeuvre. A number of the contributions dwell on the idea of 'origin' or 'cause' in people's perception of relationships. There are certainly more questions to be asked of the way persons are felt to impinge upon one another than our contradictory idioms about intentionality and the possession of power can deal with. 'Agency' provides a helpful preliminary focus on the manner in which social action is conceived. It yields something of a neutral purchase on the social depiction of causality: the exercise of agency may or may not indicate personal power and may or may not be predicated on inequality. This does not throw out the attempt to grasp systemic inequalities. All it indicates is that among the data through which to approach the issue of inequality is the manner in which this or that effectiveness or competence is attributed to certain actors. This entails in turn the question of whether competence is perceived as a matter of personal action at all – whether indeed acts register 'actors'. Or whether we need to take account of indigenous theories of relationships. What will be of interest is the point at which a difference between maleness and femaleness matters.

If gender ideas really do act as a reflexive code in a moral or evaluative sense, then we might expect them to deal with the perception of social causes, and the conceptualisation of cause itself. When two categories of persons are held to have an impact on each other, the ability to influence can appear to come from the construction of the (gender) difference between them. It may seemingly inhere in the very division of labour, in cycles of food production, the ability to induce shame, who eats what and is prevented from eating what, and in beliefs about strength and speech.

The hope was that a newish term would give scope to slough off assumptions and premises which might obscure our grasp of indigenous presuppositions about social action. Such a grasp is a necessary complement to the Westernised concern with inequality. At the same time, it also alters the grounding of that endeavour. If gender relations gives an entry into considering wider issues of equality and inequality, and vice versa, then agency gives an entry into considering whether or not in their depictions of themselves 'persons' can be abstracted from relations. The remainder of this section consequently takes the chapters in reverse order. Differentiation into the same sets highlights certain themes, but in fact many of the same issues occur in each. This interchangeability suggests our analyses are at a primitive stage.

(1) **Excision and detachment.** Chapter 10 is good to begin with, since Foi men would appear to have a specific set of notions about the moral or cultural imperative of maintaining proper distinctions, and sustaining proper social differentiation itself. Illness is the penalty for failing to do so. Although Weiner uses the language of intentionality – Foi men have a responsibility to combat illness, maintain fertility – this characterisation is derived from an understanding not of individual motivation but of Foi society as a whole. From an examination of their exchanges, rites and cults one can classify Foi acts into those which are held to channel and direct power, and those which are innate evidence of power itself. A gender divide marks the difference. Women embody a procreative capacity, of which the act of giving birth is evidence, conceived as a flow of substance between maternally related kin, while men deliberately create a counter-flow using wealth items. They thereby create male collectivities, such as men's house communities, whose acts are constructed in relation to these two flows. Their special agency is the ability to cut or chop up bits from the flow of innate substance (as in arranging the marriages of women between male groups) so that the detachable value of such bits becomes utilised in the course of their exchanges. These exchanges are not based on private property: men are not appropriating

female power in the sense of taking it and converting it to some other use. Rather, Weiner's account shows that the exchanges only make sense as constructed *against* and thus also preserving the self-sufficiency of this flow; hence his concept of analogy. The point is repeated in the context of death. Detached through the exertions of men, male ghosts are analogous to wives, inactive repositories of the power that activates living men. Evidence of this activation is given by the symbol of the head man and by the collective male life which men create for themselves.

Cutting, chopping and extracting body parts are a theme of the myths examined in Chapter 9. Kalauna and their neighbours envisage two drastic penalties; (1) on inappropriate cutting, mistaking as detachable something which belongs intrinsically to a person; and (2) on either failing to perceive proper attributes in disguised form or desiring to see what should remain disguised. Women's bearing of children is power or value revealed. Like Foi, Kalauna male agency is directed towards the channelling of objects of value, and this channelling activity by men corresponds to the innate efficacy which women evince in their persons. Although women do not have transactional responsibility for their own value, nevertheless the myths suggest that they ward off the misappropriation of it, as when men make fatal cultural errors; women themselves are penalised when they fail to appreciate what it is that men's wealth transactions do stand for. It is interesting that Young reports that Kalauna women are collectivised as 'mothers'; and that although men's transactions have a social dimension, fathers are hypothetically singular, individual actors.

Tubetube is a Massim society which seems to take to extremes a dogma of matrilineal identity which provides several possibilities for the combination of individual aggression and group interest. Either men or women can be seen as acting only for themselves. Macintyre (Chapter 8) describes how women normally activate their own powers as agents of the matrilineage, both a capacity to make men warriors and a capacity to create life. Sanctions rest on a divide between harmful and beneficial action: when a woman acts for herself only, as an archetypical flesh-consuming witch, she becomes a danger to others. In order to act either for good or ill, however, men have to be empowered, or empower themselves, as sorcerers. On Tubetube we may further note, wealth exchanges are not bound up with a distinctive male capacity, and either men or women can organise prestigious transactions. The difference between them lies rather in modes of causing or empowering persons to act in reference to collective matrilineage interests. Whereas women appear to embody that ability to cause (so that it takes deliberate malevolence to subvert this power), men's strength rests in their ability to *acquire* powers such as sorcery. Women, as matrilineage agents, can thus be the significant cause of men's actions, especially in affairs beyond the island. A warrior had to be strengthened by his matrilineage through rites which only a female relative could perform on its behalf.

Hoskins' analysis of Kodi (Chapter 7) puts a similar division into a different perspective. Women emerge as the sources of action, delegators: men as executors, as visible active agents. But this division seems to define whole areas of life, to the extent that women are prototypically passive and men active. Kodi, like Foi, construct men as givers of life and women as the life that is transferred. Among men's roles is again that of individuation. Thus a contrast between unalterable substance connection, via women, and socially negotiated group membership, which men validate by exchange, forms the difference between two types of descent reckoning. The details of the mortuary ceremonies which Hoskins gives are important. Whereas Foi would seem to view the corpse itself as only partially detached and lifeless, complete detachment and transformation into a ghost being necessary for the dead soul to embody life-flow again, Kodi separate the transformation into two distinct processes. The 'female' life-force which animated the particular individual is extinguished at death. Life is replenished however by the feminisation of the deceased's 'male' soul or destiny which is detached from the person and joins the generalised ancestral body that stands to the living as a diffuse source of blessing. However, in the few cases where the soul is re-attached to the living community, it enjoys a particular social involvement in men's affairs. An explicit analogy is drawn with the passage of women in marriage and, one might add, with the distinction in social effectiveness between those who remain attached to their ancestral village and those who must be detached. Through decorating the deceased and making it the object of songs, Kodi fashion the corpse like a female person, the soul like a bride, composing them together as a container of life-bestowing powers. Indeed, in personifying these aspects of the deceased, women personify themselves. On the one hand, the official mourner bodily accompanies the corpse; on the other hand the singer breaks the customary silence of women and, in taking a crucial role in the soul's transformation, gives evidence of their animating capacity.

(2) **Separation and control.** Nash's chapter (6) returns us to paired categorisation which does not rest on a passive/active distinction. Both talk and strength are themselves actions and are the cause of actions. At the same time, a threefold relation exists between husbands who labour and nurture, wives who talk and take decisions and children who are seen as the final reason for men having to work. Men here embody

energy; women emerge as a social source through their talk. Yet the children are a 'cause' in the marital relation because they are also evidence of the mother's work in another capacity. In relation to her matrilineage, and thus to her brother, a woman embodies matrilineal strength and procreativity, and here it is the brother who is the decision-maker and talker. If children 'cause' fathers to act, then, it is because they have been 'caused' by the mother and her brother (an affinal relationship). As on Tubetube, cause entails responsibility. Were a man to be injured in the course of his exertions for his children, they would owe compensation to his matrilineage; wives do not just assist the husband's actions, but take responsibility for what they bring about. In so far as Nagovisi women enter into exchanges, this type of responsibility is marked by their talk as wives, that is, their decision-making powers in relation to the husband's exertions. But they do not directly empower matrilineage males: in respect of these men, the brothers who emerge as guardians socially significant in the disposition of lineage assets, they are silent.

Kove women (Chapter 5) are involved for most of their lives in a cycle of affinal debts and repayment. This flows from their marriage, which puts a special value onto their pivotal position as producers of shell wealth and of food. In spite of the rhetoric of child payments, Kove make women out to be the chief cause of affinal exchanges. It is significant that women always therefore occupy a specific relation in respect of particular men. A woman's own handling of wealth items (mats and baskets) and of the shell valuables claimed by men consequently arises in the context of their assisting husbands and brothers. Chowning notes that men's and women's interests coincide in that to be a respected member of society everyone, regardless of sex, must obtain wealth. But in supporting both spouse and brother, whose interests as men do not usually coincide, women inevitably have interests particular to themselves. Kove appreciate this. Thus marriage gives a wife access to shell wealth, initiated ideally by a dowry, with which she helps her husband. At the same time, her brother's 'gifts' to her over her lifetime must be repaid, and for this she needs her husband's help. It is illuminating that Kove regard both marriage partners as wanting a same-sex replacement. Whatever the ethos of male domination, the concerns of women are no simple subset of men's.

Bell (Chapter 4) introduces notions of possession; the Aboriginal material makes it clear that categories of persons are defined by their ownership of ritual, sacred sites and song. Each sex is thus empowered only to the extent that it exercises its own knowledge of these things. Knowledge cannot be exercised in relation to a site or myth which one does not properly 'own'. From the point of view of the continuity and prosperity of any one country, then, different categories of owners must separately and severally fulfil their obligations. Bell is concerned to show what a mistake it is to assume that an Aboriginal community can be represented by its men alone. For our purposes, this presents a striking negative elucidation: a situation where one sex cannot in fact empower the other to act, nor presume on its passivity. Each must act in its own way. If each acts out its own identity, it also follows that the one does not stand for some value with which the other transacts, as one could perhaps say that Nagovisi wives transact in taking decisions over the disposition of male energies.

(3) **Responsibilities and debts.** Devereaux (Chapter 3) depicts a very different property situation, where peasant women have to purchase extra labour to help with large families, and where marriage and death are bound up with inheritance. Zinacanteco siblings compete with one another. Setting up a household at marriage forces the parents of both bride and groom to make a partial property settlement. This is the significance of her concluding section. The household emerges as a sign of autonomy, paralleling autonomy as an attribute of the individual person. The autonomous person is one who controls his or her own property and commands the labour he or she needs. Devereaux suggests that the difference between men and women does not rest in one sex carving out an area of interest in opposition to the other; persons of either sex seek self-fulfilment through similar interests. Yet whereas men negotiate their independence against senior relatives, women can only achieve independence from them through entering into a new dependency in respect of their husbands. The Zinacanteco emphasis on outward form is important. Intentions are not at issue in the assessment of behaviour, nor it would seem are powers (labour, procreativity) attached as values to persons. People do not transact with values embodied in persons of the opposite sex; rather, in so far as they control property, they have the ability to release the labour of others in relation to it. Hence they realise 'themselves' through labour exercised in relation to property. They are judged then by what they do. The distinctiveness of gender thus has to be registered in distinctive modes of doing.

Chapter 2 returns us to Melanesia, and to a different debt situation. Zinacanteco debts (as between affines) entail a notion of bondage in so far as what is owed (labour) can also be utilised for the self; men can look forward to re-possessing their own labour for themselves, even though women never really can. Errington and Gewertz's Chambri, however, do not link wealth to autonomy, but to the possibility of enmeshing one another in social networks. The authors elaborate the Chambri idea that those who cause life are more important than those whose life is caused, so that the source of a person in his or her relations with maternal kin and wife-giving affines must for ever be acknowledged. People perceive a life long debt to these kin. By the same token the debt can never be paid off: the relations could not be utilised for some alternative purpose. As in the case of Foi or Kodi, where a flow of wealth signifies this debt it passes between men – to male maternal kin and to male affines. Men create this particular flow, so that it is men as wife-givers who are superior to men as wife-takers in so far as they have power to extract wealth. Women do not seem to be marked out as particularly responsible or empowering in ritual terms. Rather, through childbirth, they themselves create that condition of indebtedness in each male individual which compels men to pay their maternal kin, and which enables other men through unequal control of the indispensable wealth items to create power for themselves. Thus women are doubly a cause – both in Chambri eyes the origin of persons, and in the authors' analysis the perpetual mover of male transactions. From the point of view of the wife-taker, however much a man pays he cannot match what was given; from the point of view of the wife-giver, nothing can replace the loss. Women, as we have seen, are not entangled in the same way. For the children they bear are regarded as direct replacements for themselves. As a consequence, the character of the kinship networks in which they are placed simultaneously makes of Chambri women social agents with obligations to others and frees them from having to meet these obligations through transactional competition.

Keesing (Chapter 1) casts agency as moral power: the responsibility Kwaio women have for keeping the 'place', for preserving proper boundaries, for 'showing the way' to the next generation, and as the force behind the deeds of their husbands. Women's talk is an important vehicle for the transmission of knowledge, in the context of relationships (especially with their daughters) which turn on social connections to and through them. This responsibility defines a different focus from that which preoccupies men. Both men and women emerge with collective interests, but with men as agents vis-à-vis the ancestors and thus in charge of public ritual, and women as agents in charge of the 'community', the owners of settlements. Above all, women are seen to have the care of rules to do with maintaining proper bodily functions. Care of themselves is equated with care of others. Bodily pollution is thus perpetual evidence of the importance of female responsibility, as negotiation with ancestral spirits is of male. Men and women alike observe taboos, and preserve boundaries: the enactment of women's powers through menstruation or childbirth situationally sets them off from the mundane world exactly as the enactment of a relation with the spirits through sacrifice sets off men. What is particular to them perhaps is that they perceive the reproduction of their society and culture, to use Keesing's phrase, as a matter of successful moral instruction. Thus the narratives of women's individual experiences also constitute exemplars of social life.

Notes

Acknowledgement: Aside from several members of the Group, Christopher Gregory kindly read and criticised both the Introduction and Conclusion. I am grateful to Diane Losche for permission to cite unpublished work.

1. However from the point of view of differences within the region, this is also an exaggeration. Thus Godelier (1982:7) refers explicitly to a 'double hierarchy' among the Baruya, 'between men and women on the one hand, and among men on the other hand'. The grade systems of Vanuatu also provide evidence of a double hierarchy. See also the Lowland Papua New Guinea societies with hereditary rank (Chowning 1977:52). These apparent contradictions to my statements about sexual inequality are considered briefly in the following section of the chapter.

2. I acknowledge the implied elision between 'we' as authors of this volume and 'we' as 'Westerners' – a category term several of the contributors use. Elsewhere one might wish to dismantle the elision. Here it serves one purpose: to draw attention to the fact that the dominant ideas of social science with which anthropologists professionally think, and which inform the way we deal with problems, have their origins in a specific cultural milieu/political economy not shared by the peoples studied in this book. I am grateful to Terence Hays for discussion on this point.

3. For those interested in problems of adjudication, Bourque and Warren (1981:ch.2) take one carefully through the minefields of such decision-making.

4. A difference between sex and gender is not necessary to the other distinctions being made here, and is ignored in the same way as one ignores the arguments of biological essentialism.

5. This is an issue in which ethnographers in the Massim have been particularly interested. I am thinking of Damon 1980; Munn 1977; and several contributors to Leach and Leach 1983. At this juncture 'exchange' refers not only to wealth transactions but also to the separation and combination of labours between the sexes.

6. I follow the contributors to this book in understanding gender relations as in the first instance speaking to relations between 'men' and 'women', undefined. For a criticism of such procedure see Yeatman 1984a:46. Elsewhere (see n.9), no doubt without complete success, I try to avoid taking 'men' and 'women' as ontological givens.

7. Lederman (1983:22) goes on to remark on the extent to which gender constructions are contested, though she is interested in the systematic social skewing of the contest rather than in utopian projections.

8. Edited collections have become such a prevalent genre, in anthropological writing, that it is time the practice of editing was subjected to scrutiny. It is hardly necessary to add that the various works cited in this Introduction provide an essential context for our own contributions. It would be condescending to register gratitude.

9. By no means all the contributors would regard themselves as having feminist interests, however, and I would not expect them to agree with this observation. M. Strathern (in press a) offers an expanded discussion of the relationship between feminist and anthropological thought, through the example of Melanesian ethnography.

10. The point is dealt with more fully in M. Strathern 1985. I see competitive intellectual positions as speaking to competitive social interests in a world self-conceptualised as plural and heterogeneous. Watson (1984) provides an intriguing discussion of some of these self-conceptualisations.

11. Atkinson sceptically wonders what a 'sexually egalitarian' society might look like. One unpalatable answer lies of course in the world Illich (1982) has shown us – the fantasy of sexed but genderless persons.

12. I keep the adjective 'theoretical' to refer to that systematising endeavour which involves the development of abstract concepts. This fuels the analytic strategies which characterise most anthropological work. But the idea of 'theory' (like 'paradigm') is chiefly of rhetorical significance, spurring us to refine our abstractions. I would be hard put to it to propound 'an' anthropological theory as such.

13. However these positions are not completely independent of the present exercise. Chowning (pers. comm.) notes that the topics covered in these chapters derive in part from the terms of the gender group and the plan for this book. I would, however, draw attention to the chapters' very differing ethnographic styles.

14. Speakers of Austronesian (formerly Malayo-Polynesian) languages belong to a family which spreads from the Malay peninsula to Polynesia. Among the peoples referred to in this book, Kodi belong to a group of Western Austronesian language-speakers, Kove, Tubetube, Kalauna and Kwaio to Eastern Austronesian-speakers. Leaving aside Zinacantan and Central Australia, the remainder (Chambri, Foi, Nagovisi) may be classed as non- Austronesian in relation to this belt but have little in common between themselves. See the discussion in Chowning 1977:11-16.

15. As also in the case of its counterpart 'social actor': in the feminist-inspired anthropology of the 1970s, this concept had a taken-for-granted status in the proclaimed need to see women 'as social actors', perilously equated with 'persons' (e.g. Faithorn 1976; Feil 1978).

16. Biersack (1984:130) and Lederman (1983:23), for instance, both employ the term, in the papers cited in the previous section.

17. Giddens is also one source for Fardon's (1985) exploration of agency; Fardon was the first anthropologist whom I heard (in 1982) using the term with analytical effect.

18. Apart from the issue of whether the actor also determines those interests, see Fardon 1985. Fardon makes a careful distinction between actors' intentions and analysts' intentions. As will be apparent, my own concern is less with the relationship between the actors' and analysts' grounds of knowledge than with keeping 'our' own minds open to an actor's perception of agency as bypassing the whole issue of intentionality. One could here go back to a long anthropological literature on sanctions and taboo, and the automatic consequence of certain ways of acting. However, as Yeatman (1984b:29-30) has already pointed out in another context, to speak of actors' points of view in contradistinction to observers' itself incorporates a 'modern' self-understanding of human beings as agents.

CHAPTER 1

Ta'a geni: *women's perspectives on Kwaio society*[1]

ROGER M. KEESING

One approach to the thorny problems of interpreting gender in non-Western societies in terms of Western concepts – of inequality, domination, exploitation, power, status – is to let women, and men, speak for themselves. Individuals' self-accounts, especially reflections on themselves, their lives and societies, can give deepened insights about how other people's worlds look to those who live in them, and provide texts which we can confront dialectically in the task of interpreting gender systems from both inside and outside.

But letting women, or men, speak for themselves is by no means a magical solution to the epistemological and theoretical difficulties of interpreting gender in non-Western settings. First there is the whole set of issues about whether women's voices can be brought forth at all, and whether women's self-accounts will be partial, 'muted' or narrowly perspectival (cf. Young 1983b). There are other fundamental problems. Such self-accounts never answer, or even address, our questions directly, since the narrator constructs an account within a context of cultural meanings and takes for granted much of what we find problematic: the division of labour, spatial and social separation of the sexes, ideas of duty and virtue, the rules imposed by gods or ancestors. Moreover it is precisely the hegemonic character of cultures that incorporate, and shape, the consciousness both of ostensibly dominant men and of ostensibly subordinate women which makes gender inequality so analytically problematic. So we must situate ourselves critically within an experienced world as revealed in self-accounts and outside it. We must read self-accounts between, and beyond, the lines; they may tell us as much in what is not said as in what our subjects say about themselves and their lives.

A series of self-accounts given by women, and recorded by Shelley Schreiner and myself,[2] provides an important complement to the mainly male-oriented focus of published Kwaio ethnography, from Malaita in the Solomon Islands. The women's accounts can do more. If we read these texts in the light of the cautions and theoretical project set out in these chapters, Kwaio women's self-accounts illuminate questions of inequality, domination and separation in gender systems; the nature and limits of male ideological hegemony, and of consensus; women's alternative perspectives and the issue of counter-ideologies; and the question of the 'mutedness' of women's voices.

The Kwaio of Malaita

Despite the rapid Westernisation of Solomon Islands, some 3000 Kwaio speakers still live in scattered homesteads in the mountains of central Malaita, defiantly committed to their ancestral religion and customs. These traditionalists preserve a numerically thinned but substantially intact social structure. Small descent groups, predominantly agnatic but often with a cluster of non-agnatic affiliants, are loci of stability and collective action in ritual, prestige feasting, marriage alliance, feuding and litigation. Cutting across the group-centric descent-based ties to ancestors and lands are widely dispersed ties of cognatic kinship and descent that give secondary interests to lands and ancestors and allow individual mobility and fluidity of residence (Keesing 1970a, 1970b, 1971). Rituals of sacrifice and progressive desacralisation after a death provide a focus of collective action by descent groups as ritual communities (Keesing 1982a). The mortuary feasts that ostensibly reward those who buried the dead provide an arena in which descent groups assert and maintain their prestige through large-scale presentations of strung shell valuables, pigs and food (Keesing 1978a). The same is true of bridewealth prestations, although outwardly these take the form of an exchange of shell valuables, presented by the groom's kin, for foodstuffs presented by the bride's kin (Keesing 1967).

Ancestrally imposed and policed rules separate men's and women's realms and activities, spatially and socially. Menstruation, childbirth and women's urination and defaecation are highly polluting and must be isolated from the living spaces in the centre of the clearings men and women share, as well as from sacred things and places. Menstrual and childbirth seclusion, separation of living and sleeping spaces for men and women, strict separation of women's food and water from men's, and the isolation of sacrifice and other transactions with ancestors in men's houses and shrines from which women are excluded inevitably suggest sexual polarisation. Indeed the tiny Kwaio settlements map out a cosmological scheme which arrays as mirror-images women's isolation and men's isolation, menstrual huts and men's houses, giving birth to babies in contexts of pollution and giving birth to ancestors in contexts of sanctity. Women are consigned the tasks of sustained labour in swiddens, raising pigs, cutting firewood and carrying water, childcare and cooking. Men's lives are centred on ritual, feasting and exchange, and the public politics of litigation.

Although Kwaio have been tied to the world economy for more than a century by plantation labour and their need for steel tools, the traditionalists in the mountains remain relatively self-sufficient, in cultivating taro and sweet potatoes in upland swiddens, meeting animal protein needs by pig husbandry, fishing, hunting and gleaning insects, and making from forest and marine products most of the material objects they need in daily life. They have managed to insulate cash from the prestige economy in which strung shell beads are the medium of exchange.

Kwaio women, largely excluded from public politics, consigned the heaviest tasks of domestic labour, seemingly marginalised and demeaned as well as controlled by rules compartmentalising pollution, would appear to be in a clearly subordinate and secondary position. But, as we shall shortly see, there is more to it than that.

Kastom and anticolonial struggle

For eighty years the Kwaio of the central mountains have been locked in struggle against Christian invasion and the imposition of alien law. In the nineteenth century Kwaio had attacked and looted recruiting ships, avenging kin dead on Fiji and Queensland plantations. In 1911 they assassinated the first missionary in their midst; in 1965 another was killed. In 1927 they assassinated the District Officer who had imposed taxation and colonial law, and massacred his entourage (Keesing and Corris 1980). In the wake of World War II they had joined other Malaitans in the Maasina Rule anticolonial resistance movement (Keesing 1978b).

The Kwaio traditionalists, beleaguered by state power, Christianity and processes of Westernisation and post-Independence internal colonialism, have elevated their culture – cast as *kastom* (Keesing 1982b) – to serve as political symbol of identity and autonomy. And they have used their own religious ideology to confront contradictions in which the shrinking power of their ancestors, the visibly growing power and prosperity of the Christians, are central (Keesing in press). Maasina Rule, in the 1940s, gained legitimacy for custom (*kastom*) both by confronting the colonial state over issues of legal jurisdiction (claiming the right for

'Chiefs' to settle disputes according to custom) and by writing down customary laws in the style of colonial legal statutes – an enterprise endowed with mystical value. As a professional chronicler of custom, I have inevitably been incorporated into this task of writing and 'straightening out' *kastom*, a task to which male ideologues, in Maasina-Rule style *bungu 'ifi* or meeting places (Keesing 1968, 1982b), have devoted vast amounts of time and energy through the twenty years of my study.

Men's talk in ethnographic contexts has thus been laden with symbolic import in relation to the ideology of *kastom*. Kwaio custom, so conceived as political symbol, has as its core the ancestors, the rituals in which they are addressed, their powers and exploits, the lands they discovered and own, and (most important of all) the rules they enforce. These rules are focused on the separation and containment of the reproductive power and substances of women, through menstrual and childbirth seclusion.

Only in terms of Kwaio men's thirty-year project of codifying *kastom* can the accounts Schreiner and I were eventually able to elicit be understood. These accounts emerged along a fault-line of contradiction in male-authored accounts of *kastom*. Male ideologues, in articulating the rules isolating the dangerous powers of women as manifest in menstruation and childbirth, were engaging realms of life and responsibility from which they are systematically excluded. Women saw their task as filling in this gap in the codification of *kastom*, of making certain that the crucial realm which *they* controlled was properly recorded. This perception of their task, shaped the versions women gave of themselves and their society. Women talked about their own lives not as autobiographical interpretations and revelations of self, but as moral texts illustrating the travails, responsibilities and virtues of A Woman's Life. In a recent examination of the micropolitical and historical context in which the self-accounts were elicited (Keesing 1985) I sketch the process through which initially reluctant and relatively inarticulate women friends became voluble and articulate, overwhelming Schreiner and me with both the quantity and ethnographic richness of their talk. That paper is a necessary complement to this chapter. More than four years of fieldwork observation have thus provided a wealth of data on how women, and men, live their lives. These data, complementing and augmenting what women say about themselves, have been drawn on elsewhere (e.g., Keesing 1982b) and will be articulated in the self-accounts in a planned longer work.

So, too, is the vast corpus of male-authored narratives, including the self-account by the Ga'enaafou feast-giver 'Elota (see Keesing 1978a), principally consisting of hundreds of hours of men's talk in 'committee meetings' and other settings where I was 'writing down *kastom*'.

Limitations of space preclude my giving extended examples of men talking about *kastom* and themselves in relation to it; rather, I here generalise about men's accounts in contrasting those by Kwaio women. I focus on what self-accounts reveal about women's perspectives on and experiences of their society, and through them on questions of inequality, domination and (less explicitly) agency, in Strathern's sense (see Introduction). The rhetorical, ideological and moral force of these self-accounts as statements of women's virtue, and, their epistemologically problematic nature as 'autobiography' must, however, be borne in mind. What they tell us about 'Kwaio women' can only be interpreted in terms of the context of their elicitation.

Women's self-accounts

The fifteen women from whom we so far have detailed accounts span a range in age from twenties to seventies (our female informants include a girl of five; see Keesing 1982a:32, 34). Initially we worked with women I had known for fifteen years as friends and close neighbours. Our immediate neighbour Boori'au, in her sixties, was regarded as highly knowledgeable – an apt spokeswoman to talk about *fa'aabunga naa ta'a geni*, 'women's taboos'.[3] But others who were early informants – Lamana, Fei'a, Gwaalau, Fa'aoria – were not regarded as particularly 'important' or knowledgeable. They did not see themselves (and were not seen by others) as appropriate spokeswomen to tell us about *kastom* pertaining to women. But partly because of this, these women were persuaded to tell us about their own selves as well as about women's virtues. Fa'afataa, forceful and brilliantly articulate, became a regular visitor to our clearing when her daughter married there in 1977. Her accounts of her life and of female virtue now run to more than a hundred pages. This sustained account in turn stimulated an equally voluminous (though more rhetorically repetitious) one by Oloi'a, another extremely forceful, and knowledgeable ideologue of *kastom* and chronicler of her life. The self-accounts changed somewhat in character as such ideologues, including tiny 'Etenga, who extolled and emulated the fearlessness of her warrior ancestresses, came forward or were put forward by other women. These voluminous and rhetorical accounts were interspersed with more low key accounts by those of others who, often as chance visitors, were persuaded to talk about what they deemed to be unimportant lives.

An important question raised by feminist anthropology is the extent to which, obscured by male-centric ethnographies, there lie women's *countercultures* that challenge the central elements of culture as male ideology. The Kwaio women's accounts of self and society interestingly illuminate this question. For Kwaio women do not, in our texts, articulate an ideology counter to the dominant 'culture'. They do not challenge the rights and rules men claim and impose, the rules of the ancestors, or male hegemony in ritual and public politics. Adult women, especially those in and beyond middle age, all proclaimed (often over and over again) the virtues of chastity, hard work, and punctilious observance of pollution rules, and bemoaned the laxity of the younger generation. That is, women almost never challenged the established order of things, what they see as ancestrally imposed rules and virtues. If that be mystification, the outcome of male ideological hegemony, they are fully taken in by it; if that simply be 'Kwaio culture' they fully subscribe to it (see Gewertz and Errington, this volume).

Yet at the same time, although few women said anything male ideologues could disagree with, their views of themselves, of female gender, of women's roles, were distinctive. Kwaio women often reveal *perspectives on* Kwaio society quite different from those of men. Whereas men depict themselves as active agents in maintaining relations with the ancestors (through sacrifice, prayer, and ritual), women often depict themselves as custodians of virtue, the moral keystones of their tiny settlements. Boori'au observed that 'a woman takes charge over the place she has married to.' Lamana, who deems herself a minor figure, nonetheless constructs a revealing picture of a woman's central place in the preservation of order:

A woman is in charge of ['minds'] the living in her clearing, the territory where she lives. She's in charge. She is the 'big woman' there. She is responsible for the *kaakaba* [menstrual area]; she's responsible for the food; she's responsible for the way people live there. If she lives properly people wouldn't get sick there [from 'pollution']. If some violation does happen to her, she'll report it and they'll straighten it out; so that sickness will be kept under control. But in a settlement where the woman didn't live properly, and things were kept hidden or not done right, eventually someone would die from it.

Fa'afataa expressed a similar theme:

If I have good sense, if I am responsible, then it's as though I'm the owner of the house [speaking metaphorically, and using the Pidgin word 'owner']. Even though I'm only young [40s], I'm in charge of our place. I'm the one who is responsible for our living. If I live properly and follow the rules and take charge of things properly, Kwalata [her husband] and I will grow old together and live to see our children grown...I'm like the 'owner' of the settlement. I'm the 'owner'; and if I take charge of things properly, our money and pigs will be used for important things like mortuary feasts [rather than expiating pollution violations, purifying curses, paying compensation].

Kwaio women are saying that they are the central agents in the reproduction of their society and culture. A woman, standing in the centre of the clearing, the middle of the Kwaio social universe, astride the generations with powers of life and death in her hands, creates and perpetuates order, maintains the boundaries which the unseen spirits police. Feeding and teaching, quintessentially social and cultural acts, are key symbols of a woman's life. The cycles that connect mothers and daughters and grand-daughters, in these constructions women place on their lives and culture, are as central as are the cycles that connect men to their ancestors through patrifilial links in male accounts. To the extent these Kwaio women challenge male ideological hegemony, then, it is a perspectival challenge, a differential evaluation of where crucial responsibility lies.

Women's self-accounts and ideologies of kastom

In seeing their task as codifying those domains of *kastom* in which women play the central part, our informants were led to relate the circumstances of their own lives to the preservation of the moral order of society, and to the key role of women in this process. Senior women recurrently contrasted the virtues of their mothers' generation with the laxity of their daughters' generation, and used this contrast to explain how and why Kwaio power has dwindled. When our subjects endlessly and repetitively recited the rules governing menstruation and childbirth, the separation of menstrual area from dwelling houses, men's things (*'ola ni wane*) from women's (*'ola ni geni*), male realms from female, they were at once emulating men's recitation of *kastom*, confronting the contradictions of recent history, and proclaiming their own virtues and centrality in Kwaio communities. Lamana's text illustrates the close relationship between self-accounts and ideological pronouncements, vividly reveals the cyclical perception of intergenerational continuity that shapes them, and gives glimpses of the threat of disorder from without that gives the preservation of *kastom* special urgency.

My mother ... was the one who taught me from the beginning. She taught me about the ways of the *kaakaba* [menstrual area]. Taught me I couldn't bring things from the *kaakaba* to the house, or from the house to the *kaakaba*. I couldn't eat men's food. I couldn't drink men's water. She taught me about those things when I was still small. I learned those ways and followed them. Then when I was bigger she taught me about working. 'You'll work like this. You'll give food to a man like this. You'll cut firewood. You'll carry water. You'll work for food.' They might sound like unimportant things, but they aren't when our parents teach them to us. Then we [women] get married. But even once we are married our parents don't just let go of us. Even if our own mother dies our [classificatory] parents still keep on teaching us. 'You have married to another territory. You must hold on to all the ways [of work, duty, etc.] that led them to choose you in the first place. Feed pigs. Work hard. Keep your clearing scraped [clean]. Carry the water, pick up the pig shit. Feed your husband. Feed pigs for their shrine. Feed pigs for the mortuary feasts for their dead. They'll say you're a good woman.' Those are the things our relatives teach us about, the important things in our lives – that's what it's all about, for us pagans.

Then when we have children, it is our turn to teach them. Because girls get married when they're still young. We are the branches on the left side of the tree. There are fully ten things you have to learn if you're a girl. If you follow them properly they'll think of you as one who would make a good wife. If you don't, they'll criticize you like this: 'That one, if we paid for her, wouldn't work for us. She wouldn't pick up the pig shit, wouldn't feed us properly, wouldn't feed pigs for the [ancestors of the] place she married to. Who would marry her?' You'd hear about it, too. So we pay attention. And someone who is old like me, if she has children, will try to make sure they learn these things too. But nowadays, with all the new foreign ways, they don't pay attention to these things the way we did. They aren't following those things. Those traditional ways might end with our generation – but if our children believe us about how important they are they'll follow them too.

The way women used these self-accounts to interpret recent Kwaio history, portraying the supposed decline of female virtues as explanation of the growing powerlessness of the ancestors and of the contemporary Kwaio who follow their rules, is particularly clear in Oloi'a's accounts. She gives these connections a special twist in underlining the part played by men in this decline:

In my parents' day – I remember this, because I went with them – if we people went down to a mission village ... all of us womenfolk would stay just at the mouth of the clearing. The men stayed at the mouth of the clearing. We put all our bags there. If a woman was to visit with some woman or man in the mission who was her close relative, she'd wait till they told her to come. Then – her pipe, she'd leave behind. Her bag, she'd leave behind. She couldn't even bring a coal from the mission village to kindle her pipe. She had to go there empty-handed. In those days when I was young, they cut paths that circled around those mission villages. I saw that with my own eyes. When we women went down to the mission, we didn't have skirts to put on. A girl who wasn't married yet had to go there naked. One who had a pubic apron [a married woman] would have only that on.

But that's not the way people follow the taboos nowadays. The mission has caused our living to go bad. Now, even a priest will go to the mission village and ask for a coal [to kindle his pipe]. People say that's the rule that governs you now. How are we to keep taboos now? We women try to hold to the taboos. But the men go on like this. When Maasina Rule came the men said, 'We have to work close to the coast now, mixing up with the mission people. And those mission people have to mix up with us non-Christians ['wicked people'].' And so bags were taken back and forth, people asked for tobacco back and forth, and for fire. Even men ate things from the bags of the mission people. And we women started to kindle our pipes from the coals of the mission people. 'The Rule governs you.' That's the way they talked about Maasina Rule: 'It has come. The Rule governs you.'

And we looked around us and said, 'Oh, the men are taking their bags into the [mission] clearing.' They were taking them into the clearing, and they were the ones who ate consecrated pigs. 'Let's us women do it too. Let's go into the clearing. When we go down to the mission, let's take our bags into the clearing. Let's leave our bags outside and peep inside the church. Let's kindle our pipes with their coals. The men who eat consecrated pigs, the "custom people", are doing it. We womenfolk should just take our bags into the mission.' The important men saw us do it and they said, 'Oh, that's all right.' That was the beginning of things turning in a different way ...

But nowadays people's living is no good. Who lives to be old any more? The young people have destroyed the senior generation. People nowadays take a bag from the mission village and just bring it back to the 'wicked'. Men take bags they have had in mission villages into their shrines. They wear the clothes into the shrines that they have had down there in the mission. Even important men, men who eat consecrated pigs ...

The mission came to our country and pacified the people. The people went to the mission; and even though their ancestors remained they no longer were punitive. The ancestors weren't quarrelsome. Because people in the mission just ate with women, because men stayed in a menstrual area. The ancestors no longer had anyone in their men's houses, no longer had anyone sacrificing to them, had no one left to feed them – there was nothing to sustain their power. It's as though the ancestors became cold.

When our subjects were persuaded to talk about themselves, their girlhood, their marriage, their children, they most often did so less to explicate a sense of self or individuality than to comment on the values of A Woman's Life (that is, in relation to ideal norms about how a virtuous woman would conduct her life in the face of its vicissitudes). One must thus be particularly careful not to project assumptions derived from our genre of autobiographical self-revelation and self-interpretation onto the Kwaio women's texts. Lamana's account of how she stayed on as beleaguered but virtuous affine after her husband (the A'esuala priest) died, despite pressures by his volatile brother Folofo'u to dislodge her, serves to illustrate the dialectical relationship between particular life circumstances and A Virtuous Woman, between self-justification and acknowledged values.

When my husband died, I did something that was important to people in the old days. When he died I stayed on here, and didn't remarry. My life with him was very good, and he left me [died]. So I took off my pubic apron [a public statement that a widow will not consider remarrying]. And I didn't remarry. I stayed on here and gave mortuary feasts. I paid bridewealth for my children. I helped my husband's people here – Folofo'u – give mortuary feasts. I fed pigs for sacrifice at the shrine on this place ...

When my husband died my brother-in-law [Folofo'u] said to me, 'Go back where you came from. Go back to your place – your husband is dead. And leave your children here with me.' But I replied, 'No, I can't go back. I'm going to stay on here with them.' I stayed on here with them. Folofo'u said to me, 'Go ahead and give a mortuary feast for your husband. That I'd like to see!' So my brother-in-law Laubasi and I tethered thirty pigs up at Naufee. They ate thirty pigs there, for the death of my husband. Three hundred valuables we got, a hundred of them major ones ... I raised pigs for the feast for my husband's death; then people said, 'Oh, she is just staying on here.' ... If they had criticized me too much about it, I would have gone to the mission ... [In what follows she is carrying on an imaginary conversation with her arch-enemy Folofo'u ...]. 'I begot male children for this place. You, Folofo'u, even though you're a grown man, you haven't done anything strong for the ritual of this place; if I had taken my children to the mission, you'd have had to go yourself. You wouldn't have been able to stay here [i.e., because you can't keep relationships with the ancestors in proper fashion]. It is my son Laeniamae who is the priest at A'esuala now. He's the one who sacrifices when people gather here.'

Such alternation between recounting circumstances of one's own life and stepping back to comment on that life in relation to ideal norms, between a woman's own responsible fulfilment and teaching of virtue and the general moral order and women's place in it, recurs throughout the texts.

Women's perspectives on Kwaio society

Thus, alternation leads to questions about the sources of women's perspectives on Kwaio society. Some, it would seem, derive from a polarisation in the division of labour that begins in childhood. Women spend their time, from girlhood onward, caring for children, fetching water, cooking, gardening, cutting firewood, and tidying the clearing; men spend their time planning and staging rituals and feasts and marriages, feuding and settling disputes, felling and fencing swiddens, and just talking. These differences in roles and paths engender different life experiences for men and women, physically and emotionally as well as socially. The physical/emotional experiences of menstruation, pregnancy, childbirth and suckling evoke distinctive self-images and social bonds; men may talk about such experiences but can never share them. This is equally true for menstrual segregation and childbirth seclusion, as both attendant and mother, and the experiences of the daily round of work. The work women do, singly and in groups, in a world of gardens, mud and vegetation, of thatch, smoke, roasting taro and pigs' droppings, vividly creates distinctive subjective experiences and orientations which emerge, if often only between the lines, in women's talk about themselves and their way of life. Oloi'a's instructions to a (hypothetical) daughter were:

Your work, girl, is to stay in your own house. And when day comes you take your burning coal, your knife, your bag, your leaf umbrella, and you go and work in the garden. You cut firewood, too, and scrape the clearing. In the morning, scrape the inside of your house clean. Then pick up the pig shit. Then go out and work in the garden. You come back from the garden and roast taro for everyone. And you fetch drinking water, feed the pigs – and feed the people. This is your work ...

Kwaio women's talk is redolent with the mundane experiences of work, of kinesic and sensory images of everyday acts performed thousands of times, even where they are left implicit in rhetoric about responsibilities and virtues.

The differences between men's and women's perspectives toward their society also derive from the gulf between the jural rights men exercise and the interpersonal influence and responsibilities women exercise. A mother, even in precolonial times, may well have exerted the major influence on who and when a son or daughter married; but the father and his male kin have primary jural rights, publicly accepting or rejecting the marriage and taking the lead in paying or distributing bridewealth. Men depict their world and their *kastom* more in terms of rights, women more in terms of social responsibilities and the shaping of others' action by precept and example.

Yet another source of contrasting perspectives lies in the distinctive cycle created by patterns of marriage and postmarital residence. A woman's double role, as wife progressively absorbed into her husband's local group and as sister bound still to her own 'side', to her brothers and her ancestors, emerges clearly in Boori'au's account:

[A woman] has two sides, equally strong. She is strongly attached to the group into which she marries: she raises pigs for her husband and father-in-law. But when her own ancestors ask for pigs, she raises them; she has strong ties still to her father and brother. And it is her own ancestors from whom she seeks strength to make her family live well, to do the things women do ... Her strength doesn't come from her husband's ancestors, but from her own ... Her husband's side is separate. For the good living of their family, his consecrated pigs and hers are just as important. A woman who is strong will raise consecrated pigs which her husband and his people will eat and [consecrated] pigs which her brothers and her people will eat ... A strong woman will take responsibility over the place to which she marries; she will raise consecrated pigs herself, will feed people, will gather together the men of the group into which she has married, will take a big part when they give a mortuary feast.

Fa'afataa's account of her life takes a different view of this two-sided orientation established through marriage:

I have to take proper care of my husband; it's as though he has taken the place of my father; and I've borne him children. I don't want to be left by myself as a poor widow ... Our husband replaces our brothers and father in our lives when he takes us off in marriage.

These distinctive perspectives are artefacts of social processes and differential life experiences; where they reinforce women's sense of their own worth and their power over and responsibility for men and children, they acquire strong ideological force.

The theme of cross-generational continuity between women and their daughters emerges over and over again in the texts, as in Lamana's earlier account. Our subjects stressed their responsibilities and connections to their daughters, in several cases newly married and facing the critical early period as affines under scrutiny and stress – and in some cases facing criticism or rejection for pollution violations that could rebound onto their mothers. Thus Fa'afataa, whose daughter had been ousted soon after marriage because she menstruated in her husband's clearing, was preoccupied with how this terrible thing (which had never happened to Fa'afataa, or her mother, or to the daughter before her marriage) had come to pass, bringing near disaster to the daughter's affines and disgrace to her family. The daughter had just re-married, to our next door neighbour's son; and Fa'afataa's talk dwelled on maternal virtue and responsibility. Oloi'a returned over and over again to the scorn and rejection that had been heaped on her by her husband's female kin when she had first arrived as a bride twenty five years earlier. She used this as a commentary on her own daughter's recent marriage and on her own career as wife and mother, which she was idealising retrospectively in answer to those who had doubted her.

The theme of continuity between mothers and daughters emerges as well in repeated idealisations by women of their own mothers as paragons of virtue and industry they could scarcely live up to. Fa'afataa's elderly mother Teobo is herself rather laconic about what she takes to have been an unremarkable life. But Fa'afataa idealises her mother's virtues, using them as foil for what, in the stylised self-deprecation of a Kwaio feastgiver, she depicts as her own inadequacies:

From the time I was young, I never saw my mother make trouble, curse, or do things like that. I never heard anyone say anything bad about her – not my grandfather, not her brothers. She was only interested in being strong for giving mortuary feasts, for feeding pigs, for paying bridewealth. When something happened [e.g., a death, a pollution violation, an elopement] and her husband didn't have any money, she'd produce some of her own and say, 'Here are some shell valuables.' 'Here is a pig.' 'Let's give a feast.' But even though my mother was strong and had resources, I'm not that way. I don't take after her. Even though I think about doing important things, giving mortuary feasts, working for a good living, I can't seem to accomplish anything. I'm just young – what can I do? I think about doing things, but actually doing them turns out to be impossible for me ... I don't have the resources, the valuables or the pigs.

Elsewhere Fa'afataa places herself in a matriline of virtue:

In all the time since [I got married] I haven't caused a single pollution violation. Not from menstruation, not from childbirth, not from cursing – not once ... From the time I was just a little girl, I hadn't done anything wrong, anything that might have caused my father's death. Then, after I was married but when he was still young, he died. But not at my hand. I had warned him against going down to those Christian villages [hence exposing himself to menstrual and childbirth pollution], but he didn't listen ... If he had, he'd still be alive. I never made a mistake [i.e., pollution violation]; and Teobo, my mother, never made a mistake. And her mother Kafuala hadn't done anything wrong in her day either – menstruating in the wrong place, stealing, having a sexual affair, defiling [sacred things]. So she raised her daughter, my mother Teobo, to be a good woman too.

There may be more to this cross-generational continuity than meets the eye, since grandmothers often provide child care for young grandchildren and form close emotional bonds with them.[4] The connection from grandmother to grand-daughter is direct as well as mediated.

Kwaio cosmology and the question of 'pollution'

Schreiner and I have been led progressively away from viewing the rules about women's bodies in terms of 'pollution' (see Keesing 1982a:64-71). It is possible to characterise Kwaio cosmology through an opposition between a men's sacred realm and a women's polluted realm; to depict women as polluted by their essential nature and bodily substances; and even to depict men as symbolically 'cultural', women as symbolically 'natural'. The seclusion of women to confine the dangerous emanations of menstruation and childbirth and the seclusion of men to confine the dangerous manifestations of sacrifice and ancestral power are transparent mirror-images. Women create infants in a context of pollution; men create ancestral ghosts in a context of sanctity. But while such a characterisation would appear to illuminate certain themes in Kwaio symbolism, it also hides a deeper coherence.

Both women and men in seclusion are *abu* [tabu], from the standpoint of those in the 'neutral' (*mola*) middle realm of the clearing where the routine activities of everyday life are centred. To see women as polluted and men as sacred would ultimately obscure our understanding of women's views of themselves and their ancestrally ordained culture. Kwaio categories deal not with substances and essences but with boundaries, invasions, dissolutions of form. It is not menstrual blood that emanates danger; it is menstrual blood in the wrong places (Keesing 1982a:72). What men do in their isolation and what women do in theirs represent processes whereby form, cultural order – disrupted and dissolved – is *re-created*. The process of re-creating cultural order is the process of becoming *mola* again, of moving back into the boundaries of the mundane. Marginalisation from the community takes place in the forest and on the outer rim of the clearing. Both men and women's lives represent alternations between order and disorder, boundaries and breaches of boundaries, the centre and the periphery. In an important sense the centre of the Kwaio social world lies not in the men's house at the upper margin of the clearing but in the dwelling houses, in the *mola* central part of the clearing: in the life of hearth and home, separated off by boundaries above and below. This view of women as agents at the centre is reinforced by the preoccupation of Kwaio narrators with their role in socialisation and the observation of ancestral rules, and thus with their place in the reproduction of cultural order.

If Kwaio cosmology were indeed based on premises of the impurity of women's substances, we might expect to find such symbolic constructions mirrored in the way women talk about themselves and their bodies. Women's lives are confined by rules compartmentalising their bodily functions and sexuality. Yet the texts give no evidence that women express negative feelings about their own bodies, about menstrual blood and other bodily substances, or their sexuality. They tend to be notably less prudish than men about sexuality. 'Copulation', as one said, 'is the mother of us all'. Although senior women extol the virtues of chastity and deplore modern 'promiscuity', the view of virtue glimpsed in some of the autobiographies contrasts with and complements a male view. Kwaio men seek to maintain rigid control over the sexuality of wives, sisters, and daughters – while envying the (perhaps mythical) Don Juans who seduce with impunity. Women if anything see their own bodies in terms of purity, not pollution – or if not quite purity, at least sacrosanct boundedness in relation to sexual invasion by male deed or word. A teen-aged girl, 'Etenga's daughter, commented revealingly about the compensation just paid by a man who had invaded her sexuality by gossiping about her:

He went around talking about me, spoiled my reputation [lit., 'put badness on me']. ['Etenga interjects: Men just accuse girls falsely. A man will brag that he is having a sexual affair with a girl. But he really isn't.] Then [her daughter continues] paying money is the only way to satisfy her mind. The minds of men are messed up. If a man wrongs a girl he must sacralize her [*fa'aabua*, 'cause-be *abu*'] with [shell] money. Sexually invasive talk is forbidden; [sexually malicious] gossip is forbidden; going around talking about a girl is forbidden. In the olden days I could have been killed because of something someone said about me. If I had had an affair, I would have been killed unless they had compensated me to make me *abu* [sacred/pure] again.

Fa'afataa also talks about sexuality and the *abu*-ness of person:

[A woman's] whole body is *abu*. Our bodies are *abu* even though we may joke and fool around. Let's take an unmarried girl. If I were an unmarried girl my breasts would be *abu*. It's all right if my close relative brushes against them or touches them by accident when he puts his arm around me. But my breasts are *abu*: if someone touches them he has to pay valuables [as compensation]. My legs are *abu*. If a man steps over them, or if a man touches me in any sexual way, my relatives will demand compensation ... Or if someone made a sexual reference about me and I or one of my relatives heard ... they'd have taken their weapons and gone straight away ... It's as though I were a sprig of *la'e* [evodia, an aromatic shrub used in magic for wealth] for attracting money.

Our texts, mainly from senior women, do not adequately represent the perspectives of a younger generation that has achieved something of a sexual revolution in the last fifteen years. Only indirectly, as targets of ideologues of a generation still deeply committed to the virtues of chastity, do the sexual mores of young people emerge through the texts.

Yet in some of her less rhetorical moments, Boori'au speaks revealingly about women's sexuality, across generations.

Women here want to have sex just as men do. A girl who desires a man will try to get him to make love to her. Or to marry her. You've seen how girls are getting pregnant nowadays – well likely as not she's the one who started it. A girl who desires a man, whether he's single or married or a widower, will proposition him. It's not just men who desire women – it works both ways ...

A man and woman who got married because they desired one another got together so they could have sex, so why shouldn't they enjoy it? They have sex, they enjoy it, they have children, they get old together. That's the way it is with us Melanesians. That's what we get married for ... The work comes second. Feeding pigs comes second. Feeding people, living in a place – that's all secondary. Sex is first of all.

She goes on to talk about the inevitability of adultery if a young husband goes to a distant plantation, leaving his wife behind.

A woman doesn't just stay [by herself]. From the time she is born a woman has a vagina. From the time a man is born he has a penis. What did they get two different things for if it wasn't for intercourse? That's what penises and vaginas are for – copulating...[Returning to an imaginary conversation with a young husband who has gone off to a plantation] 'You married her, why did you go off and leave her? ... Is she just supposed to stay home with her vagina? A vagina needs to eat too. What does it eat? Only a penis – nothing else will do. She can stay home and eat taro or sweet potato or cabbage. But what is her vagina supposed to eat while you're away? You've got the penis that belongs to her. If you take it away she'll look around for another one!'

In other contexts she proclaims the virtue of chastity and condemns its decline. But here and elsewhere in the texts our subjects depict women as active agents of their own sexuality rather than as passive objects of male attention who must be kept under vigilant control by the men with jural rights over them. Kwaio men's accounts acknowledge the latent power of female sexuality but portray it in terms of a woman's inability to resist a man's sexual advances: hence women must be policed and men who transgress killed – or, now this is no longer possible, heavily fined.

Seclusion, independence and solidarity

Whereas men usually depict the seclusion of Kwaio women in menstruation and childbirth and their recurrent marginalisation in ritual in negative terms, the texts give clear glimpses of an alternative view in which women in seclusion are substantially freed both from direct male control and burdens of daily work; and in which considerable solidarity among women emerges. A number, in response to our queries, harkened back to adolescence as a time when girls of a neighbourhood visit back and forth during their menstrual isolation, when they discuss (often ribaldly) one another's partners and sexual adventures. Lamana's narrative will serve to illustrate:

Four or five, or even ten, girls would gather down in the *kaakaba* [menstrual area] and we'd talk about dating.[5] We didn't talk about serious things. Dating and things, going to feasts – we'd talk about those things, about fooling around. The girls would say things like this: 'The man you're dating with is no good.' Her girlfriend would say, 'What of it?' Another would say, 'Well, the boy I'm dating is really nice.' Everyone would just laugh when we'd talk like that. That's the way of young people. The young women would talk in the *kaakaba*, on the path, in the garden; and there was nothing else they'd talk about – just dating, and people's [sexual] affairs. Those are the things they'd talk about. They'd be careful where and how they'd talk about those things: sometimes a sexual affair a couple were having in the bush would be known to her girlfriends, and they'd talk about it. But if the adults found out, it would cause big trouble. So we'd only talk about those things among ourselves, along the path, in the *kaakaba* when we were menstruating ... If it came out [that a couple were having an affair] we could talk about it openly. Even though we were just young, we could bring trouble down on ourselves if we disclosed such a thing we knew about. In those days most girls wouldn't have had a sexual affair with the man who took them in marriage; so mostly we just talked about dating, in the *kaakaba*. We talked about the men we were dating. We just laughed about it. We'd joke that so-and-so wasn't any good [as a dating partner]. That kind of joking has always been the way of unmarried young women. My grandmother got married because of that kind of talking. Arumae and Tafulao and Tolongee'au and Guanga'i were in the *kaakaba*, at Tala'aa. They were gossiping. One of the girls farted, and another said, 'That's the bald man's fart.' One of the men up in the clearing heard them and reported it to Ri'imolaa, the balding man Arumae was dating: 'They swore against you. You're dating with Arumae and the girls down there swore against you. One of them said, after someone had farted, "The bald man's fart".' The men talked about it and went to Arumae, and 'seized' her [*laua* an infrequent variant form of marriage], and took her with them to Uo. They got there and demanded compensation to purify the curse. 'You swore against me, you'll have to purify me.' They paid three pigs as purification. And then Ri'imolaa paid bridewealth for her. It was Arumae who gave birth to my father. And it all started with that talk by the girls in the *kaakaba*. A bride came because of that talk.

A woman may become *abu* (in a sense we can gloss as 'sacralised') if an ancestor intervenes in her life and imposes special restrictions on her. These rules parallel those governing a ritually mature man (Keesing 1982a:93-94; 207-08), in restricting her contact with menstruating women, childbirth and other sources of danger associated with the female body. Usually a woman is sacralised after menopause, but sometimes young women are singled out (for example, in being saved from a life-threatening illness or coma). Boori'au describes her own sacralised state:

A woman who has lived well and grown old will be made *abu* by her ancestor. She will plant an *'otofono* [consecrated magical shrub] for her ancestor and call it her *abuabu* [the area by a men's house where sacred plants are kept], though it is in the clearing. Then she is *abu*. She can't clean up infants' shit, can't go into the menstrual area, can't babysit for an infant. She can't be cursed by children or she'll get sick. She can't eat food touched by a menstruating woman, can't touch anything associated with the menstrual area ... She's *abu*, like men. If she breaks open a coconut [a canonical ritual act], no woman can share it with her – only boys.

She in effect enters a separate, interstitial, gender category. The parallels with priestly taboos are transparent. Fa'afataa, who is not yet sacralised, describes this state hypothetically in characteristically vivid fashion:

A woman's life is just going along and the thing that happens to men [as a normal part of the life cycle] happens to her. Her ancestor demands her; wants her to be [by] herself ... 'I want you to be *abu*.' ... Say the ancestor says 'I want Fa'afataa to be *abu*.' So that if I touch or eat anything upon which a curse has been placed – even though I may not be past menopause – I'll get sick ... It's not that I choose myself to be *abu*: the ancestor chooses *me* ...

Even though I don't know that ancestor's magic, the ancestor says 'You are my woman: I claim you.' ... Even though we don't know his magic and ritual, he wants our bodies – as though he wants to have a special bond with us ... It's as though, if it were me, the ancestor had taken aim at me and said 'You're the woman I want, I want you to be *abu*. I want you to observe all my rules.' If the ancestor makes me *abu*, if I put my legs across someone's way, no woman can step over them or she'll have to purify and sacralize ['cause-be *abu*'] me. Because it's as though the ancestor is in my body, is specially bound to me.

Although women are excluded from sacrifice and many phases of ritual, some have not only an encyclopaedic knowledge of ritual procedure (in which senior women perform several key parts), but also penetrating insights into an underlying symbolic grammar beyond the view of many male ritual officiants. Normative statements that it is men who are responsible for relations with the ancestors and for the performance of descent group rituals must be tempered by the way women approach their ancestors directly, command magical and ritual knowledge, and in some cases understand the symbolic system more globally and incisively than their male counterparts. Kwaio men and women cite with approval a case concerning a woman whose husband was priest for a shrine where the congregation had mainly died out or become Christian. He died when his son was still a teen-ager and had not yet learned the procedure and magic for sacrifice, the lines of ancestors whose names must be recited. The boy's mother, though from a different group, commanded so much of her dead husband's ritual knowledge that she taught her son the required procedures and magic, then stood at the edge of the shrine and prompted him while he addressed his ancestors.

Fenaaori, deeply respected by both men and women for her knowledge, gave me a penetrating analysis of the taboos that apply to women in menstrual seclusion in terms of the mirror-imaging of women's marginalisation and the seclusion of men after sacrifice. The procedures (such as eating of taro and coconut pudding) the men perform in their men's houses would be defiled if women performed the same acts 'on top of them', in their menstrual huts. This remains the clearest folk exegesis I have yet recorded of a complex that lies at the heart of Kwaio religion.

Fa'afataa talks about how a woman can become repository and custodian of the ritual and magical knowledge of a dwindling group, and pass it on to her son:

A woman whose talk is straight and proper, who commands curing magic and the knowledge it entails, is the one people will turn to [as opposed to one whose powers have not been confirmed by success]. 'So-and-so is the one I like. She knows about curing, she knows about divination, she receives true messages in dream. *She* knows how to get the truth [through divination or dream], the way her father and grandfather did.'

A woman who is the last of her group, where no men are left – like Boori'au or Faifanaageni – will be responsible for all the knowledge for good living. She will command the knowledge passed down from her father and grandfather, and if she has a son she will teach it to him.

These extracts illustrate both the extent and the limits of women's control of ritual knowledge: they can, under unusual circumstances, take the crucial part in preserving and interpreting knowledge of ritual procedures. But they do so as custodians on behalf of the sons who are the appropriate links to ancestors. A key part of a woman's role is to pass on her duties and virtues to her daughters; a key part of a man's role is to pass on his ritual and magical knowledge to his sons. A woman may, of necessity, be left to act in lieu of dead husband or brother as best she can. Note here an interesting contradiction, in terms of women's quest for status, for prestige and respect. While a strong father, brothers, and descent group provide security and resources and status, it is the *absence* of senior men that opens the widest challenges for a woman to become powerful, to succeed her father and preserve her group's magical and ritual knowledge.

A passage from Oloi'a's account represents a creative, philosophical extrapolation of Kwaio symbology. She develops a simile in which the earth, as symbol of origins, is seen as source of the good and bad in human life:

We sprouted from the earth like leaves: the land is like our mother. We sprouted from the earth – and death originated along with us humans. It's as though they put us here [the 'they' is impersonal and rhetorical] and they put dying here along with us ... All the things we die from sprouted beside us from the earth along with leaves and stones and trees. It's as though the earth created [lit. 'gave'] death along with us humans.

All the things we can die from – those are all things the earth put here with us. 'You and the things you die from are to live here on the land.' [Again, 'earth' is personified as a kind of abstract agent.] Everything that happens to us for the worse and everything that happens to us for the better sprouted with us from the earth. 'Bad things are to sprout here with you. Good things are to sprout here with you. These things are to befall you; these are the things that will come to pass.' So both good things and bad things stand with us here, with us who sprouted from the earth, with the leaves and trees and stones ... The earth is like our mother. It put everything here with us. If you do good things you will live well. If you do bad things, it's as though the earth itself will destroy you.

Women and the quest for prestige

Kwaio gain prestige by giving, not receiving. Cycles of exchange of shell valuables, in mortuary feasts and bridewealth, are a major preoccupation. Mortuary feasts, ostensibly to reward those who buried the dead for their acts of kinship service, provide an arena for descent groups and individuals to display their largesse, gain and maintain renown. Bridewealth prestations provide another setting where descent groups and individuals can publicly demonstrate their strength. Rights to bury the dead, and individual presentations in mortuary feasts are carefully kept track of, subject to eventual reciprocation. Bridewealth contributions in one generation establish rights to receive bridewealth in the next (even though each wedding feast is cast as an exchange between valuables from the groom's side, food from the bride's).

Women, wives and sisters and daughters, contribute to these prestations, both as members of a feastgiving group and as members of the kindreds of individuals giving the feast. Except in the case of children, the valuables they give usually represent their own earnings, accumulated through sale of craft goods, pigs or produce. The importance of such prestations as a path to self-esteem and 'renown' (*talo'a*) for a woman emerges clearly from the texts. Structurally, a married woman has a double role, as wife and as daughter/sister. In each capacity her contributions have special import. Fa'afataa uses the cast of characters created by marriage of her daughter to talk at length about how a married woman able to present her own valuables and pigs alongside those of her husband accrues special prestige and radiates special virtue, both when she and her husband contribute to mortuary feasts given by her kin (in which case her pigs are tethered first and she takes centre stage to give speeches) and when she stands with him while he and his group give a feast to honour their dead. She highlights the latter with characteristic reference to her own mother's special virtue:

My mother gave mortuary feasts, paid bridewealth. Her brothers gave a mortuary feast and she'd tie up her own pigs and hang up her own valuables with them. They'd hang up their valuables, she'd hang up hers. When her husband gave a mortuary feast he hung up his valuables and she hung up hers. She was really a strong woman ... Some strong women, who end up marrying insubstantial men who can't accomplish things themselves, are the force behind their husbands' deeds, using valuables they earn [by selling] taro and pigs and tobacco. When her husband does something [as an assertion of strength] she says 'Here are my valuables I earned with my own hands.' Someone who does that, who acts as a major partner in staging a feast, would be called *suarilobo* [something like 'right-hand man']: it was like fighting at the right hand of a warrior. A strong woman would earn her own money, stand beside her husband holding her own valuables ... What's important is that their two sides, the husband's and the wife's, be separate when they stand together to stage a feast, pay for a woman [with bridewealth], give a purificatory sacrifice.

An alternative perspective on women's own contributions is presented in Bioana's depiction of herself as feast sponsor.

When I've given mortuary feast, I've given speeches. I've given six or seven mortuary feasts myself ... When I wanted to give a mortuary feast for the death of my mother's sister Siifela, Ba'efaka [Bioana's brother] quarrelled about it and made a ritual injunction against it. 'No, I'm going to do it at my place. People will make their contributions to me.' I borrowed a pig to purify his injunction, then ... gave the feast ... He [her brother] wanted to give it down at his place, but I said 'I'm an outmarried descent group member [*ino ruma'a*, lit. 'affine woman'], I'll give it at my place.' So I did. A strong woman who has started off in life giving mortuary feasts with her mother and father, with money she has earned, won't be afraid to do something important herself. She'll get pigs and feed them, earn valuables herself, and give a mortuary feast. It's not hard. We can do it!

A woman may, under unusual circumstances, act as sponsor of a mortuary feast, though in normative accounts it always appears to be a man who sponsors feasts.

Blood feuding and virtue

Although in these texts Kwaio women do not squarely challenge the ancestral rules and conceptions of virtue that constrain their lives and extract their labour, they occasionally show a clear insight into contradictions of the precolonial social order which male ideologues gloss over. Women's retrospective interpretations of blood feuding serve to illustrate how women have been both victimised by and caught up in cultural legitimations of male power.

The most common immediate causes of killings were seductions and other transgressions of women's sexual purity (and men's rights over their sexuality). While the male perpetrator became the primary target for vengeance, the girl or woman whose purity had been invaded (even if only verbally) was often killed as well. Women were also killed for violation of pollution rules or accusations of theft. Fei'a, who as a child had seen her mother, victim of her father's adultery, cut down by bounty-hunting warriors for 'purification',[6] spoke with understandably deep feeling about the events in late 1927 when the feared Kwaio warriors were scattered, disarmed, and in some cases shot or hanged. Fei'a went on to recount the powerlessness of women, in the days of blood feuding, to save their innocent sisters, victims of men's sexual violence and greedy intrigues. Her account shows how women were enmeshed in the cultural and social system in ways that led them to participate in vengeance against equally innocent 'sisters' in other groups:

Women were often killed for things men did. The men would accuse a woman of stealing taro or greens, or urinating in the house and not reporting it. And so they'd kill her. Or a man would proposition a girl, and the men would say 'Let's kill her.' ... The men ... would lie about a woman. They'd find some excuse to kill her; but what they were really after was the blood bounty – the money and the pigs. 'That woman had an affair with a relative.' 'That woman urinated in the house.' 'Let's kill her for purification.' I saw that when I was young ... The women talked about that. They said to the men: 'You have to accept compensation for that sexual offense, not kill her.' 'No, we have to kill her.' So they'd kill her and then put up a blood bounty to avenge her death ... The women mourned the death of their sister or their daughter or their mother. They cried, saying 'They've killed our sister.' Then they'd say, 'I'm putting up my pig for the bounty to get revenge for her ... I'll put it up for the death of the man who caused the death of my sister.' Another woman might get killed then. That's the way killings went on and on.

Women were not mere onlookers of male violence. They might also intercede . 'Elota's autobiographical account tells of a girl who was raped by her boyfriend.[7] The girl came home and told her kin, expecting to be killed by her warrior brothers. But the brothers were away, and before they returned the girl's mother interceded to save her – spiriting her away to her boyfriend's maternal uncles, who negotiated a bridewealth payment. An even braver intervention emerges in Fa'aoria's account:

My grandfather Lafuria was walking in the bush and he saw that a girl named Orinaauata ... had felled a tree ... on his land. So he came up to her and grabbed her and raped her. She went back and told her father. He was enraged: 'A widower, having sex with my daughter! I'll strangle her!' They put her up in the men's house and were going to strangle her. A woman there named 'Ofa said: 'No, Orinaauata is my friend, I have to talk to her.' 'You can't, she's dead.' 'They're going to strangle her.' She went up to Orinaauata [who was in the men's house] and [reaching in the door] she took Orinaauata by the hand. 'Let her come out to me. She's my friend, we've shared the contents of our bags, eaten from the same tray. She's crying, about to be killed – let me at least talk with her.' So they let Orinaauata come out. But 'Ofa had her brothers waiting in the scrub at the path entrance, and as soon as Orinaauata came out 'Ofa threatened the men with a piece of wood and ran down with Orinaauata to where her brothers were hiding. They took her by the hands and ran away with her – and then bridewealth was paid for her.

References to blood feuding and the threat of execution are often cast in terms of female virtue. Thus Fa'afataa, projecting herself back into her mother's girlhood days, warns how a girl had to take special care to avoid situations (especially visiting other peoples' houses or gardens alone) where she could be (falsely) accused of theft: you would be killed – then your innocence discovered, if at all, too late. Or the accusation could rebound on the accuser, or on an innocent kinswoman. Fa'afataa recounts how a man named 'Alakwale'a accused her grandfather's kinswoman Osini of stealing taro. Fa'afataa's grandfather Obosiaba'e demanded compensation for the insult and 'Alakwale'a refused.

So Obosiaba'e left. On his way he met 'Alakwale'a's sister Ka'o weeding in the garden. He took his club and said, 'Here's yours, Ka'o.' And he killed her. When he got home he said to Osini, 'I killed Ka'o for your purification.'

Men's killing clubs, and volatile anger fuelled by greed and notions of honour, could scarcely be challenged: they defined the spaces within which women had to live. The relaxation of these daily threats must represent the most profound change of the colonial period; and one which, the supposed decline of virtue notwithstanding, women can scarcely mourn without ambivalence. Fa'afataa went on, with metaphoric eloquence, to contrast the old days with the new:

People nowadays don't realize what it was to live amid people who lived with threats and anger, who killed and seduced and fought. The taro had stinging crystals then, but now it is all soft and sweet: soft with foreign ways. ...

The customs used to stand straight up, but now they've been dug out and set askew. What is there to be afraid of, to keep you from taking what you like and doing what you like? You slip and slide about, doing anything you please.

Individual lives, individual women

A final point that bears underlining is that Kwaio women's views of themselves and their lives are diverse and uniquely individual. Differences in personality and life experience preclude any stereotypic view of 'Kwaio women'. Stances towards virtue in following pollution rules will serve to illustrate. Whereas Boori'au or Fa'afataa can point toward surviving husband and children to depict herself as virtuous, Tege – who has outlived three husbands – constructs a view of herself as victim of circumstances. A senior woman's prestige, recognised virtue, and sheer force of personality may seemingly deflect the attribution of irresponsibility onto others. Boori'au, a senior woman respected for her knowledge, is wife of charismatic, angry Folofo'u, leader of the most bitterly anticolonial faction in contemporary neotraditional struggle – a man from whom others retreat. Yet in talking about her life she forcefully insisted (in his presence) that the death of their child was caused by a ritual error he and his brothers committed rather than a pollution violation on her part. Folofo'u deferred to her interpretation – indeed, as an important diviner he had presumably fashioned that interpretation with her.

The wide differences in self-conception, as well as life experiences and the constructions culturally placed on them, are vividly illustrated in Fa'aoria's narrative. Now in her fifties, she lives with her affines, the kin of the great feastgiver 'Elota, far from her home territory. In Fa'aoria's early childhood she had seen her father, father's brother, maternal uncle and two older sisters shot down by police in a dawn massacre during the 1927 punitive expedition. The construction she places on her life builds on the experiences of a girlhood when scattered survivors of her group gathered to reconstruct as best they could the group and way of life that had been destroyed.

If it hadn't been for my mother I'd have turned out to be a wild animal. If we are left in the nest by ourselves – if a piglet doesn't have its mother to raise it, it will just grow up wild in the bush. It will just eat any way in the bush. A man will pick it up, feed it, and then call it a woman. That's what happened to me. I was like a pig. I was still *ria* [bad, but here meaning unsocialized] when they killed my father and all my people. My mother showed us, when my brothers came back [from prison], how to feed pigs. We ate them at the mortuary feast for the death of the men who were killed [in 1927] and a child who died. She gave three mortuary feasts for the death of her husband and children. She showed us the way; we worked. We fed pigs. I kept the taboos with her.

... My mother died ... six years after I got married. She had taught me how to live properly, like this: 'You must work hard for food and for money. You must feed pigs. You must work hard so your living will be good. You don't have sisters. Where are your father and brothers and sisters?' That's the way she taught me.

[Her voice starts to get very emotional.] Now it's as though I am going back to the time when I was a girl, when all my family were killed. Now my people have all died out [her brothers, with whom she was quite close, have died]. You ask about my people and all I can do is cry ...

When I got married, my mother released me, saying 'You're just a little girl and you've gone with a man in marriage. They'll pay me for you.' I went off then with my husband and I've been with him ever since ... My mother gave me this advice and I believed her. I tried to raise pigs, work hard, keep the taboos; I wanted to live properly. Here I was, moving to a different place. But the man who had paid for me ['Elota], my brother-in-law, said to me: 'You, the woman I bought for this place, you don't pay any attention to me. When I tell you something it falls on deaf ears.' I thought that way too. 'It's true, it's as though I'm a wild unsocialized animal – you're the ones who paid for me, because I'm good looking ... It's as though you've bought a young pig that looks good. But I've grown up by myself in the bush; I'm like a wild animal. You saw that its body was good looking and bought it. The ways ... a girl's father should teach her I couldn't learn about. I just grew up by myself.'

Yet while no single 'women's perspective' emerges from the voluminous texts, the accounts together provide a rich complement to the views articulated through the years to me by Kwaio men.[8] Kwaio women have certainly not proved 'mute' or 'muted' in their views of self and society once a context was established in which they were willing to talk to outsiders.

The perspectives the texts reveal are situated in the structural frameworks and experiences of women's lives. In that sense they are partial, a woman's stance toward Kwaio society. Men's accounts are of course similarly situated with respect to their roles and experiences; but both men and women classify these realms of ritual, war, politics and feasting as the core of Kwaio 'culture', and women's work as in this sense peripheral. The contradiction lies in the fact that it is women's proper compartmentalisation of their bodily functions that most preoccupies the ancestors; what men do is only possible when women strictly follow the taboos that govern their lives. It is this crack of contradiction into which women's alternative ideologies drive a wedge. Women use it, in the accounts recorded to themselves depict what they do as reproducers of society and cultural order as the core of social responsibility. (Under the circumstances in which the accounts were recorded, it is a moot point whether men could or would challenge such depictions; see Keesing 1985.)

We see in the texts further contradictions that allow of counterinterpretation. Women in menstrual isolation are by their marginalisation placed temporarily out of men's control; thus they are able to establish and use solidarity, and to use their labour for their own ends. Women's freedom from male control has certainly increased through the disarming of men. With the threat of execution now gone women are freer to act independently with respect to their sexuality, their economic pursuits and their domestic interests. The ambivalence female ideologues express in these texts runs deep. Women face the contradiction that the very virtues they would extoll – which constitute their essential contribution to Kwaio *kastom* – were sustained by threat of male violence as well as ancestral punishment. One of the fascinating elements in the transformation of Kwaio society since imposition of the *Pax Britannica* in the 1920s is the way young men and women have gradually broken free of the constraints on their sexuality and mobility imposed by the threat of execution; while at the same time women have remained in the grip of the rules imposed and policed by the ancestors, which they can escape only by taking refuge in Christianity.

The accounts Kwaio women have given cast in doubt any interpretation of their society in terms of a sharp and mutually antagonistic polarisation of the sexes. In the textures of everyday social life, the more closely examined details of cosmology and ritual, the organisation of the prestige economy, and partly submerged alternative models of social structure (Keesing 1970b:1015-18; 1971), it is clear that Kwaio women are not being marginalised or rendered passive. Nor as jural minors, as polluting beings or as dangerous outsiders in their husbands' armed camps are they being subordinated. They are important social actors who see themselves as complementary to and sustaining of their brothers and husbands. Yet these accounts do not, we must remember, constitute direct evidence on how our narrators actually live, and experience, their lives. They are in many respects normative statements about how women should feel and act; it is in relation to such ideals of conduct and responsibility that our informants talked about themselves as individuals. They tell us some of the things we would like to know about Kwaio women's thought and experience; but they do *not* tell us, except perhaps by indirection and extrapolation, many of the things we would ideally like to know.

Inequality: subordination or complementarity?

We come back, then, to the problems raised at the outset. Situating ourselves in Kwaio women's lives and worlds through these texts, we see that women perceive themselves to be crucial agents in the maintenance and reproduction of cultural order. They must do the things that are women's responsibility conscientiously and well if they are to preserve the lives of loved ones, to marry, to be respected. These narrators recognise that people have different life chances. Yet they proclaim that by inner strength, virtue and hard work any woman could go beyond success in female pursuits to acquire prestige through mortuary feasting and bridewealth contributions.

Seen from within the framework of Kwaio culture, the complementarity of men's and women's lives argues for difference, perhaps for inequality. But we cannot go on to infer, without serious qualification, that Kwaio women were subordinated, exploited or powerless. The texts give no evidence that Kwaio women see themselves as lifelong jural minors, exploited workers, passive objects of male jural control and manipulation – though prior to the *Pax Britannica* many must have been at best ambivalent about the threat of male violence directed against them. Our women informants see themselves as agents in producing the conditions of their own lives and in reproducing cultural order in the next generation through their daughters.

But the dialectical task foreshadowed at the outset is also to step outside the texts and their matrix of cultural meanings: to ask whether in shaping their lives around ancestrally imposed rules and definitions of virtue that extract their labour for the benefit of men, women are victims of ideological hegemony. It is precisely the power and the role of dominant ideologies to render contingent social/economic/political relationships as eternal, self-evident, beyond doubt or change. Gender systems, conceptions of duty and virtue and the 'proper place' of women, act both to sustain particular forms of male domination and to reproduce the social formations of which they are elements.

Do we step back from the Kwaio texts, then, to see ancestral rules as 'celestialised' instruments of male oppression, to see women's labour as appropriated for male ends in the name of virtue, to see the authors of these self-accounts as trapped in a hegemonic ideology? Step back we must, I think. But as M. Strathern (1980, 1984b) has warned, there are hidden traps awaiting every backward step. With each step we make precarious assumptions, not only about what constitutes inequality, oppression or exploitation and about what a more just and liberated society would be like, but about what work is, what constitutes personhood, agency, power, what subjects are and objects are.

Gender relations pose questions about culture-as-ideology in a particularly acute form, since they present us with an analytical field defined by a cleavage — whatever its special cultural form — between men and women, the lives they lead and their perspectives on those lives. Yet the problem is more general. Anthropological theories of culture and society — functionalist, structuralist, symbolist — have in general lacked an adequate conception of ideology and of the ideological force of cultural symbols. Marxist theory, in its varying forms, has yet to integrate a concept of ideology with adequately developed conceptualisations of culture. The two bodies of theory do not meet in the middle: and it is this gap, as well as the special epistemological and perspectival problems of the anthropologist's field encounter with another people's world, that confronts us in asking whether Kwaio women's values are caught up in a hegemonic cultural ideology.

Perhaps in the long run we can develop a set of theoretical concepts less bluntly crude than 'subordination', 'exploitation', or 'oppression' to examine the social uses of cultural ideologies in comparative perspective. I have suggested elsewhere (Keesing 1981: 304-05) that more precisely developed conceptualisations of consensus, appropriation, exclusion, control and constraint are needed. The Kwaio case illustrates the difficulties in assessing whether, in examining male and female in a society very different from ours, gender differences can be read as inequalities, and inequalities can be read as implying domination and subordination. There are sharp differences between (adult) men and women in control over resources (valuables, pigs, magic) both sexes value, in access to public stages on which performance brings prestige, in jural rights over persons and things, in rights and powers over one's own life and sexuality, in norms of kinship, descent and residence, and (perhaps most importantly) in control over the weapons that constituted ultimate sanctions in a society where, on a tiny scale, might made right. Together, these differences clearly (to me) argue for inequality, despite the considerable room they allow for women to see themselves, and be seen, as central actors on the stages of everyday life and as paragons of domestic virtue, and to gain prestige in exchange and feasting. They less clearly argue for domination and subordination. Kwaio women are subordinated to (some) men in some contexts, particularly contexts of litigation and rights over women's sexuality and contexts where men mediate and direct relations with ancestors. But any interpretations of dominance and subordination must be carefully framed in terms both of contexts and the social identities of participants. Moreover, we must deal with special care with the problematic disjuncture between the assignment of rights and the way actual social interaction unfolds.[9]

Are Kwaio women oppressed by men? There is a salient difference between rules and sanctions imposed by physical force or threat of violence to keep people from making choices they would otherwise like to make and sets of cultural assumptions so pervasive that for members of the society there are no alternatives perceived, no choices to be made. In the Kwaio case, we can regard as constraints of a different order those which were imposed by actual or threatened violence and those which were assumed to be imposed by ancestors or to be self-evident and unquestionable facts of human existence. Thus I am prepared to find oppression where Kwaio women and children were victims of male violence, particularly for punishment or purification of acts they did not knowingly commit or willingly instigate. I am not prepared to define as oppression norms about women's domestic duties or rules compartmentalising women's bodily functions, even though they manifestly result in inequalities (that go beyond mere differences) in the ways men and women are able to live their lives. This is a line we may want to cross as political activists – as feminists or revolutionaries; it is a line I find difficult to cross wearing the garb of an anthropologist.

In the end I believe that a critical comparative anthropology can avoid the excesses both of a self-indulgent and ultimately nihilistic relativism that sees each cultural world as unique and demands we view it only in its own terms, and of crudely ideological analyses that see mystification, false consciousness and oppression in the deepest commitments and values of other peoples. There can be no easy middle ground; but we learn much from reflecting about unexamined concepts, our own takens-for-granted, and learn from our own missteps and plunges as well as those of others. The value of the Kwaio women's self-accounts is that our dangerous but necessary steps backward to take an external and critical view of Kwaio society can alternate with steps forward, into the texts, as rich expressions of subjective experiences and individual perspectives.

Notes

1. Field research during which the women's self-accounts were recorded was supported by The Australian National University; previous Kwaio research was supported by the US National Institute of Mental Health, the National Science Foundation, the Social Science Research Council, and the University of California. For helpful comments on an earlier paper incorporating some of this material, I am indebted to Thomas Greaves. Valuable suggestions for revision of the present paper were contributed by members of the ANU research group on Gender Relations in the Southwest Pacific, and in particular by Terry Hays, Marie Reay, Shelley Schreiner, Marilyn Strathern and Jill Nash.
2. The work sketched here is very much Schreiner's and my joint project. Her insights are reflected throughout, and the texts could almost certainly not have been elicited had the context not been defined as talk by women to a woman, as well as to me. However, I alone am accountable for the interpretations that follow.
3. As in most other Oceanic languages, *tapu* (Kwaio *abu*) is not a noun but a stative. Here it is used with a causative prefix and nominalising suffix to form 'causing to be *abu*'. *Ta'a geni* is 'women', lit. 'female humans.'
4. My 1964 photographs show Teobo minding and fondling her five year old grand-daughter Geninaatoo – who as I recorded Fa'afataa's account fourteen years later was a young bride in our settlement.
5. I use 'dating' to gloss Kwaio *arunga*, the traditional mode of customary courtship in which a young man and girl meet in the forest at an arranged time and exchange presents and small talk, in what are supposed to be chaste rendezvous.
6. This case was anomalous even by the rather tortuous logic of Kwaio homicide and vengeance. Fei'a's father committed the worst sort of violation of the strict sexual code, in running away with his wife's sister (in what is tantamount to incest). When repeated attempts to kill him failed, the aggrieved wife was murdered, in what was rationalised as purification.
7. He penetrated her while she slept, when he was late for a forest rendezvous. He should have taken her home so a marriage could be negotiated, but instead let her go home, hoping she would remain silent.
8. Men's views of Kwaio society are reflected in many of my writings, including 'Elota's autobiography (Keesing 1978a), quoted passages in my book on Kwaio religion (Keesing 1982a) and my writings on Maasina Rule and ideology (Keesing 1978b, 1982b).
9. Even where rights are defined according to Kwaio norms, successful assertion of these rights, in conflict situations, becomes a test of strength. A striking case in point, recounted in 'Elota's autobiography, is a dispute between Fa'atalo and his sister Maebata over distribution of an opening bridewealth payment. As guardian of the bride, Fa'atalo had the right to distribute valuables among the claimants, who in turn had claims based on their contribution to the bride's father's bridewealth (Keesing

1970b). His sister Maebata, who had raised the bride from infancy as foster daughter, raised a claim for a substantial valuable as recognition of her nurturant role. Both Maebata's claim and Fa'atalo's right to make ultimate decisions over bridewealth payments were culturally legitimate. But Fa'atalo threatened to kill his sister with a tree branch, and she in turn threatened to invoke a curse against the marriage; 'Elota intervened by presenting the valuable she demanded, on behalf of the groom (against whom such a claim vis-à-vis the bride can legitimately be imposed). Asserting rights successfully, in Kwaio society, entails political action, not simply enactment of law.

CHAPTER 2

The remarriage of Yebiwali: a study of dominance and false consciousness in a non-Western society

FREDERICK ERRINGTON AND
DEBORAH GEWERTZ

Anthropologists have thought for some time that even those societies which they have termed 'egalitarian' are characterised by considerable inequality between men and women. In most of these societies, men are described as dominating women and women as suffering from 'false consciousness', misapprehending the nature of their domination (see A. Strathern 1982 and Keesing, this volume). However, it seems to us that the generality of male dominance and of female false consciousness cannot be easily established given cultural diversity in the bases, mechanisms and forms of dominance, as well as in the ways dominance is experienced. Unless dominance can be accurately discerned in its various cultural guises, we cannot know how general a phenomenon it is nor, therefore, be able adequately to interpret its causes and consequences in our own or in any other culture. Before inequality – the central moral and political preoccupation of contemporary Western consciousness – can be dealt with, dominance must first be recognised.[1]

As a preface to the problem of diagnosing 'dominance' and 'false consciousness' in culturally diverse contexts, we reopen one of the cases which was first used to address the topic of cultural differences in gender inequality (see Mead 1935:258-62). Our ethnographic focus is upon the remarriage of Yebiwali, a young Chambri (Tchambuli) widow of Papua New Guinea's East Sepik Province. Mead believed that Chambri women dominate Chambri men by reason of their economic activity, and Chambri men misapprehend the nature of their subservience to their women. Despite the widespread interest this view of the Chambri evoked, anthropologists have come largely to ignore Mead's conclusions because they found no comparable cases elsewhere. Moreover, Mead's own data appeared inconsistent: while arguing that Chambri women were supposed to dominate their men, she also describes, for example, the widow Yebiwali as compelled by men to abandon her lover and marry a man considerably older than herself (see Mead 1935:260-2).[2]

Although the analysis by which Mead makes the Chambri appear so unusual is flawed by inconsistency, it does not necessarily follow without further investigation that the Chambri conform to the more frequently described pattern in which males are dominant and females connive in their domination. However, any reinvestigation of male–female relationships among the Chambri would still misconstrue patterns of domination unless it took more careful account of the culturally defined objectives of men and women. Indeed, we shall argue that relations of dominance among the Chambri – and among other peoples – can best be understood with reference to those sociocultural forms which prevent individuals or categories of individuals from becoming what is culturally defined as persons of worth.

The concept of dominance in Western culture

Mead, we think, misread male-female relations among the Chambri because of the manner in which she applied to their case the definition of dominance widely held in Western culture. She follows the view that dominance is a relationship between individuals or groups in which one unjustifiably deprives the other of its capacity to make and enact what are regarded as reasonable decisions. Not all forms of constraint are thus considered expressions of dominance. Few Anglo-Americans, for example, would so interpret parents' insistence that their children eat with knife and fork.[3] To the extent that the constraints are regarded as reasonable and normal, they will be interpreted as acts of legitimate control rather than of dominance.

There may of course be different perspectives within a culture on what is regarded as appropriate constraint and choice. Thus, even those subscribing to the same general definition of dominance can well reach different conclusions about whether dominance has occurred. A hypothetical example will make the point. Consider the North American 'secretary' who, in the late 1950s, dressed in slacks when her 'boss' insisted that she follow the then contemporary fashion imperative by wearing a skirt and blouse. If she complied but only under protest, or indeed refused to comply at all and was subsequently penalised, relatively few would sympathise with her. Those who thought the behaviour of her employer as reasonable would not regard him as seeking to dominate her; nor, therefore, would her response be interpreted as an effort to escape domination, but would be seen as irrational, perhaps even as the loss of emotional control thought to be characteristic of women. Yet others might interpret the conflict between the boss and his secretary in a very different way, by arguing that the culturally current definitions of what is 'reasonable' and 'normal' are imposed by those in power for their own benefit. These definitions, themselves, become part of the mechanism by which dominance is expressed and cannot be regarded as the objective standards by which reasonableness and normality should be judged. That people regard it reasonable and normal that most bosses are men and most secretaries are women would, from this perspective, render invalid prevailing cultural definitions of what constitutes reasonable and normal standards of conduct for bosses and secretaries alike. Virtually any approved interaction under these circumstances between superordinates and subordinates would be regarded as an act of dominance.[4]

However, as divergent as these perspectives are likely to be in their interpretation of particular cases, they nonetheless share certain key cultural assumptions about the nature of persons and the achievement of personal worth: from either position it would be reasonable and normal for anyone, bosses and secretaries included, to seek satisfaction in what they do – to establish personal worth as subjectivities through self-expression.[5] Moreover, from either perspective, control of economic resources is believed essential to achieving personal worth. Those who failed to sympathise with our hypothetical secretary would probably regard the boss as reasonable for looking after his business interests, and the secretary as irrational for choosing self-expression in dress at the cost of her job, thus sacrificing the economic viability which is the most general Western prerequisite for choice. Those who did sympathise would no doubt sympathise with all secretaries, regarding their capacity for self-expression both on and off the job as contingent upon, and inherently limited by, the economic interests of others.

Our disagreement with Mead is not that she subscribed to this general definition of dominance as an unjustifiable constraint on a person's capacity to make and enact what could be argued as reasonable decisions. Rather, we contend, she did not recognise that those assumptions which even allow members of our own culture to debate whether constraint in particular cases is unjustifiable or decisions reasonable are not assumptions which would make sense for the Chambri. In our view, Mead misinterpreted the bases, mechanisms, forms and experiences of dominance among the Chambri to the extent that she viewed men and women as subjective individuals seeking self-expression through an economically derived individualism (see Gewertz 1984). Consider the following passage from *Sex and Temperament* where she elaborates upon what she regards as female dominance:

Here is a conflict at the very root of [a Chambri male's] psycho-sexual adjustment; his society tells him that he rules women, his experience shows him at every turn that women expect to rule him ... But the actual dominance of women is far more real than the structural position of the men, and the majority of Tchambuli young men adjust themselves to it, become accustomed to wait upon the words and desires of women. (1935:271)

Mead implies that, if left to their own devices, Chambri men would not act as they do. She sees their behaviour as an abnormality, manifesting a psycho-sexual conflict which Chambri men would like to resolve by acting according to the structural principles of their society which tell them that they should rule women. Instead, they are compelled to wait upon the words of their wives, mothers, and sisters, because it is women 'who have the real position of power in society' (1935:253). It is women, Mead suggests, who dominate their men by compelling them to act in ways that the men, because they fail to understand the nature of power in their society, find confusing and inappropriate.

That women can so compel is, moreover, a function of their control of 'the underlying economics of life':

For food, the people depend upon the fishing of the women ... For traded fish they obtain sago, taro, and areca-nut.[6] And the most important manufacture, the mosquito-bags, ... are made entirely by women ... And the women control the proceeds in kinas and talibun.[7] It is true that they permit the men to do the shopping, both for food at the market and in trading the mosquito-bags ... But only with his wife's approval can he spend the talibun and kina and strings of conus shells he brings back ... Real property, which one actually owns, one receives from women ... Once one has obtained it, it becomes a counter in the games that men play ... The minor war-and-peace that goes on all the time among the men ... [is] supported by the labour and contributions of the women. (1935:254)

Women according to Mead, then, dominate their men because women control the significant economic resources. Men are unable to be themselves: they are forced to act against their own inclinations which in turn produces a crisis in their subjective experience of themselves – a psycho-sexual conflict which, in some cases, becomes a neurosis (see Mead 1935:265-75).

Mead's culturally induced error is double. She starts with the economic sphere as distinctive and primary whereas it is neither for the Chambri. It is socially embedded and serves as an index of social relationships rather than as a cause of social relationships (cf. Sahlins 1972; Gregory 1982). Economics in Chambri social life reflects, but does not determine, dominance. Moreover, the relationships of constraint prevail between persons whose primary objective is not to establish themselves as distinct subjectivities, but to enmesh one another in social networks.

To be a person among the Chambri is to belong to a patriclan, whose members assume corporate interests in affinal debts and credits and assert common ownership of totemic names. These names both provide and indicate the social networks which afford men, women and their children basic identity and protection from coercion and assault. (See Weiner, this volume, for an interesting discussion of a highland people who also define themselves as persons through the possession of names.) Of even greater importance, the totemic names allow both men and women to pursue, respectively, their culturally defined preoccupations of political competition and the bearing of children. These are preoccupations, as we shall see later in more detail, in so far as they provide the means for men and women to repay those who have caused their physical and social existences. Both men and women strive to redeem themselves from ontological debt: a man competes with others to acquire power equivalent to those who have engendered him; a woman reproduces children to replace those who have engendered her.

The totemic names available to men, therefore, convey different sorts of powers and resources than do those available to women. The names men hold provide the possibility of gaining power over others and are the focus and basis of political competition. Men seek to augment their own power through gaining control of the names of others. Since, for men, the social relationships between – and within – clans are manifestations of relative power, and since social relationships constitute personal identity, men define themselves as persons primarily in terms of relative control over names – over that which gives them power.[8] Women also define themselves by names. However, the power conveyed by their names cannot shape social relationships as does the power of the names men hold, but, instead, ensures reproduction.[9] Because the power of women cannot be transferred into the male sphere of politics, women do not compete with men for political eminence. At the same time, the interests of Chambri men and women are not inevitably opposed. Chambri men and women each have a partially distinct sphere of activity, and each allows the other to pursue partially distinct strategies. Consequently, women are not caught up in the politics of names, power and sorcery to make them, as a category, the usual targets of male efforts to establish power over others. Women are not, thus, to be regarded as the followers of particular men, nor as their usual victims.[10]

If dominance can be defined as an unjustifiable constraint on the behaviour of another by depriving him or her of the capacity to make and enact reasonable decisions, the form dominance takes among the Chambri rests on the control of the social relationships and totemic powers which determine action and are the basis of Chambri identity. Moreover, a significant part of the cultural meaning of dominance for the Chambri is that only those deprived of power consider it unjustifiable that another has incapacitated them. Particular cases apart, Chambri men consider it perfectly reasonable, indeed essential, that they seek to dominate one another.

Dominance thus characterises the strategies of men as they compete with each other to become equal to those who have caused them. Women, in contrast, neither compete with men nor with each other to repay their ontological debts. Nonetheless, both men and women, on important occasions, do focus their distinctive strategies of validation on marriage, the particular social context which produced them and their relationships of indebtedness. It is in these cases, where the strategies of men and women impel each to pursue their very different objectives in the same arena, that we would most expect to find the members of one sex attempting to dominate the members of the other. It is in this context that we would expect to appraise whether Chambri men dominate Chambri women, or, as Mead would have it, the reverse.

Of valuable widows

We examine the nature and relationships of male and female interests with the analysis of a men's house debate concerning the remarriage of Yebiwali, a debate recorded by Mead during 1933 in her unpublished field notes. The immediate ethnographic problem we face is to determine whether Yebiwali was, by Chambri standards, dominated. Could it at least be argued that in terms of the key Chambri assumptions about persons and their objectives that when she abandoned her lover Tchuikumban to marry the considerably older Akerman, she was unjustifiably deprived of the capacity to make reasonable decisions? Mead decribes the circumstances of Yebiwali both in *Sex and Temperament*, and in her unpublished field notes. We first cite these field notes where, under the following heading, she describes the debate over a Iatmul's desire to marry the woman:[11]

> Debate over who should marry a widow
>
> For some days Moi [who was a Iatmul originally from the neighboring island of Aibom] had been howling for the hand of a widow, Yebiwali, whose husband, the son of Kwosaivon, he and two other PBs [police boys] had buried at Marienberg, asking for the widow to wash his hands [to be given to him as payment for his action]. Moi says that this a good Sepik custom that if a man dies in a faraway place, he who buries him deserves his hands washed and that the

widow is suitable pay. Tchuikumban had given goods to his tambu [brother-in-law] to give to the woman. She is the sister of this brother-in-law, Megodimi ... The widow had been living in her father's house, both father and father-in-law being of Yangaraman HT [ceremonial house] ...

Moi got a kerosene box, took it to Yangaraman and opened the debate with about five or six stalks of ginger to beat the stool with ... Moi debated solemnly, aggressively and vigorously. Everybody else either conciliatory or with short and impotent-like angry flashes. Moi demanded the woman. Girl's father, Saman, did not talk. Girl's father-in-law, Kwosaivon, did all the talking ... Moi said he wanted to wash his hands. He described the funeral. Father-in-law spoke again, declining agreement. Tana [Kwosaivon's in-law][12] spoke very impassioned about sorcery and Aibom, how they had challenged an Aibom boast of having killed this boy, by threatening calaboose [prison], and Aibom had backed down ... Moi said he belonged to Tchambuli finish, that he was making a garden here. Walinakwon [Tana's adopted son] said Moi had refused his food. Moi excused himself by saying that he had already eaten our [Mead's and Fortune's] food. Walinakwon said then he didn't belong to Tchambuli, he didn't eat his food.

Moi reiterated that he wanted the woman. Father-in-law said that the girl had not 'sat down good' as a married woman. Megodimi, [Yebiwali's brother] fixed an apparently angry accusation upon Tchuikumban, of being the widow's sweetheart. (Note he had helped to effect this so he wasn't really angry.) Tana said that this love negotiation, i.e. of Tchuikumban's, had proceeded upon the private bush roads not along the public roads which lead to the shore, alleging mysterious and private doings.

Moi described the funeral services which he performed again. Walinakwon said Moi didn't eat his food. Moi advanced further arguments of same nature as to why he should have the woman. Father-in-law flushed angrily and said that his son didn't die nothing. (More direct statement than remark that girl hadn't sat down good, meaning that some lover had been responsible for the sorcery.) Wapbivali spoke. Walinakwon spoke, repeating former remarks. He finished by taking half of the kawa [ginger stalks] and crushing it under his feet. Moi took up the kawa that was left while there was still some left and tried to keep debate going, and broke his kombon [lime gourd] by accident over box.

Megodimi, Tchuikumban's tambu [affine], spoke saying how he and X had some years before recovered the widow from Ambunti where some police had framed her and taken her. His associate in this then spoke, and finished by kicking the box over and over. Debate broke up; people broke up into groups. Father-in-law and father went to talk with Moi and father-in-law gave Moi a new kombon. They and their brothers then went and talked among themselves. Note, quite a number of speakers, Megodimi, Wapbivali, and father-in-law had constantly thru debate been saying, it would be a good thing to give Moi some terubon [talimbun shells] to wash his hands, a suggestion which Moi never took up, clinging to woman idea.

Asked Tchuikumban if groups would come to decision. He said of course not. (Mead n.d.)

In *Sex and Temperament* Mead alludes to this debate with only one line. Within the story of the thwarted love between Yebiwali and Tchuikumban, she mentions 'offers for Yebiwali's hand from a man from another tribe' (1935:262). That these offers provoked accusations of sorcery and group betrayal proved not as interesting to her as did the story of Tchuikumban and Yebiwali itself, for in this story she saw illustrated the freedom young women possess to determine their own fates. She wrote:

With a young widow also, it is the girl's choice that is decisive, for men will not be foolish enough to pay for a girl who had not indicated her choice of a husband by sleeping with him. It will be, as they say, money thrown away. A young widow is a tremendous liability to a community. No one expects her to remain quiet until her marriage has been arranged. Has she not a vulva? they ask. This is the comment that is continually made in Tchambuli: Are women passive sexless creatures who can be expected to wait upon the dilly-dallying of formal considerations of bride-price? Men, not so urgently sexed, may be expected to submit themselves to the discipline of a due order and precedence. (1935:259)

Mead also reports in *Sex and Temperament* that Yebiwali makes a number of overtures to Tchuikumban. She attempts to capture his attention by claiming to another woman that he had given her two bead armlets; she sends him the head of a fish to indicate her interest in him; she requests that he give her the new white belt he had acquired indirectly from Mead and Fortune. All of these make sense to Mead as initiatives which reflect Yebiwali's freedom to choose her own mate, as indicative of her self-sufficiency and independence.

Mead also explains the failure of the love between Yebiwali and Tchuikumban to eventuate in marriage in terms of self-sufficiency and independence. Tchuikumban, although

tall and straight and charming [was] an orphan; his father and mother having both been killed in head-hunting raids, he belonged to a vanishing clan. (1935:260)

His relatives refused to help him pay bride-price for Yebiwali because 'she did not know how to make mosquito-bags' (1935:26l).

His foster-father was merciless: 'You are an orphan. How can you expect to marry a wife of your own choice? This girl is no good. She is worn out with loose living. She cannot weave. How will it profit for you to marry her?' (1935:261)

Yebiwali, correspondingly, without the skill to weave mosquito bags, had also less personal autonomy than she needed to effect the marriage she desired. Since her father had decided, however, that 'the need to remarry her was urgent' (1935:261), rumours of her liaisons being rife, she

was led away to marry Akerman, followed by the consoling word of an older woman: 'The other wife of Akerman is your father's sister. She will be kind to you and not scold you because you do not know how to make baskets'. (1935:261)

Thus, believing that economic independence could have prevented the lovers from falling under the dominance of their elders, Mead concludes that 'the love-affair was defeated because his relatives shamed Tchuikumban in terms of his orphanhood and because Yebiwali was not able to provide for a young husband' (1935:262).

To make her economic interpretation more convincing, however, Mead would have to address such questions as: Why would Tchuikumban have been shamed because of his orphanhood into giving up his claims upon Yebiwali? Was the source of his shame simply that he lacked sufficient resources to pay for her bride-price? Would he have pressed his claims if, for example, Mead and Fortune had provided him with the requisite number for the most prized valuables – *kina* (pearlshell), *lin* (necklaces of cowrie and coral) and above all *talimbun* (greensnail shell)? And why did Yebiwali pursue Tchuikumban at all? Did she not suspect that her inadequacy as a producer of mosquito bags would make it difficult for the young orphan's classificatory relatives to support his desire for her? Moreover, even if Mead could provide answers to these questions using her economic perspective, it is far from evident that she could account in these terms for what the Chambri were actually expressing during the debate as their concerns. It is in this debate that we will best see from the Chambri viewpoint what is primarily at issue in the remarriage of Yebiwali.

Moi, it will be recalled, wished for Yebiwali's hand to 'wash his own.' Something was owed him because he had buried the dead young man, something for which he considered Yebiwali but not the valuables offered him to be adequate compensation. Thus Moi's act of burial was associated by him with the wife of the deceased – and at least from the perspective of some of the debaters – with *talimbun* shells.

The association made in the debate between Yebiwali and *talimbun* shells is plausible to the Chambri because in most important social transactions the various kinds of valuables exchanged among Chambri men denote women. The *talimbun* shell, for instance, offered to Moi by some of the debaters, is explicitly associated with wombs. During male initiation ceremonies, these shells are employed as water receptacles by the mothers, mothers' sisters and sisters of the young initiates. As these women rinse the body paint from the initiates they refer to the water contained within these shells as the blood within their wombs. Even now that banknotes have replaced shell valuables in affinal prestations, this money is not simply currency under these circumstances; it assumes the form of symbolic women. The money is attached to sticks inserted in the spines of the sago palm to form a money tree, which is then decorated with a net bag. The sago palm is explicitly regarded in Chambri mythology as comparable to women and the net bag is characteristically used by Chambri women to carry their infants. Moreover, the ceremonial setting in which valuables are used, whether in the traditional form of shells or the more contemporary form of the money tree, makes clear that each not only is given for a woman but is itself a kind of woman. (Gewertz 1982 discusses how these money trees serve to give cross-cousin marriages the appearance of sister exchanges.)

Unlike the ubiquitous currency which provides Westerners with self-sufficiency and independence, Chambri valuables establish and mark social relationships, particularly, as in the context of affinal exchange, relationships of enduring obligation and debt. Unlike the secretary we described earlier, who would have had little to fear from her boss if her choice to flout his fashion-imperative was backed by an independent income, a Chambri who was affluent in shell valuables would neither have been able nor have desired to assert independence by severing social relationships. Such an objective would have been inappropriate for him in a world in which identity is determined by social connectedness.

This is not to say that Chambri wish to be dominated by others. In both our own society and theirs, individuals wish to avoid domination. But for Westerners with a fundamentally individualistic definition of person, the best guarantee of self-sufficiency is to possess enough resources to be able to break social connections.[13] For the Chambri, with their positional definition of person, the only guarantee that they have to avoid domination by others is to establish adequate social alliances.

As a Iatmul from the neighbouring island of Aibom, Moi undoubtedly subscribed to the same general definition of person and of valuables as did the Chambri he buried, debated with and wished to marry. Both peoples define persons in terms of their names, powers and kin, and both establish crucial social alliances through exchanging women for the same types of valuables. The debate in the Chambri men's house concerned the kind of Chambri identity Moi wished and would be allowed to establish. He was accused by Walinakwon of not really belonging to Chambri society, of not eating Chambri food, but he was nonetheless offered a *talimbun*. For Moi's part, he wished to have Yebiwali rather than a *talimbun*, recognising, as did everyone else, that although women and valuables are analogous they are not identical. Because women are significantly different from that by which they are denoted, a different kind of social identity would have been constructed through a relationship established by the presentation of Yebiwali rather than a *talimbun*. In the differences between these items of exchange through which debts are established and paid it is possible to locate Moi's rejection of *talimbun* as adequate compensation for his having buried Yebiwali's husband.

The nature of male indebtedness

Chambri men and women are permanently indebted for the fact of their lives to their affines who have provided their mothers and their wives.[14] Despite repeated payments, these affinal debts can never be fully settled: irrespective of the generosity of any individual, wife-takers remain indebted to their affines. The primary reason for this rests on the assumption those who have caused life remain more important than those whose lives they have caused.

Indeed, perpetual indebtedness is implicit in the very mode in which Chambri meet their affinal obligations. The fundamental inequality between wife-givers and wife-takers is reflected in the cultural arrangement that the exchanges between them be made through items of an incommensurate nature (see Forge 1972:537). Although all Chambri understand that the valuables they exchange represent the women that they also exchange, they recognise that the capacities of the latter to 'cause' the birth of children cannot be compensated by any number of shells or shillings. Wife-takers must, nonetheless, do the best that they can to redeem themselves, and valuables thus continue to move in one direction in exchange for the women who move in the other. That the two are never equivalent denotes and perpetuates the inequality between the groups linked through these exchanges.

We can now return to the question of why Moi demanded Yebiwali's hand to 'wash his own'. Although it is true that had he been given Yebiwali in marriage he would have been assured of permanent incorporation within relationships of affinal debt, enduring social alliances would also have been established had he accepted *talimbun* in compensation, but social alliances of another kind.

Whereas the impersonal nature of Western money allows it to be used to dissolve all social relationships and thus appears to create complete self-sufficiency, valuables are enmeshed within social relationships, and what is received for them is also socially entailed. Within Chambri society, these socially enmeshed valuables are most frequently given and received within the two social roles of affine or of agnate. As an affine, one receives valuables from members of another clan in compensation for women given in marriage; as an agnate, one receives valuables from members of one's own clan to acquire women in marriage or to repay affines for the children these women have produced. Thus as an affine, a man receives valuables because wife-takers are indebted to him; as an agnate, a man receives valuables because his father and brothers are obliged to assist him in order to maintain themselves as clansmen. When Moi was offered *talimbun* by members of Kwosaivon's patriclan, he was thus offered agnatic status as a member of this clan. From the perspective of men of this clan, Moi must accept their *talimbun* as a prerequisite to his marrying Yebiwali. He would have to be turned into a brother before he could become a husband to their sister-in-law,[15] and, as we shall see, for reasons more extensive than that of the levirate.

Because Moi must have known that he was not entitled to the woman as compensation for having buried her husband, unless he first became an agnate of the deceased, we are left with the perplexing question of why he pressed this case? Why did he refuse the *talimbun* shell, which as the basis of bride-price conveyed the promise that he would be helped in the future to acquire a bride, insisting instead that it is a 'good Sepik custom that if a man dies in a faraway place, he who buries him deserves his hands washed and that the widow is suitable pay?' Since this is not a Sepik custom anyone else then (or now) seems to have heard of, why was he associating the widow and the burial, suggesting that they could be appraised as comparable values for exchange?

Hoskins (Chapter 7) analyses the Kodi association between marriages and burials. To understand the specific association Moi was making between a widow and a burial – and to explain why Yebiwali eventually married the considerably older Akerman – we must examine the process through which inequalities between affines are transformed into inequalities between other non-related groups. Although the Chambri consider individuals and groups that are not linked through marriage to be potentially equal, differences in relative status can be established and maintained between groups of men when those who are 'more than equal' assist their 'less than equal' neighbours to meet their affinal debts. When a Chambri and the members of his clan cannot amass sufficient valuables to compensate their wife-givers in a creditable manner, they will seek assistance from an unrelated clan. Members of this clan, in return for their assistance, gain power over their clients – over their land and water rights, their totemic names and other valuables – until the debt can be repaid to them either by the client clan itself, or on its behalf by yet another clan. In the latter and more frequent case, the client clan has simply found another patron. Indeed, wealthy clans compete with each other to acquire new clients, either from clans freshly distressed by their obligations, or from clans which are already clients of other clans. The inequality inherent in affinal exchange ensures that each clan will be politically ascendant over one other clan. However, as the system works out in practice, this inequality ramifies in so far as the affinal relations of some provide others with the opportunity to prove themselves ascendant over most – not only over their clients but over other only moderately wealthy groups which have been able to acquire fewer clients.

That a clan wins or loses at the politics of affinal exchange is, from the Chambri point of view, completely attributable to the control of totemic names. These secret names, when used effectively, enable a man to establish identity with his ancestors and to become the embodiment of their power. For a man to remain powerful, he must ensure that these names remain secret lest their power be alienated or diluted through use by others. It is improbable, however, that a man will lose control of these secret names while he retains social power. If he is recognised by virtue of his network of social relations as having power, no one is likely to risk his retribution by attempting to use his secret names, nor is he likely to reveal them through insufficient vigilance. Moreover, a rival is unlikely to receive the amount of public support necessary to become an effective incarnation of a particular clan ancestor provided another continues to receive social definition as the lineal descendant of this ancestor.

When a clansman dies, however, it is clear to everyone that the names and the powers they convey have been lost. Under most circumstances young men have sufficient totemic power to protect themselves and insufficient numbers of enemies to warrant ensorcelment. When their deaths do occur, their senior agnates view them primarily as attacks upon themselves. From Kwosaivon's perspective, thus, to have had his son killed meant not only that his names had been stolen, but that a social process had been instituted in which Kwosaivon's own relationship with both living and dead might become critically impaired.

In the politics of affinal exchange, individuals and clans can be assisted in their competition by women who have learned of totemic secrets through their close association with their husbands and their husbands' agnates. Moreover, men are particularly vulnerable to the theft of their totemic names when they are asleep and dreaming, or when they are ill and dying. Thus, Moi and Yebiwali were posing the same threat to Kwosaivon, the girl's father-in-law, and to his clan. As we will see, it was with the understanding that each might have learned disabling totemic secrets that Moi pressed his demand that he be compensated for his burial of Yebiwali's husband with the widow herself.

On public and private roads

Although Kwosaivon could not have been sure who had taken which private bush road to effect the death of his son, he was convinced that the death was contrived through sorcery. One possible private bush road could have been travelled by Yebiwali and her lover Tchuikumban, another by Moi. It was Kwosaivon's purpose during the debate over who should marry his dead son's widow to ensure that whoever had gained access to secret totemic names would do no further damage.

The debate over who should marry Yebiwali makes clear Kwosaivon's concern. Although it was Yebiwali's father who 'decided that the need to remarry her was urgent' (Mead 1935:261); although it was her 'male cousin, Tchengenbonga, whom she called "brother"' (1935:261) who was sent for in order to negotiate her marriage, and although men of Yebiwali's patrilineage had been extremely active in pressing for her wedding, nonetheless her father-in-law 'did all the talking during the debate'. Whatever of political significance was taking place that day in the Yangaraman men's house concerned Yebiwali's affines and not her agnates. Their concern was best articulated by Kwosaivon's in-law, Tana, who spoke 'about sorcery and Aibom, how they had challenged an Aibom boast of having killed this boy, by threatening calaboose, and Aibom had backed down'.[16] That men from Aibom would have boasted at all, however, justified Kwosaivon's fear that Moi may have done more than bury his son; he may also have learned the totemic secrets necessary to kill him through sorcery. And, if he had learned these secrets he was in a position to attack other members of this same clan. Indeed, Moi's insistent claim upon Yebiwali could have been meant only as an assertion that he was sufficiently dangerous to Kwosaivon that he must be placated. Like the men's house debates of the Iatmul, those of the Chambri are won by individuals who can 'judge whether to expose [their] opponents' secrets or merely to indicate by some trifling hint that [they know] the secrets ... [and can judge] whether [others] really know any of the important secrets of [their] clan or whether their trifling hints are only a bluff' (Bateson 1958:161). Kwosaivon, we imagine, was anxious during this particular debate to refine his judgement concerning the extent of Moi's knowledge.

From the very beginning of the debate it must have been clear to all present that Moi's demands were simply too great to be accepted. By proposing this marriage to Yebiwali, Moi was attempting to further weaken and, in fact, to humiliate Kwosaivon's clan. He was insinuating that Kwosaivon's clan had already lost so much of its power that it could not prevent him from augmenting his knowledge of its names by hers.

Moreover, if they agreed to his demands Kwosaivon and his agnates would lose the rights over Yebiwali which they had gained through their affinal payments to her agnates. To have acceded to Moi's demands would have been to relinquish all claims to social viability.

Moi, in his turn, refused compromise. If he had accepted the offer of *talimbun* he would have been incorporated as an agnate into Kwosaivon's patriclan, and would have occupied the same social position as the man he had buried. This incorporation would have neutralised the significance of any totemic secrets he may have learned from Yebiwali's dying husband. As a junior agnate, he and his totemic knowledge would be subject to Kwosaivon's control. That he refused the *talimbun*, but continued to press for Yebiwali, was a clear indication that his intentions toward Kwosaivon continued to be fundamentally antagonistic. (We can only speculate why Moi remained so intransigent throughout: why, if he were interested in social incorporation into Chambri society, did he not eventually accept the *talimbun* which would have, at least, gained him clan membership? As a Iatmul, and one, moreover, from the linguistic group which had in their last military encounter devastated the Chambri, he probably felt much their superior. Perhaps for these reasons he thought it appropriate that he join Chambri either as the leader of Kwosaivon's clan or with that clan as his client.)[17]

That Kwosaivon distrusted Moi, and Yebiwali as well, is clear from the debate: Moi was from Aibom and villagers from there had boasted of the sorcery; Yebiwali 'had not sat down good as a married woman' and together with 'some lover ... [might have] been responsible for the sorcery'. Mead's account of these events, however, ignores Kwosaivon's response to Moi, and would have us understand his distrust of Yebiwali as the rational male response to the active sexuality of Chambri widows. 'A young widow is a tremendous liability to a community. No one expects her to remain quiet until her marriage has been arranged' (1935:259). But Chambri sexual politics imply a different view. For both men and women believe that sexual initiative on the part of young women is indicative not of their highly sexed natures, but rather of the totemic powers of the men to whom the women offer themselves. If widows are tremendous liabilities to the community, it is not because their knowledge of sex may lead them to 'sleep around', but rather because their knowledge of totemic names may lead them to 'speak around'. Since widows know about the totemic names of the patriclan into which they have married, they become of concern to the agnates of their dead husbands.

Kwosaivon would never have agreed to a marriage between Yebiwali and Moi unless he had first neutralised by agnatic incorporation the threat Moi offered, for both Yebiwali and Moi could have known a number of his totemic secrets. Together they might have been able to use these with devastating effect against him and his clan and, as well, to convince a significant number of others that their knowledge was sufficient to empower them against him. Nor was he likely to agree to a marriage between Tchuikumban and Yebiwali. This was not because Tchuikumban was a young orphan without resources to pay sufficient bride-price. Tchuikumban did have, after all, classificatory relatives willing to look after his interests, relatives who arranged, we might add, a perfectly satisfactory marriage for him after Mead and Fortune left the field. Rather, it was precisely because Tchuikumban had probably been Yebiwali's lover that Kwosaivon objected to their marriage. If Tchuikumban had succeeded in his desire to marry Yebiwali, this would have demonstrated that he was also powerful enough to have caused the death of Kwosaivon's son. The extent to which Tchuikumban got his way would provide social verification of the weakness of Kwosaivon and his clan.

The remarriage of Yebiwali

But what of Yebiwali? Was she constrained from marrying her lover, Tchuikumban? Was she compelled to marry the considerably older Akerman? Certainly she posed a threat to Kwosaivon, since she had perhaps learned through his son of totemic esoterica to which she had no right. And certainly it was in Kwosaivon's best interest, as this interest was defined in Chambri society, to have her married to someone like Akerman, an ally who was not, at least at that time, likely to use the secrets Yebiwali may have brought to her new marriage as political leverage against him. But did he compel Yebiwali to agree to this remarriage?

This remarriage would figure quite differently in the lives of Yebiwali and Kwosaivon because Chambri men and women each appraise experience from a different perspective. Although both perceive of themselves as members of patriclans, only men are preoccupied with the political relationships which are established through the system of affinal exchange. Men, we have seen, are trapped in relationships of enduring obligation and inequality, because they can never fully repay those who have provided the women who have given them life. Women, however, are under no such perpetual obligation, since they can in fact compensate those to whom they owe their lives by bearing sons and daughters. That is what Gewertz's Chambri sister meant when she told her that 'the business of men [i.e. affinal exchanges] is to pretend that they can bear children. Women don't have to pretend because they can.' Women, therefore, are little involved in the politics of affinal exchange in which their husbands and fathers engage with such obsessional intensity.

The concerns about the relative power and hence political viability of particular clans expressed by the men in their debate with Moi did not engage Yebiwali. While women are not indifferent to the deaths of their relatives, they are unlikely to occupy themselves with the kinds of political affairs which lead men to threaten, enact or suspect homicide. Yet, the separate interests of men and women may each on some occasions be satisfactorily served by the same social action. If the decision of the men had directly affected Yebiwali – had they capitulated and given her in marriage to Moi – it is likely that she would have found this decision acceptable, though for reasons other than theirs. She probably would not have objected since their decision would have demonstrated his relative power and would have meant, therefore, that any children she might have had by him would be well situated. Comparably, she did not have to be coerced to marry Akerman rather than Tchuikumban since either marriage would have satisfied her interests as a Chambri woman. Tchuikumban's capacity to have attracted her indicated that he probably possessed strong totemic support, but Akerman's powers had already been amply demonstrated. He was wealthy and well-established, with wives who would assist her in her domestic tasks. Any children she bore to him would become integrated within extensive social networks. Tchuikumban certainly had potential to emerge as a man of social importance, but Akerman was, for her, also an excellent choice as husband. The overtures she made toward Tchuikumban did not mean that she objected to her eventual marriage to Akerman. If she had in fact found Akerman distasteful, she would not have been compelled to marry him since as a discontented wife she would be likely to steal his secrets and give them to a lover of her choice.

*   *   *

Yebiwali is now the only Chambri alive who prefers to sleep in a mosquito bag rather than under a mosquito net.[18] The one she uses, she wove herself, although once when she was a young girl, Mead tells us, she refused to weave at all and was therefore regarded as unable to provide for a young husband such as Tchuikumban.

When we visited her in 1983, accompanied by three tourists, she was about eighty.[19] The tourists – teachers of French, two from Sydney and one from Paris – were interested in handicrafts. They were spending their vacation travelling throughout New Guinea, and hoped to see one of the traditional Chambri mosquito bags. Resplendent in orange army surplus jumpsuits, with mottled green netting draped from their pith helmets to protect them from the mosquitos which were more ferocious than usual that particular December, they were escorted by us to Yebiwali's house to see her mosquito bag. We had sent word that we would like to see it, and were met by Yebiwali's grandson, Clemence Akerman, a primary school teacher, who quietly advised Gewertz that Yebiwali would consent to sell her mosquito bag for K300.00 (almost U.S.$360.00).

Most of the other Chambri we met on our way to Yebiwali's house found our friends amusing and novel, but Yebiwali, at first, ignored them entirely. She fastened her gaze upon Gewertz, tottered over to her and, calling her *aiyai* – 'mother', crawled through her legs. She then turned to her other visitors, and explained several times in Chambri, with evident satisfaction, that she was to be called the 'wife of Akerman'.

Yebiwali, some twenty years after Akerman's death, was still defining herself by the social relationships which her marriage helped to establish. She had, it is true, belatedly learned to weave the mosquito bags which Mead believed to be the most important Chambri item of manufacture, responsible in large measure for the position of power she felt Chambri women held in their society. But Yebiwali had always known that her personal validity was not determined by the production or possession of objects like mosquito bags, but rather by the social context created through her own relationships and those of her children. As the 'wife of Akerman', Yebiwali had the considerable pleasure of crawling through the legs of her children and grandchildren – as she had crawled through those of Gewertz. By calling them 'mother', she was reminding them all that they were repaying her debts by replacing those who had produced her. Through the role of these children in social reproduction she would be able to repay those responsible for her existence: no one had through sorcery interfered with her social reproduction. She had been able to conceive, carry to term, and raise two sons and a daughter to maturity.[20] From her perspective, hers had been a well-formed life.

Because Clemence Akerman had spent much of his life away from home while being educated by Europeans, he had, we suspect, a completely different view of debts and credits in mind when he offered his grandmother's mosquito bag for sale, a view more akin to the one Margaret Mead held when she argued that Chambri women possessed an unusual degree of self-sufficiency and independence because their husbands were economically dependent upon them. Clemence, who usually lives in the town of Wewak, would have probably agreed with Mead that earning sufficient money to pay bills on time, with some money left over for investment, is the most important component of independence. He was, nonetheless, confused by the lack of autonomy he experienced whenever he returned home to his village. Although he was the money earner, his senior agnates were frequently the investors of his money, and in networks upon which he continued to depend in a manner that puzzled him.

Yebiwali could probably have resolved his confusion for him, if he had mustered the patience to decipher her archaic Chambri. She understands the social meaning of wealth, and knows that junior males rarely possess a sufficient number of totemic names to have political control over their own lives. But Clemence Akerman is not likely to seek instruction from her and she apparently does not care if he learns from her or not. From her perspective, he has already satisfactorily fulfilled his function by marrying and siring children. She is glad that Clemence pleases her sons by earning as much money as he does, but she knows that valuables never promised women their freedom from debt, neither before, when they were shells, nor now when they are money trees. And moreover, she likes sleeping in her mosquito bag, which is why she wove it, and is quite content that the orange and green water spirits did not decide to purchase it.

Toward a general definition of dominance within particular cultural contexts

But was Yebiwali dominated? By Chambri cultural standards of the reasonable and normal she was not. But to have demonstrated that according to these standards Yebiwali was not dominated is still to leave open the possibility that she was dominated in actuality, but that she and other Chambri failed to recognise this fact for reasons of false consciousness. Even though her behaviour was uncoerced by Chambri standards of what constitutes coercion – no one, after all, prevented her freeing herself from debt through reproduction – perhaps her choices were constrained by such standards to the extent that she was prevented from knowing, much less from following, her own 'best interests'. Perhaps, as some would say, she was in much the same circumstance as the secretary who, following the dress code endorsed by her boss, mistook her interests for his?

We would certainly wonder whether Yebiwali's domination was implicit in the cultural patterns which shaped her understanding and action if, for example, she had wished to express her views directly to the men debating her remarriage, and had found her entry into the men's house checked by the culturally appropriate response of collective rape. Yet, from the perspective of those who define dominance in relation to

accepted cultural standards – those failing to understand why any
secretary would choose to flout her boss by rejecting a reasonable and
normal dress-code – this would not be viewed as an act of dominance
since to enter the men's house would be defined by Chambri as culturally
inappropriate. But how, after all, from the perspective of *any* contemporary
Western sensibility, could collective rape ever be anything other than
an act of dominance?

We leave the story of Yebiwali – and others like her in non-Western
societies – uncertain about what kind of connection to make between her
life and our own. Sharing aspects of Mead's vision of the nature of
anthropology, we sense that Yebiwali's life has something to do with
ours: that because her life and our own constitute part of the human
condition, she should have both moral and intellectual significance for
us.

But when we speak as anthropologists about issues of contemporary
importance to members of our own culture, how can we be both relevant
and fair? On the one hand, we know that people in different societies do
things differently – in which case anthropologists tend to have the role in
our own society of showing how the ways of other societies contrast to
our own. Under these circumstances what is learned about other cultures
often seems to have little applicability to our own. On the other hand, in
trying to generalise across cultures, anthropologists tend to elevate their
own cultural definitions to the level of universals. Under these circumstances, the particulars of non-Western cultures are frequently not only
distorted but judged according to Western political and moral sensibilities. Because Mead saw Chambri women as economically independent
and politically self-sufficient actors she applauded them for their competence. It is difficult in cases such as these to relate anthropological
understandings about other cultures to our own without betraying those
very understandings.

In particular, how can anthropologists speak to feminist issues important to contemporary Westerners? Understanding a subject as complex as
dominance proceeds most readily when we can compare 'ourselves' to
'others', as we have done throughout this chapter. This is so in large
measure because the degree of interconnection between the elements of
any social system makes comparison of the variant forms and arrangements of elements which appear in distinctive but still comparable social
systems the best way to discriminate between contingent and causative
relationships. If, in other words, Yebiwali's life cannot speak to our own,
on what basis can we hope to appraise our own? How can we begin to
determine the best interests of women living in the contemporary West

without at the same time beginning to determine what the interests are of women living in sociocultural contexts different from our own?

Best or real interests derive from what is, according to the perspective of the authors of this chapter, the universally applicable political and ethical premise that all people should be able to lead lives which provide them with satisfaction. These interests, in our present non-Utopian view, cannot be perceived in a completely culture-free manner. They must be seen with respect to definitions of what constitutes satisfaction. The reference against which best interests are to be discerned must, therefore, concern the nature of experience. The most that radical or reformist anthropological thought can hope to accomplish, if it values cultural differences, is to provide an understanding of the kinds of social arrangements, actual or potential, feasible within a particular cultural context. If it wishes to alter experience, yet preserve any degree of cultural integrity, it cannot expect to make precipitous or substantial changes to the ways of thought of the experiencing entity. It would not be feasible to suggest that contemporary North American women could be made to think like a Chambri. Nor can contemporary Chambri be made to think like an American. And whether Yebiwali was or was not oppressed, she must be seen as a Chambri woman, with a Chambri epistemology and metaphysics, for this judgement to be reached.[21]

Dominance, in these terms, should be recognised with respect to its effect on the experiencing agent. Thus, the meaning, consequences and manifestations of dominance will vary according to the cultural definition of person. It should be added that to use the cultural concept of person as the reference point for determining the presence of dominance does not imply that such a concept exists apart from a sociocultural system of coercion. The point is that the best or real interests of a person like Yebiwali, who defines herself as a product of her social position, will not be the same as those of an individual who defines herself as a subjectivity, the product of a set of unique experiences. Yebiwali could not and would not wish to have a private self which acquires a unique perspective and individuality over time. Such a self would make her profoundly disoriented in Chambri culture.

If it is the case that real or best interests can most appropriately be understood with reference to a culturally constructed definition of person, our general definition of dominance can be expanded to include more clearly the fact that dominance will take different cultural forms in different cultural contexts. Dominance, in our reformulation, is a relationship in which individuals or groups are impeded or prevented from following the strategies necessary for them to meet the cultural standards which define persons as having worth.

Following from this definition of dominance, false consciousness is a form of domination: more specifically, the incapacity to recognise the fact and the means of dominance. Thus, for example, if Chambri society is structured in such a way as to hinder some individuals or categories of individuals – perhaps women – from establishing themselves as persons of worth in positional terms, then these individuals are in relations of dominance. If they do not recognise the nature of this domination, they suffer from false consciousness. False consciousness is the failure to understand that or why the self has been diminished. Dominance and false consciousness would thus appear in at least two distinctive clusters – one centering on the varieties of subjectivist, and the other on the varieties of positional, views of self. Sorcery, disruption of kin networks, loss of names, humiliation in debating, are some of the forms dominance might take in positional kinds of societies. The loss of economic autonomy, through which individuals sustain viability as self-sufficient persons, could be a source of dominance in subjectivist kinds of cultures.

But could the very definition of person itself be a manifestation of domination, and our use of it as a primary reference point, be a form of false consciousness? This possibility arises in two different circumstances. The first involves cases in which there may be more than one culturally salient definition of self, whereby members of a social category may meet the cultural definition of what their sort of person should be, but still define themselves and/or be defined by others as of much less value than the members of other categories within the society. That people may be aware of more and less favourable definitions of self presumably diminishes the amount of satisfaction to be gained for those bound by the less favourable definition.[22] Domination becomes the restriction of favourable definitions of person to certain social categories; false consciousness becomes the failure to recognise the nature and basis of this restriction. Relations of dominance between systems can also be analysed in terms of such differentially valued definitions of person.[23]

The second circumstance involves the possibility that all definitions of person within a culture, whether one or several, are manifestations of false consciousness. Should, for instance, the American definition of self in terms of a privatistic subjectivity be viewed as manifestations of false consciousness? And would class consciousness better be furthered through a positional definition of self? If so, would adherence to a subjective view of the self be to subscribe to a form of domination? Since our perspective is not Utopian, this latter possibility does not deter us from our project: irrespective of whether a culture's definition of person contains an ideological distortion, if all who share in the culture are equally subject to this distortion, then domination does not exist within that context. Thus, for example, individual subjectivism may indeed be an ideological component of advanced capitalism, but were no members of such a society to be deprived of the means of realising themselves as persons of worth, then relations of domination would not exist.

To return in conclusion to the domination of Yebiwali, we need to consider both what did and did not happen. If marriage to Tchuikumban had been in her best interests, and if the men debating her marriage were indifferent to these interests, this would have been an act of dominance. If she had under these conditions entered the men's house to act as an advocate of her interests and had been raped, or if she had desisted from advocating her interests from fear of rape, the men's dominance of her would have been compounded. If she did not realise that she and other women would be punished much more severely for such social and ritual infractions than would men, then she was suffering from false consciousness. Since it seems that she neither wished nor needed to act as advocate, nor was deluded by cultural misunderstandings, we believe that although not dominating others herself, this particular Chambri woman was not herself dominated because she was not denied access to cultural standards of worth.

Notes

1. Our primary concern here is not to review the immense literatures on dominance and false consciousness which have been generated in fields ranging from ethology to moral philosophy. Instead, we wish to explore through an exercise in anthropological reflexivity those sociocultural influences which have shaped our own perception of the nature and sources of inequality.

2. The data we analyse in this paper come both from the unpublished field notes of Margaret Mead and our own field research among the Chambri. The Department of Anthropology of the Research School of Pacific Studies at the Australian National University helped sponsor our two-month field trip during 1983. Gewertz has made two previous trips. The first, in 1974-75, was sponsored by the Population Institute of the East–West Center, the National Geographic Society and the Graduate School of the City University of New York. The second, during the summer of 1979, was sponsored by the National Endowment for the Humanities and by Amherst College. Gratitude is expressed to each of these institutions, as it is to the Wenner-Gren Foundation for Anthropological Research, which allowed Gewertz to investigate archival material during 1981. We also wish to thank Carolyn Errington, Leslie Devereaux, Mervyn Meggitt, Jill Nash, Edward Schieffelin, Donald Tuzin and James Weiner for their substantive comments and editorial advice.

3. Thus, it is not an act of dominance for members of American society to be socialised to speak English; it is, however, at least arguable that immigrants to New York City from the American Territory of Puerto Rico are being dominated if their children are prevented from advancing academically because they must be taught in English rather than in their native Spanish.

4. The question of why particular relations of dominance should exist is not the focus of this paper. The forms dominance takes in various cultures must first be examined.

5. Marxists such as Braverman (1975), for instance, are explicit on the point that under advanced capitalism workers are alienated from their humanity because work cannot become a form of self-expression for them. Neither the conditions of their work nor the

product of their work express their subjectivity, and as regimented producers of partial products, they remain themselves incomplete.

6. The history of exchange relationships between fish-producers and sago-suppliers of the Middle Sepik is the focus of Gewertz 1983. Until recently, the Chambri have bartered surplus fish for their staple, the starchy sago flour leached from the pith of the sago palm, *Metroxylum rumphii*, by Bisis and Mali speaking women from the neighbouring Sepik Hills.

7. Types of shell valuable. Before the European introduction of cotton and nylon netting, cylindrical mosquito bags some 10 to 15 feet long were woven by Chambri women from sago shoots and bast. In Mead's view, these bags were the most important of Chambri trade items. However, it appears to us that the stone tools produced and widely traded by Chambri men were at least as important. We also must qualify her statement that women controlled the shell valuables received by their husbands from the sale of these bags. Based on Mead's observation that women did possess some valuables, Gewertz (1983:91-2), suggested that these were the revenue from the sale of the mosquito bags. We now think it likely that most of these valuables held by women were entrusted to them by their fathers at the time of marriage, to be given eventually to their sons. Since such valuables could only be used in the male realm of affinal exchange, we doubt that women would own many of them in their own right. Thus, as far as we can establish, Chambri men returned few, if any, of the shell valuables that they acquired in exchange for the mosquito bags woven by their wives or sisters. Yet, we think it inaccurate to argue that Chambri men alienated the products of female labour. No evidence exists suggesting that any Chambri man could do more than urge a woman to produce a bag for him. Whether a woman wove a bag to oblige a husband or brother or to please herself, she did not expect to earn shell valuables for her efforts.

8. Errington and Gewertz (1985) describe how names are acquired and lost; see also Harrison 1982, for an important discussion of the political use of totemic names in another Sepik society.

9. That Chambri women become persons of worth through reproduction suggests a parallel with the circumstance described by Weiner 1976, for the matrilineal Trobriand Islands. In this influential analysis of Kiriwina women and men as, respectively, persons of value and of renown, she argues that women reproduce the unchanging substance which gives matriclans their continuity, while men distinguish among themselves and their matriclans according to the degree of eminence achieved through exchanges. The most theoretically significant of the many ethnographic differences between the matrilineal Kiriwinans and the patrilineal Chambri concerns the relationship between the objectives of men and of women. Among the Kiriwinans, both men and women share the same vision of the social whole but recognise that each has a distinctive role in the implementation of this shared society. Among the Chambri, both men and women pursue separate objectives and their society is a negotiated balance between separate interests of each.

10. Chambri men are much more frequently the targets of sorcery than are Chambri women. A woman is only ensorcelled in order to attack her male kinsmen. However, it is rarely clear whether the primary target is her affines or her agnates. Since the purpose of sorcery is to demonstrate that power has shifted from the victim to the attacker, the ensorcelment of a woman is unsatisfactory because in these cases, the identity of both true victim and attacker is uncertain.

11. Margaret Mead, believing that social scientists build upon the work of their predecessors, wished her field notes to be placed within the public domain upon her death. We are privileged to have been among the first to study these notes, and are grateful to Dr. Mary Catherine Bateson for granting us permission to do so before they were catalogued by the staff of the Library of Congress in Washington, D.C. Although the conclusions we draw from Mead's field notes differ from hers, we are profoundly indebted to her for in this sense allowing us access to them. We could not have written this paper if it were not for her generous commitment to the future of her discipline.

12. When Mead transcribed her account of the debate, she thought that Tana and Kwosaivon were brothers. (To simplify matters, we have adopted the spelling of names that Mead employed.) Actually, Tana, referred to as Tanum in Fortune's field notes,

was Kwosaivon's daughter's father-in-law. Indeed, the relationship between Tana and Kwosaivon's daughter had generated a considerable scandal. Although the girl was married to Tana's son, it was generally acknowledged that Tana had 'made the first hole in this woman' (Fortune n.d.). This scandal is described in detail elsewhere by Gewertz (1983:176-85).

13. Although all individuals define themselves in some measure by their social context, the degree to which an individual is subsumed by his social position is culturally variable. Thus, Chambri are more completely their names than the English their class or Americans their profession.

14. A discussion of the contrast between the pattern of perpetual indebtedness found among the Chambri and the oscillating indebtedness found in the New Guinea Highlands appears in Gewertz 1977.

15. Although *talimbun* are sometimes used to pay for services and to acquire commodities without establishing enduring social relationships, we doubt that one was offered to Moi simply to pay him off and, thereby, get rid of him. Because Moi probably knew too much, and pressed his claim with such audacity, Kwosaivon and his agnates would not have thought that they could so easily dispose of him.

16. Most Chambri and Iatmul debates are occasions for the expression of several social issues. In this case, a subsidiary dispute involved Tana and Kwosaivon and the scandal described in note 12. Tana's boast that he quelled the Aibom who had bragged of causing the young man's death, while ostensibly a defence of Kwosaivon, was also a statement of Tana's own power. It could thus be seen as a challenge to Kwosaivon because it suggested that Tana himself was powerful enough to have ensorcelled Kwosaivon's son.

17. Although several Iatmul from the Parambei dialect group have moved to Chambri, Moi does not appear in any of our genealogies, and we do not know what happened to him after he failed to acquire Yebiwali in marriage.

18. With the European intrusion at the turn of the century, the commodities the Chambri produced ceased to be valued by their neighbours since mosquito bags and stone tools had become less desirable than cotton nets and steel tools. See Gewertz 1983 for a discussion of the drastic socioeconomic changes wrought by these replacements.

19. Although we encouraged Yebiwali on this and other occasions to recall the circumstances of her remarriage to Akerman, she could remember virtually nothing.

20. Women compensate those to whom they owe their lives by bearing sons and daughters. Sons compensate a woman's agnates for their having bestowed on her the names and powers which have contributed to her identity and viability: as sister's sons, they serve as mediator between their mother's brother's clan and other social groups (see Harrison 1982). Daughters provide social replacement of those who produced their mother, particularly if patterns of restricted marriage are followed.

21. Although revolutionaries aspire to create new kinds of persons, we would question the morality and practicality of this objective: the people who would enact the revolution are unlikely either to frame or wish to respond to revolutionary aspirations which are unintelligible to them.

22. A poignant example might be found in the position of a sweeper in Calcutta, whose satisfaction at being a sweeper is likely to be curtailed by the realisation of the way sweepers are regarded by members of other castes. Lukes (1974), for instance, in a discussion about how one can determine what the members of a relatively powerless group regard their interests to be when they are afraid, or think it futile, to criticise those who control them, briefly discusses the case of the Indian caste system. He refers both to the process of Sanskritization, whereby the members of a lower caste attempt to raise the position of their caste in the hierarchy through such methods as adopting strict vegetarianism, as well as to occurrences like the mass conversion of Untouchables to Buddhism in 1956. These instances, he argues, indicate that the relatively powerless, even in a system premised upon inequality, may, in fact, object to their low status.

23. Our discussion of the differences between Clemence Akerman and his grandmother suggest that under the conditions of rapid social change accompanying colonial rule there may be a shift for some from a positional to a subjectivist definition of person. Domination under these circumstances would be the restriction of access to the more

valued definition of self. Thus, dual educational systems may, in these respects, become mechanisms of domination.

CHAPTER 3

Gender difference and the relations of inequality in Zinacantan

LESLIE DEVEREAUX

Gender is strongly differentiated in Zinacantan, a Mayan community in the highlands of southern Mexico. Women and men, girls and boys dress in sex-specific, highly distinctive costume, and undertake very different tasks within a rigidly defined sexual division of labour. Men and women also move differently in space, both in demeanour and forms of locomotion as well as in the spatial arenas which they habituate. The Zinacanteco ideology of gender, overtly articulated in some ritual enactments, tales and in the formal talk of court cases and ceremonial occasions, produces a view of male and female as different, without emphasizing essence or substance as the source of difference so much as stressing action and appearance as appropriately displaying difference. Man and woman in Zinacantan are conceived of as ideally complementary and formally unranked in social evaluation within the social unity of marriage, the union of male and female labours. The gender ideology casts men and women as adult social actors, as two necessary parts of a social whole. Each part is incomplete without the other; each part expresses itself through its characteristic labours which find their needed complement in the labours of the other.

Zinacanteco gender ideology, then, with its emphasis on the harmonious union of different labours and the mutual rights and obligations of men and women, would seem to provide *prima facie* support for the 'different but equal' thesis. But men and women are not equal in Zinacanteco; men's interests, autonomy and life prospects enjoy greater scope than do women's. The question arises then as to how women who are overtly conceived to have the same motives for action, find that their objectives are not equally available to them.

My approach to this issue differs from that taken by some other contributors to this volume who focus on motives and/or the ideological construction of gender-appropriate forms of agency. I argue, by way of contrast, we must take care not to conflate motives with action itself and that we must analyse action as always effected within structural arenas. As actors, Zinacanteco men and women have differential access to the institutions in which their interests can be represented and pressed. There are many reasons for this and to grasp them it is necessary to situate the household – the main social unit in Zinacantan – in the context of the wider social relations of which it is part. This task involves identifying the groups who control the ideological mechanisms which define life goals and allow some people to press their interests more effectively than others. Gender differences provide a convenient social division for these groups to exploit in the pursuit of their ends. Women's subordination, then, should be seen as the outcome of this process and not as an intrinsic quality of gender difference.

Gender ideology: difference and complementarity

Zinacantecos live as members of a cultural group which is first among its peers of indigenous communities, but has never been free of external hegemony, whether lowland Maya, Aztec, Spanish colonial or modern Mexican. Zinacantecos make use of their geographic location to supplement subsistence swidden horticulture with perspicacious and often long-distance trading. In the pre-Columbian era Zinacantecos ran lines of slaves bearing cacao, salt and feathers from lowlands to highlands; in the colonial epoch first as bearers themselves and later as muletrain drivers Zinacantecos transported wheat, sugar, cotton and mercantile goods as far as Guatemala and Tabasco. Today Zinacanteco truck owners and traders buy perishable vegetables and flowers where they are plentiful and carry them to regions of scarcity and high prices. Zinacanteco men combine this trade with a variety of regimens of wage labour, subsistence and market farming, the bulk of which is carried out on rented lowland cornfields which they clear, sow, weed, and harvest in a yearly gamble with weather, herbicides and the variable avarice of non-Indian landowners.

Before the Conquest Zinacanteco horticulture was confined to its own communal highcountry lands. Afterwards, encroachments by would-be *hacendados* (lordly ranch owners) and the trickery of agents of labour-short lowland ranchers made many Zinacanteco families into debt farmers outside Zinacantan, a diaspora in some cases of 200 years' standing. For as long as records can inform us, then, Zinacantecos have had to take cognisance of powers to tax, to enslave, to appropriate, to promulgate canon law, conscript labour and require votive offerings, to set land tenure laws and National Military Service regulations which emanated from authorities whose force vastly outmatched their own. Throughout these eras Zinacantecos have actively maintained and promoted their distinct ethnic identity, and an ethos of internal social and political unity.

In Zinacantan gender is rigorously marked in all areas of human activity, but it has little conceptual force as a code through which the non-human world is ordered. Zinacanteco constructs differ from those of the Melanesian Nagovisi (to be described in Chapter 6) who encode modes of action through gender, males acting with strength, and females through speech, but who only lightly connect this gender code to the tasks of production and the maintenance of life. Among the Indonesian Kodi similarly, (Chapter 7) highly elaborated notions of male and female principles operate in the politico-spiritual realm, but leave the work of the daily world only partially organised by a gender opposition. Foi and Kwaio, however, (also Melanesian, see Chapters 10 and 1) have well-developed notions of the tasks appropriate to male and female; violation of these notions strikes at the very physical well-being of the person, the group or the crop, in part because these gender ideologies construct males and females as both physically and spiritually different kinds of beings.

Zinacantecos recognise and symbolise male and female as physically different. Theories of health in Zinacantan contain ideas about the hot and cold natures of foods and of persons; ill-health can be brought on by an imbalance in hot and cold, and restoration of the balance can often restore health. Women in general are prone to the cold end of the spectrum; during menstruation and following childbirth women should not violate their cold natures by consuming hot foods such as oranges, chillies or chicken. Men are generally more hot, on the other hand, and consume and tolerate hot foods better than do women.

Male and female hardly exist lexically, however, as abstract biological concepts separated from roles. Male and female animals are distinguished as mother and father animals, for example. People, as in the sense of human being, are refered to as *kristyano* ('Christians', equated with persons, ungendered). One can only refer to children as *k'oshetik* (little ones, ungendered) or as *zeb* (daughter) or *krem* (son). When they marry, socially conferred sexual maturity begins to make them *anz* (woman) or *vinik* (man). For purposes of identifying someone in a story being told, in the role of child of their parents, even an octogenarian will be *zeb* or *krem* in a possessed form ... so and so's daughter or son. Parents are socially responsible for their children until the children set up their own households as married people. This happens after the birth of one or two children, and is the point at which a person will be easily referred to as an *anz* or a *vinik*. The most productive gender terms in Tzotzil are *me7*, mother, and *tot*, father. These, with their core referents of biological parenthood, are metaphorically extended but not in a wholly parallel fashion. *Me'*, extended, carries a causative element of meaning, which has to do with the origins of things:

> *me' tak'in*, the source of treasure;
> *me' 'ik*, the origin of the wind;
> *me' unen*, afterbirth (source of the infant);
> *me' chamel*, source of sickness;

Tot, on the other hand, is used in metaphoric extension to convey the notion of authority, overlordship:

> *totil*, father authority, as in *totil PAN*, head of the PAN political party;
> *Totilme'il*, parents, refers to ritual advisors, and to the tutelary gods.

There are clear male and female roles, but little talk or symbolic suggestion that because males and females are, in their essence, different types of creature, they then behave as they do as a consequence. Indeed, there is instead the suggestion that men and women share, in their common humanity, common proclivities, such as sexual appetites, ambition for prestige, personal wealth and social power. What is strongly evident in the Zinacanteco social ideology is that these goals can only be achieved (perhaps one should say can best, or most appropriately be achieved) by couples, acting in concert through their complementary work skills.

Thus the overt ideology of gender in Zinacantan, as it is articulated in ritual performances, in tales and in formal speeches, stresses the complementarity of roles of adult men and women and assigns no hierarchical order of value to these roles. Nor is there any particular conceptual elaboration to the physiological differences of male and female. Rather, an action-based or role-oriented elaboration of the different reproductive labours becomes a rigid and rigorously defined sexual division of labour.

The social and economic organisation of Zinacantan is built upon the unit of one male and one female adult labourer, plus their dependants. This is the ideal living unit. Only marriage confers adult status upon members of either sex; it is a requisite condition for most ritual service (except curing) and is the expected state for all adults. Life is labour in Zinacantan, and marriage is overtly formulated as the union of complementary labours.

One of the most significant moments in a wedding ceremony is the instruction of the newly married couple by the godparents of their marriage. This obligatory, but extemporaneous, speech is devoted to exhortations to the bride and groom to work hard in their separate roles as husband and wife. A wife is expected to keep the hearth, to feed her husband whenever he is hungry, to be waiting by a hot fire whenever he returns to the house, to spin and weave sturdy clothing for him, to look after him when he is drunk, and not to scold him unnecessarily. A husband is expected to work hard to produce enough food for the family and to provide for the necessary materials of weaving and sewing, not to lose or waste his money, and not to beat his wife when he is drunk. Male labour clears the land and builds the house; it produces the staple foods of corn, beans, chillies and squash. It is allied with the transformative capacities of women, who raise sheep and spin the wool and cotton into yarn, dye it and weave it into clothing and bedding, who sew garments, who cook and grind the corn, boil beans and serve meals, who tend the small domestic animals of sheep, pigs, chickens and turkeys. The native conceptual schema is that male labour produces the raw materials and female labour transforms them into objects of use and consumption. Working hard is the primary mark of the virtuous person in Zinacantan (controlling one's emotions is the second).

A marriage is about work, then, and is a cooperative economic and social enterprise. It is an alliance of work to which the component of sex is added; the notion of wife (*ahnil*) or husband (*malal*) is applied whenever there is an exchange of sex and labour between a man and a woman, whether or not their arrangement has been solemnised by a ritual wedding, and all the rights of a wife or husband apply in such a case if problems arise and the couple go to court. Since sex is presumed to occur whenever a man and woman are alone together, it is the man's receipt of food and clothing from the hands of a woman which critically defines a functional marital arrangement in an anomalous case, in gossip as well as in public dispute settlement.

The central notions which define acceptable activities are *'abtel* (work) and *k'op* (talk). Work is the defining quality of human beings in Zinacantan. It is that activity to which there is no gainsaying, no exception to be taken. A person's waking life is properly spent in work, in a paced manner much of the time, but often in very intensive and exhausting bursts. Men and women have almost mutually exclusive forms of work, but subsistence work for both is extensive of labour and extensive of time. Work contrasts better with notions of idleness and sleep than with the non-existent idea of leisure. When people are not pressed by urgent tasks they keep busy by less urgent ones, and this is a product both of the deeply held belief that working is what one does when one is not asleep, and of the deeply held fear that to be seen not to be working is to be thought lazy, and up to no good. Work also refers to ritual work – taking a religious post or helping someone in such a post by errand running or providing expert advice. If asked, for instance, if she were going to the fiesta next week a person could as easily say, 'Of course, I have my work', meaning I have ritual duties to perform, as she could say 'Oh no, I have too much work', meaning I am too busy with weaving or other subsistence tasks.

Ritual work takes many forms, but its most spectacular and studied variety is the arduous and expensive care of a saint throughout a year by members of the ritual hierarchy of religious officeholders, referred to in the mesoamerican literature as *cargo*, or burden, holders.[1] This ritual work is often spoken of in anthropological accounts as the work of men, who, incidentally, must be married in order to carry it out. The description echoes the talk of men in Zinacantan themselves, who remember their own and others' ritual careers in this way. But it is in fact the practical case, as any Zinacanteco cargoholder would be the first to admit, that the necessity of a wife is far from a merely formal requisite. The duties of the cargoholder (and they vary enormously) always include the serving of meals, an essential feature of all ritual occasions, and meals cannot be served without the labour of women. In ritual (public) contexts, in fact, the complex timing of the labour and time intensive preparation of food depends to such an extent on the experienced skills of women that official cooks must be recruited for most cargo posts, and the wives of cargoholders become in their later years essential advisers to young wives at the start of what anthropologists regard as their husbands' careers.

Beyond the essential skills of women, allied to and backstopping the ceremonial duties of the men, there is also the need to recruit large numbers of general dogsbodies to run errands, light lamps, serve drinks, light firecrackers, carry home drunks, pat tortillas, produce prodigious amounts of food, sew up costumes, and so on. These people are recruited from the families of both the husband and the wife; they are too numerous, and their duties too onerous, to come repeatedly over the course of a year, unsung and unheralded, from among patrilineal kinsmen alone. In fact, going through a fiesta with a cargoholding household is perhaps the single most eloquently demonstrative experience one can have in the complementary division of labour in Zinacantan.

There is no getting round the fact that it is the men who have a public presence. But everyone in Zinacantan knows the essential labours of the wife, and the essential availability of her kin, without whom none of this public activity could possibly come off. It may be an ideological requirement of the Catholic Church that the caretakers of saints be in a state of sanctioned wedlock, but it is most definitely a matter of practicality that cargo holders have female counterparts at work in the kitchen. Social value and prestige accrues to the wife for this work well done, and she may have considerable power in later life to direct ritual activity herself.

The category, *k'op*, along with other kinds of speech, refers broadly to the necessary role of talk in social life, highly valued and highly dangerous. Ritual speech (as in prayer) and political talk (as in oratory and gossip) are essential skills to maintain health and well-being. The capacity to talk well is an individual gift, no more likely to characterise a man than a woman, but the arenas of talk and style in speech are highly sex differentiated. Attending to gossip (hearing talk) and listening in to the political affairs and court cases, are important things to do in a day. Men routinely cruise past the courthouse, picking up news, while women, for whom the courthouse is not an appropriate spatial domain, watch the lanes of the village for people involved in current affairs, and waylay them by the gate of their house to pry out of them what news they can. In a well-functioning household, the men return regularly with news gathered from the masculine domain of the plaza and cantinas. Within the privacy of the house, around the fire, in voices that will not carry beyond the walls, they match this to the news gathered through women's channels, picked up at the well, overseen or overheard on the path, whispered by a friendly relative as she passes the gate, her mouth covered by her shawl. As they sit weaving or spinning in the yards of their houses women keep a continual watch on all the visible paths up and down the mountains, tracking the movement of other people, speculating on what they are carrying and where they are going. This is not idle; it is essential social work, without which a person or household would be ignorant of the social and political dangers and opportunities lying in wait for them.

Defining interests and situating action

The anthropological enterprise does not end with the arduous tasks of discovering what people do and recording what they say. It must be pushed one step further; as Weber long ago made clear, the rule or law, the enunciated, official way things ought to happen, is something upon which people fall back when the capacity to press one's interest fails. Thus we must ask what is done, what is said to be done, and the reasons for it, but also in whose interests does this happen. If ideological mechanisms can be seen to be controlled by one group over another (and in otherwise homogeneous societies this question is likely to be missed until we look at gender), then ideological hegemony exists (and we have a good case for false consciousness). If the political and economic mechanisms work better for one group than for another, then we have a good case for inequality.

Gender ideology can be the locus of hegemony; this is the force of one part of the modern Western feminist critique. Women's interests can be so defined that a woman's own actions render her confined, socially helpless or culturally inarticulate. Thus, the cultural definition of interests and the personal understandings by actors of their situations and their motives to actions comprise a realm of gender relations which may underlie asymmetries in the social powers of the sexes. But I would contend that this is not the realm in which we can assess equality. By its very nature, gender ideology encodes differences, and these differences are refractory to the easy application of notions like equality except in those cases where the gender ideology itself orders difference in hierarchical ways. In asking about equality and inequality, then, I am concerned specifically with the arenas of social action which are available to men and women, with the relative capacities of men and women to effect action, to influence the circumstances of their own lives, and to determine the circumstances of the lives of others. Each society presents to analysis, as well as to actors, possibilities for action which differ from those available to actors in other societies. In assessing the degree of equality between the sexes within any society we must determine the nature of social action for all actors, and then weigh the dimensions of action for differences which affect men and women.

Zinacantecos are extraordinarily conscious of the possibility that more for you could mean less for me, and they behave toward one another with the suspicion appropriate to this attitude. Envy of good fortune is believed to lead to witchcraft, something which is within the power of anyone with sufficient ill-will to undertake in order to cause harm to someone else. There is also the belief, of less constant application, that by selling one's soul to the evil Earth Lord one can obtain earthly riches in exchange for ultimate debilitation of the person.[2] Thus, deviation in gender terms is as dangerous as deviation in ethnic terms; non-conformity renders one susceptible to attack by witchcraft, or by outright political bullying, and leaves one potentially without allies.

Both in describing, and in evaluating social action, Zinacantecos are preoccupied with the surfaces, or appearances of things. There is far less apparent concern with motive and intention than there is with effect, both in talk about social actions and in dispute resolution.[3] Both private and public talk about other people's actions turn on putative strategising over interests and gains, construed as concerned with social power or with the accumulation of property. People refrain both from inquiring about inner states – feelings, intentions, wishes, hopes – and from offering them as reasons for actions, either in explanation of themselves or of others. This is not to say that inner states are unintelligible, but that they are rendered somewhat irrelevant by social convention. One observes another's anger, or grief, and may remark on it, but one does not offer it as a reason for action, or as an excuse. Inner states stand in the background of Zinacanteco perceptions of other people's action, and do not enter into social practice as legitimations.

In analysing a similar constellation of attitude and behaviour among villagers locked in petty competition Bourdieu (1978) has suggested that this disinterest in analysing the inner reasons for another's actions stems from the overall homogeneity of the conditions of existence. Certainly Zinacantecos exist under conditions which are objectively homogeneous. This is felt to be so by Zinacantecos themselves, to whom each half *peso* is a significantly differentiating sum. More important is the Zinacanteco attention to maintaining homogeneity of behaviour through prescribed form, backed up by the penalties of social abandonment, and by the ethos of egalitarianism which is given voice in the ritual and political mechanisms. The historically imposed religious cargo system of hierarchically ranked yearly religious offices and the government-imposed civil offices both force on families extensive expenditure of time and money. The return on this expenditure is both self-perceived and socially perceived piety and virtue, since the effort is carried out for the good of the entire community, and is one of the few occasions when action for the communal good is ever believed. Both systems maintain the appearance of egalitarian relations within the community, an equality of economic consumption and an ethos of achievement-based and noninheritable social rank.

Politics and gender conformity

We could choose to regard the division of labour itself as incorporating an ideology of gender. It is unfeminine in Zinacantan to hoe in the cornfield or to drive a truck; Zinacanteca women blush even at the thought of doing such a thing themselves, while they are all fully aware of women in other ethnic communities who engage in just such activities. It is unmasculine to bake tortillas, even to pick up a loom or, usually, to cook for oneself. People are prevented from doing the work of the other gender sometimes by its very inconceivability, but more often by a well-developed sense of shame. One is not the sort of person (say a *Ladino* or Chamula) who regards such work as acceptable for a member of one's sex. One would shudder at being seen doing such a thing. These feelings have to do with maintaining ethnic credibility as much as gender credibility; ideology clearly does not go far enough as an explanation, then, of the persistent rigidities of the division of labour. The social relations which are built on this division, like marriage, are one source of strain; the social relations of power which attack one politically, with economic consequences, or attack spiritually, damaging the health of one's family, are another.

The priorities of a well-lived life are not opaque; insulation from political assault is guaranteed by wealth and social prestige, and these are assumed by everyone to be the aim of everyone else. That is, everyone is capable of assault on others, by social means, in the interests of financial gain and social self-aggrandisement, and only a fool would proceed on any other assumption. Thus, a person who does not protect herself from such assault is also a fool, *sonso*. To be a fool is to become the target of everyone else's self-aggrandising efforts, as well as to make oneself unattractive as a person worth being courted in social alliance. Many people live out their lives so defined socially, but it is not a desirable or particularly secure condition in Zinacanteco terms. Shame, in a society very concerned with appearance, is a strong negative impetus to gender conformity, but it is firmly backed up by the constant politics of gossip and ruinous court cases.

This is as true for women as it is for men. Interest, in this general social sense, is identical for members of either gender in Zinacantan . What is differentiated are the actions and behaviours through which one pursues these interests. The ways in which men and women press their interests, guard them, and get in the way of competing interests are not the same.

The dimension of interest has already been raised by Errington and Gewertz (Chapter 2 of this volume), and they have succeeded in liberating this notion from its ethnocentric moorings. Without deciding in advance what the interest of an actor will be, it is still possible to look at the ways in which actors can press their interests when they wish, can frustrate the interests of others, can articulate their interests, can effect them. This requires a simultaneous concern with action, always specific, and with the systemic forces which may give certain actors advantage over others, may pit an actor's particular interests against others, or relativise long-term and short-term interests. One very important question is the structural allocation of interest between the sexes, the ritual, legal or other structures which determine who 'has an interest' in a given matter. Regardless of the way a person construes his or her own interests (as goals, or desired outcomes) social forces may construct legitimated interest in specific ways.

Ethnicity, gender and the form of action

Caution to be seen to be doing the correct thing, and to see whether or not others are similarly invulnerable to reproach, is closely connected to the Zinacanteco attention to form. Every gesture, action and word must be patently Zinacanteco in appearance, a concern which is itself the product of modern and historical pressures in a hierarchically ordered multi-ethnic region under Spanish cultural and capitalist hegemony. Ethnicity, allied to a pervasive economic scarcity created through colonial expropriation, has produced in the highlands an intense preoccupation with membership in a community as the only source of land, credit, social achievement, even physical and social safety.[4] In the highlands of Chiapas, membership is principally a matter of acting like a member: wearing the ethnic dress, speaking the dialectical variant of the community, participating in the ritual offices, working in the manner of the community. This is not to say that no one takes note of ancestry, but that ancestry foreign to the community can be overcome by conforming action. Historically there has been a great deal of movement in the highlands since the Conquest; many modern villages are the products of migration, return from debt peonage, and recent recovery of lands under land reform legislation.[5]

Thus, in this region, ethnicity is not construed so much as a matter of biological continuity as it is a matter of the appearances of things. To be a Zinacanteco one must dress like one, eat like one, work in the same manner, speak correctly, walk in the way Zinacantecos do, and use the same tools as everyone else. This would be necessary to establish membership; it is essential to maintain membership. The subjugated relationship of indigenes to the Spanish-derived colonial and post-colonial classes, the movement of individuals as traders, and as migrants, and long periods away from home for both men and families occasioned by work on distant plantations has created a situation in which it is always a possibility that a person may become a different sort of person, a town dweller, a deculturated peon, a Chamula instead of a Zinacanteco.

Attention to appearance makes gender membership and ethnic membership inextricable. To be a woman, one must be a Zinacanteca woman; to be a man, one must be a Zinacanteco man. All social signs of gender are ethnically marked; to deviate from conventional form in an item of dress or a mode of work is to call into question simultaneously one's gender membership and one's community membership. Thus, the gender system of Zinacantan can be characterised as highly sign-oriented. The consequence of this attention to form, a strictly well-defined ethnically correct way of doing things, is a cultural emphasis on what people do, which then defines what they are. Gender, like ethnicity, in Zinacantan is in this sense highly external, and is attached to the surface of the person.

The concern with form apparent in the gender ideology is given expression in the ritual cycle carried out yearly at the fiesta of *nativirat* (Nativity). Certain religious officeholders dress in costumes which are caricatures of women's clothing, and enact ritualised dramas in the churchyard, behaving in outlandishly non-feminine ways. This public spectacle is hilariously funny for several reasons,[6] the first of which is that anyone would dress in any costume and appear in public other than in the most solemn manner. All fiesta spectacle in Zinacantan partakes of this vicarious thrill of embarrassment when the most dignified of people, seriously and with great personal expense, enact public vignettes in bizarre costume, cavorting in ways no Zinacanteco, drunk or sober, ever would otherwise do.

This particular spectacle cycle, which has the most overt gender significance in Zinacantan, has two additional and reciprocal humorous elements. Men who are dressed as women, but with less than perfect imitations both of dress and demeanour, are funny because of the highlighted impossibilities: the grosser body imitating the more delicate, the hairy imitating the smooth. The Zinacanteco men in this instance overtly instruct the young women in the audience in spinning; in their gross ineptitude they point (in a somewhat archaic manner) to the significance of this once essential female productive skill. At another juncture the actors dressed as men purchase a bull, but they do so with the bizarre objects of soaproots, vegetables and woven cloth. What is significant here is that these are all the products of feminine labour, and pointedly not normal objects of exchange. One of the messages in the humour of both these inversions is the essential connection of female productive labour to male productive labour in any successful life. Yet the really laughable point for the audience lies in the dress, action and demeanour of the actors in the drama; the men move in grossly non-feminine ways, have trouble with their skirts and shawls, all very much on purpose. The sense of this becomes clearer when the male women engage in a mock horserace and fall off their horses because their skirts get in the way. The actors playing men make much of this in remarks to the effect that people dressed in women's clothing should not ride horses.

This spectacle, which purports to instruct in feminine ways, as Bricker

(1973) noted, quite pointedly remarks on the incongruity of people dressed in feminine clothing doing masculine things, even while the apparent joke is about the hilarious inappropriateness of masculine persons dressing in feminine ways. Another writer has recently suggested that one of the messages of this drama may have to do with the historical absence of Zinacanteco men and their late return to reclaim their masculine places in society (your feminine work is valuable, so give us back our horses and hoes; Wasserstrom 1983).

Either interpretation is commensurate with the more general point that gender and ethnicity are coded together in Zinacantan. There is enormous cultural value in the highlands of Chiapas in acting like the right sort of person, and one must do so as a gendered member of an ethnic community, where every item of dress, each gesture, each action is simultaneously marked for gender and for cultural loyalty.

Action, then, in Zinacantan is always demonstrably Zinacanteco and demonstrably male or female in form. A sexual double standard is one of the most convincing bits of evidence for the asymmetry of sexual complementarity in Zinacantan. In the same ritual cycle as the spinning lesson and horserace already described, another humorous vignette is played out. A man, dressed as a woman and playing the role of a bonesetter (a curing speciality as commonly female as male), in a clever and obscene parody of ritual speech, calls upon the 'bone', quite obviously to every listener a circumlocution for phallus, to find its hole, to stay in its hole, never to leave its hole empty. This is not merely an injunction to husbands to be sexually faithful; it is a clear command to them to be sexually gratifying to their wives. Men are as obliged as women to provide sexual activity for their spouses; appetites are basically the same. But Zinacantecos believe firmly in the differential outcomes of these common human proclivities, by virtue of the fundamental differences in what men and women in fact do.

Women's sexual appetites are considered dangerous both to themselves and to the men they may engage themselves with. Girls are rarely told directly about menstruation, sex or childbearing, although ribald joking and gossip is not particularly inhibited for the benefit of innocent childish ears, and the information children of both sexes pick up around the evening fire is considerable. Still, the facts of monthly cycles are positively hidden from girls, and it comes as a frightening shock. Similarly girls are not allowed to attend childbirth, and are sent away from the house, an otherwise very unusual circumstance. Pubescent girls must rigidly maintain an overt attitude of frightened modesty, a falsely uncomprehending blankness toward sexual joking and a stance of fearfulness toward the opposite sex. They never go anywhere unaccompanied by someone whose testimony about their modest and innocent behaviour will be believed. On the other hand, young men are expected to make eyes at girls, to try to engage them in conversation, to catch them alone on the path, even though speaking to a marriageable girl is tantamount to rape, and can easily end up in court.

Unbridled female sexuality is believed to drain a man, draw out his 'animal spirit companion', a form of soul essence, and weaken it. Unbridled male sexuality weakens women by too many pregnancies. One of the most fearful tales told round the fire in Zinacantan is of the *h'ikaletik*, black creatures of winged, man-like form with penises as long as a horse's, which used to inhabit the forests and sit upon the housetops at night, ready to swoop upon women outdoors alone, and to carry them off to their cave homes where their potency causes the women to bear a baby a day until they die of it. Similar tales are told of sirens in the woods, who copulate with unwary men who allow themselves to be seduced, until the men stagger home, mere husks, and die. Men and women are as dangerous as they are necessary to one another in their uncensored desires.

Access and agency

These considerations lead directly to the dimension of access: the relative availability to men and women of important spaces, arenas, audiences and resources. Differential access clearly results in asymmetrical success in negotiating the realisation of one's interests. In fact, issues of access count among the most significant social forces which constrain and promote actors and their interests. They will define some actors as more significant than others, thereby affecting the agency of persons in regular and analysable ways.

Gender ideologies may specifically empower men or women, as categories, with particular forms of agency, assigning by gender the capacity to act in one situation or another, to create things or situations. Or gender ideologies may define access and interest in ways which indirectly curtail or enhance the agency of the members of one sex over the other. As the discussion of gender in Zinacantan will show, these dimensions are never extricable except heuristically in order to reveal the ways inequalities are reproduced through practice. The ethnography which follows describes how a community whose gender ideology stresses complementarity, and which accords equal social valuation to the rigorously differentiated roles and behaviours of men and women, can produce nonetheless significant inequalities in social practice.

The canons of the division of labour make access to resources, and to wealth extremely asymmetrical in Zinacantan. Since it is only men who farm corn and beans, the staple crops, women are not bequeathed farming land except in those families so rich in land that sons are not disadvantaged by their sisters' inheritances. Women do not wield hoes in Zinacantan, and do not travel to lowland ranches to find land to rent, clear and sow. Boys, and not girls, have for the past two generations been sent to village schools to learn a modicum of Spanish and literacy, and thus women have less ready access to the markets and shops of the towns. Male labour has also for centuries included commercial trading and transport, buying cheap and selling dear through judicious marketing, often involving considerable travel. This is explained nowadays as masculine work because women could not safely, or reputably, spend nights away from home. It would be hard to ascertain whether this reflects the dangers to women imported along with Iberian suzerainty and whether Zinacantecas were once as confident to travel as are the women traders of Tehuantepec. It is certainly the case, however, that modern Zinacantecas take care never to be away from home overnight, never to be unaccompanied whether by day or night, and only a few engage in trade which takes them to distant towns. No Zinacanteca woman drives a truck, or even owns one in her own right.

This cuts women out of the principal means of capital accumulation. Together with their inability to farm for themselves whether on their own or rented land, it leaves women incapable of creating a stable or growing economic base for a household except through the agency of a man, typically a son or a brother.

Women who have left a marriage usually support themselves and their children through intensifying traditionally feminine production: taking in weaving, spinning and tortilla-making for the chronically overburdened married mothers of young children who cannot perform all the labour-intensive services of feeding and clothing their families.[7] This work can provide subsistence, but it can never produce either security or wealth. Men who have left or been left by a wife can continue their economic activities relatively unaltered,[8] but they become helpless domestically, and truncated ritually, as only half of the necessary pair. Such men remarry as soon as possible unless they have a married daughter, or daughter-in-law, in their household.

Speaking well is a skill of primary social importance in Zinacantan; to tell a good story, to be deft at puns and double entendres or to be a good conversationalist are the qualities which confer all the benefits of conviviality and social value in this gossip-ridden and joke-loving community. Men and women are equally likely to possess these qualities, but they exercise them in somewhat differentiated arenas. When men are not working in their fields or markets they are listening in to the proceedings at the courthouse, or gathering in the cantinas or around the town plaza. These all are grouped in the central area of the village, and none is a place where a woman would go unless forced to by circumstance. In so far as all serious disputes are brought to the courthouse, including land battles, inheritance complaints and divorce cases, the inappropriateness of women in these places both restricts women's direct access to information of potential importance to them, and places them at great disadvantage when they themselves must appear to contest their interests there. In fact, most women litigants in a courtcase appear, but speak through a man whenever possible. What is most interesting is that it is clearly a matter of access, to both place and audience, for these same women in the more private contexts of the household, or even of a dispute taken to the home of a local elder, will argue with ease and articulation. Indeed, informal neighbourhood dispute settlers are nearly as often women as they are men. What prevents women, then, from representing themselves in higher courts is the masculine character of these spaces, and of the audience to them.

The matters I have presented here as primarily emanating from decisions of form, or access, critically impinge on the agency of gendered persons in Zinacantan, indirectly empowering them to certain acts, to modes of efficaciousness and depriving them of power in relation to others.

For example, their own interests may be at issue. Women cannot act directly as economic entrepreneurs in the same manner as men: they cannot farm corn themselves, or lead their hired workers to lowland rented fields and work there in concert with them. A woman who wishes to farm corn for her own consumption or to sell in the market does so through a brother, a son, or another agent who will share with her in the profits. A woman only very rarely travels to distant markets, which means that she cannot engage in the high-profit gamble of the long-distance flower trade. This is partly a matter of guarding her reputation, and also her safety in a non-indigenous world of actual, ready rape. It also is a matter of access to indigenous masculine spaces; for a woman to break in to established male travelling partnerships or semi-cooperative male market monopolies would be very difficult. Some do this, but they are exceedingly few. Most women who want to sell flowers (and the majority of flower growers are women in Zinacantan) or to trade in them, do so through a son or a brother.

Similarly, a woman who wants to fight for a share of the family inheritance in court, who wants to oppose the encroachments of others on her land, who wants to divorce her husband or to harass a neighbour will act through a man if there is one in her extended bilateral kin group likely to be able to talk for her. Few, even the best talkers of them who are ritually competent at prayer and curing in their own right, will go to the town hall before the panel of male civil authorities and plead their cases without men to back them up. This is a strategy designed to deal with both the masculine power structure and the masculine audience, to whose reactions the civil authorities are very sensitive.

That the civil authorities are today male and have been for centuries, is at the very least the requirement of the Mexican, formerly Spanish, ideas of government and gender; Mayan or Zinacantecan gender attitudes toward authority are too deeply buried to resurrect. Whatever the origin, modern Zinacanteco public authority is firmly male in personnel. Women influence this realm through their power in the nuclear family household, where the actual and ideological complementarity of labours accords women authority over children, expenditures, their own produce, and virtually all consumption, as well as power produced by the combination of their monopoly over domestic skills. Their wifely rights to divorce are slightly more socially acceptable than are the rights of their husbands.

For communities such as Zinacantan there is a strong temptation to dismiss the value of local politics in the face of the overwhelming influence of state and national governments in setting the parameters of land tenure, prices, credit, political eligibility and labour opportunities. These all are as heavily determined by forces outside of Zinacantan as they are in any peasant community; this means that a great deal of the political and social interactions of men in the town plaza are wholly without efficacy to set or to change the parameters of existence within Zinacantan on a systemic scale. This does not mean, however, that the politicking has no effect on village lives. For while it is beyond the power of politically active men to change the market forces or the rules by which legal and political matters can proceed, it is well within their power to harass the members of their own communities, to bully, to obstruct, to form inside factions, all of which make the difference between success and failure within one's reference group. In the highlands of Chiapas this is one's ethnic community.

Thus Rogers' apt observations on the empty content of male politics in rural France are rewarding to contemplate in the context of Zinacantan, for here, if anywhere, the tyranny of the household is paramount (Rogers 1975). The household is the only enduring social unit in Zinacantan; this union of adult male and female is the single efficacious unit, socially and ritually. All other groups are fragile aggregates of nuclear family households, with only an ephemeral capacity to unite in common interest. Thus, the power of men in local politics in Zinacantan is heavily curtailed, on the one hand, by the strength of the non-indigenous forces which lie outside the community and, on the other, by the socio-economic strength of the household within the community. Men, however much they argue and plot in the plaza, have an exceedingly limited ability to shape the parameters of the life of the community, and they also have much less autonomy than it would appear in representing interests in those political battles in which the local political organisation can take effective action. This autonomy is limited by the actual power and the authority of women within the household, power which women hold by virtue of their crucial part in the division of labour. Women can and routinely do withhold labour in order to influence their husbands' action in the public realm. Men are agents for their households in politics, marketing, and formal social life, but they are accountable to women in ways which makes their agency more representational than autonomous.

Nonetheless, it is important not to mistake accountability for identity of interests and agency. Rogers is right in pointing to the emptiness of authority when power lies elsewhere, as in the state of France or Mexico, and she is also right in reminding us that in a community of households, women have the likelihood of substantial power to influence the men who are their agents, as well as the authority which flows from their frequent leadership in the domestic realm.

But influence, however valuable, is never the same as outright agency. In so far as men are consistently agents for women in Zinacantan they enjoy regular advantages over them in defining, articulating and pursuing their own interests. Male and female interests are not, per se, different in Zinacantan, but any one person's interest is construed as opposed by all other interests in the native understanding of the social universe. Given the rigorous difference which people maintain in the doings of men and the doings of women, that a woman's interest as she conceives it is only poorly represented or articulated by a man is not surprising but inevitable.

Marriage: interest, access and agency in conflict

Perhaps the best way to clarify this connection of access and agency is to consider the complexities of marriage arrangements in Zinacantan. Here we can perceive the ideology of gender in this community in its most clearly stated form.

Marriage is effected in Zinacantan by a lengthy courtship, by brief brideservice, and by the gradual payment of bridewealth, which is specifically regarded as purchasing the consent of the bride's father to a period of cohabitation by the groom with his daughter. To meet this payment, socially and financially, a young man must have the active aid and consent of his own parents, and any other relatives, male and female, lineal and collateral, that he can manage. Young women, by contrast, properly await the advances of a suitor, advances which have the feel and appearance of an assault, as he and all his spokesmen surround her house and harangue her parents for as much of the night as is required to erode their will to the point of consent. The consent of the girl in question, however, is considered only insofar as her parents, and specifically her father, choose to entertain it.

Following this visit of request are two years, during which a proper bridegroom pays visits of respect, bearing gifts to his prospective parents-in-law at every significant point on the church calendar. What is at issue in these visits is the accustoming of the parents of the girl to his person, and the impressing on them of his upright, hardworking intentions. At the end of approximately two years the young man wins the right of 'house entering' in which he begins his short period of brideservice in the home of his parents-in-law, and also cohabitation with his wife-to-be. After this period, the wedding, including church nuptials, is properly arranged, and the bride moves formally to the home of her new husband to reside there until they set up their own independent household some years hence.

Nowadays, and I strongly suspect formerly, all this can be quite effectively short-circuited if the pair (ideally virtually unknown to one another, but frequently actually first or second cousins on a current, if secret, speaking basis when unobserved) arranges either to elope outright, or to be observed speaking to one another without chaperones. Such behaviour precipitates a courthouse confrontation between the two parental households and a hasty wedding, with great irritation on the part of the senior generation, often not unmixed with relief at the reduced expenses, in spite of the loss of social face involved in having wilful and disobedient children.

This is a move made in direct affront to the interests, and rights, of the parental generation in the social disposal of their offspring. These interests include controlling their children's labour and its produce, and continuing to use children as agents of the parents' own social and political alliances. Such an affront is possible only by virtue of the capacity of young men to find wage labour without the aid of their senior relatives, a situation quite distinct from the former ideal in which the trading expertise of parents was necessary to acquire the prestige goods for the proper prestations. The self-willed actions of young women are possible to the degree to which their position in the parental home of their new husband is not prejudiced by their unorthodox arrival; this is, in turn, a function of the equanimity of the woman's family itself. They are her only allies in future disputes, and she can toy with their interests only so far as she is willing to sacrifice their goodwill. Both sons and daughters are regularly cut off in Zinacantan without further speech or inheritance by angry parents, something young lovers are often unprepared to predict.

It is apparent that in the proposition of marriage, which is the only avenue to adulthood for either sex, young men exert considerably more agency than do young women. They have the capacity to choose the moment and the object of their intentions, while girls await being chosen. Nonetheless, the senior generations are essential to the successful bid to adulthood by any young man, and could be said actively to deny agency to youth and to monopolise it for themselves. Indeed, the purported complementarity of the social division of labour by sex is transformed into inequality by the effect of the age hierarchy. Zinacantecos have an ethos of egalitarianism and achieved rank; adults, ideally, are equal to one another, except for deference to age. For all Zinacantecos know their relative ages with respect to one another, and all social activity acknowledges age with formal deference behaviour. Sibling terms are marked for older and younger relationships, and almost all ritual positions are paired in senior/junior (literally, older and younger brother) couples. There is a preoccupation with gate-keeping at the entrance to adult status. Both men and women are obliged to marry to gain adult status, and the terms are controlled by those already adult, specifically their parents.

Men must acquire adult consent to succeed in their bid for adult status. Women, by contrast, cannot attempt, let alone achieve adult status by their own volition. Further, they have only passive resistance at their command to effect their fate; it is the parents of the girl who accept the arrangement, accepting the gifts, visits, labour and money, not she. Girls thus are at a disadvantage, relative to boys, in acquiring the ability to pursue their lives as independent adults.

Brideservice, rendered by the boy for a period of weeks, places him ultimately on equal terms with his father-in-law. Once married, he assumes a status of adulthood undifferentiated except by continued deference to the individual calculus of relative age. Bridewealth, whether in cash or in traditional goods and sociality, is the means whereby the senior generation relinquishes its formal claim on the labour of the junior female generation and transfers this claim to the parents of the husband. Egalitarian politics motivates continued social control of juniors by seniors; after marriage, the bride owes her labour to her parents-in-law, and a degree of personal service to her husband, to whom, ideally and usually, she rarely speaks except in whispers in the dark of night. The husband owes social loyalty both to his new parents-in-law as well as to his own parents, and he continues to work as a member of his parents' household. He can claim private property of any significance only after the birth of his children, whose patrimony his labour becomes.

Parents use the resources which will eventually be inherited to control their adult children through delayed bequests. When a daughter marries, her parents will settle on her a part of her share of their property. A married son receives part of his inheritance at the time he and his wife establish their own household separate from his parents. The remainder of the parental property remains the stakes for which adult children compete until the death of the senior generation. Competition is carried on through loyalty to the parents' political aims, gift giving, reciprocal ritual aid, obedience, and both formal and informal sociality. Married sons and daughters compete for the parental inheritance, but daughters have fewer economic resources of their own to bring into play. Sons-in-law can become essential in this competitive drama, therefore, although they may well have interests of their own at stake.

A woman who does not marry remains a junior in her father's house, with only a potential claim to inherit: the success of this claim rests on her parents' goodwill, and on her good relations with her brothers. A widow, on the other hand, who does not remarry, can claim her childrens' patrimony in trust from her husband's land, and can set up independent life, at a minimal level, subject to the depradations of the powerful. The divorcee who takes the option to return to her parents' home returns to her junior status, and suffers the fate of having dragged into the house the additional mouths of her children. If, however, she finds the resources from her parents to set up her own home, she must eke out what subsistence she can through traditional female labour exchange, which is paid at approximately one third the rate of unskilled male agricultural wage labour.

As single divorcees or widows, women can and do refuse to remarry, usually by appropriating the labour of a son, or by paying men, whose farming efforts are already squarely in the market economy, to raise their corn and beans for them. Married women with children always need to purchase additional labour at certain times in their lives, because the domestic labour of women is so time consuming that a mother of three cannot accomplish it all on her own. Women in need of income take on weaving, spinning, and food preparation for pay, and have done for generations. But this labour is still conceptually linked to marriage, and is sexualised in such a way that propriety dictates that these exchanges must be made between women.

A man, conversely, cannot live without the daily services of a woman. Only very old men with daughters remain unmarried; all other men must take wives. A man must have his food cooked and his water drawn, his fire lit and his clothes woven, and while these labours can be paid for, or borrowed from kinswomen, this is not regarded by Zinacantecos as a stable situation. For instance, a man can really only receive clothing from the hand of his mother or his wife. If a woman is paid to weave his clothing, his mother or wife must arrange this service; for the man to do so is a sexual slur both on himself and on the weaver. Thus women's domestic labour is subject to restricted circulation, and while it is paid, it is not in the same labour market as men's farming labour or corn production, which circulates freely according to market price mechanisms.

The interaction of the division of labour with the strictures of gender-based access to the resources of the Zinacanteco world and their monopoly by the senior generation render the possibilities of life quite different for men and for women, different in ways not hard to characterise as unequal. In this relatively homogeneous society, with its ethos of egalitarianism, subsistence, let alone achievement and rank, is not equally available to men and women. The ideology of complementarity – which avoids putting differentiated value on the highly differentiated labours of men and women – hides the extent to which the complementarity is asymmetrical. It in fact accords to men much more autonomy and flexibility in meeting the changing requisites of the world than it does to women. Nonetheless, this inequality springs from what it is that women and men do, and how that intersects with the structures of the Zinacanteco and the non-Zinacanteco social worlds. The ideology of complementarity, while lying, as do all ideologies, about the nature of reality as actors encounter it in the social universe, does not itself encode the hierarchies which produce inequality. But it does encode differences which are used in strategies of both Zinacantecos and non-Zinacantecos to accumulate power and economic status, which in turn create for men and women in Zinacantan social outcomes of great inequality.

Notes

1. This system is extensively discussed by Cancian 1965, Vogt 1969 and J. Haviland 1977, among others.
2. Not unlike the beliefs analysed by Taussig 1980, as deriving from inexplicable external sources of wealth in capitalised, Colonial conditions.
3. See Collier 1973 for the negotiated forms of courtcase settlements.
4. Very recently some Zinacantecos have discovered and begun to use legal and financial mechanisms made available by government Indianist agencies, but the use of these mechanisms is by virtue of their ethnic membership, by the ideology and policy of the agencies themselves.

5. To appreciate the complexity of continuity and historical changes in the region see Wasserstrom 1983.
6. A discussion of some of these and a detailed description of this ritual spectacle and others is given by Bricker 1973.
7. This appears to have been a customary and necessary exchange for at least the past four generations. Indeed, based on the remembrances of women married before 1920 I would contend that young women must always have taken in the excess work of mothers, whether for pay, as they do today, or for reciprocity within kin networks.
8. For example, they have to pay or cajole other women into bundling flowers for market or baking the crispbread which they carry for themselves and their workers to eat at their lowland cornfields.

CHAPTER 4

The politics of separation[1]

DIANE BELL

At a Law Reform Commission meeting in Alice Springs in 1982, Aboriginal women from various town camps and Aboriginal organisations addressed the problem of law and order in their communities.[2] To kerb access to alcohol, their most immediate and pressing problem, they suggested restricted outlets and trading times. To alleviate the high level of interpersonal violence, they suggested the establishment of separate women's camps. If we could withdraw, as women, they argued, we would not be the subjects of violence and there would be no recriminations, no need for intervention from police and we would be safe with other sober women. The concept of women having the right to live in an area which is under their control and which is taboo to men is not new, but the reasons for and the value placed on the separation are. It is within the context of the 'politics of separation' that I wish to locate my discussion of changing gender and spatial relations in Central Australian Aboriginal society and to draw certain parallels with feminist analyses of separatism.

In understanding the dilemma facing women in an urbanising context in the 1980s, it is necessary to have some knowledge of traditional local and social organisation and some understanding of the nature of the changes wrought in the lives of desert people through a century of colonisation of their lands. Here I offer the briefest overview both of the traditional situation and social change. Although attempts at reconstruction are fraught with difficulties, I sketch the pre-contact situation of desert people in Central Australia and describe the contexts within which these people have come into contact with non-Aboriginal Australians. From there I shall move to a discussion of two very different urbanising situations wherein Aboriginal women seek to exercise their right to retreat: the one in Alice Springs and the other in Alicurang (Warrabri).[3]

Several factors influenced my choice of situations. Firstly while the

Eastern Aranda of Alice Springs and the Alyawarra and Kaytej of Alicurang are both of the Aranda cultural bloc, and thus share similar systems of land tenure, ceremonial practice, kinship and marriage, their contact histories are very different. Here we have a good basis for comparing the nature and direction of change. Secondly, as I have field experience in the area which spans some ten years, I feel more in touch with the aspirations, interpretations and opinions of the women in these communities than in others further north where my field experience is more limited.

Brief history

In the 1870s, with the building of the north/south telegraph line and the establishment of telegraph stations in Central Australia at places such as Alice Springs, Barrow Creek and Tennant Creek, Aborigines came into contact with non-Aboriginal settlers. Previous contacts with explorers, although traumatic, were fleeting and provided few insights into White society (see Bell 1983:60-2). It was the telegraph station which provided a focus for continuous and sustained Aboriginal interactions with Whites. The Aboriginal ambush of the Barrow Creek station in 1874 changed the character of the interaction. Two Whites were killed and punitive parties scoured the country on a hundred kilometre radius, killing as they went (see Gillen 1968:107-9).

The late 1870s and early 1880s saw increasing pastoral activity in Central Australia, the establishment of ration depots at telegraph stations and the growth of semi-permanent Aboriginal populations focusing on the infant towns and cattle stations. Other groups were attracted to missions such as that established at Hermannsburg in 1877. In response to pastoralists' requests for protection from 'the Blacks' who were not prepared to relinquish their access to water in favour of cattle, police were stationed near trouble spots. Thus began the era of pacification. Willshire, the leader of a pacification party of the 1880s, provides an insight into white perceptions of Aboriginal society. He wrote of Aboriginal men as lazy, treacherous and dirty. Of the women he wrote:

[White men] would not remain so many years in a country like this if there were no women [i.e. dark women] and perhaps the Almighty meant them for that use as He placed them wherever pioneers go. (Quoted in Strehlow 1971:587)

There were many Aboriginal attacks on white encampments – the ones at Frew River station in the 1890s are given as reasons for the abandonment of the station in 1896 (see Bell 1983:65). For the Aborigines, the toll of their attacks and the counter attacks by Whites was great. One report of

1898 states that there were '45 bucks and 460 gins' in the Frew River area (see Hartwig 1965:411). We have no statistics with which to compare this for a decade earlier but the implications of the sex imbalance, even if over-stated, and especially when read in conjunction with the Willshire sentiment, are horrendous.

From this so-called period of pacification, we enter the era of protection. During the first quarter of the twentieth century, Aborigines were forcefully removed from their country in order to offer nominal protection from the expanding pastoral industry of Central Australia and mining endeavours at places such as Wauchope and Tennant Creek. Regulations forbad Aborigines from engaging in work in mining centres and living in towns. However, if the reports of men such as Beckett, Chief Protector of Aborigines Darwin (Northern Territory), are any indication, these rules were not strictly followed. In 1914-15 he recorded a growing part-Aboriginal population and their engagement in (unpaid) work at the mine (Beckett 1915:26-8).

Thus the Aborigines of Central Australia came into sustained contact with Whites within very different contexts. For the Aranda of Alice Springs it was mission, mining and telegraph lines; for the Kaytej and Alyawarra of Alicurang it was pastoralism and only marginally the telegraph stations and mining. The one common thread in all these situations was that the communities were predominantly male, and there was little opportunity to observe the family life of Whites. On cattle stations a common pattern was that the run would be established by a man whose wife would not arrive for several years. During that initial period, Aboriginal men and women recall that they worked in very similar jobs. Aboriginal women were engaged in fencing, horse-breaking and branding, as were their menfolk. It was the arrival of the 'White missus' which created the category of domestic labourer and brought women into contact with the hearth and home of settler families.

In the 1940s, under the assimilation policy, large government settlements were established where Aborigines were to be taught the values of White society (see Rowley 1970:383-403). Alicurang was such a site. The population of these settlements has run as high as 1200 and the organisation of such situations tells us something of the way in which Aborigines accommodate such intensive settlement. The sedentary life style of Aborigines in the towns, on missions, cattle stations and large government settlements severely undermined the hunter-gatherer mode of subsistence. No longer were Aborigines in control of the goods which were distributed in their communities. Constraints on behaviour lay outside their mode of subsistence production, outside their control.

What then has been the impact on gender relations? I have argued that popular characterisations of Aboriginal women as second-class citizens, as pawns in the games of the male gerontocracy, can only be understood in an historical framework. The nature of sexual politics on the colonial frontier, I suggested, had been fundamentally transformed by the impact of the changes wrought by a century of intrusion of non-Aboriginal persons into desert lands. What had once been negotiable had become fixed. In place of the complementarity and interdependence which once underwrote the relation between the sexes, there was now sexual asymmetry (see Bell 1983:94-106).

For the women the changes were manifest in a loss of autonomy and independence. In the shift from the hunter-gatherer mode of subsistence to a sedentary lifestyle, Aboriginal women had lost much of their independence. No longer were they critical to group survival. Their role as contributor of 80 per cent of the subsistence diet had been usurped by rations and welfare payments which defined household units as male-headed and located women as dependants within such structures. The implication for men was that a marriage no longer meant economic wellbeing, but rather liability. Wives, once assets, became dependants. If we are to give any credence to the reported sex imbalance of the 1890s, men would have been able to activate claims to more wives than had been possible several decades earlier. In pre-contact times, with a more even sex ratio, men could not expect to enjoy the benefits of plural marriage until in their forties. The change in the productive relations within marriage would have added further stress. Indeed on the colonial frontier of Northern Australia, the wide ranging skills of women were deemed inappropriate and through a consistent denial of access to domains within which they could have learnt new skills and adapted old ones, they were further removed from productive activities. By missionaries and administrators alike they were defined as wives and mothers, not as owners of land. Their role in decision-making was deemed non-existent and, on the predominantly male frontier, Aboriginal men were groomed as spokespersons while Aboriginal women were relegated to a domestic domain.

A clear distinction between what is men's work and what is women's work persists. It is the value placed on these activities which has shifted. The result is a skewing of gender values, a shift from complementarity to hierarchy, which is masked by continuity in the maintenance of separate men's and women's domains of action. This analysis is as appropriate to activities in the economic domain as it is to those in the politico-religious. Where once women had been engaged in ceremonial activity which complemented and paralleled that of men, they now find that limited access to resources such as vehicles means they cannot participate in ceremonies held away from their home community. While men extend their political networks through ceremonial involvement, women are constrained. Few women own cars and even fewer hold licences. They have limited access to funding for travel. It would be both inappropriate and dangerous for women to attempt to share the same transport as men on occasions of ceremonial visits. It is telling that the very recent phenomenon of a women's 'cultural tour' is one of which women have quickly taken advantage in order to extend their networks. Past promotions of 'Aboriginal culture', as song, dance and art by various entrepreneurs (both Black and White but nearly always male) provided men with opportunities of religious and political import which until recently were not available to Aboriginal women.

Instead of a woman's separate domain of action providing a power base and ensuring her a place at the negotiating table, the separation has provided the means for her exclusion from decision-making arenas. I have explored this erosion of women's power base and the differential impact on gender relations for different groups in Central Australia elsewhere (Bell 1983, Bell and Ditton 1984). The issue to focus on here is spatial relations.

Spatial relations: settlement

Understanding the nature of relations to land is critical to an appreciation of group structure, residential choice, decision-making and gender relations. Central Australian Aborigines trace descent-based rights to land through two major lines: that of the father's father and the mother's father. They also trace an important relationship through the mother's mother. In all these 'countries' people enjoy rights, albeit qualitatively different rights, and indeed may wish to live in any one of these 'countries'. There are also ties to land established in more individualistic ways. Where one's grandparents are buried, the place where one was born, the place where one lived as a young married woman – all are important. Too often we emphasise the descent-based aspects of relations to land and forget the sentimental ties. Without this dimension, group composition is difficult to understand.

People lived in small family-based groups, the size and composition of which fluctuated, but the core was probably a husband, wife or wives (often sisters), the wife's mother, the wife's father's sister, unmarried children and married sons and daughters (until the birth of the first or second child). (See also Peterson 1970:9-16.) This core group could amalgamate with another core group from a larger constellation linked through either husband or wife. It would not be uncommon for the husbands to be brothers or the wives to be sisters. In the case where a man is married to sisters, the bond between these women both pre- and post-dates the marriage. With the death of an elderly husband, sisters/co-wives may still be in their middle age. The underlying kinship bond of these co-wives or co-widows, and the common interests which they share in land, are themselves a cause for solidarity rather than for conflict (see Bell 1980:239-69).

Because within any one group there would be diverse and multiple relations to different tracts of land or 'countries', the group could move across a vast area of land. Choice of camping site would be constrained by the availability of food, family obligations, ceremonial responsibilities and relationship to land. The pattern which emerges is one in which no one individual has an obligation to stay in one place with any particular group. It is possible to survive in a number of situations in a number of different 'countries'.

This has important ramifications not only for the exploitation of resources and residential patterns but also for the resolution of conflict. In the past one common strategy was to withdraw. If conflict within the group became too stressful there was the possibility of fission. If an individual's membership of a group became too vexsome, then that individual could join another group. However, whichever group one chose to join, one could be assured that there would be close kin and country relations which would provide a secure base and map out the nature of the obligations, rights and responsibilities for and between group members. Banishment from one's country was another matter. If someone had seriously transgressed the Law, that person could be sent to a community where there were no kin or country ties. Such a person would be, in a sense, outside society. At the level of interpersonal disputes, an individual may appear to sulk in a solitary fashion, while others ignore his or her existence. When good humour returns and he or she rejoins the group, there are no charges to answer because no harsh words have been spoken.

Within such small family groups there was a strict sexual division of labour. Women spent most of their day in the company of other women and men in the company of men. Much hunting and gathering and even sociable activity was done in such single sex groups. It is in the evening that husband and wife come together as a unit, the time when experiences of the day are shared. That women are absent from a family camp for much of the day is not, as men sometimes provocatively suggest, an indication that they are engaged in extra marital affairs. They are always in the company of other women who can bear witness to their activities. Of course there can be conspiracies between women, but most hunting parties would include women with the right to sanction such behaviour in others. For most of the year people lived in these small fluid groups. It was not possible to maintain a higher density of population in one place, save at times of abundance. It was at such times that people were able to gather for ceremonies. However, even at such large gatherings where upwards of 300 people may be camped in any one area, there was still a clear separation of camps based on kin and country relations. While much interaction at such times was clearly structured according to well-known rules, there was no overarching political structure (Meggitt 1964a).

It is on large government and mission reserves and in the towns, that we may observe the contemporary strategies for overcoming the tensions generated by a population-intensive sedentary lifestyle. *Daughters of the Dreaming*, describes how the camps at Alicurang were organised in terms of an east–west division which encoded information concerning traditional affiliations to land of the Aboriginal population. People with ties to the land to the west oriented their camps in that direction, while those with ties to the east, the Kaytej and Alyawarra, oriented their camps to the east (see Bell 1983:73-89). The other major division within the community was that between the Aborigines and non-Aborigines. Those engaged in servicing the community (teachers, nurses, police and administrators) lived in a core area around which the Aboriginal camps were located. Each institution within this core area was classified as a male or female domain and thus embarrassing encounters were minimised. For example the hospital was a female domain whereas the office was a male domain.

Located within the broader division of east and west side were several large family camps within which there were smaller units. The one on which to focus here is that known as the *jilimi* or single women's camp. In the past, in small family camps, there would have been maybe two or three women to form a *jilimi*, but on settlements the residents of the *jilimi* may number upwards of 20. Thus the possibility of women forming larger and potentially more powerful *jilimi* has increased. That women have chosen and, in ever increasing numbers, are choosing to live in the *jilimi*, instead of entering into second or third choice marriages, is I think indicative of women's perception of and responses to the changed life in the 1970s (Bell 1983:259-62).

Forming the permanent core of the *jilimi* are those widows who have chosen not to remarry and other women who, although married, are not domiciled with their husbands. These women are today the active ritual leaders and repositories of religious knowledge. They are old enough to have reared children to adulthood and to have acquired the necessary knowledge befitting the status of ritual leaders. Joining them in the *jilimi* are single girls who are reluctant or too young to go to their promised husbands; women who are seeking a safe environment while visiting the community without their spouses or who, following a dispute, have temporarily vacated the swag of their spouse; women who are ill or in need of emotional support, and those not yet through their final stages of mourning. Accompanying all these women are their dependent children and charges. During the day the married women from nearby camps come to the *jilimi* to socialise but at night they return to their husbands' camps. The atmosphere within the *jilimi* is usually pleasant and supportive; conversations centre on family, recent hunting expeditions, local scandal, ritual business and health.

The *jilimi* are proof of women's separateness and independence. It is from the *jilimi* that women's ritual activity is initiated and controlled, and it is in the *jilimi* that women achieve a separation from men in their daily activities. A refuge, a focus of women's daily activities, an area taboo to men, a power base, an expression of women's solidarity, the home of ritually important and respected women, the *jilimi* is all this. Women have clung tenaciously to certain key values and institutions and in so doing have found continued meaning for their self image as independent and autonomous members of their society in a crumbling world.

The physical separation of the sexes which the *jilimi* represents is a mode of expressing the continuity of a key facet of relations between the sexes. The *jilimi*, like the east–west division of the Alicurang population, elaborates a traditional form. In the past, separation allowed each to demonstrate independence without compromising the essentially complementary nature of male and female activities in the maintenance of their society. Today, the separation of the sexes and women's independence no longer refer to mutually reinforcing values. As I have suggested, the persistence of separate domains of action effectively denies women participation in the emerging political and economic spheres within which power and authority have come to reside.

Any assessment of Aboriginal male–female relations must be located within the context of the wider society. We can see that women's rights to impose certain sanctions have been severely undermined by settlement life. In the past women could live close to sites from which they derived power. Today, because of their limited access to vehicles and residence on settlements many miles from their special places, they no longer enjoy easy access to sites from which they derive power. Aboriginal men are relieved in a sense that women no longer have some of these powers and attempt to brush aside and joke about those which women have retained.

On settlements men have further opportunities to gang up on women, not a possibility when family groups were smaller. I believe we can see the women's response to enhanced male solidarity in their increasingly living in the *jilimi* which provides a focus for female support and solidarity. *Jilimi* life thus constitutes a complex interplay between women's needs for a refuge in a strife-torn community such as Alicurang and a woman's proud assertion that she is an independent member of her society.

We are faced with something of an enigma. On a settlement as large as Alicurang, the women have been able to retreat to the company of other women. Indeed the women of the *jilimi* are relatively independent in terms of income, for it is here that older women who are in receipt of old age pensions camp. Thus, while the basis of independence has changed, women may still remain substantially independent in economic terms. They do not, however, exercise the same degree of control over their produce as was possible in the past. The goanna they once caught and the seed cakes they once prepared have been replaced with food bought in a store with money from Social Security cheques. The independence of the women of the *jilimi* is illusory in another sense: it keeps them out of the arena in which decisions are made. They may still exercise informal power through kinship networks, but they are not members of the newly formed village councils and thus are outside important formation networks.

Spatial relations: other communities

What of the politics of separation in other Centralian contexts? There is a general tendency for people to attempt to form residential units which are consonant with the small family groups of pre-contact days. Within the towns this tendency is marked strongly in the pattern of special purpose leaseholding. In the Alice Springs town camps, groups with common affiliations form themselves into communities. Interpersonal disputes may be settled and day-to-day life organised within a well-known system of rights and obligation to kin and country. This system is of course under threat and changes have occurred: the fixity of camps and proximity to the town itself are considerable constraints. Yet the tendency for people in the town camps to coalesce into small groups within which law and order may be maintained has much in common with the homeland (sometimes called outstation) movement.[4]

One striking characteristic of this movement is that women do not feel that they are left out of the consultative process. On homeland centres they are present when decisions are made. Often they are camped on their own land; they are once again providing staples in the diet; the ritual statements concerning their role as nurturers of people and land are vindicated, in short they have a power base and their authority is respected. There is no need to create 'representative structures' such as village councils to make decisions and there are no excuses for men to forget to consult with their womenfolk. But for several reasons the position of women in the town camps is less secure.

An organisation called Tangentyere represents the interests of the town campers. It was through this organisation that special purposes leases were negotiated after the needs basis claims were removed from the Whitlam Land Rights Bill as it became the Aboriginal Land Rights Act under the Fraser regime (Heppell and Wigley 1981:172-95). Thus Tangentyere shouldered the burden after the Aboriginal and Torres Strait Islander Housing Panel folded in 1978. A fascinating initiative of the Whitlam administration and under Fraser a clear thorn in the side, this Panel was responsible for the design and monitoring of housing programmes. The architects employed by the Panel saw their task to be a social one, and the establishment of priorities, as in the town camps of Alice Springs, bore them out. Area lighting and fencing – so that people could control their own boundaries – were given as the first shelter needs of the first group to obtain assistance. Obviously spatial relations to other communities and within the camp were seen as linked to issues of law and order (1981:128-51).

But the consultation was male oriented. Thornton, the sole Aboriginal woman working as community adviser to the Department of Aboriginal Affairs, regarded the situation of women in the Aboriginal communities of Alice Springs as one of 'the most overlooked areas' in Aboriginal affairs (Thornton 1979:1). She saw the payment of benefits to men as at odds with the traditional role of women caring for their own children and those in need of care following, for example, the death of a parent. Women in towns were burdened with an ever-increasing responsibility to care for children but had little support. She urged the special appointment of a woman as Area Officer to coordinate programmes in different areas where women community advisers would be located. Appeals to staff ceilings were initially used to put down this heresy, and when that failed White feminists were blamed for creating unrest and imposing a foreign ideology. The fate of the Women's Centre in Alice Springs was one of the casualties of this debate.

In 1977 several White women, concerned with the lack of access to abortion in the Northern Territory, formed a health group. A local refuge was suggested as a suitable venue. Women from the health group assumed control of the refuge, and in 1978 it became the Alice Springs

Women's Centre. Its reputation had been as a racist institution – Black women were not admitted, but then neither were many White women. Those few middle-class women who did use the refuge argued that they could not admit Black women because they did not understand them. Under the health group, the refuge was run as a collective and several Aboriginal women who worked in the Aboriginal organisations of Alice Springs and who came into contact with these White women began to take an interest. Indeed, in its second year of operation the dominant group became the urban Aboriginal women who formed an *ad hoc* advisory group. There was much discussion concerning the needs and aspirations of the Aboriginal women. In its third year of operation the dominant group became the women of the town camps and bush communities – women stranded when they were in town, ill, discharged from hospital with no way to get home. These women co-existed with the urban women who at no stage moved out. There were cross currents and heated discussions between these groups of women with very different needs and backgrounds, but seeking very similar solutions. They all needed a place which was set apart. They all needed a safe place to which they could retreat in time of stress. A *de facto* parallel structure began to develop within the centre, but the potential for this arrangement was not realised because the refuge folded after a further six months.[5] The refuge had come under increasing criticism; White women accused Black women of misusing government resources by dominating the refuge. The reverse had never been an issue. To certain bureaucrats and administrators the refuge was politically dangerous for it provided a basis from which Aboriginal women, already discontent with their lot, could engage in wider political protest. Criticism of the American installation at Pine Gap was one clear example.[6]

It is interesting to speculate what would have happened had the latent parallel structure been able to develop. The refuge could have become two self-sustaining structures located within outside supporting structures. This would have entailed developing a system of transport to bring women to the refuge and to return them to their bush communities. It also would have allowed the burgeoning argument for the setting aside of land for single women's camps within the town communities to have been pursued more rigorously. Instead through Community Development Schemes the women were given assistance to become good homemakers. One of the facets of the homemaker service in the camps was to set up a system of bulk buying on pension days to assist in budgeting. After several months the system broke down. Drunks (mostly men, but sometimes women) would demand food; food was stolen; the budgeting did not help the families of the women to survive until next pay day. The alternative for these women was to buy food daily, involving investment in transport and time. There were no buses servicing the town camps and taxis were expensive. There have been more recent attempts to set up women's councils with the same general representative basis as Tangentyere, but as soon as the women become a force in Alice Springs politics, the organisation becomes the brunt of jealous fights or a straight out political 'White ban'. The current attempts to establish more specialised bodies within the land councils have also experienced a checkered history. The women's council of the Pitjantjatjara Council has its own adviser/anthropologist and representation on the decision-making body but access to resources always remains an issue; women are included as an afterthought. They do not have any outright claim on the resources of the organisation (Bell and Ditton 1984, esp. appendices 4 and 5).

In summary, attempts to find a way of participating in decision-making arenas, of ensuring the political representation of women, have varied. Alice Springs women have tried to form organisations, albeit with differing rationales, to represent women as a group and to provide a place where women may be separate. All thus far have failed but the experience gained is evident in the way in which women's meetings are now conducted. At a women's meeting in Alice Springs (in May 1984), the delegates passed several motions which outlined the structural changes necessary in the Land Council. They were no longer content with an informal role.[7]

Aboriginal women and feminist politics

Through their participation in the Pine Gap protest and more recently at the Women and Labour Conference in Brisbane, Centralian Aboriginal women have begun to clarify and explore not only the basis of their right to be separate but also their relationship to feminist politics. At the Brisbane conference some Aboriginal women expressed the view that it was inappropriate for White women to undertake research in Aboriginal society. They contended they had been over researched, and under consulted, and demanded that a conference paper which traversed published material they considered non-public should be withdrawn. Not all demand such drastic measures. There are points of contact with feminists which range from those personal and work relationships established in the field to more diffuse relationships through federal organisations.

The Aboriginal Women's Task Force, an initiative of the federal government, established within the Office of the Status of Women in late 1982, provided links to femocrats. But the Task Force suffered the same lack of funding that has stifled other women's projects. Two Aboriginal women set out to consult throughout Australia and report in 12 months on an impossibly wide range of issues. Under the Hawke government the Task Force was restructured: it became a body with a national representation. But, as women both Aboriginal and White have pointed out, it is government funded and government controlled. It answers questions which perplex governments. The terms of reference preclude a full explanation of issues within a self determination context.[8] About the same time another organisation emerged – the Federation of Aboriginal Women – whose tactics have been quite different. If the women want action, they go directly to the organisation involved: the need they argue is obvious – they do not need an enquiry to tell them. Further they address a wide range of issues felt by some bureaucrats to be adequately covered by other organisations. But, they reply, the organisations are male dominated. Their role is to bring women's opinions forward. Under the current administration, the Department of Aboriginal Affairs has not been prepared to recognise the need for such an organisation.[9]

One way to explore the relationship between Aboriginal women's strategies and those of White feminists is in terms of a clash of modes of decision making. In White society a common strategy has been to seek incorporation within the dominant power structures in order to work towards an equality of action. In Aboriginal society we have a model of decision making based on negotiated agreements underwritten by differentiation of the sexes. In the process of clarifying issues and emphases, the separation of women and men is important. In achieving consensus, complementarity between the sexes is critical.[10] But we cannot leave it there for such interaction now occurs at the interface of Aboriginal and White society. As yet no strategy which ensures that Aboriginal women will be both informed and heeded as well as safe has emerged. In the past the right to retreat did not need to be asserted; by retreating women were not living a less meaningful or impoverished life. The retreat afforded them space. Today it locks them out of arenas in which decisions affecting their lives are made.

Yet Aboriginal women have not been prepared to endorse the ideology of those White feminists who seek equality of action in male dominated areas. They have given different reasons for their reticence. In Central Australia, Aboriginal women have sought to have their distinctively female contribution to their society recognised and that entails a role in decision making. Superficially we appear to have a variation on the 'different but equal' theme. This has proved a dangerous platform for White feminists, and given that the constraints on Aboriginal woman's participation in decision making derive from the nature of gender relations in the wider society, it is a dangerous position for her also (Hartmann 1981:29).

Black activist Roberta (Bobbi) Sykes (1975:313-21) writing in the early 1970s, stated that Black women would not join White women's groups because there was no shared experience. For her the common ground was that all Black women had been raped, literally and metaphorically. The racism of White women was apparent in their inability to respond to or even address such facts. Rape was a taboo subject. Sykes' position was very much that of Black America and it is significant that she says 'Black' not 'Aboriginal'. In Sykes' view White women sought the right to say 'yes' to sexual advances without social condemnation, while Black women sought the right to say 'no'. This is a generalisation which most radical feminists would reject: they too sought the right to say 'no'. The focus on sexuality is, in a sense, reactive. It was an issue with which White feminists struggled in the 1970s but in my experience of Central Australia, the key issue was decision making and political representation, not sexuality.

A theme not fully developed in Sykes but given full weight by barrister Pat O'Shane (1976:31-4) is that of the special relationship of Black women to Black men in their joint struggle against racism. The argument runs that for Aboriginal women to seek liberation in terms of the feminist platform is divisive, a further cause for injury of their menfolk. The major fight O'Shane concludes is against racism, not sexism. 'We don't want to put men down, they have suffered enough.' She does however see a situation in which all women may work together.

When the white women's movement takes head-on the struggle against racism, which is the greater barrier to our progress, then we've got a chance of achieving sisterhood and, through our combined struggles, liberation of all humankind. (1976:34)

Marcia Langton (1982, 1983:11-16) in her enunciation of the dynamics of what she calls 'the Black gin syndrome' provides a most devastating account yet of Aboriginal women's perceptions of White women. She argues Aboriginal women recognise the taboos of White women and violate them. They mock and satirise White women's response to men. But, as she rightly points out, their strategy is, in the end, incoherent. They are jailed for offensive behaviour (see New South Wales Anti-Discrimination Board 1982:31).

I think I have said enough to indicate that Aboriginal women respond to White feminists in a number of ways. After all Aboriginal women are in very different situations in different parts of Australia.[11] To this point I have spoken of feminist strategies as if they were endorsed by all White feminists. Of course this is not so. In conclusion let me briefly draw some comparisons with features of separatism in our society. Superficially, the radical separatists of the 1980s appear to be advocating a solution similar to that of Aboriginal women. They concentrate on the establishment of institutions which look remarkably like the *jilimi*. Encapsulated in their catchcry, 'women have no country', is the recognition that women need space which is theirs. Further they share the dilemma of Aboriginal women in that if they are separate, how will their voices be heard? No doubt some would respond that men have never listened so not much is lost. There is little point in attempting to convince the enemy of your right to equality of opportunity. Political lesbianism, by isolating the heterosexual couple as the basic unit of the political structure of male supremacy, and refusing to engage in heterosexual activity, seeks to undermine the power of man as a class (Leeds Revolutionary Feminist Group 1981:5-10).

There is, however, a significant difference in the politics of separation as pursued by the Aboriginal and White separatists. For Aboriginal women a retreat to the *jilimi* is not a retreat from heterosexual activity. Many women in the *jilimi* maintain relationships with men: some marital, some more casual. Celibacy is not a feature of *jilimi* life. For the Aboriginal women with whom I worked sexuality is not and never has been associated with the responsibility of the wife in marriage, nor was it tied to her economic wellbeing. A retreat to the *jilimi* does not threaten her economic wellbeing. A husband enjoys no automatic control over a wife's sexuality any more than he has the right to distribute her produce. Her sexuality is hers to bestow, and further, she has real choices. A young wife may withdraw to the company of other women or return to her family. She is not bereft of social and economic support. She can expect sympathy from both male and female kin. An older woman may leave a husband and her retreat could occasion both shame and fear in the man. Aboriginal women may move in and out of sexual relations with men without undermining their relationship to other women and without suffering economic deprivation. The emphasis on denial of sexual access to women's bodies is not a defining feature of Aboriginal women's separation, though it may motivate individual instances of retreat.

It is interesting to note that one of the arguments for closing the Women's Centre in Alice Springs was that it encouraged 'deviant' relationships: that men were not allowed access to their wives and that the family was not promoted as the basic structuring unit of society. Here the threat was not celibacy but lesbianism; it was not the withdrawal of women from heterosexual activity but the existence of an alternative which affronted the sensibilities of certain influential Women for Christ in Alice Springs. For White women generally the separation usually implies a negation of heterosexual activity, it is a retreat from what Cheryl Hannah has aptly termed 'the heterosexual battleline'.[12] Here we have the nub of the conflict of models. Historically any 'women only' groups must necessarily be deviant because to withdraw is to pose a threat to the right of men to define women in terms of sexual access. If the all-women's community also achieves a measure of economic independence, the threat is compounded. This becomes clear if we compare two accounts of closely related yet very different women's communities: a nunnery and the beguinage of Medieval France and Germany.

Of these two the threat posed by the nuns was considerably less than that of the politically and economically independent beguines. For many a nunnery may appear to constitute an artificial or 'unnatural' community (Williams 1975:105-25) but the women do not violate the principle that all women are either daughters or wives, that is, women under the control of a male. At the head of the Church is the 'father', the nuns themselves are 'the brides of Christ', chaste wives whose sexuality poses no threat. While particular orders may have exercised a degree of autonomy in the handling of their affairs, ultimately they were subject to the dictates of a religious code which categorically denied them the right to assume the position as head of the Church.

Unlike nuns, the beguines were not initially subject to direction from male clergy. Against the background of the religious revival of the twelfth century, certain women who wished to develop a lifestyle separate from men, to uphold Christian values, to pursue independent careers in the cities where women were in a majority, formed communities which provided a supportive and powerful alternative to family life or the life of a nun (see Clark 1975:72-80). The organisation of the beguinage had much in common with the *jilimi*. There was a core of women who were living without men but they were joined by others in need of a safe environment. Meetings were secret and the women discussed matters of intellectual and spiritual import in a way not possible for those women subject to male control. Families sent their daughters to the beguines to be educated in reading, religion and other matters before marriage (1975:78). However the strength and number of women choosing a life of chastity outside the church eventually proved too much for church authorities who succeeded in dispersing the women and absorbing the remaining groups within the church structure. The tactics and the reasons given were in essence very similar to those members of the Alice Springs Christian community who sought the dispersion and absorption of the Women's Centre in 1982.

The position to which the women of these separatist communities retreat and that from which they retreat are fundamentally different for White and Aboriginal women. Perhaps to use the word retreat pre-empts the issue. White women who withdraw permanently from the heterosexual battleline threaten not only men, but also many of those women who remain in heterosexual relationships. Those women who retreat occasionally tend to use the 'women's camps' of the separatists for brief respite. Not surprisingly the women who have chosen to live there permanently are skeptical of the visitors' motives: they see little point in returning. Further the occasional visitors in need of recharging the batteries before re-engaging in combat on the battleline, engender resentment (see Leeds Revolutionary Feminist Group 1981).

The battleline is an artefact of White society and it is one which Aboriginal women recognise and treat with a wry scorn. Those Aboriginal women who see some common ground in feminism and their own struggles direct their energies at attempts to create both a basis on which a dialogue between men and women may fruitfully occur and a context within which Aboriginal women may talk to White women. By focusing on the nature of the changing gender and spatial relations in two specific situations and comparing strategies of White and Aboriginal women, I have sought to provide the basis for a better understanding of the dynamics of the politics of separation in both societies.

Notes

1. Discussions with colleagues in the Research Group, of which I was a member in 1983, sharpened my awareness for the need to explore further the issue of spatial relations in Aboriginal society. A request from Sophie Watson in the Urban research Unit, at ANU prompted me to write a paper on the topic, but on that occasion I focused on the 'Right to Retreat' in two urban contexts. An invitation from the Australian Historical Association to present the keynote address in the Aboriginal History section of their biennial conference (Melbourne, 1984) provided an opportunity to extend and refine the paper. Discussions arising from these presentations have been extremely helpful and in particular I acknowledge the contributions made by Michaela Richards, Diana Gribble, Jill Matthews, Sophie Watson, Cheryl Hannah, Sue McGrath, Pam Ditton and Marcia Langton. I also acknowledge the permission of McPhee Gribble to draw upon material in *Daughters of the Dreaming* (Bell 1983).
2. See Australian Law Reform Commission 1982:29-30. The Australian Law Reform Commission reported on the customary law reference in late 1984. I have acted in the formal capacity of consultant to the Commission on this reference since 1982, and in an informal capacity since 1977 when the question of recognition of customary law was first referred to the Commission by the Attorney-General.
3. Alicurang is a rendering of the Kaytej name, Alekarenge, for the area formerly known as Warrabri.
4. Since the 1970s the movement away from populace intensive centres to country to which people have traditional affiliations has intensified. See Bell and Ditton (1984:55-62) for an account of women's perceptions of one homeland centre near Alicurang and Bell (1982) for a more general account.
5. The history of the closure may be traced through the pages of the *Centralian Advocate* (Alice Springs, Northern Territory) 7/2/80, 14/2/80, 21/2/80, 23/2/80, 6/3/80, 20/3/80,

27/3/80, 10/4/80, 17/4/80, 24/4/80, 1/5/80, 15/5/80. The engineering of the collapse of the refuge was one of the dirtiest pieces of Northern Territory sexual politics I can remember. At the time I was engaged in research on the role of Aboriginal women in the maintenance of customary legal systems (see Bell and Ditton 1984) and the power plays of those months were of great practical moment.

6. On 11 November 1983 a number of Aboriginal women joined White feminist groups in the 'Close the Gap' campaign which focused on the issues of land rights, peace and nuclear disarmament. Inspired by the Greenham Common peace camp, the women established a Peace Camp at Pine Gap, the USA communication base near Alice Springs. For discussion of the event see *Chain Reaction* (Melbourne), No. 34, 1983:26-9 and No. 36, 1984:12-17.

7. See Toohey 1984:49-50. In his review of the Aboriginal Land Rights Act, Mr Justice Toohey, the former Land Commissioner, concluded that it may be necessary to amend the legislation to give effect to the principles of greater representation for women on the Councils. However, he stressed it was for Aborigines themselves to decide. The women in the Central region have decided: they wish to be represented.

8. The Task Force is due to report in late 1986. Its handling of the terms of reference will then be clear.

9. The Minister, Mr Holding, in response to a question from a member of the Federation at the Aborigines and International Law Conference, Canberra, November 21-22, 1983, stated that organisations already existed through which women would make their opinions known on the matter of the proposed national land rights legislation.

10. See Australian Law Reform Commission 1982:47-8 for an example of such a negotiation.

11. Striking parallels are evident with the New Zealand experience. Dominy (1986) explores the cross cutting affiliations between Maori and Pakeha women, the alliances which are forged within contexts of social protest and the consequences for lesbian gender conceptions.

12. Coined by Cheryl Hannah in the discussion following the presentation of a work in progress paper in the Social Justice Project seminar series, Research School of Social Sciences, The Australian National University, June 1983 by Virginia Novarra, 'The Man Question: some reflections on female separatism'.

CHAPTER 5

'Women are our business':
women, exchange and prestige in Kove

ANN CHOWNING

When I first went to Kove in 1966,[1] it was the fourth Papua New Guinea society in which I had done fieldwork, but the first with a patrilineal descent system. Although the main reason for going there was a desire to understand the reasons for their reputed resistance to mission and government influences, I also intended to pursue an interest in social organisation, with particular attention to kinship and relations between the sexes. These had been the focus of my first fieldwork, among the matrilineal Lakalai a short distance to the east of the Kove. In Lakalai I had learned that there was no simple correlation between type of descent and the ways in which men regarded and treated women. When I was writing up the Lakalai material, little had appeared apart from the speculations of the early evolutionists concerning possible relations between descent, marriage patterns, and the position of women as wives, sisters and mothers (nor had I read Richards 1950). Accordingly I was not surprised to find that matrilineal descent gave Lakalai women little advantage; that they were not inevitably torn between their husbands and brothers; or that marriage was extremely stable once children had been born (contrast Keesing 1981:231). Male domination[2] of women was like that described for many Melanesian societies which combined matrilineal descent with virilocal residence (for example, see Hogbin 1964:84), but unlike that found in most Massim societies (A. Weiner 1976; Macintyre, Chapter 8) or in some others which favoured uxorilocal residence (Nash, Chapter 6).

In the years that followed, during which I worked in two societies lacking unilineal descent groups, an increasing volume of material appeared suggesting links between descent systems, marriage patterns, rights to children and the 'position of women'. Some writers (e.g. Friedl 1975:67) assumed that with patrilineality a wife is valued primarily because she will bear children for her husband's descent group, whereas with matrilineality it was equally often assumed that the children are not even kin to the father. Simplistic conclusions were then drawn about the consequences for women: 'Whereas the position of females is quite variable in patrilineal societies, it is almost universally high in matrilineal ones' (Martin and Voorhies 1975:224). 'The lack of authority [of women] must be related to the rules of exogamy, virilocal residence, and patrilineal descent, through which women bear children for groups other than their own' (O'Laughlin 1974:312). If the 'position of women' seemed relatively poor in a society with patrilineal descent or relatively good in a society with matrilineal descent, the type of descent system rather than the particular form it assumed in that society was often thought to be responsible. Thus even so careful a writer as Keesing could say that: 'compared to women in many patrilineally organised societies, [Trobriand] women enjoy substantial autonomy over their personal lives and sexuality' (1981:236). Given my experience in Lakalai, I remained sceptical about the putative advantages of matrilineality to women, but probably had been affected by some of the common generalisations about the consequences of patrilineality. Although I did not expect to find that Kove women would necessarily be put at a disadvantage by patrilineality and virilocal residence, I was still surprised to hear Kove men repeating how much more important sisters were than brothers to a man seeking renown. In addition, they kept saying, 'It takes a real man to be married to a Kove woman.' Soon it was made clear that much of the value given to both sisters and wives had to do with their role in the system of affinal exchanges. These exchanges were the principal topics of conversation and dispute among Kove of both sexes, and women echoed what men said about their importance. It took me a long time to realise that talk of the importance and value of women had little to do with the actual lives they led. To understand how Kove women are viewed and treated, it is necessary to understand above all how the exchange system operates.

Social organisation and affinal exchanges

The Kove (or Kombe) live on the north coast of West New Britain, just to the west of the Willaumez Peninsula. Most villages are located on sandy islets, the only vegetation a few coconut palms; long canoe trips are needed to reach the mainland gardens and to collect fresh water and firewood. A village is usually composed of several hamlets, each with family houses and a men's house containing ritual paraphernalia which women may not see. In theory, the men of a hamlet comprise a single exogamous patrilineage but residence shifts resulting from divorce, adoption and internal quarrels produce a more complicated mixture. Each men's house is headed by a *mahoni*, a wealthy and powerful man who has reached his position through a combination of achievement and ascription. Until recently, sanctions ranging from shaming to sorcery made it difficult for anyone who was not close kin to a previous *mahoni* to become one himself (Chowning 1979:70), and each village contained only three or four *mahoni*. Nowadays, however, many men aspire to the title, and there is less distinction between simply demonstrating that one is a 'real man', worthy of respect by the community, and being acknowledged as truly outstanding, a *mahoni*. The newer *mahoni* have little if any power, lacking the seniority, knowledge of sorcery and ability in warfare that characterised most of the previous ones. What they can acquire is prestige, by the traditional method of sponsoring ceremonies for their children at which large amounts of shell money (*vula*)³ are dispensed, particularly to the wife's kin. Increasing pressure on men to provide *vula* to a wide range of affines and kin has produced both the similarity between *mahoni* and ordinary men, and the peculiar position of the modern Kove woman, caught between her husband, her brothers, and her own desires regarding herself and her children.

Almost all women speak of marriage as a desirable state, and it is expected that every woman who is not severely handicapped will marry. Single women other than widows are often subject to strong pressure to marry by their kin, including mothers and grandmothers, who wish to receive a share of the marriage payments. In the past almost all first marriages were arranged with little consultation of the partners, who might be small children. More recently greater attention has been paid to the desires of the couple, but no young man can finance his own marriage, and he still needs to ensure that his choice is acceptable to his kin. Equally, he must prove himself acceptable to the wife's kin. The process of demonstrating that one is likely to be a satisfactory son- or daughter-in-law is much the same in all cases. If both sets of parents agree, the first payment consists of a few strands of high-value *vula* delivered secretly to the woman's family. There follows a trial period during which the woman is still largely under the control of her parents but works for the groom's parents, spending lengthy periods with them if they reside in a different village. (The rate of local endogamy is high; often spouses come from different hamlets of the same village.) Meanwhile the groom may live with her at her parents' house, and helps his parents-in-law with house-building, gardening and canoe transport. The bride is said to be married but not paid for during this period, which sometimes lasts until one or two children have been born. During this time the bride's family constantly sends small gifts of food to the groom's family, and receives *vula* in return. The exchanges are intended to cement relations between the two families. The labour provided by the bride and groom for their parents-in-law is simply part of the obligations of marriage, and a demonstration that both individuals are hardworking and obedient. One man said that the groom's father contributed to his son's marriage in explicit payment for the food given him by the bride and groom during this period, but added that if she did not produce this food, the marriage arrangements would be terminated. Other Kove seem simply to assume that the father's contribution is part of his duty to his son.[4]

The groom's side collects goods for the marriage payments from men and women who are close consanguineal kin through both the father and the mother. The patrilineage, which may have branches in other villages, does not act as a unit in marriage, but the groom's hamlet does; all residents, including in-married women, are expected to help. Men donate *vula* and cash, while the female contribution consists primarily of sewn pandanus-leaf mats, supplemented by plaited baskets. Some women may contribute *vula* as well. Ideally each recipient of *vula* on the woman's side should also receive mats, while additional mats recompense women who receive no *vula*. In return the bride's side produces more pandanus mats, other minor valuables such as wooden bowls and tortoiseshell bracelets, raw and cooked food, pigs and dogs. Cash may also pass to the groom's side. All contributors from the groom's side should receive something in return; the bride's father is not a 'true man' if he cannot manage this. If the bride's family is really wealthy, her kin also give her a set of special elaborate household utensils such as carved bamboo tongs, and escort her formally to her husband's household, displaying the goods that will belong to the bride as well as those that go to her affines. Being accompanied by these special goods is a continuing source of pride for a woman, often mentioned in later arguments with her husband and his kin as evidence of the importance of her family and herself. Ideally the bride's father gives her additional *vula* to serve as a basis for repaying the debt which she and her husband owe those who paid for his marriage. Without such a dowry, she can only begin sewing mats as her continuing contribution to life-long cycles of debt and repayment in which she will be involved as wife, sister and mother. Meanwhile her husband must begin obtaining *vula* to fulfil his parallel obligations, first to his kin, then to hers, the latter being included in his obligations to his children. However, Kove do not share the Chambri belief that such debts can never be paid (see Chapter 2).

The large payment gives the husband the right to have his wife living with him and to share the regulation of her behaviour with other members of his family and the senior men of his hamlet. The wife is now expected to identify herself with her husband and his interests, and to behave respectfully towards his kin. Initially she has a specific obligation to repay the women of the hamlet for their contribution to the marriage payments by bringing them firewood and fresh water from the mainland and preparing the stone ovens on which food is cooked. Once this period of work is finished, she has a continuing responsibility to join the other women of the hamlet in supplying the men's house with cooked food and water for the unmarried men who normally sleep there, the married men who often eat there, and outside visitors. Cooking only for one's own household is strongly disapproved and may lead to divorce. At the same time, the woman has not severed ties with her own kin and hamlet. She almost always goes home to have her first child, and may be buried with members of her natal hamlet, just as her ghost is said to return to their sacred place. Furthermore, her husband is obliged to continue paying for the marriage until all of the children are grown, even if his wife has died in the meantime. The primary recipient of these payments is the wife's eldest brother (who would also have received the largest amount of the earlier payment if he was already grown). The usual occasions for payments to the wife's kin are ceremonies celebrating stages in the life of the first-born child of the marriage, such as the first haircut or first visit to another village. The most important ceremony celebrates the donning of earrings peculiar to one's patrilineage, after the earlobes have been slit on an earlier occasion. Because of pressure from mission schools, boys no longer have their earlobes slit, and although a ceremony is held when a boy undergoes the obligatory superincision of the foreskin, nowadays the major ceremony usually focuses on a daughter[5] (see Chowning 1978b).

The first-born is still singled out if he or she is injured as a child, especially if blood is shed. The father should kill a pig and give *vula* to the child's maternal kin on each such occasion. When the foreskin and earlobes are slit, payments must be made for each child. They are said to 'wash away the blood', but Kove insist that all payments to the wife's kin are 'really' for the wife; the child is just a pretext. The childless must find or manufacture occasions (such as the construction of an elaborate family house) to make the same kinds of payments. The worst insult to a man is to tell him that his wife is not paid for. His most difficult task is ensuring that those payments will be adequate. In order to continue paying for his wife, he must call on a wide range of other kin, while his wife tries both to help him and to fulfil her own somewhat different set of obligations. She is also a sister, and the ideal way to obtain *vula* is from, or more accurately through, a married sister. Difficulties arise because a man sponsoring a ceremony does not only want to pay his wife's kin and his other creditors, but to make a name for himself by dispensing an exceptionally large amount of *vula*. Since most men share this ambition, his wife's brother may not be content to wait for the would-be sponsor of a ceremony, but will try to get *vula* as soon as possible for use in his own ceremony. He does this by demanding from his sister repayment of 'gifts' made to her in the years since her marriage.

These 'gifts' are viewed as part of normal cross-sibling obligations; Kove women expressed disapproval of my society when I said that with us brothers do not constantly 'give' things to their sisters. The goods range from those which men obtain by trade (such as wooden bowls) and manufacture (such as tortoiseshell bracelets) to the products of wage labour such as bags of rice and drums of kerosene. The woman, however, knows that she will have to repay these gifts, and that she cannot do so alone. Accordingly she should always share the goods with her husband and his kin. When her brother wants to sponsor a ceremony, he calls on her for repayment, which should be in *vula* somewhat in excess of the cash value of the goods; repayment of the exact amount removes the profit margin which makes the transaction worthwhile. The sister has to obtain most of the *vula* from her husband and his kin, and she is best able to do this if she has not only shared the gifts with them but contributed mats and other items to their exchanges.

The feast sponsor has other ways of acquiring *vula*, particularly by calling for repayment of loans he has made to his male paternal kin when they were sponsoring ceremonies, and by soliciting loans from other male kin. All such loans, however, should be repaid at 100 per cent interest unless the lender is a true father or brother. A man who is not a renowned sorcerer may find it difficult to collect this interest or even to get a loan repaid, and he incurs a heavy burden of debt if he accepts many loans. It is much more profitable to call for repayment by his sisters. For this reason, men now say that the greatest aid to becoming a *mahoni* is to have many sisters. These must, however, be sisters that have married well. Although men talk of requesting *vula* from their sisters, it is not usually expected that a woman alone can produce the necessary amount, and it is taking a risk to give gifts to an unmarried woman. The reasons for this expectation reflect traditional rather than modern ideas about the relation between gender and goods.

Gender and property

Early in the century *vula* came only from male sources, particularly trade, and most of it was manufactured far outside Kove (see Chowning 1978a). The old sources eventually dried up, and in recent decades the

Kove started making their own out of local shells. The job of manufacture has fallen increasingly to women, who now do most of the work of collection and manufacture, and can do it all. Nevertheless, *vula* is still regarded as primarily male wealth, and women are expected to use almost all that they make to satisfy the demands of their husbands and brothers. Although neither simply takes wealth from her, they tend to regard their claims as overriding her desires to spend it in other ways, as by buying rice rather than relying on the garden. The goods preeminently identified with women are mats and baskets. A virtuous woman should spend all of her spare time manufacturing these, and a woman who is respected as wealthy has a large supply of such items stored in the rafters of her house, mostly intended for exchange rather than use. A young woman married to an aspiring *mahoni* said specifically that mats are the 'strength' of women, as *vula* is that of men, and mat-making the female complement of a man's trading for *vula*. (When I pointed out that women also make *vula*, she said, 'Yes, that's not straight.') Mats do not, however, have the importance to women that *vula* does; they either supplement *vula* payments, on a decidedly lower level, or balance them, so that each fathom of *vula* is repaid with two mats but, ideally, with other objects as well. These other objects, such as clay pots and tortoiseshell bracelets, all originate from men. Perhaps mats were more highly valued in the past, before the amount of *vula* in circulation became so inflated, but nowadays women prefer to receive *vula* at wealth distributions. When the amounts of *vula* available are small, as often happens at a hastily organised ceremony (for an injured first-born child say), men receive all the *vula* and women receive only mats, baskets, clothing and similar items. They are more pleased when enough *vula* is available for them to receive some too. Moreover, however essential it is for women to have a supply of mats for exchange, excess ones are simply sold at Kimbe market or traded for goods such as tobacco. In contrast to *vula*, and certainly in contrast to women's wealth in Kiriwina (A. Weiner 1976:118-19), mats do not figure prominently in the competitive part of wealth distributions. Instead, they are used to demonstrate that a woman is able to meet all her obligations; her possession of many mats primarily contrasts her with the poor and feckless.

As we have seen, the Kove divide most goods into men's and women's, but assignment to these categories is made in different ways which do not wholly coincide: how they are (or were) obtained, who uses them for everyday purposes, and their role in exchange. (In no case is direct gender symbolism involved; goods are not male and female in themselves.) Some goods, such as tortoiseshell bracelets, can be classified by all of these criteria: made by men, usually worn by women, usually exchanged accompanying women's goods such as mats. Similarly mats are made by women, used for sleeping by both sexes, and distributed by and to women. Other goods, such as pigs, are classified by only one criterion: they may be acquired and owned by either sex, but in affinal exchange are part of the masculine contribution. (Women can and do dispose of their own pigs on other occasions, such as at funerals.) Particularly in the case of *vula*, there are discrepancies between theory and practice. As was noted above, most of it is now manufactured by women rather than being acquired by men. In fact, women were always able to obtain some *vula* for themselves. The mother of a bride would receive part of the initial marriage payment, and in time other close female kin of the bride would also receive *vula*. Women can also lend mats or food to other women who need these items for ceremonies, and then will eventually receive *vula* in payment of the debt. Furthermore, women who are experts in certain forms of magic are paid in *vula* by other women. The amounts a woman would hold cannot, however, be enough to meet the demands of a brother wanting to sponsor a ceremony. Anything received for the marriage of a daughter is usually put aside to help finance the marriage of a son, and the payments received for small transactions fall far short of the 50 fathoms that a man is likely to request of a true sister. Only masculine activity can bridge the gap.

The norms regarding the direction in which objects move and the sequence of exchange are not always adhered to. A man may ask a sister to give him *vula* first, promising to deliver goods later, or a woman may help a brother in need by simply 'giving' him a pig, *vula* or cash. She expects repayment in kind, with a small increment (such as a female pig in exchange for a less valuable male), but not the high interest demanded by most male kin. A brother cannot, however, coerce a sister to make such loans, and is unlikely to receive them unless he has already shown considerable generosity to her and her husband.

A man who has made substantial gifts to his sister is in a much stronger position. He can demand repayment in *vula*, starting by simply reminding the couple of all he has given them. If necessary, he then tries to shame them as ungrateful and poverty-stricken, and finally he can threaten or attempt to break up the marriage, if the fault clearly lies with the husband. But if the couple make common cause against the creditor, he threatens to kill his sister or her child. Kove women say, 'Our brothers love us and constantly give us gifts, and then we give them *vula* in return, and if we don't, they sorcerise us.' The woman is likely to support her husband if the couple are trying to save *vula* for a ceremony of their own, or if the brother's demands are considered excessive. Otherwise she will try to induce her husband to help pay the debt by scolding him, refusing to cook for him or sleep with him, or theatening to leave him for a 'rich man'. Her ultimate weapon is to 'poison' the husband by putting sexual secretions into his food or by helping her brother practise a male form of sorcery against him (Chowning 1987).

The brother who threatens to kill his sister or break up her marriage is of course subject to identical pressures from his wife and her kin. A man's failure to give adequate *vula* to his affines is the most common reason given for a woman's leaving or turning against her husband. Men also say that they would kill a sister (by sorcery) rather than be offended by seeing her 'walking around not paid for'. (Women are considered physically weaker and so more vulnerable to sorcery than men; the death of a married woman is almost always ascribed to a grudge against her husband.) In turn, a woman can scold her brother for failing to pay all his debts – most often, for not making a further payment of mats and other women's goods in return for the *vula* she gave him to repay his initial gifts. Most of these goods will be passed to her husband's female kin to repay them for their help in collecting the *vula*. Men complain that their sisters are paid twice for *vula*, but also say that they fear their sisters' tongues if the second payment is not made.[6] But unlike the doubling of *vula* demanded by male creditors, mats used in this second payment come directly from women. The debtor's wife has to assemble them, calling on the women (her sisters and her brothers' wives) who received *vula* in payment for her marriage.

In dealing with men more remote than her husband and brother, a woman has little ability to collect debts or shame a defaulter, and no means other than resort to a government court[7] to compel payment. Occasionally a widow will attempt to continue sponsoring a ceremony begun by her husband, but men agree that she will find it particularly difficult to collect the necessary amount of *vula*. However this is also true of some men; many more ceremonies are planned and begun than ever come to successful conclusion, regardless of the sex of the sponsor. Where a woman does have power is in her ability to withhold *vula* from a brother to whom she is not indebted, or to pay a debt exactly without adding the needed increment. At this point she can express her own desires and choices without danger or loss of prestige. When a man in debt after sponsoring a ceremony demanded that his lineage 'sisters' help him by giving him *vula*, an old man, 'father' to all those involved, commented '*Vula* is hard work for women. They'll give it if they want to, and not if they don't.' Because of the competing claims of husband, other brothers, and personal plans for the disposal of *vula*, a brother can never be sure that a sister will produce what he needs on demand. Consequently he prefers to be able to call on a large number of sisters. If they are true siblings, so much the better; otherwise he will have to rely on cousins who may be subject to stronger claims from nearer kin.

Women as mothers, daughters, and sisters

The desire for offspring of one sex or the other varies somewhat with the sex of the parent. Married couples agree that they want children of both sexes to help the same-sex parent, given that the sexual division of labour tends to be rigid. In addition, every Kove wants a replacement of the same sex who will ensure his or her immortality. Adoption is not a satisfactory substitute for a child of one's own, but an own child of the wrong sex somewhat relieves the yearning for a replacement. Women are just as eager to have at least one son as men are, and couples are rarely at odds about the ideal balance, though the woman may be reluctant to keep bearing children in order to achieve it. They agree that so long as one or two sons have been born, it is preferable to have a greater number of girls. Because of the marriage payments, too many sons are a financial burden; it is advantageous to be able to use the *vula* received from a daughter's betrothal and marriage to pay for those of her brother. Furthermore, daughters are considered more likely to care for the aged than are daughters-in-law, and residential choices by the elderly often reflect the desire to be with a married daughter. There are no pressures from the patrilineage to keep up the number of males. Young (1983b:481) has described Kalauna neglect and depreciation of daughters as 'a classic rationale for patrilineal descent and succession', but Kove, when told of female infanticide in other societies with patrilineal descent, are flabbergasted, saying that someone would always be willing to take a girl if the parents do not want her.

All men prefer to have more sisters than brothers. Although brothers should cooperate, they are also rivals; an old adage states that there should not be two *mahoni* in one men's house. Quarrels, including physical violence, between full brothers and between more distant male lineage mates are everyday occurrences, and tend to centre on property. Given the Kove ethos of male domination, which women accept to some degree, a man feels that he has a better chance to control the behaviour of a sister than a brother. In particular, he expects to have the principal say in the marriage of a younger sister, if he is old enough at the time, and also to influence not only how much he profits from his sister's marriage, but whether it should continue. The reality may differ; a woman may defy her brother or brother-surrogate to elope with the man of her choice, stick with a poor man who fails to deliver *vula*, or refuse to remarry after a divorce despite her brother's complaints. Nevertheless, most women comply with the desires of their brothers, and try to induce their husbands to do so as well.

The outstanding exception is the female *mahoni*. In the past, this title was occasionally conferred on a first-born daughter by a father who was himself a *mahoni*. (I know of no very recent cases.) Such a girl was shown very special treatment, including remaining naked until she was full-grown, like a man in the traditional society but unlike other girls. Her father would reveal to her all the rituals associated with the men's house, which other women are still afraid to discuss openly, and would teach her important masculine magic such as weather control and sorcery. At the same time, she was kept ignorant of the most elementary female tasks, such as drawing water and cooking. The one way in which she behaved like a normal woman was in marrying and bearing children. When first married, she was assisted by a retinue of female retainers until she learned feminine tasks. In one or two such cases, she never worked like an ordinary woman, but put her energies into directing male activities such as the construction of men's houses and warfare. She is sometimes referred to as a 'man-woman', and it is also said that her father 'made her a man'. The descendants of such a woman speak of her with great pride, sometimes mixed with shock. By contrast, a male 'man-woman' is a transvestite who 'makes' himself in the face of much opposition by his male kin, and although women may talk admiringly of how well he carries out their tasks, he is regarded as somewhat ridiculous or even so shameful that his brothers kill him (see Chowning 1973; 1987).[8]

The female *mahoni* has real power, but it is conferred on her by a man. The only other women with such power are a few who have not been put through the formal process, but are believed to have been taught masculine magic by a father renowned for its use. This is the case with one contemporary woman I know, who is not a first-born but who is reputed to share with her one brother knowledge of their father's sorcery and weather magic. This woman, who carries one of the badges of a male *mahoni*, a highly decorated lime spatula, is feared as well as respected.

Lacking such special privileges, other women occasionally achieve exceptional prestige, but not power. Again, the support of male kin is necessary. For example, a woman called Supu managed to reach her present position partly because her male kin supported her desire to remain unmarried after she was left a widow with six sons and one daughter. Using her husband's wealth and aided by his male kin, she managed to finance the marriages of her older sons and mission education for the younger ones. By working outside Kove for many years, the younger ones managed to contribute especially large amounts to their own marriages. Exceptionally hard-working and energetic for a woman in her 70s lamed by elephantiasis (blamed on sorcery by her frustrated suitors), Supu is allowed various privileges ranging from the ordering of funeral ceremonies to uninterrupted speech-making at public assemblies. At the same time, she usually depicts herself as a compendium of specifically female virtues, and is genuinely devoted to her often neglectful children and cantankerous brother. She frequently scolds girls and women for departing from the traditional female role, as by playing basketball when they should be collecting firewood or cooking. She reproaches a young woman (admittedly her affine) for quarrelling with her husband, saying that he has paid for her and now owns her, and she should not answer back even if he curses or beats her. She often expresses fear of physical attack by men if she is working in the garden alone, and of male sorcery. Furthermore, she tells of once having had the opportunity to learn rain magic from a kinsman and abandoning the idea when other male kin said it would be inappropriate for a woman. Yet she seems always to have been willing to depart somewhat from expectation, as when, before her husband's death, she challenged another woman with whom she had quarrelled to a game of football for which she wore shorts and a singlet and carried a bone dagger in her (husband's) belt.

This is a case in which the individual's personality has made possible recognition of exceptional ability. Supu has been granted high status because she fulfils all the expectations for a virtuous woman and then does other things as well, rather than like the female *mahoni*, substituting male tasks for female ones. The loss of her husband, while certainly creating difficulties for her, made it easier for her to achieve individual renown. It is virtuous for a widow to remain unmarried, as it is not for other women. No matter how exceptional she may be, a married woman usually finds her efforts and abilities ignored by comparison with those of her husband. The nearest equivalent to a widow is a woman whose husband has left her for someone else, but only if she is not thought to be at fault. It is interesting that Supu's daughter, long divorced, has managed to sponsor a major ceremony in her own right, while her eldest brother's attempt to do the same failed because of his inability to collect debts.

Wife and mother, wife as mother

A woman's decision to marry a particular man may not be her own. Either the marriage is arranged by her father or brother, and she agrees to obey (or risk beatings), or she presents herself as the helpless victim of the man's love magic. Women are said to have weaker 'bellies' than men, and may be made so sick by love magic that they risk death if not allowed to marry the man. On the other hand, women also practise love magic, and are often reported to initiate sexual advances and to request marriage. They may also defy the desires of their kin and elope, hoping to gain assent once tempers have cooled. Although it is not unknown for a couple to be at odds from the beginning, if the marriage lasts until it is time to sponsor ceremonies for the children, it is probable that the couple will be in full agreement on matters that concern the children (apart from those that reflect modern concerns, notably schooling). Although the ceremonies are the occasion for the husband's paying for his wife, they also honour (lit. 'stand up') the children, whose prestige as they grow up depends to a great extent on the magnificence of these ceremonies. Children of both sexes are taught to boast of being so honoured when trying to win an argument (see Chowning 1974:189), and very old people continue to describe the ceremonies centred on themselves. They talk only of the father's accomplishments, not mentioning the mother.

In planning the ceremonies, a woman can request that the rituals held for her, and peculiar to her patrilineage, also be held for her children. Her brothers will consent as long as her husband can pay for the privilege. Otherwise the wife's role is wholly subsidiary to her husband's. She should help him with everything he undertakes, and before the *vula* is dispensed, reminds him of her precise debts over the years to her various 'brothers'. Failure to repay these adequately will be blamed on the woman. If she plays a more active role in deciding who is to get what, this is likely to be ignored or discounted by the general public. Their attitude was shown when a young woman died in childbirth shortly after she and her husband had sponsored a large ceremony for their older children. It was widely suspected that she had been killed by sorcery practised by her first cousins or her half-brother, angry because they had received less *vula* than more remote kin. The victim had made no secret of the fact that the decision to withhold *vula* from the cousins was as much her own as her husband's; she had been offended because they had refused to help with the ceremony and had publicly sneered at the possibility of its being brought to a successful conclusion by a pair so young. During a quarrel which also resulted from the cousins' disappointment, I saw her acting more vindictively than her husband, who said he 'felt sorry for his affine'. Another theory held that the woman was killed by men envious and resentful of the husband's boasting of his achievements. Nevertheless, in discussing the death, people constantly suggested that the woman had been the innocent victim of misbehaviour by her husband or possibly her father. Only her next-door neighbour pointed out that she too had boasted excessively. Everyone else seemed to feel that if she had been killed by sorcery inspired by discontent over *vula* transactions, she bore no responsibility for inspiring that discontent. By contrast, those who did not attribute her death to sorcery thought she might indeed have brought it on herself (see below).

A woman's clearcut duties to her husband and his kin can conflict with her duty to her brothers. Another potential source of conflict is her children. A nursing mother must resist her husband's advances if he approaches her while her baby is too young to be weaned. Women have been badly injured or even killed by men whose sexual desires overcame their consideration for their offspring. Conversely, if she is not known to have resisted her husband, the woman tends to be blamed for badly spaced pregnancies, particularly if she shows excessive jealousy and 'keeps her husband near her all the time'. Care for children should outweigh all other considerations for a woman. It is proper for a woman to nag her husband to sponsor the ceremonies for the children, especially to ensure that a son's foreskin and, usually, a daughter's earlobes will be slit.[9] Today she also tends to be the one who tries to make sure that the man sets aside money for school fees for his sons. (Few parents are much concerned about formal education for their daughters, since they do not want them to leave Kove.)

Towards both her children and her husband, the woman's main task throughout her life is providing food. She is acknowledged to be the principal source of it, not only doing most of the garden work but collecting firewood and water and cooking everything except meat that men consume alone in the men's house. Furthermore, she alone can supply animal protein throughout the year. The Kove wish to eat some every day, but it is often too stormy for men to fish, and the men acknowledge that they are supported by women who collect shellfish in all weathers. The rigid sexual division of labour makes it impossible for a man to feed himself without female aid, whereas a woman has no difficulty.[10] Both sexes consequently agree that a widower suffers much more than a widow. Interestingly, old men sometimes say that a wife is really like a mother, but more greatly mourned when she dies than a mother would be because she has cared for the man for so much longer. 'Care' here refers specifically to feeding. By implication, it includes not only giving a constant supply of nutritious food (and not refusing to cook even when angry) but abstaining from poisoning her husband at the instigation of another man or of her own desires. A virtuous wife avoids harming her husband, telling him if she 'no longer thinks of him' so he can counter the love magic that is turning her against him.

Autonomy

The boastfulness of the young *mahoni* was condemned because he talked as if he had achieved success without the aid of others (apart from his wife, whose contribution was taken for granted). Nevertheless, Kove of both sexes, particularly the children of *mahoni*, are encouraged from early childhood to show pride in themselves and their families and disdain for others. Arrogant behaviour is displayed even when it is dangerous, as when a woman rejects a suitor so insultingly that it is considered natural for him to retaliate by raping or sorcerising her. The frequent male emphasis on the inferiority of women, who should submit to men, is accompanied by the knowledge that women are as capable as men of wilful behaviour. Usually a man simply tries to influence a woman by magic, persuasion and the accumulation and dispensing of wealth, so that she feels it is economically and socially profitable to continue interacting with him as wife or sister. If these techniques fail, he tries intimidation or force. Nevertheless, a woman may follow her own desires, insisting on marrying a man of whom her kin disapprove, evading her creditors, going on a trip while her husband just says, 'She herself', when asked why he did not keep her home. Moreover, men often complain that their wives persuade them to act against their wishes, not only in sending away a second wife but in abandoning jobs outside Kove or in shifting residence to look after the wife's parents. So long as her behaviour does not shame her husband or other kin (as sexual infidelity or promiscuity inevitably does), and so long as she does not neglect her children, a woman has considerable freedom to follow personal inclinations. If she comes to grief, she has only herself to blame. In one case those who did not attribute a death in childbirth to sorcery suggested either that the woman concerned was being punished by God for not observing a day of rest,[11] or that she had ignored medical advice about her earlier gynaecological problems. Thus her death was on her own head.

What is not tolerated is a woman's taking over, without the agreement of others, certain male prerogatives. A myth tells of a sister who dressed as a man in order to lure to her village a wife for her brother. When discovered, she was scolded by her sister-in-law for not remaining a woman, as 'we women' should be content to do, and was transformed into a kind of veined growth on trees called by the word for scrotum. On the other hand, behaviour that is generally condemned on the part of women but tolerated in men, such as drunkenness and engaging in protracted public quarrels, may still be repeated by some women who are largely indifferent to criticism, not to mention fines and beatings. They cannot, however, be so indifferent as not to manufacture valuables if they wish to remain accepted members of Kove society. All Kove of both sexes assume that everyone wants respect, and preferably prestige, in the eyes of other Kove, and at present achieving these requires *vula*.

In 1983 I heard for the first time the assertion that '*vula* work' actually holds the society together; everything the Kove value would collapse if it was abandoned. Older men said this when a few younger ones argued for more time devoted to earning cash. The conservatives particularly mentioned the possibility that without the need for *vula*, women would turn to prostitution, obtaining cash which they were not obliged to share with anyone. Men all seem to agree that female autonomy cannot be allowed to lead to financial independence. Interestingly, one unmarried (though twice divorced) woman announced that the best aspect of being single is that you can keep your property for yourself. Conversely, one old woman suggested that unseemly greed for money led me to work so far from my kin. A number of older people of both sexes, however, criticise modern young women for choosing husbands on the basis of their possession of cash and Western goods, asserting that a young man is appealing only if he is educated or has a good job, and otherwise a well-off older man will be preferred even if the woman has to make a polygynous marriage. The young women themselves, however, still talk of deciding to marry only because of sexual attraction or obedience to their kin; they do not represent themselves as being influenced by the possibility of material benefit. Their behaviour once married is a different matter.

Women and wealth

Given that women now actually manufacture most of the shell *vula* themselves, and that it is an all-purpose currency, it struck me as surprising that men did not worry that women might achieve independence of them and of social restraints through *vula* alone. The reasons for male lack of concern are probably two. First, however it is acquired or produced, *vula* remains primarily the type of valuable that *men* receive and dispense. Second, whatever its other functions, *vula* takes its real value from transactions of cultural importance, and women usually agree with men that the most important transaction is paying for a wife. Conversely, a woman's social value is demonstrated[12] by the amount of *vula* that is paid for her. The only socially esteemed use a woman can make of *vula* is to give it to her brother in recompense for what he has given her. Women in fact often complain that *vula* is rubbish because it cannot be used to buy Western goods. Some men agree, saying that they too would like to abolish *vula* work but fear the vengeance of their creditors – shaming from women, sorcery from men. Those who support the system can say little in its favour except to suggest that it binds Kove villages together in a network of interdependence; they do not mention the quarrels centring on *vula* that sunder the closest kinship ties.[13] They do, however, dampen female complaints by 'giving' women trade store goods, not in return for *vula* but as justification for requesting it. In specific cases, however, a wife is likely to complain[14] that almost all the goods her husband acquires are going to his sisters while his own wife and children may actually be short of clothing or, after periods of drought, food. It is at this point that a man has to stress his ultimate goal: proving himself a proper man, worthy to be married to a Kove woman, and simultaneously honouring the children of the marriage. Women accept the validity of these goals, and in the long run are most likely to show dissatisfaction only with a man who is either unable to make the gifts to his sisters and sister substitutes in the first place, or who cannot induce these women and their husbands to pay the debts when he needs the *vula*.

Kove men regard marriage as essential both for proving one's personal worth and for ensuring one's immortality through offspring; ideally, it also replaces a nurturing mother with a nurturing wife. At the same time, marriage brings onerous and even dangerous obligations. 'Men die only because of *vula*', or, 'only because of women', men complain, referring to the same thing; the usual cause of death is assumed to be someone's dissatisfaction with affinal exchanges. When Kove men say that women are their business, they are referring to the sisters (and daughters), who are not themselves property but the sources of it, subject to manipulation by the arrangers of their marriages who hope to use them to put pressure on their husbands. Wives, on the other hand, simultaneously put such pressure on husbands to satisfy brothers, and join husbands in producing the necessary goods. The woman's role as helper is played down or even ignored when a ceremony is made and the child's father publicly supervises the dispensing of *vula*, whereas the role of the sister's husband is equally ignored when a man talks of receiving *vula* from his sister, not his brother-in-law. Sisters deliver *vula* openly, but without the public shouting aloud of the type and amount of transaction that accompanies loans and repayments by men. The degree of acknowledgement of male and female roles in *vula* transactions may relate to the publicity of the event. In Kove there are many rituals from which women are wholly excluded; sometimes they must leave the village while these are held. Furthermore, women are normally strongly discouraged from taking part in public debates, other women joining in reproaching them for interfering in men's affairs. To a greater extent than in the other societies I know, these separate male and female domains are kept apart by force.

To understand Kove male attitudes, it is necessary to appreciate the parallels they see between *vula* work and the role of money and money-making in Western society. Frequently the two are contrasted, particularly by those who wish to be free of the network of *vula* obligations and debts in order to earn cash to fulfil personal desires. Equally often, however, men make such statements as the following: 'Our women are like your [European] coconut plantations; they are the way we make money.' Or: 'Having *vula* is for us like your having money in the bank; a man is respected if he has it and not otherwise.' Now Kove of both sexes look down on those whom they exploit financially, such as the outsiders they overcharge in trading. As the tenor of these statements indicates, women may be no more respected as a source of wealth for men than plantation workers are respected by the plantation owner. As a category, then, women are not esteemed. They have to work as individuals to overcome the view that they are or should be simply at the disposal of their male kin and affines.

Moreover, in contrast to Tubetube described in Chapter 8, Kove, both men and women, emphasise female physical weakness. This produces the ritual separation, compels women to obey men or risk ferocious beatings (even from sons seeking *vula*), and makes them the appropriate victims when their husbands have offended. My own first impression of Kove, exacerbated by my assignment to a Kove female role,[15] was that treatment of women was exceptionally repressive by the standards of other societies I knew best. Furthermore, women agreed with male statements about proper female behaviour, apart from a few girls who wanted more formal education, and they never talked as if they had abilities or strengths not acknowledged by men. On the other hand, they did not echo the frequent male remark that women are of no value, nor suggest, as men did, that male desires automatically outweighed female ones. Young women, in fact, sometimes boast of their power (in the form of sexual attraction) to lead a man to act against his own interests, as by staying with a wife despite her adultery. As was noted, a woman can also shame a brother and actually kill an unsatisfactory husband. But what she cannot do, while remaining married, is to keep for herself what she produces. Furthermore, she has no real reason to do so. *Vula* is only needed for the exchanges centring on children, and even if her contribution to the success of the ceremony is publicly ignored, it is privately acknowledged. A Kove woman who wishes to have the pleasures and advantages (including children), the support as well as the demands of her kin, and the prestige of being viewed as a good woman, has no option at present but to accept the restrictions, denigration, and occasional physical abuse that reflect a value system subscribed to by all Kove.

The picture is not in fact so gloomy as it first appeared to me. Traditional values that are not sex-limited, such as the encouragement of independent action and of pride in oneself, often lead women to act much more freely and openly, as in choosing sexual partners, than I had expected. The constant acknowledgement by men of their dependence on women for achieving status, counter-balances their equally constant depreciation of women's desires. Since to achieve self-respect men today need to put on the same kinds of ceremonies that were once reserved for aspiring *mahoni*, they are now far more dependent on women than in the past. A woman cannot achieve full equality with men unless her father makes her a *mahoni*, but a man cannot even gain the esteem of other men, on which self-respect depends, without the assistance of several women. By contrast, although a woman has a head start if her father sponsored ceremonies for her (just as a man does), her status in the eyes of other women and of the community does not depend on how men treat her. Whether she is well housed or has access to luxury foods such as pork and rice may vary according to what kind of husband she has, but if she makes mats and *vula*, and feeds and cares for her husband, children, and the men of the hamlet, her reputation is secure. The frequently mentioned strength and 'hardness' of Kove women derives from basic self-confidence; they are evaluated in terms of how they operate as individuals. Men are evaluated in terms of their ability to influence women as well as other men. Women may feel physically vulnerable, but they do not feel economically exploited, whereas men do. When men talk of women as the business that can make them rich, they are referring to a possibility that will be realised only if men give full credit to female autonomy. Without the women, the man is nothing; with their help, if he can secure it, he may become a real man. In the stress on self-achievement, patrilineality counts for almost nothing, and successful affinal relations, only achievable if women are satisfied, for almost everything.

Notes

1. Fieldwork in Kove was supported by The Australian National University (1966, 1968, 1969), the University of Papua New Guinea (1971-2, 1972-3, 1975-6), and Victoria University of Wellington (1983). In 1978 I visited the area at the request of the Papua New Guinea Department of Environment and Conservation.

2. In contrast to Errington and Gewertz (Chapter 2), I use the term to designate a spectrum of socially accepted behaviour ranging from forced marriages to rape and killing of women who intruded on male secrets.

3. *Vula* is all-purpose currency composed of disc-shaped beads; one type, 'gold' *vula*, is worth twice as much as the rest. *Vula* has long been pegged to the national currency; in

1966 one fathom of ordinary *vula* was worth one Australian dollar. In this chapter, 'cash' designates Papua New Guinea money. *Vula* is accepted in lieu of cash at trade stores, including those run by non-Kove.

4. In turn, the son and his wife have a life-long obligation to give food and other goods to his father (and mother). Although members of the lineage should help, the financing of the marriage is the father's responsibility.

5. The daughter may in fact not be the first-born. The reason is that a man often is not able to collect all the goods necessary for a truly impressive girl's ceremony until he is middle-aged, by which time his first-born may already be married.

6. Men frequently talk of being shamed by women, but they cannot be driven to suicide by what women say (as Lakalai men can be). On those rare occasions when men commit suicide, the reason is usually a wife's adultery. Female suicides are more frequent, and are triggered by adultery, excessive beating by the husband, and parental refusal to allow a girl to marry the man of her choice.

7. In the past, these were conducted by patrol officers; at present, official village courts hear such cases.

8. Herdt, in his recent study of homosexuality in Melanesia, misunderstood information that I gave him about Kove. At least the contemporary 'man-woman', about whom I have the fullest information, is a lifelong transvestite who longs for female genitals, apparently a case of what Herdt (1978:74) calls 'primary male transsexualism'. For that biological male, a Kove woman's life appeals more than a man's. He is reported not to engage in homosexual behaviour, unlike at least one Kove man who is not a transvestite (compare Herdt 1984:76).

9. It is shameful for a man to be called 'stinking penis', and usually another male kinsman will sponsor a ceremony for a boy whose father is neglectful or poor. In theory a girl's earlobes should be stretched before she is married, but this operation is more often neglected than the male one. Nowadays a girl may just have the ears pierced for European style earrings.

10. On the other hand, only men make sago, the staple in time of drought. One woman told of having been well-fed by her husband when everyone else was hungry at such a time.

11. Some Kove are Roman Catholics and some Seventh-Day Adventists, so that alternative 'days of rest' are available.

12. It is not determined by these payments, however. In effect a husband who fails to pay adequately does not show proper appreciation of his wife.

13. For a detailed account, see Chowning 1987.

14. She makes the complaint to other women. No man would sympathise.

15. This had not happened on my previous fieldtrips, where I was not subject to normal female tabus nor excluded from male ritual secrets. A few older Kove men did not share the common assumption that I should be classed with Kove women, but did threaten me with sorcery if I talked of what I was told or shown. Meanwhile women constantly pressed me to spend my spare time making baskets.

CHAPTER 6

Gender attributes and equality: men's strength and women's talk among the Nagovisi

JILL NASH

This chapter attempts to explain gender equality among the Nagovisi, a people of southcentral Bougainville, North Solomons District, Papua New Guinea.[1] It describes gender attributes in terms of cultural conceptions of agency and efficacy – that is, what each sex is assumed to do and be capable of. These constructs have implications for other, non-gender forms of social differentiation.

The matrilineal Nagovisi may be seen as a 'low production' society with some degree of achieved 'big man' leadership (for reappraisals of Melanesian political organisation, see B. Douglas 1979; Hau'ofa 1981; Godelier 1982; Modjeska 1982; Keesing n.d.). Low production societies in Melanesia have until now been identified among the fringe Highland populations, these generally being agnatic in orientation. However, matriliny in other parts of the whole world has long been associated with what observers perceive as low production, namely, conditions in which the material base and the relations of production do not lend themselves to the development of social inequalities without ultimately destroying their matrilineal character (Murdock 1949; Aberle 1963; Gough 1963; Allen 1981, 1984; but see also M. Douglas 1969). Nevertheless, my intent here is not to contribute to a discussion of the effects of intensified production on matrilineal institutions, but to connect gender notions to the ideology of balance and the practice of reciprocity which characterises Nagovisi matriliny. Also of significance to the issue of gender equality here is dualism, based on the perceived similarities of pairs. Here the sexes, like other cultural pairs (e.g., moiety eponyms), are neither logically nor otherwise opposed to each other, but follow a model of sameness (Rosaldo 1980b; Atkinson 1983).

Matrilineal by contrast with patrilineal societies have long been assumed to make possible what was once called 'high status' for women (Martin and Voorhies 1975); in the previous chapter, Chowning challenges the universality of such association. Nagovisi women do have substantial and important rights. However, these do not come at the expense of men's rights. Rather there is an equality between men and women, the source of which I hope to elucidate in this essay. This equality is neither a matter of identity (as in Lamphere's definition of sexual equality 1977:613), nor, although it results from reversing gender attributes in the different contexts in which men and women must act, is it to be understood in terms of 'complementarity' (Schlegel 1978b; Hoskins, Chapter 7).

The south Bougainville groups (non-Austronesian speaking Buin, Siwai, Nagovisi, Nasioi and the Austronesian-speaking Banoni) probably shared important similarities pre-contact times as they do today. Settlement pattern was one of dispersed hamlets, based on a matrilineal,[2] probably uxorilocal, core of females and their spouses and children. Subsistence activities involved swidden horticulture with taro (*Colocasia esculenta*) as the main crop. Pigs were raised for ceremonial pork feasts, and the diet was supplemented by the hunting of feral pigs, possum, flying fox and various birds, fishing in the streams, and the gathering of fungi, miscellaneous wild greens and yams, nuts and insects. Political leadership was achieved and men's activities involved feuding, head-hunting and feasting in the club-house. Other ceremonial occasions included feasts marking events in the life cycle of individuals: these were managed by women. Shell valuables, traded from the islands to the south, were used in certain kinds of exchange, such as pig-acquisition, marriage and compensation payments.

Among their neighbours, Nagovisi seem to be at one end of a continuum. H. Thurnwald's work (1938:232f.) on the Nagovisi of the early 1930s, based on information supplied by the resident Catholic priest, makes clear the 'importance' of women, the underdeveloped rank system, the relative scarcity of shell valuables and the lesser emphasis on pig-raising as compared with Buin. In his visit to the Nagovisi area in the late 1930s, Oliver found that in comparison with the Siwai, the Nagovisi were less politically organised and more kinship oriented, with dual organisation and cross-cousin marriage, more strictly uxorilocal and less materially well-off. He noted the comparative 'freedoms' that women enjoyed (1943:57-9). Thus, although in common with other south Bougainville societies Nagovisi is characterised by certain features associated with big man political organisation (such as feasting, pig husbandry, and achieved leadership), comparatively speaking the working of these social features is unorthodox and fits a society with low production and low political development.

Low political development, low production

Nagovisi place great stress upon reciprocity and balance (cf. Ogan 1972; Hamnett 1977), not simply in the exchanges between groups on public occasions, but in other areas as well: individuals seem motivated to maintain parity and balance in a variety of contexts. Accompanying this desire of balance is an ambivalence toward leaders. Indeed, negative attitudes toward leaders are frequently encountered, and people who 'go ahead' too much fear for their lives.[3] In the past, informants claimed people might wreck a big man's house to make him 'as poor as us' or his adherents might actually kill him. There are articulated desires to cooperate ('We only work together when someone dies', was the complaint of one man), but many plans come to nothing (cf. Oliver on similar problems in Siwai, 1955:475-6). What cooperation exists is based largely on mechanical solidarity – individuals wish to participate because of some benefit to themselves which is much the same as the benefits that other participants envision – and little gets done by groups of people. Community scale is small: named lineages might have as many as 80 members but the signs of segmentation into identifiable minimal lineages were evident when a named lineage reached the size of 40 or so persons. Nagovisi predicted a future separation for such minimal lineages. Settlements ranged from small hamlets of 1 to 4 households to larger villages (up to 30 households). The latter were unusual, however, informants holding that larger settlements bred disruption and illness. Feasts, although frequent (especially since the change to sweet potato as the staple following the taro blight of World War II) are small by many Highlands standards (e.g. A. Strathern 1971), generally no more than twenty pigs at a large feast. Resources are always being shifted in small amounts in the context of conflict resolution, accompanying the fine tuning of relations between people.[4]

There is maximum opportunity for personal expression and action, and action generally proceeds in the following manner: someone first proposes a plan and then others, hearing of it, either agree or disagree. Or: someone acts, and others protest; action must come to a halt then until agreement is reached. No one seems to be able to force anyone to do anything,[5] and attrition is a major political tool. Of course, using it oneself also places one at the mercy of others who act in accordance with this principle.

Exchanges of all kinds were supposed to equal out. Feasts were not intended to be competitive, with hosts successively striving to outdo one another (this was a 'Siwai custom', according to informants; but see Connell 1977). Post-feast evaluations turned upon whether appropriate recompense had been made, with excess bringing criticism, just as insufficiency did. The desire for balance extended beyond the context of feast-giving between affinally related groups to the everyday and personal; for example, adultery on the part of one's spouse might be satisfactorily avenged by taking lovers of one's own. In former times, killing someone to restore the balance was more important than keeping up the numbers of one's own group. Informants told of men who, for this reason, in the course of feuds had killed their own lineage mates on behalf of their affines.

The use of shell valuables, also, stressed equivalent exchanges, rather than investment or profit-making. Informants stated that shell valuables were 'like people': important non-exchange uses of these items included decorating infants and destroying valuables at someone's death. There were no forms of currency valuables as there were in Siwai (Oliver 1955) or Buin (R. Thurnwald 1934); Nagovisi knew of these but thought they were 'trash'.

Marriage prestations have a long history (Nash 1974; 1978a), but for the present purposes the following points are significant. In the past, shell valuables were used for marriages of the children of high-ranking people only: most other marriages were made without exchanges of any kind. Probably many Nagovisi would agree with Ogan's Nasioi informant who said of past marriages, 'Basically we just exchanged people' (personal communication).[6] Even the high-ranking favoured a kind of exchange called *aparito* (that is, equal numbers of identical pieces). Any marriage exchange would figure in the later calculation of mortuary payments made for children of the couple and between spouses' survivors. Although groomprice was practised up to the mid-1930s, marriage prestations today consist of universal bridewealth; shell valuables are not used to control the young. I recall only one instance in which a man was threatened (quite justifiably) with the denial of shell valuables in order to block a non-exogamous union, and the threat was not carried out.

Another traditional use of shell valuables was in fights – recruiting allies and paying compensation for those killed in one's cause. Heirloom jewelry, never used in transactions today, was said to be exchanged only in the forging of a permanent truce between two hostile lineages. The belief today is that the widespread distribution of shell valuables (nowadays there is scarcely a household which does not control some strands of it) has permitted people to indulge in misbehaviour, secure in the knowledge that they can buy off whomever they offend, whether this be by insult, blows or adultery. Thus rather than, or perhaps in addition to, being seen as investment in pig production or in the means to pigs (i.e., spouses), shell valuables are seen as enabling one to act upon one's impulses – to express anger, or obtain revenge and sexual gratification.[7] The things for which such valuables were most readily given were matters involving human beings – their feelings, their work, their sexual favours, their blood – not other material items.

Nagovisi society, then, may be characterised in Fried's (1967) terms as one of low political development, where the desire to be the equal, rather than to be the superior or inferior of others, is strong. Social life was concerned with circulating, rather than accumulating or increasing, things and obligations, ranging from shell valuables to personal names. Reciprocity was a way of restoring, replicating and replacing, not of increasing or profiting. Money tokens were anthropomorphised as individuals with peculiar characteristics and idiosyncratic histories. As such, they were not fully or primarily mediators between things or people (cf. Schieffelin 1980; Modjeska 1982); in transactions, shell valuables were seen as substitutes rather than equivalences, often subtly creating a new dimension in a relationship, rather than cancelling a debt.

At the same time, the desire to act on one's own, the general social approval of this stance of individualism, and the awareness of inequalities implied by rank relationships, provided the internal contradiction which makes the ideology of reciprocity and balance consistent with political aspirations typical of big man politics: for those who wished to try, well, good luck to them. As long as others did not object, an ambitious person might well succeed in organising others – as well as his own reputation. Individualism here is consistent then with an achievement ideology: people should do as they please, in so far as others do not mind.

The material basis of life and the social relations of production were consistent with such low political development: there is evidence that Nagovisi gardening produced fewer pigs than either Buin or Siwai gardening did. Pigs are fed on what amounts to surplus human food: scraps and the less desirable of the roots. Both Oliver (1949b:28; 1943:57) and my informants indicated that there were fewer pigs in Nagovisi in the past. Oliver made his comparisons with the Siwai of 1938, whereas my informants said that there were fewer pigs in the pre-war taro days than there were in the period after the sweet potato was adopted as the staple food. One informant said, 'Sweet potato turned everyone into a big man', that is, allowed them to produce sufficient garden food so as to raise and trade pigs. Oliver (1949a:13) implies that pig raising was also more important in Buin. Horticultural output was evidently greater in both Siwai and Buin than in Nagovisi, allowing a larger pig population to be supported. Nagovisi say that because of the scarcity of pigs in the past, many feasts included smoked possum meat and that mourners (who today are given gifts of pork) may have been sent smoked possum or bamboo tubes of almonds in the days before sweet potato became the staple.

It is difficult to compare the efforts that women in these different societies give to their gardens. Although active, Nagovisi women do not give the impression of being overworked, and rarely go to the garden more than three times a week (Mitchell 1976). To count 'hours in the garden' is misleading, for women by no means get down to their tasks in a businesslike manner – they stop at villages en route to chat and chew betel, and once in the garden, they cook snacks, tend to small children, bathe, and so on. In other words, 'work' is not well differentiated into a separate category. However, one observation indicative of intercultural differences in Melanesia comes from the work of a woman from Mt Hagen married into a village just outside the study area: all aver that she far exceeds Nagovisi women in her gardening efforts.

As Godelier remarked for Baruya, the effect thus is that for the ordinary person 'one has no need to accumulate wealth in order to reproduce life and kinship relations. There is thus no internal articulation or direct connection between material production and the reproduction of kinship relations. In this logic, the production of pigs, like subsistence activities, remains of relatively low value' (1982:31).

Dualism and pairs in Nagovisi

I have stressed that Nagovisi are much concerned with reciprocity and balance between individuals and social groups, however defined. Such concerns relate to the maintenance of relationships between pairs and an emphasis on dualism. My first field trip to Nagovisi was made in the wake of dual organisation studies, and since the Nagovisi were reported to have exogamous moieties (Oliver 1949a:13), I was prepared to find an elegant dualistic cosmology. Alas, I sought long and fruitlessly for the evidence.[8]

Nagovisi moieties are exogamous and totemic; yet their eponyms (Eagle and Hornbill) are not logically opposed to one another, but thought instead to be similar (cf. Lancy and Strathern 1981). Both birds are seen to be 'like people' in that they are believed to be monogamous, have 'houses', and produce only one offspring at a time (although this fits the hornbill case, Nagovisi know little about the habits of eagles; they are rarely seen in the area). Moieties are also associated with the sister-in-law ancestresses, Makonai and Poreu/Poana. Makonai was 'good' and Poreu/Poana was 'bad' – she killed children and cooked her taro by exposing it to the sun, until Makonai showed her about fire. There is no well-developed set of complementary oppositions drawing on the relationship between day/night, good/bad, sacred/profane or male/female. Genderising of the world is minimal.

A male–female distinction is, however, applied in a logical, extended way to differences involving physical strength. The right hand is said to be male, because it is stronger;[9] lightning is either male or female – female lightning flashes across the sky and male lightning kills things – people and trees, for example; fish which jump over weirs are believed to be male, whereas those which cannot, a big-mouthed variety, are said to be female. These notions are more support for ideas of male strength than ways of dichotomising men and women. Logical extensions do not employ gender as it is employed, for example, among the Maring of New Guinea, where women are associated with death, decay, cold and slime and are hence polluting (Buchbinder and Rappaport 1976). Hertz (1973) argued that while oppositions may give the appearance of symmetry (his example was the two hands) they imply an asymmetry (as seen in the abilities of the hands) and in fact constitute value judgments. This construction of dualism is not typical for Nagovisi; indeed, it can be argued that an ideology which favoured male-female asymmetry was lacking.

As in the case of the moiety eponyms, Nagovisi dualism involves an emphasis on pairs which are seen as similar; actions between paired entities consist of reciprocity, reversal (as in *awaitowai* in kinship terminology and behaviour[10]) and interchangeability, which comes from a 'model of sameness' (Rosaldo 1980b; Atkinson 1983 provide Austronesian examples of this phenomenon). Pairs are not constructed as halves of a whole (as would appear to be the case in Kodi, described in the next chapter), but as two of a kind with certain differentiating qualities.

The different kinds of pairs which Nagovisi link together include brothers-in-law, who are portrayed as different but similar animals in just-so stories, sometimes antagonistic and other times helpful. Two examples follow:

The rhinocerous beetle and the firefly were walking along one night. The beetle said to the firefly, 'Isn't it fortunate that I have this light so we can see the way?' The firefly said, 'Sorry, brother-in-law, but it's my light.' The beetle said, 'It certainly is not yours; it's mine.' So the firefly turned his light off for a moment and the beetle tripped in the dark and broke his mouth on a cane thorn. That's why the rhinocerous beetle's mouth is split as it is.

The millipede was going to give the centipede all his strength and they went down to the garden where he started, but the sun got very hot and the millipede had to retreat before he could finish. That's why a centipede only makes you sick instead of killing you; he didn't get all the millipede's strength.

Neither has the advantage at the beginning of the story, but in the first account, one pays the other off for 'offending' him. In the second, the unsatisfactory outcome of an incomplete transaction makes reference to the important quality of strength.

Things which are the same may also be described as brothers, differing only in relative age. Man and woman are usually construed as husband and wife with a difference in one dimension;[11] here, too, the idea is a kind of sameness. People claimed that a large sacred stone in the river had two wives, which were adjacent smaller stones. Someone jokingly referred to a small sore as the wife (meaning, similar to) of a larger one next to it. As one informant put it, 'married people are like one person in two skins'. The qualities which differentiate the sexes understood as husband and wife are strength and talk. These qualities are not opposed to one another, that is, they are not considered together to form a single whole. Although attributed separately to men and women, it is important to note that they are reversed when referring to brother and sister.

Men and strength

Men provide the primary energy source: they are supposed to have physical strength. The justification of groomprice was to buy the strong hand of the man for work in the gardens (H. Thurnwald 1934:168, 1938). Masculine physical strength (especially upper body strength) is as 'natural' a characteristic of men as the ability to bear children is for women: all men have this strength (barring some abnormality[12]) and all men use it. The term strength also refers to the ability to know and control powerful spells. Women were not expected to be strong like men.[13]

Men were also strong enough to kill people.[14] In pre-contact days, some young men were fighters, killers, and had violent tempers (cf. Keesing n.d.). Sometimes these people were able to get their way because others were frightened to confront them. Anyone making such a person angry risked getting killed, and occasionally people were said to have killed others simply because they were in bad moods. Perhaps people who were troublesome laid themselves open to be killed, because there was no other effective way to make them change their behaviour. The term *pikonara* was used for these angry killers. The word derives from the term *piko*, a magical substance made at cremations and mixed with lime which was said to 'sharpen a man like a knife'. Its purpose was to 'make trouble', to make a person 'angry', and to make a person 'strong' in fights. The term used to mean 'to smite/kill' (*tavi*) is also used in the construction 'to make (something happen)'. For example, I feel sad, *ni piapiamoi*; it makes me feel sad, *te piapiamotavi*; my father is making him stop, *mmake te kametavi*. It means, then, not only to kill/smite but 'to cause', that is, to apply force to make something happen.

Usually, of course, strength was directed not towards killing people, but towards doing ordinary jobs on behalf of one's wife and children. Heavy horticultural work was the main thing: the felling of trees and, in the old days, garden fencing. Doubtless, these jobs were more difficult and time-consuming in the past (until after World War II) than in present times, because of the comparative growing requirements of taro by contrast with sweet potato (up to five harvests of sweet potato may be taken from the same plot; taro depleted the soil after one crop), and the fact that pigs foraged freely, requiring that all gardens be fenced against their depredations. In pre-steel tool days (the latter part of the nineteenth century), the work would have been more onerous still. Men's work enabled women to do their work; they protected the family from ambush during times of feuding. Earning shell valuables also came from strength,[15] but was a kind of bonus. Men's ability to do this on behalf of their daughters would be acknowledged in the course of mortuary exchanges.

Women's talk

Women's power to make things happen is through talk. Not only do women play an essential part in lineage discussions and decision making with regard to pig distributions, land use and compensation settlement in a more general sense their talk greatly influences public opinion. The differences between these kinds of talk and oratory, by and large a male concern, are discussed below.

Women are said to be 'strong in the mouth', referring to their inclination to talk and the effect of this talk. In matters involving pigs and shell valuables, as one informant put it, the wishes of women cannot be ignored. No doubt rights to plan the disposal of wealth items derive from matrilineal rules which make women the repositories of shell valuables and important actors in pig raising and the production of feasts. Women also take part in the discussion and planning of these events. But they can stay out of the active side of planning and make their wishes known in the form of a veto. A man once remarked to me during a dispute over the details of a feast, 'The women want to have the feast now – we know this because they haven't made any objections.' Objections by women are efficacious, and those women who are forthright or even outspoken help to change the rank of their lineages. If a woman's talk 'goes ahead' of other, more genealogically senior women, the former may find her lineage rising in prominence. This means that the renown of that lineage increases, and the involvement of its members in the community and clan affairs is greater. Such events may attract the resentment of others, since the exercise of power or advantage is frequently resented. Women here compete with other women, not with men.

Women's tongues are said to be 'sharp'. The term *iri* is found in a number of relevant contexts: *irida*, acid (as in oranges); *take iriwo*, the sun is hot; *irimoi*, I feel angry; *irimas*, sharp (knife, tongue). Sharpness, heat and anger are evoked here as primordial energising qualities which create action. Angry words can be goads, insults, one-liners, and these generally will set a series of events into motion. Talk which took the form of insults could get a person injured or killed in pre-contact days. Sometimes, one insult would set off a series of killings and counter-killings. Today, there is a constant round of small suits, including many for slander and hurt feelings, which arise from women's talk. The Nagovisi seem not to have changed much in this respect from the way they were described in 1934 by H. Thurnwald (1938), who wrote that they were 'extraordinarily sensitive to insults'. Talk can be the major reason for the failure of trial marriages – people do not want their children to marry into a place where the women 'talk'.

Talk in this sense is political. The substantive has the primary meaning of dispute – something subject to litigation. When it does not lead to an actual court case, talk still has the effect of fragmenting plans and making revisions necessary to accommodate those who have objections. Talk as such means that revisions are required. This may sidetrack or throw off course the plans of the group, whether a lineage, a group of lineages attempting to cooperate, or a few households. These effects of talk relate to the low level of political development and the difficulties in cooperation which Nagovisi readily acknowledge. Individuals, however, achieve satisfaction for themselves. They air their complaints and may even see something done about problems they perceive. People rarely have to do things that they do not wish to do, although they may be prevented from doing some of the things they want to do.

The power of talk in preindustrial societies is often located in oratory (Bloch 1975). Nagovisi women do not orate; this is a style that men may use. However, oratory is not explicitly associated with men as an attribute of gender, but is rather seen as a special ability that some people have.[16] Many men shun public speaking, and those who try but flounder are relentlessly imitated in jest long after. Furthermore, oratory is a limited kind of talk, heard largely in court settings. It summarises, gives generalised sorts of good advice, or repeats in a personal and stylised way information which has been said before or decisions which have been made elsewhere. Thus, it is not at the heart of decision-making, and women's non-participation here means little with regard to their impact on public affairs.

Around nearly every event of importance, a veil of versions[17] is built up through (non-oratorial) talk. These begin to have an existence which may itself cause problems. The local big man used to advise, during times when sorcery accusations were circulating, that people in our village simply not talk about a particular subject at all. It is notable that he did not advise denying one version, or trying to find out 'the truth', but rather guided discussion. Nagovisi women spend much time together in the village meeting house[18] where daily events are discussed and where passers-by rest if they are travelling the road through the village. That their behaviour may be atypical among their neighbours is suggested by the following anecdote:

A Siwai man told my male informant that if he [the Siwai] were married to a Nagovisi woman, he would probably kill her because she would make him so angry. The named infuriating practice was Nagovisi women's habit of going around to other women's houses and talking with them in groups rather than staying at home. My informant retorted that Siwai women had their faults, too: he alleged that unlike Nagovisi women, Siwai females won't greet you if you pass them on the road, but look down and say nothing. 'You think they're angry at you', he said.

Actually, Nagovisi men sometimes complain about Nagovisi women's talk themselves. They complain about their 'indiscretion' (Nash 1978b). For example, according to men, there is always the risk that should one invite a woman to copulate that she will answer in a loud voice so that others can hear, 'What? So-and-so wants to have sex relations with me?' Rather than attributing this so-called indiscretion to a lack of self-control as men are apt to do, perhaps this can be seen as a matter of women's use of their talk to register events. Men guard their talk and believe themselves to be discreet; women bring things out into the open and earn complaints from men when talk is not managed to masculine advantage. So women's talk is a kind of freedom of expression they feel entitled to exercise and a way of protecting their interests by broadcasting information.

Nagovisi reversals: 'men' and 'women'

When Nagovisi say that men are strong and women talk, they are referring to husband and wife. When we look at the interactions between the other important pair – namely, brother and sister, members of the same matrilineage – and note expectations for the behaviour of each, these gender attributes appear reversed.

Women of the descent group are called just that – *maniku* means 'women' and the male members are referred to as the 'men' (*nuga*). Husbands are collectively *motai* (the coconut eaters). Because of uxori-local residence, 'men' and 'women' do not see each other on a daily basis as adults. They meet on descent group occasions, however, and have certain common interests. Both are believed to own descent group property, but only sisters use it and add to it; brothers advise about its future. Thus, women have the material and labour involvement with matrilineage assets, land and shell valuables.[19] They are the ones who plant food and cash crops on matrilineage ground with which to support their families. Trees with edible or useful products are also planted on matrilineage ground; while unmarried brothers have a right to use the produce from these trees, after they marry, their sisters may ask them not to take it any more. It is quite within the sisters' rights to take all the produce for themselves, their children and their husbands: brothers ought not get angry about this. Sisters can also deny unmarried brothers the use of matrilineage shell valuables for dubious projects of their own;[20] again, this is entirely within their rights.

In the 1930s while still a bachelor, Lapisto intended to remove a self-imposed taboo on eating pork he had assumed as a sign of mourning. He asked his parallel cousin Piskaro for a high-valued shell strand in order to buy the pig with which to do so. She refused to let him have it. He got angry and went away to work on a coastal plantation, but told me (years later, of course) that she had been perfectly within her rights to act as she had.

Brothers talk about matrilineage assets.[21] A brother is an adviser to his own lineage: he should be consulted as to the disposition of descent group assets and in matters affecting the younger members of the group (e.g., marriage prestations, or when young people get themselves into difficulties). Should he and his sisters fail to reach agreement, bad feeling will result, and such a situation is to be avoided. Males act as guardians of descent group morality and avengers of affronts of an immoral nature towards both male and female members of their descent group. Men testify on matters concerning the traditions of their descent groups in court; however, a man must not testify on behalf of his own lineage if such testimony would conflict with the interests of his wife and children.

Thus, we see brothers using the supposedly 'female' talk and women using the supposedly 'male' physical strength when it comes to lineage assets. To some extent, these equations are submerged: men and women are not characterised by these practices. But talking women, who roundly insult husbands and other women, should not insult brothers: they cannot use offensive language to a brother, it being shameful to do so. Strong men, who work hard for wives and children, cannot work in their sisters' gardens on a regular basis: it would be embarrassing and suggest a highly improper sexual connection. Shame constrains and is powerfully felt.

Gender attributes in Nagovisi are consequently dependent on the context of men's and women's actions. As husband and wife, a man is strong and a woman talks; these characterise their efficacy as individuals. Men's garden work, and killing or defence in earlier times, are visible and external, as is the talk of women, whether as 'political commentary' with sisters and friends, in arguments or in statements about how the household resources will be used. The context for these is the routines of daily life, the social realities which relate to stereotypes uppermost in Nagovisi conceptions of gender. As brother and sister, however, 'men' and 'women' (*nuga* and *maniku*) reverse styles of agency within the matrilineal unit. Now 'men' talk and 'women' are strong. These associations are muted and taken for granted, with attention focused not so much on individual actors but on the effectiveness and cooperation of the matrilineage. Rules of shame which govern broad sexual and economic matters explicitly bind the concerns of the matrilineal unit from other interests people have (especially as husband and wife, and in the related world of 'big man' politics).

The reversal of male and female attributes through the devices of opposition and complementarity of the sexes appear to typify many Papua New Guinea societies (Bateson 1958; Clay 1977; Gewertz 1981; M. Strathern 1981; Lutkehaus 1982 are but a few examples). The contexts in which male–female reversal or transformation takes place are frequently the temporally bounded activities of play and ritual. Bateson's description of initiation among the Iatmul is perhaps the first and best known description and analysis of this phenomenon.

Recognition of two contexts where actions, meanings and symbols are reversed implies a kind of elusive equality: that whatever men and women may do in the course of daily life, there are settings in which these behaviours are abandoned and reversed. The reversals are short-lived (bounded in time) but routinely repeated (traditional). Indeed, Errington states that for Karavar in New Britain such episodes reveal cultural themes more tellingly than does everyday life (1974:32). And yet there is something flimsy as well as powerful about these reversals. Female supremacy in ritual contexts does not afford women a material basis to resist male meanness in everyday life, nor do amicable everyday relations between the sexes mitigate the asymmetrical male-oriented excesses of ritual (Tuzin 1982). Yet ritual makes a powerfully felt, naggingly insistent connection to a world of emotion which cannot be dismissed, even though it has paradoxically little effect on the ordering of daily life.

For Nagovisi, matrilineage matters in which the brother–sister pair (with their 'reversed' gender attributes) operate are also bounded and short-lived – in the sense of organising mortuary feasts, for example, or deciding what to do about young people fornicating – but there is little that is indirect or in need of deciphering; instead, there is prolonged planning in meetings and then intensive deployment of concentrated (meat or shell) resources. Men do not bow out or give over centre stage to women during these times as 'context' changes, as in the ritual reversals mentioned above, or for that matter as it appears in Hoskins' account of Kodi women's participation in mourning (Chapter 7). Daily life is not suspended as on a holiday or during a period of mourning: bounded activities do not replace daily life; they are instead added to it.

And so, for Nagovisi, the two conceptions of gender (husband/wife and brother/sister relations) appear mixed up in time and space, such that a different kind of 'balance' is achieved – not an oscillating balance, but one made up of many strands woven together. Life lived only in the matrilineage or in the household is not conceivable; they must exist simultaneously. What gives women efficacy in the household is their position in their matrilineages and what lets men talk in the matrilineage is their claims on wives' property (such that they are not competing with sisters for the use of matrilineage resources). Thus, to speak of 'complementarity' and 'balance', as Schlegel does for the matrilineal Hopi as a stand-off (or indeed as unrecognised female advantage)[22] between female-oriented household and clan and male-controlled community organisation (1978b:347; also 1978a) does not reflect the Nagovisi situation. This is why distinctions between the domestic/public or ritual/secular domains cannot employ gender constructs and indeed make little sense in Nagovisi (Nash 1978b).

Reproduction and procreation

Nagovisi gender is associated with traits not directly connected to reproductive difference. The resultant relationship between men and women is to be contrasted with that of societies in which gender differences do rest on anatomical or physiological characteristics. Gender always involves mystification, but in Nagovisi, it is not primary sexual characteristics which are mystified, as in other parts of Melanesia (e.g. Herdt 1981; and the essays in Brown and Buchbinder 1976).

What about the perception of primary sexual differences, then? Nagovisi appear to consider sex to be what we in the West might recognise as a drive: it is part of human nature.[23] All people are believed to enjoy and seek heterosexual activity (perhaps not on all occasions, but no one is reluctant all the time). Heterosexual activity is not seen as a distasteful social duty to procreate children or please insatiable wives, as in parts of mainland Papua New Guinea (e.g. Gewertz 1982:314; Kelly 1976; Meggitt 1964b). Sex is a force of great attraction, but also disruption, and must be controlled. Conduct between persons of the opposite sex is predicated on sexual availability; etiquette of avoidance has sexual overtones and exists to prevent what would otherwise be likely but wrong. Avoidance etiquette conflates blood relations and forbidden affines on grounds of the impropriety of sexual relations with all such persons. It applies between opposite sex siblings and many affines. Men and women are said, after all, to be like dogs and meat. Joking relationships between men and women involve numerous ribald references to copulation, real and imaginary.

Adultery is common and almost expected. When detected, it is infuriating (therefore always causing action), but it is fixable, however, and in uncomplicated cases is thought to be a private matter (between husband, wife and correspondents). It usually does not threaten the marriage bond, men's relationships with other men, nor women's with women. Rape is practically non-existent; indeed, in response to my queries, people could not quite imagine how it would work ('the woman would cry out [and people would help her]'). Group rape is unheard of; it is not a punishment for wayward women (Berndt 1962; M. Strathern 1972). Promiscuous women may be gossiped about or openly teased, but no attempt is made (beyond urging marriage to one of their lovers) to restrain or correct them.

An extremely common form of insult in Nagovisi is to accuse or suggest mismanaged copulation: for instance, a man who complained that his wife did not go to the garden enough was told by her to 'stop screwing me so much, then, and I won't have all these children to take care of'. A woman angry at her husband for giving her tobacco to another couple told him to go copulate with them instead of her. The classical insult in Nagovisi refers to copulation with an opposite sex sibling. One obscure and now defunct sexual custom in Nagovisi involved women paying men either for their attractiveness or in the course of a context in which a man would demonstrate control over his sexual urges (Nash 1981:112). Men's sexuality and women's desire, men's attractiveness and women's appraisal of it, were thus given recognition. Other details can be briefly mentioned. There were no beliefs in pollution from sexual fluids, including menstrual blood and lochia. Married couples inhabited the same house, and this was in fact a sign of marriage; there were no separate residential men's houses for married men. There are surely many areas of sexual practice on which I have no information from Nagovisi, but from other societies in the region, the evidence is suggestive. In pre-contact Siwai, heterosexual orgies were said to be held before enemies were attacked (Oliver 1955:415); sexual activity was energising, not depleting. In Lesu on New Ireland, heterosexual orgies were held in connection with a stage of male initiation (Powdermaker 1933:136).

Regarding beliefs on reproduction,

Our [Rosaldo's and Atkinson's] initial hunch in 1975, inspired by Ortner's influential 1974 article, was that an emphasis upon childbearing would play up the differences between the sexes. The Wana represent a case in which sexual reproduction is heavily stressed. But instead of emphasizing the physiological differences between women and men, Wana's concern with procreation appears to deny differences and to assert an identity between men's and women's reproductive roles. (Atkinson 1983:6)

Much the same can be said for Nagovisi. Husbands (*motai*) can be described as 'the ones who make children'. Father–child ties are predicated on the obligation to nurture: father cares for his children when they are young and they for him when he is old. Children are 'between' parents and must, for example, observe both parents' clan food taboos until they are older. Men say that they have freedom before marriage, whereas after it, they must always think of their children.[24] The importance of the father and his responsibility toward his children are seen in men's legal liability for certain kinds of sexual indiscretions: violating the post-partum sex taboo, supposedly causing miscarriages through sex relations, making sickly wives bear too many children,[25] having sex relations with a woman who was still passing lochia. Both partners are believed at fault, but the husband usually pays the fine.

Injury fines and mortuary payments which pass between affines are also testimony to this connection. Whenever a man is injured (e.g., cuts himself with his machete, falls off his bike on the way to work) the children must pay for this blood: they must pay fines to his descent group (that is, his wife and children pay his sisters). The children are considered to be the reason the man was hurt – they are his reason for exerting himself, the reason he acts. The same is true of the bigger mortuary payments which articulate with all the outstanding debts and obligations between affines.

The ceremonial focus of traditional religion was to protect children of both sexes while they were growing up, to encourage a proper rate of growth (not too slow), and to mark their 'firsts' (for example, first bath, first visit to the garden, first taste of pork) with public feasting and ritual. Women were in charge of these affairs. Their female orientation can be seen in a number of ways: they are held during the day, when women are free to attend, women comprise the majority of the assembled, women bring their shell valuables to decorate the honoured persons, women evoke the ancestral spirits, Makonai or Poreu/Poana, depending on the moiety affiliation of the person being honoured. The association of women and growing-up rites is clear in Siwai (Oliver 1955:140f.) and Buin (Keil 1975:105).

Pregnancy and childbirth were a focus of herbal and magical attention, and children might be strengthened or killed by the performance of magical acts upon the mother. Women showed stoicism in childbirth; to cry in the pain of labour was ridiculed. A post-partum sex taboo was observed by both parents in order to space children and protect them, and contraceptive herbs and magical acts were also used with this intent. Infanticide might be practised to insure the older child's survival if births were too close (Ogan, Nash and Mitchell 1976). Despite the great concern for the health of children, sterility was not a cause for divorce. Indeed, there was little sterility:[26] such as existed was believed to result from a consciously performed magical act on a girl in her childhood. Sorcery was believed to cause infant mortality, especially more than one death in a group of siblings. Atkinson describes the magical properties attributed to the relics of reproduction among the eastern Indonesian Wana; in this connection, one might note in conclusion that in south Bougainville, the club-house demon (spirit familiar of a big man) is manifested as thunder in Buin, a large snake in Siwai and the ghost of a dead child in Nagovisi (see also Wheeler 1912:45).

The relationship of sex and gender to other social differences

As gender ideas do not mystify primary sexual differences (namely, reproductive or anatomical ones), does this mean that other discontinuous, immutable attributes of persons are also played down, while changeable traits are emphasised? Besides sex and gender, in Nagovisi persons are distinguished by rank of lineage, relative age and absolute age. There are ways to treat these potential differences as negotiable: immutable characteristics may be ignored or played down.

Nagovisi apply an idiom of rank to both lineages and people. In the latter case, rank involves added responsibilities, being in the nature of an exemplar rather than implying domination over others. Thus the first-born is a woman who is expected to act as leader in lineage affairs. She has much to do with carrying out funeral obligations – both those concerned with members of her lineage who die and in returning obligations to other lineages where there are affinal ties. She approves the scale of operations and decides whether or not to enter into payment of claim for mortuary dues at this time. Female leaders are named as 'the one who buried/cremated so-and-so', even though clearly many other people are involved in the actual work done. Female leaders also played major roles in the growing-up rites. A leader controls heirloom shell valuables and may destroy them to show anger or sorrow. She is nominally in charge of garden lands, but her actual impact here is curtailed by traditional rights that other women in her group have to make gardens where their mothers did.

Seniority within and between lineages is supposedly a genealogical matter and thus gives the impression of fixity. But Nagovisi say that in addition to the lineage or person which is high ranking because of being first-born, there are the *kaskelo* groups and people – those who became high ranking by effort. The most senior woman of the lineage will not be considered its leader unless she is energetic and has an active and intelligent husband. A younger sister or parallel cousin will supersede her if she lacks these other qualities. Rank thus changes because of the personalities and circumstances of the members of the descent group.

Age differences between persons might seem difficult to manipulate: Nagovisi say they always know who of a pair of persons was born first, even though they did not keep track of birthdates in traditional times. How does one become older than, say, one's father's sister? Here, details from the kinship terminology are relevant. Kin terms may be manipulated easily to create special effects, generally fitting the ways that particular people wish to act toward one another, rather than requiring people to behave in certain ways because of their kinship relationship. Thus, persons of different ages may be able to call each other by chronologically inappropriate terms, for instance, a nine-year old boy may call a 70-year old woman 'wife'. Chronologically younger and kin-categorically junior persons should normally defer to their elders and seniors. A style of 'respect/avoidance' behaviour may be prescribed for certain classes of relative. However, Nagovisi act as though people have the fundamental right to obviate these hierarchical behaviours if desired. Sibling terms incorporate the elder/younger distinction, and these are the ones with the most heterogeneous denotata; for example, *mama* (eZ) is also used for MZeD, FBeD, eBW(ms), WeZ, MBD, FZD, FM, and thus 'elder sister' occurs in both moieties (namely, WeZ) and in alternate generations under ordinary ways of reckoning. The same is generally true for eB, yZ, and yB.[27] This in and of itself scrambles the very chronological relations to which the term supposedly makes reference.

A practice called *torowaiwatata*, 'return of the elder brother', involves men matrilineally related to one and the affines and children of such men. Under *torowaiwatata*, a sibling relationship between a man and his MMB is postulated such that the ZDS calls his MMB's children by the same terms as he calls his own (as he would for any brother) and so on for other relatives (see Table 1 for changes). Such changes affect people of adjacent generations only, because reckoning by the *torowaiwatata*-imposed terms and by ordinary application of kin terms becomes identical at distant, i.e., minus-two from Ego and lower, generations. *Torowaiwatata* relationships depend on ties of descent; both the MMB and the ZDS must belong to the same lineage. Thus, such relationships are never postulated between younger men and others of the plus-two generation who are *tata*, e.g., FF, MFZH, etc., unless such men are MMB as well. The effect of the manoeuvre is not so much on the 'siblings' thus created, but on the relatives of the 'siblings'. By means of *torowaiwatata*, people can justify less formal relations: a man treats his daughter very differently from his father's sister or mother-in-law.

The system of namesakes creates similar opportunities for scrambling chronological and categorical age. Names are moiety-specific, sex-specific, and must alternate by generation. Most people have several names. When a child is given the same name as another person, whether or not the person has asked that the child be given this name, a relationship between the two and their circles of kin is created. Each of the namesakes is identified with the other, such that A1 calls A2's mother, 'mother', his father, 'father', etc. and vice versa. Thus, a middle-aged man may call a little girl 'grandmother' and so on.

The notion of *awaitowai*, mentioned above, might also be pointed out again here: since marriages do not always take place between persons in the appropriate generational kin categories, again, possibilities for correct use of several kin terms, sometimes from adjacent generations, between particular individuals is likely for most people. What happens is that the issue of elder/younger – seemingly straightforward and unchanging – gets confounded.

Youth was not disenfranchised. Juniors and children were expected to be deferential to their elders, but had political and property rights equal to adults: the big man's eight-year old son owned a pig of his own, and little boys who did a day's work with the men were always paid the same, despite the fact that they clearly did less work. In traditional times, killing a child counted the same as killing an adult in the system of balances and

Table 1: *Changes caused by* Torowaiwatata

Genealogical referents	Ordinary term	*Torowaiwatata* term	Reciprocal changes
MMBD	*kabo* (FZ, MBW)	inola (D)	*inabalum* (BS, WS) to *mma* (F)
MMBS	*mma* (F, FB)	*inuli* (S)	*inuli* (S) to *mma* (F)
MMBDD	*inalamada, mama* (female cross-cousin, MD)	*inobe* (GC)	*inalaman, tata* (male cross-cousin, WS) to *kaia* (MF)
MMBDS	*inoli* (male cross-cousin, MS)	*inobe* (GC)	*inoli* (male cross-cousin, MS) to *kaia* (MF)

retribution of feuding. A man claimed in a court case (where it is true one hears exaggeration sometimes) that his daughter at age two had distributed pigs on the occasion of her grandfather's mortuary exchanges. Another man came home a little drunk one night and announced that he had chosen a name for his newborn DD meaning 'she doesn't own property', a barb reflecting his view that land distribution subsequent to a recent large mortuary feast had been mismanaged to his children's lineages' disadvantage. Children are in a very real way counted as descent group members. Indeed there was no initiation in Nagovisi of the kind in which groups of boys or girls undergo an experience from which they emerge as different sorts of persons. There was 'first eating in the club-house' (the one I witnessed was run by the women) and 'first killing or first ready-to-kill' (it was not clear which from informants' accounts) for boys, but their ceremonies were individually performed and they were not universal: only the high-ranking could organise them, and usually only the first-born were honoured in this way. The same was true for girl's puberty, which consisted of a feast which took place while the girl apparently stayed inside the house, embarrassed by the whole thing.

Perhaps the emphasis on mortuary exchanges, rather than marriage exchange (a typically 'matrilineal' rather than 'patrilineal' phenomenon, as Gregory 1982:195 has noted) also means that there is less interest in seeing youth as a category to be used in the interest of adults.[28] It is difficult to identify a category analogous to 'legal minor', with a diminished capacity to act. There was a lack of interest in celebrating the transfer of rights over young people in marriage. As I have noted, marriage did not actually require any gift exchange in earlier times. In Nagovisi, the important thing was to 'use' the whole adult life, so to speak, in mortuary assessments. The sorting out and exchanges were done after a person's earthly productive accomplishments were unarguably completed, that is, after death.

Sharing similar qualities

I have tried in this chapter to cite possible relationships between gender equality and the factors which make for low political development and low production with its entailed emphasis on reciprocity. Nagovisi is a society in which we see a dislike of imbalances, whether gain or loss, and its material-productive basis and relations of production (especially before World War II, when taro was the staple) were inadequate for the development of material inequalities.[29] We get some idea of this by comparing pig production for instance, with neighbouring groups: in Nagovisi, pig production was low. The work of women gives further hints about production level. There is a preference for balance in exchanges. Exchange between pairs which are minimally differentiated (whether this be moieties, brothers-in-law, siblings, or spouses) and who may reverse themselves and who may change places under a variety of circumstances seems the model of action.

Complementarity, opposition, dualism and so on are concepts often used in connection with a cultural emphasis on pairs: these are also much stressed in studies of gender. A major analytic tradition for understanding dualism is Hertzian (see Needham 1973) – pairs as unequal parts of a whole. Asymmetry is built into this conception. However, dualism may stress equality and reciprocity, rather than opposition, and this is the kind of dualism we see in Nagovisi. Indeed, there seems almost to be a resistance to making the 'obvious' oppositional connections (cf. the moon and sun example above).

Men and women are usually thought of as playing their normal adult roles as husband and wife, although it is brothers and sisters who are terminologically marked as 'men' and 'women'. The qualities associated with men and women are physical strength and talk respectively; these create action in social life and are motivated by a similar source – heat/anger/sharpness. And there is a stress on sameness here through the device of reversal. Wives talk and sisters use their strength, husbands are strong and brothers give advice. In terms of the multiple roles they play, people are not divided by absolute criteria, but in fact share the same range of qualities.

When it is reproductive differences which divide men and women culturally and socially, the important thing is not the supposed content of these differences. What is important is that nothing can be done about them: they are considered for all practical purposes to be unchangeable. This point is at the core of feminist criticisms of naturalistic explanations of sex differences – although specific attacks may be made upon the substance of allegations about the sexes, the real problem is with the idea that certain attributes are regarded as genetic rather than as a product of experience, so that reproductive differences apparently have the power to confer permanent status. Nagovisi avoid this whole problem by not making reproductive differences the core of gender notions. The attributes of the sexes are not in this sense sexual, and in terms of the range of actions performed by men and women, there is overlap between them, as there is between people of different age and rank.

Notes

1. Many persons and institutions have aided me in writing this chapter. Of course, without the cooperation and hospitality of the Nagovisi people, I could not have attempted to write this at all. For financial support during the periods of fieldwork in Nagovisi, I thank the National Institutes of Mental Health (USA) and the New Guinea Research Unit of The Australian National University. My colleagues in the 'Gender Group' during 1984 – Fred Errington, Deborah Gewertz, Leslie Devereaux, Terry Hays, Janet Hoskins, Roger Keesing, Nick Modjeska, Marie Reay, Marilyn Strathern, Jimmy Weiner and Michael Young – have all been helpful.
2. With the exception of Buin.
3. During my period of fieldwork intermittently from 1969 to 1973, prominent men eschewed ordinary sociable offers of betel nut from others, since lime is traditionally the place where poisonous substances were allegedly put to murder people.
4. Nagovisi have a preference for solving conflict in court-like settings, i.e., where each party tells its story and a third person assesses wrong and sets damages. This may involve extremely minor disputes, for instance 10 cents worth of betel pepper taken without permission by a classificatory grandson, as well as more serious matters. To bring conflicts to court changes the nature of these arguments, converting them from situations of inequality and interdependency to ones of reciprocity, the latter evidently being perceived as a more satisfying way of resolving arguments between people, however related (cf. M. Strathern 1984a).
5. This may have been less the case in pre-contact times, when the possibility that a frustrated person might murder a balker was recognised.
6. Central mountain Eivo do not make marriage prestations, either, and see cross-cousin marriage as a substitute (Hamnett 1977:77).
7. One kind of magical substance is said to increase the general rate of adultery and fornication, with the result of making the shell valuables circulate.
8. A typical incident reveals my attempts: on a clear chilly night, the moon appeared to have a reddish ring around it. A man standing outside with me said, 'The old people would have said that the moon is menstruating.' Eagerly I asked, 'Is the moon a woman?' 'Yes, the moon is a woman', my informant patiently responded. I continued, 'Is the sun then a man – perhaps the moon's huband?' For a moment there was silence. Then he said, 'The old people didn't tell us *that*.'
9. In Buin, the right hand is associated with the maternal relatives and has the palm lines which are said to identify one's descent group. In Nagovisi, both hands are believed to have such lines.
10. The term *awaitowai* means 'reversal' or' reciprocal'. Because people can be related to others in a number of possible ways, it often happens that two persons will be able to trace their relationship to one another in a number of equally valid ways and be able to use several different pairs of kin terms toward one another. This is called *awaitowai*, and it is normal and unavoidable.

11. Faithorn (1975, 1976) has criticised anthropologists for identifying male and female with husband and wife, but the Nagovisi themselves do this.
12. The only impediment to marriage for a man is lack of physical strength; thus, the robust mentally retarded were invariably married whereas the pusillanimous retarded were said to have no chance of finding a spouse. Nagovisi also claimed that because old men lacked physical strength, young Nagovisi women refused to marry them. They believe such matches are possible in Siwai, especially with elderly 'big men'.
13. I misunderstood this cultural expectation for a long time. Because the Nagovisi do not quantify things as we do (e.g., shell valuables are ranked rather than convertible, the language itself lacks true comparatives), the term 'strong' is largely a qualitative one. When Nagovisi say that 'men are strong', they do not mean that women are either less strong, or weak – in fact, they usually say, 'Women are not strong'. This confused me since women were evidently capable of a great deal of work and seemed to me to possess some percentage of men's strength. But I was wrong to think that women played the 'strong' game at all.
14. Women might select whom to be killed in compensation arrangements, but men did the actual murdering. Exceptions caused approving wonderment: one woman killed a Japanese soldier in her garden during World War II.
15. Shell valuables themselves were considered to have strength, too, ' distinct from other value such as scarcity or quality' (Mitchell 1976:38). The loss of this strength was part of the reason for the reluctance to convert or spend such valuables, especially by women.
16. Nagovisi are well aware that young women teachers may be skilled at speaking in public to large groups.
17. I avoid the use of terms like 'gossip' and 'rumour', which may connote falsehood and pettiness.
18. On a side-trip made to Nagovisi in 1938, Douglas Oliver's Siwai companions were reportedly scandalised to see women in Nagovisi club-houses (Oliver 1943:57).
19. One lineage has some sacred shell valuables and an allegedly petrified snake's heart, which, when looked at, confer power to earn more shell valuables. Only the women of the lineage (and their husbands) may view these; men of the lineage may not, lest they gain the ability to earn shell valuables (i.e., for their wives' lineages) at the expense of their own (and sisters') groups.
20. Married brothers, of course, use their wives' matrilineage resources.
21. The testimony of the *nuga* is preferred to that of the *motai* in court cases involving land, because it is believed that the *nuga* have nothing to gain by lying about the extent of the holdings, the position of borders, mortuary transactions in the past, whereas the *motai* are the 'men who want ground', i.e., for their wives' and children's matrilineages.
22. It is curious that Schlegel implies that equality results from institutional female strength plus institutional male weakness:

    The strength of the matrilocal household and the matrilineal clan and the relative weakness of male-controlled community organization are important factors leading to sexual equality in this society. Another is female ownership of houses and control of land, which, although usually allocated by men, is held in usufruct right by women. Women also control the allocation and exchange of agricultural produce, which is not only the staple food but also a major product for trade with other tribes. These factors provide the material structural bases for female equality, which is reinforced by the cosmic principle of the female as the source of life. (Schlegel 1978b:347-8)

    In the absence of any clear way to match or measure the balance alleged to exist between men and women, it seems as though Schlegel arguing that what is required for sexual equality is in fact female superiority. Does this assertion hide an assumption that men are somehow naturally inclined to dominate women and that their tendencies must be culturally overbalanced?
23. It has been noted in anecdotal and impressionistic ways that matrilineal societies evince fewer stresses with regard to heterosexual relations than, for example, patrilineal ones (Friedl 1975:73). There are more 'freedoms', fewer constraints – but it must be stressed

that attributes of matrilineal societies are not 'natural' (as the evolutionists of the nineteenth century thought (Bachofen 1861; Morgan 1887; McLennan 1865) and as Allen seems to be saying (1981, 1984)): they are cultural phenomena.

24. When a young man left his wife shortly after their child was born (an extremely unusual occurrence), a big man talked to him and said, 'Don't you want to give some money to buy your child some little things (i.e., clothing)?' The young man said, 'Absolutely not'. According to the big man, who recounted this exchange to me, this response indicated to him that the young man was crazy. Two other alleged indices of craziness (from the behaviour of a man who seemed perhaps to be schizophrenic) were (1) asking a classificatory daughter to copulate with him and (2) refusing to attend his mother's funeral. Lapses such as these are taken as signs of a serious disorder.

25. One informant claimed that in the past, a woman's father might kill her husband for repeatedly causing pregnancies at short intervals. Other less drastic sanctions involved extensive destruction of property.

26. Combining the figures of Chinnery for Nagovisi and Siwai (referring to 1929 but published in a report dated 1924) and Thurnwald (1934:164), re-examined by Jared Keil (1975, 1979) for Buin, female sterility in Siwai ranged around 12%, at least 12% and perhaps more (but probably not 35% as Thurnwald claims) in Buin, but only 3% in Nagovisi (see Nash 1981:124). Does this suggest that as Friedl has argued (1975) when fewer stresses and strains cluster around heterosexual intercourse, impediments to conception are reduced?

27. I follow anthropological convention here: M mother, F father, Z sister, B brother, D daughter, S son, e elder, y younger, etc. Thus yZ = younger sister.

28. Mortuary exchanges have proven stable (unchanging in form according to reconstruction of past events based on informants' accounts) whereas marriage exchanges have varied widely in the past 80 years or so. Mortuary feasts involve a series of occasions and sizeable expenditure; marriage is a single event (now often Christian) and costs much less.

29. Nagovisi seem to like moving assets around through work and talk rather than creating more assets. There is always the notion that things should be circulating, whether this is kin terms, names, shell valuables, or today, cash.

CHAPTER 7

Complementarity in this world and the next: gender and agency in Kodi mortuary ceremonies

JANET HOSKINS

Eastern Indonesian societies are often depicted as pervaded by 'complementary dualism', a characterisation of social difference in terms of contrasting pairs which together designate a single whole. Gender is perhaps the most consistently evoked structuring principle within these systems. From the dyads of ritual language to the description of objects exchanged in ceremonial prestations, a metaphoric opposition of male and female qualities is used to express relations of contrast and interdependence. Exactly what is constituted by the 'complementarity' between male and female domains? And what implications does the division of categorical oppositions offer for effective social action?

At its most abstract level, 'complementary dualism' could be applied to any system of classification in which various elements are linked in contrastive association with an opposing particular (Needham 1980:41). When applied to contrasts such as day/night, sun/moon, or living/dead, gender identifications may serve as a simple 'principle of difference', signalling the halves of a whole conceptual entity. But when applied to persons, to the description of the appropriate roles of men and women, they acquire the capacity to differentiate potencies and values. The personification of the dead as male or female creates a possible asymmetry between men and women in the ways that they may act towards their ancestors, and differentiates human agency as well as cosmological divisions.

The complementarity which is observable in the everyday division of labour and friendly mixing of the sexes in most endeavours is paired with a series of more complex notions about appropriate forms of male and female action in relation to the afterworld. I shall examine indigenous notions of gender and agency among the Kodi people at the western tip of Sumba in the Lesser Sunda island chain. As speakers of an Austronesian language who are also heavily involved in traditional feasting and

174

exchange, they bear strong resemblances to many groups in seaboard Melanesia, and particularly the Massim (see the chapters by Macintyre and Young). But the elaboration of gender complementarity in oral traditions and dyadic verse seems a particularly Indonesian characteristic. Since some 80 per cent of the 45,000 Kodi speakers still cling to the worship of *marapu* or ancestral deities, the regulation of relations with the spirit world is seen by them as crucial to harmonious social life. Complementarity of male and female in this world is linked to maintaining the balance of complementary forces in the world to come, and both domains must be explored simultaneously to reach a better understanding of how gender structures Kodi notions of inequality and agency.

The specific context on which this discussion will focus is mortuary ceremonies, where a contrast between two types of agency emerges most clearly. Several scholars have noted that women often have prominent roles in death rituals, even when their presence is muted and less visible in other public contexts (e.g. Bloch and Parry 1982; Huntington and Metcalf 1979). More specifically, women in many societies – including the Kodi – seem to have been designated the vessels of kinship emotions, and the most vocal sufferers in mourning. In other societies, such as the Trobriands, this association has been linked to 'control over the regenesis of human life', and the continuity of life and death in the widest sense (A. Weiner 1976:283). But before we rush too eagerly into the mystical embrace of this idea of women as 'innately tied to the continuity of life' and 'the locus for the means by which human survival transcends itself' (A. Weiner 1976:234), I suggest a detour through Kodi mortuary ceremonies, where the dynamic is slightly different. Like Trobriand women, Kodi women are brought into the forefront of attention at funerals, and play important roles as singers and ritual actors. Women are the agents who separate the soul from the living and from its particularistic social position, but their share in the division of spiritual labour does not necessarily put them in a position of 'control' or superiority. A diarchic balance is established between the passive authority of female actors and its delegation to male executors, so that women serve as 'sources' for a life whose exchange is then negotiated and transferred by men.

Death brings women out of the shadowy recesses of the back of the house into the public eye in ways which contrast highly with everyday divisions of space and work. Groups of women gather around the corpse in the front vestibule (a part of the house usually reserved for men) and keen, expressing their grief loudly and emotionally, while men stay at a slight distance away, beating the drums and gongs or talking quietly. When guests have arrived for the funeral, a few women, particularly renowned for their clear voices and skills in ritual language, may sing the elaborate death songs which are the high point of a Kodi funeral. Cast as a long lament or dirge sung by the mother or widow of the deceased, these songs are considered a challenging art form, and also the form of traditional verbal expression most deeply moving to the spectators. The words of the song are arranged in parallel couplets[1] which refer to the particular sorrow which women feel in seeing the dissolution of the flesh that they once contained in their wombs, or shared with in the production of children. While women do not usually sing in public, and particularly not in the formal cadences of ritual couplets, at funerals they are 'given the voice' and allowed to break their usual silence to perform in a highly prestigious genre.

But, while these songs stress the shared experiences of 'womanness' which give the singers a privileged insight into the processes of life and death, they also lift the emotional experience of loss onto a cosmic level where the individual attributes of the deceased are cast off. The singing of death songs is an important stage of the Kodi funeral because it provides an emotional catharsis which allows the living to loosen the bonds which tie them to the dead soul, and allows the soul to become 'light' enough to begin its long journey to the village of the dead. Women are called in to sing the death songs because they are regarded as being able to generalise the experience of emotional loss, dissolving the various important categories of social differentiation into a shared cosmology. As such, they help transform the deceased from the vividly remembered personality that he or she was in his life into one of the nameless 'spirits of the dead' (*ndewa tou mate*) invoked as a source of the 'cool and fresh waters of blessing' (*wei myaringi, wei malala*) provided for the living. Men's participation in funerary rites contrasts sharply with that of the women in focusing not on the separation of the dead soul from the living, but instead on its reincorporation into the community of the ancestors. Through the mediations of men, a few of the dead can be lifted out of the general category of the 'spirits of the dead' and transformed into named ancestors or *marapu*. The *marapu* are the sources not only of life but also of law, of the ordering of social groups and the shaping of social relations.

This difference is a crucial one because it separates the dead into two different categories, undifferentiated spirits and named ancestors, with consequences for the community of the living. The important roles given to women in mortuary ceremonies are related, I shall argue, to what Forth has called 'the symbolically feminine aspect of the dead' (Forth 1981:93) in Sumba, in contrast to the masculine character of the *marapu*. But, whereas Forth sees this distinction as a static one rooted in the oppositional logic of a classificatory scheme, in Kodi at least it operates in a more dynamic sense: the dead are moved from the undifferentiated category of spirits to the more clearly articulated category of the *marapu* by the actions of the living. The intervention of male and female actors is crucial in determining the future career of the soul, and the consequences which its eventual destination will have on its living descendants.[2]

Sumbanese express the symbolic equation between women and the dead by saying that 'dead souls are like brides' – they must be carefully ushered out of the ancestral house and (despite a certain emotional wrench) prepared for a journey to another home. The ritual incorporation of the dead into the village of the ancestors provides an exact parallel to that of the bride. The resemblance is perhaps even more striking in East Sumba, because a substitute for the bride is dressed and displayed in the same way that a corpse is prepared for burial. As Forth has described it: 'Both assume the same position, sitting motionless in the right front corner of the house; the heads of both are veiled in red cloth; both are attended by women who weep and perform exhortatory chants in anticipation of the addressee's departure; and both are carried from the house by men while the women attempt to hinder their passage' (Forth 1981:201). The bride substitute is not used in Kodi, but the bride herself assumes this position before being transferred at marriage. Two specific women (the singer and the mourner) explicitly identify themselves with the corpse in the course of the mortuary ceremonies, and the transfers of marriages and funerals are clearly patterned after each other.

It will be my argument that we should interpret the femininity of the dead as socially constituted in their detachability and transferability. If women themselves are seen as partible and alienable, their movement is also related to the shifts in the ethereal parts of the person which can be attached and detached at death. The person is created initially by a double gendered supreme being, The Mother Binder of the Forelock, Father Creator of the Crown (*Inya wolo hungga, Bapa rawi lindu*). In its female aspect, this great mother binds the *hamaghu* or life force to the head at the forelock, while the great father smelts the harder fate or destiny (*ndewa*) at the crown. The *hamaghu* is the part which can be detached from the person during life, usually when someone becomes seriously ill, loses consciousness after a fall or becomes delirious. It can wander around on its own and have various adventures which cause severe mental confusion to its owner. The *ndewa* (destiny), by contrast, presents an unalterable life pathway which is only gradually revealed to the person as the years go by. At death, it is only the female-created life force which is lost irrevocably when the body is no longer animated or breathing. *Ndewa* persists, but must undergo a gender transformation.

The male-created soul must, in its immortal aspect, be 'feminised'. It must be separated from individual attributes and turned into a spirit of the dead, offering passive nurturance and cool waters of blessings to the living. The spirits of the dead are turned from male into female (whatever the sex of the deceased), and the transformation occurs at the time that the *ndewa* is detached from the community and sent off to the land of the dead, in much the same way that the bride is detached from her natal home and sent off to her husband's village.

The social background of gender concepts

The prescribed roles of men and women in mortuary ritual are, of course, rooted in wider conceptions of male and female as agents and as markers of social position. The first important arena to examine concerns the kinds of ties traced through male and female links. Kodi social organisation has been the subject of considerable controversy in Dutch structuralist literature, because of its early characterisation as a system of 'double descent', with both matriclans and patriclans (Kruyt 1919; Onvlee 1980). It was here that Van Wouden (1935), author of the most complete survey of eastern Indonesian forms of social organization, hoped to find what he believed to be the original proto-Austronesian form of dual organisation. Alas, since the Kodinese differ from many other Sumbanese peoples in their failure to observe a rule of prescriptive marriage, they did not bear out the famous 'Leiden hypothesis' (Van Wouden 1956). Although the asymmetric relation of wife-giver and wife-taker was the model for exchanges of land payments, fines and funeral gifts, as well as bridewealth, women could marry into any of the other patriclans without any fixed directionality. 'Complex' systems such as the Kodi one are in fact more common in Eastern Indonesia than the famous 'elementary' ones, but the area remains distinct for its development of two types of 'descent' which organise very different modes of social affiliation.

The kind of descent which passes through males is referred to as membership in 'houses' (*uma*) which make up ancestral villages (*parona*) united in the worship of a common body of named *marapu*. The *parona* refers not only to a ritual centre where important ceremonies are held, but also to a corporate group which transmits rights to land, ritual office, livestock, and the gold heirlooms which form the patrimony of individual houses. Although people spend most of the year living in huts near their gardens, they return to their houses in the ancestral villages to negotiate marriages, build megalithic graves and hold feasts dedicated to the spirits of the dead. The village forms an exogamous unit which arranges alliances with other villages. Women are transferred between them, along with the exchange of many other valuables, and eventually incorporated into the ancestral village of their husbands.

Descent traced through women is, by contrast, seen as a transmission of bodily substance ('blood') and personal characteristics (including some talents, weaknesses to disease and witchcraft), but no corporate rights or obligations. Certain types of magical knowledge, food taboos and skills in weaving and dyeing cloth may also be transmitted, but there is no formal occasion on which members of the named matriclans (*walla*) will come together. A patriclan is named by the location of its ancestral village, and often by the kind of tree planted in the centre of the village which serves as the communal altar of the clan's 'elder spirit' (*marapu matuyo*). The matriclan, in contrast, bears the personal name of its founder, or the name of a region from which she is said to have come. The term for the matriclan is the 'flowering' (*walla*) of the descendants of a given woman, whose 'blossoms' appear along the boughs of the great trees planted in various ancestral villages.

Although both the matriclans and patriclans are exogamous, incest within the matriclan or *walla* is considered the more dangerous. Members of the *parona* frown on extra-marital liaisons within the village, but acknowledge that they do occur. If it becomes desirable to turn a liaison into a marriage, a legal fiction must be used to adjust the receipt of marriage payments. On such occasions, the girl concerned will generally be 'adopted' into another village, which agrees to receive the bridewealth given for her and act as wife-giver. No such ritual mediation is considered possible in the case of sexual relations discovered between members of the same *walla*. Marriage itself is flatly impossible, and after initial sexual contact it is said that the blood of the two parties will 'rise up in protest' and cause high fevers and haemorrhaging.

Ties established through women are inalienable and permanent. They cannot be manipulated through prayers to the *marapu* or the performance of specific ceremonies. By contrast, ties traced through men establish membership in a social community with important political and economic functions. Although people should, as a general rule, remain faithful to those *marapu* who have been worshipped by their fathers and forefathers, some flexibility is allowed within the system. All relationships defined by *marapu* worship are part of a manipulable social system which receives its full definition only in terms of a more overarching pattern of exchanges negotiated between different villages, and between the human community of the villages and the invisible *marapu* spirits who serve as their guardians.

The affiliation of women within this system changes more often than that of men. Most women will, in the course of their lifetimes, be shifted from the community of worshippers defined by one ancestral village into the village of their husbands. The transfer is, however, not complete until the main instalment of bridewealth payments (usually five buffalo, five horses, and a sword and spear) has been made. Children who are born before these payments are completed may be shifted into their father's village only after at least ten head of livestock are paid. In cases where the minimal payments are never made, mother and children will continue to be affiliated with her village. Men may also change their village affiliation later in life through adoption, usually into their mother's village of origin, if there are no descendants born to carry on the house line, or if a particular affection has developed between the mother's brother and sister's son. Such adoptions are relatively rare, but have occurred in a significant number of cases where the transmission of a key ritual office required specific abilities or talents. Each movement of a person from one village to another is defined as a change in the *marapu* worshipped, and must be sanctioned with offerings dedicated to the *marapu*, and an augury which shows their agreement to the change.

The significance of these institutions for mortuary ritual lies in the fact that the bonds established through women are seen as the direct result of a shared physical substance (referred to as blood), while those established through men are only given form by exchange relations contracted between persons and legitimated by sacrifices made to the ancestral spirits. While women carry within their bodies the possibility of creating new life, the social group which will control that life and the cult of ancestors to which it will be associated are all determined not by her transmission of substance but by later transactions between groups defined in reference to paternal forebears. Thus, the descent system creates a conceptual separation between relations of unalterable substance (the *walla*) and those of socially negotiated group membership (the *parona* or ancestral village).

The death songs

The death songs which we shall discuss here are presented as the words of one woman, sung by another. There are therefore two crucial ritual roles which women assume in Kodi mortuary rites, roles which are significant in terms of a complementary division of labour in mourning. The first is the silent woman, the *tou kalalu* or 'official mourner' who respects the heaviest mortuary prohibitions. She is confined for a period of four days after the burial, and usually also guards the corpse during the interval between death and burial. Usually the widow or mother of the deceased,[3] she is forbidden from walking around outside the house, bathing, cooking, laughing or even speaking in anything but a low, inarticulate moan. She lies immobilised at the back of the house, wrapped in old mats, with tangled, unwashed hair. During this period, she is still close to the spirit of the dead man, and able to receive messages from him through dreams. Her confinement does not end until the dead soul is brought a final meal of rice steamed in coconut leaves, and allowed to fly away, carried on the backs of bats and butterflies.[4]

The person who sings for her is called 'the weeper', *tou hoyo*, and is often a complete outsider. My informants told me that in former times there were many older women who specialised in the singing of funeral dirges, and could be summoned from afar. Before singing, each woman would retire briefly to kill a chicken and examine its entrails in order to 'ask permission of the dead soul' and assure its cooperation in her singing of the mourning songs. Nowadays, it is more often a distant relative of the deceased who sings, someone not resident within the house and therefore not close enough to assume the mortuary prohibitions herself. It is said that the silent one gives her voice over to the singer, who then expresses her sorrow in the traditional couplets of ritual language. This is a sort of mediated communication, but not one where the words are directly delegated to another speaker, as in a divination. Rather, there is an assumption that the feelings of the silent one are somehow undifferentiated and diffusely shared, so that although the woman who feels her loss most directly cannot state it, she can listen to her own feelings expressed on the lips of another. Many women told me that they had been very moved by the beauty and skill of the singer who sang at the funeral: It had 'lifted a burden from the heart' to hear their own experiences transformed into such a lovely text.

What intrigued me about this division of labour between the two women was that it seems to deny the individuality of the dead person, and replace personal memories with evocations of socially appropriate emotions – how a mother feels at losing her child, how a wife feels in grieving for her husband. Sorrow is 'generalised' in terms of categories rather than worked through in terms of personal experience. The person who has the most vivid memories of the deceased is forced into an institutionalised silence: she must imitate the corpse in its inaccessibility and pollution-ridden existence, becoming in many ways as distant and inarticulate as the wandering soul. Another woman sings in her place to articulate this sorrow in a poetic idiom which generalises the experience of loss, and denies the significance of individual biographical detail.

This cultural process goes very much counter to Western expectations; we tend to see mourning as the gradual exteriorisation of grief, as the living come to accept the fact that the deceased is no longer among them.

Freud has referred to this as the 'work of mourning', and he describes grief as a process whereby memories are re-lived over a certain period of time until the ego is able to accept the separation: 'Each single one of the memories and hopes which bound the libido to the object is brought up and hyper-cathected [given a new attachment] and the detachment of the libido is accomplished' (Freud 1925:154). Kodi death songs, in contrast, do not focus on the content of individual hopes and memories but rather on their links to enduring social roles (as mother, daughter, wife or sister) and the culturally specified emotions and attitudes which go with these roles. Moreover Kodi do not lose all of their dead as thoroughly as we do. Certain named ancestors continue to hover as invisible presences in the village, enforcing ancestral laws and continuing a dialogue with the living through divinations. Others, the nameless 'spirits of the dead' (*ndewa tou mate*), recycle their essences to their descendants through the 'cool waters' of blessings of health and prosperity. Living and dead are members of the same enduring social community, and since the dead do not vanish completely at death, the most important change that they undergo is a transformation in the forms of agency which they may exercise towards the living.

Mourning is defined by the Kodi as mourning the loss of the *hamaghu* (the 'life force' or vital energy which was bound to the head at the forelock). The house and paternal descent group is portrayed as attacked: death is said to 'tear holes in the walls and rip gaps in the floorboards', breaking through the protective shell provided by friendly spirits. At each death, those resident in the hamlet have lost a crucial locus of health and vitality. The more enduring part of the person, however, the *ndewa* or fate at the crown, remains in the body after death, and must be acted on in the funeral rites. It must be detached during the period of mourning and transformed from its living, acting power (presented as conceptually male) to a more passive, nurturant force (presented as conceptually female). For this reason, the task of mourning is entrusted to women, and women attempt to make the dead soul one of them, identifying with its fears of the dangerous transition ahead, and guiding it with words which make the process a more familiar one.

I shall discuss two specific texts, given in the appendix (see pages 200-6). Each is of only moderate length, and composed of standardised couplets which refer to the age, category and personal characteristics of the deceased, as well as drawing a vivid picture of the shock of receiving the news of death. When a very important person dies, longer and more elaborate dirges may be sung, detailing the many stages of ritual preparations for the funeral and describing the ancestral village where it occurred. But the stages of grief portrayed remain basically the same, and most embellishments are added only to enhance the prestige of the patriclan.

The first text is presented as a daughter's mourning for her dead mother, and begins with a conventional disclaimer. The singer argues that she has neither the wisdom contained in the liver of the pig nor the eloquence in the throat of the snail. She humbles herself before the larger forces of the cosmos, and feels unable to speak appropriately to the occasion of death. She refers to death as especially unbearable because of the shock produced on the members of the house: 'This is why we cannot wipe away. The mucus flowing on the corpse ... This is why we cannot set aside. The tears falling on the body'. She wonders why the house itself did not shake with the impact, the boughs supporting the roof shifting with the sound. Her denial of the news of death is presented as a failure of perception ('But I didn't even hear it. Carried away by the winds. But my ears did not sense it. Swirling in the whirlwinds') and of interpretation: small premonitions (the mouse pinching at the side, the rat who sends a warning twitch) took the form of minor problems which were neglected, and not heeded properly to forestall the more major disaster to come.

Any death, even that of an elderly person who has been ailing for many months, is seen as the result of a temporary lapse in ancestral protection, a momentary vulnerability which exposes the residents of the hamlet to the dangers of death and disease. There must have been a reason to 'let the piglet slip from the armpit ... let the chick fall from under the wing', so that death could swoop in like a bird of prey and steal away her vulnerable life-force. Thus, the death song begins a process of self-questioning and self-blame within the community, as various members try to find who among them may have committed the infraction which proved fatal. Kodi notions of guilt and causality admit that one person's sin may be responsible for the death of another. In the absence of a concept of individual guilt, responsibility for this loss may be born by anyone of her co-residents. In this song, the singer first searches for the person who may rightfully be blamed ('the fault in the hamlet', the 'sin in the settlement'), then turns to reproach the mother herself for not resisting more strenuously. Feelings of abandonment and helplessness ('You left us drifting in the river ... You let us wash away in the tides') alternate with the uneasiness of guilt.

Towards the end, this anger and confusion is transformed into an instruction to the dead mother to speak well of her kinsmen on her arrival in the afterworld. The unity and forcefulness of the house is re-asserted with references to its ability to defend itself and avenge her death, had the death been caused by an earthly agent instead of a spiritual one. The 'many knives ready to cut' show preparations for a vengeance killing. But the final lines signal a fall back into despair as the singer is reminded that it was a *marapu* who caused the death, an ancestral killer whose deeds cannot be so directly reciprocated. The lethal nets of the *marapu* trap men in their own mortality, from which they are unable to defend themselves. Their helplessness and passivity is given its strongest expression in the restrictions of mourning – the skin left unwashed until it is coated with filth, the hair left unbound until it is tangled and dishevelled.

The process of mourning as presented in this song begins with hearing the news of death and denying its reality, proceeds to a questioning of what has gone wrong, then asserting people's anger and unity, finally stepping away from decision-making into the proscribed restrictions of mourning. The refuge which the singer seeks focuses on the traumas of rupture and separation. Her account is notable for the fact that it makes no mention of themes of continuity and renewal, and carries no invocation of ancestral precedents or the specific path of the soul on its journey. The experience presented is an emotional wrench which ends with detachment and loss, not the regeneration of life or the survival of an enduring social identity.

These themes of an irrevocable transfer are linked, I have argued, to the ways women perceive their own lives as transferred, thus making them particularly appropriate mediators between life and death. The Kodi death songs can be contrasted with other mortuary chants, found in neighbouring societies in Eastern Indonesia, which are performed by male chanters. The Rotinese *bini*, extensively documented in Fox (1971, 1974, 1975), are composed in similar sets of parallel couplets and also reflect upon the themes of loss and separation. The chanter himself never expresses these feelings directly, however, as the whole chant is structured to praise the deceased by likening him or her to a mythic protagonist. The loss of a young boy of several months is compared (in the text cited in Fox 1971) to a mythic figure who was stolen away by an eagle and a hawk, to avenge an egg eaten by the mother during her period of pregnancy cravings. Here, it is the eagle and the hawk, takers of life, who assert that they also loved their egg, and who present a parable of balance between life given and life taken away. As in the Kodi songs, the deceased is de-particularised by being equated with others in the same general category, but the grief and distress of his close kin are referred to only obliquely. Male mediations stress the continuity between the deceased boy and an ancestral forbear, and the order which must emerge after death, while the death songs sung by Kodi women focus on the suffering of the survivors and their confusion in the face of a new transition.

The stages of an initial funeral

The stages of grief outlined in the death song are to a certain extent paralleled by the ritual stages of mortuary ceremonies. The dead person is physically detached from the community and buried in a series of events which oppose female nurturance and identification with the dead to male control of social continuity and differentiation. Most persons receive only a single burial, either in an earthen grave or a stone chamber in the central courtyard of the ancestral village. Those who have died a 'bad death', however, cannot be buried within the village until special ceremonies have been held to call back their souls, and they may linger as ghosts for several years awaiting a second burial. Prominent persons whose descendants wish to raise them to the status of named ancestors may also find that their bones are disinterred and moved, some years after death, under the more prestigious stone slabs designed to 'make their names live'. The initial funeral is concerned with detachment and separation of the living from the dead, however, and presents the general model for these transformations.

As soon as an important man or woman dies, messengers are sent to bring the news to kin and affines. The corpse is brought close to the hearth and bathed in warm water by a woman relative (usually the official mourner), then laid close to the fire with its knees bent up under the chin. The clothes which were worn during the period of illness are removed, and the corpse is dressed in a new set of fine textiles. A man receives two loincloths of good quality, and a woman two sarungs. The first is said to be the loincloth worn as a garment in the afterworld, the second the loincloth used to cross over the water which separates the world of the living from the dead.

The dead live in a village located at Sasar, a large and dangerous cape along the northern coast of the island, the point where the first Sumbanese were beached when their canoes were torn apart on the reefs. Life in the village of the dead is much like life in an ordinary hamlet, except that no children are born so that the community can only renew itself by recruiting new members from among the living. The souls of the dead leave their own villages after the last funeral prestations, but may stop at specific spots along the seashore to wait for companions to join them in the long journey to Sasar.

The dead person is dressed in a headcloth of three colours, tied in a way which is similar to the bride's headcloth in the most elaborate forms of marriage. The corpse is first placed lying beside the hearth, where an uncertain maiden might wait nervously for her presentation to her future husband and in-laws. As guests arrive, they bring fine textiles to be used for the shroud. The gesture of presenting the textile, which is ceremoniously draped over the corpse as soon as they enter the house, is a token of mourning. An important person may be buried in more than forty or fifty sarungs or loincloths, but there will still be many cloths remaining to be re-distributed as partial compensation for those who brought gifts of animals for the funeral sacrifices.

Affines also come, bringing with them appropriate contributions to the mortuary exchanges. The wife-givers (*ghera*) are delegated to handle the corpse throughout the course of the funeral, and oversee the sacrifices which feed the souls of the dead and allow the dead person to be detached from the human community. As 'givers of life' and of women, they bring along pigs and cloth, the usual counterprestation for bridewealth payments. Those in the category of wife-takers (*nobo vinye*), by contrast, bear the heaviest economic burden, providing horses and buffalo for slaughter, just as they provided them for exchange in the marriage prestations. Sacrifices must be performed every day of the funeral to feed those guests assembled. Usually a day or so after death, a buffalo is killed 'to move the corpse to the front platform', and its meat is distributed to all. This corresponds to the moment in a marriage negotiation when the official sword and spear are presented, signalling agreement to the stated brideprice, and allowing the bride to be transferred to her husband's home. The corpse is shifted up, so that its head rests against the divination pillar in the front of the house, in the same place that a bride comes to sit beside her husband, dressed in all her finery and ready to assume the role of an obedient wife.

Each night the corpse spends on the front veranda new pigs or buffalo must be killed. Many guests may spend the night, the women wailing and dancing, the men receiving the mortuary gifts and deciding on how they will be shared to cover the expenses of the funeral sacrifices. During this whole period, the offical mourner, *tou kalalu*, remains beside the corpse or in the rear of the house.

On the day set for burial, representatives from one of the wife-giving clan villages, usually that of the dead person's 'origin' (the *lete binye*, or village of his mother's clan, if he is male, or her own village of birth, for a married woman) are selected to be the *nggaba pa tanongo* or counterparts to bury the dead. This task is associated with the overall importance of the mother's brother in all life crisis rites. He is addressed as the *lete binye* or 'steps and doorway', from the couplet which refers to the origin village as the steps that came down, the doorway that was left behind. Seen as a source of life, health and vitality, his association with the lost *hamaghu* qualifies him to assure the safe passage of the dead soul into the afterworld. His assistance at the mortuary rites also has another sense, however, in that death payments mark the final stage in the series of alliance payments begun with the betrothal of a young girl. Only by receiving the riding horse and the heads of buffalo killed at funeral feasts for her sons can the great 'debt for life' contracted by the wife-taking village be paid off. Although the mother's brother may play a crucial role in the funeral, the payments he receives are in fact not intended as recompense for that service, but for the much earlier 'gift of life' which brought the mother of the deceased into the clan where he has now died.

Just before burial, the dead person's horse is paraded in front of the crowd. Ornamented with a fine bridle, a good textile on the back and occasionally even gold jewelry, the horse is led into the slaughter field and presented to the mother's brother. He can, at this point, choose to either kill the horse and dispatch its soul off to the afterworld, to carry its master on the long trip to Sasar, or to spare it and bring it home to his own village. Nowadays, especially when the horse is a fine riding horse, usually the second course is followed, although a brief blow at the neck with a sword must be made to signal the transfer of rights. The horse is held by the son of the deceased, dressed in all of his finery at the moment that he surrenders the animal to the representative of his own origin village.

Immediately after the horse is brought out, the dead person's body is carried down from the front veranda. Drums, gongs and high-pitched yodelling by the women accompany this moment of dangerous transition, and more dancers crowd into the field. The women continue to sway and undulate their arms, while the male dancers do a vigorous war dance – stomping their feet, shaking spears and swords in their arms, and rolling their eyes furiously. Stereotypical expressions of anger and rage at the unexpected death are often yelled by the male dancers. 'If this were the work of a fellow Sumbanese (i.e. another human being, rather than the *marapu* spirits), then I would charge towards him with my shield and swing at him with my spear!' The war dance itself is a vain display of bravery and the desire for vengeance, as all men lose in the final struggle with the *marapu*. But it is significant that men, confronted with the loss and suffering of death, respond by asserting their fierceness (*mbani*), while women, confronted with the same loss, stress their helplessness (*pemo*). The words of the dirges that they sing describe a sense of being tossed by the waves, swept away in the river current, deprived of any sense of volition or purposiveness. Their concentration on the beat of the drums and gongs is intended to blot out more personalised responses, while male kinsmen seize the occasion to display their own personal rage and fearsomeness.

A mock battle between men and women ensues at the time that male kinsmen come to take the body out of the house and move it to the grave. Female mourners (both affines and kinswomen) remain clustered around the corpse, resisting the attempts of the men to remove it, and even striking out at them in anger as they do so. They told me that they felt that the dead person had become 'one of them', and should not be taken away to the grave. The men in attendance at funerals, although also obviously moved by the spectacle, never expressed such a close identification with the dead, and seemed to feel some embarrassment at this effort by the women to prolong their emotional and dishevelled mourning wails. Whether the deceased was male or female, women unfailingly assert that this moment in the funeral provides the deepest wrench for them, because it reminds them of the cruel separation that they felt when, as brides, they had to leave their natal homes and marry. For that brief instant, the dead soul is as nervous and hesitant as the uncertain maiden, and the sufferings of transition are most deeply felt.

The body is carried out of the house and towards the grave by close kinsmen, and then inserted into the stone chamber of a megalithic grave (if one is already built; if not, it receives a provisional earth burial). The knees still tightly bound, it is placed lying on the right side, in much the same position that it had assumed within the house. The dead person is buried with his or her betel pouch, and one earthenware dish and a wooden spoon are broken on top of the body, then scattered off to the west, so that they can be brought along with the deceased. A wooden plate used to scoop up the earth is also shattered and cast off to the left. Once the grave has been sealed, the sacrificial animals are brought out for the slaughter.

Any important adult should have at least one mature buffalo killed at the funeral feast, and the number of animals provides a clear index of social position. The sons of a dead man may compete for the number of buffalo killed at his funeral as a way of making claims on the estate, which will be divided by the eldest. The animals provide the cortege which follows the deceased on his journey to the afterworld. After the death of an important man, it is said that one can hear the roaring of the waves (echoing the sounds of gongs) and the beating of the winds (echoing the sounds of the drums), signalling his journey along the seashore to the land of the dead at Sasar and his greeting on arrival there. Thus, the dead soul retains in death the status achieved in life. Most adults merit the killing of at least one buffalo, but an important figure may see as many as ten or twelve killed to 'carry on his name' to the afterworld.

The person from the origin village or wife-giving group who has been designated as the 'counterpart to bury the dead' receives the thighs of buffalo meat. His closeness to the deceased has been shown by his willingness to receive the body when it is placed in the stone grave, and his taking the share of rice and sacrificial meat intended for the deceased and placing it beside the grave. When the burial is finished, he 'cools off' the grave by storing coconut leaves and a few firelogs on top of it. The pollution associated with handling the corpse is thus not specifically delegated to women (as it is in many other societies, cf. Bloch 1982), but is mainly assumed by the man most clearly linked to the earlier transfer of women into the village. He can bear it because of his stronger position as a 'giver of life'; the woman in mourning bears it from a position of weakness and vulnerability, through her identification with the 'life' that is being transferred.

The official mourner remains confined and secluded, in the four days after the burial. She must let her hair hang loose and refrain from washing or combing it, so that she comes to share the filthy and restricted condition of the dead soul still trapped within the grave. At the end of this period, small portions of sugar cane, cassava, sweet potato, taro and other tubers are prepared to bring to the dead along with his final meal of boiled rice packets. A dog is sacrificed, called the 'dog that rides the rice packets', in explicit parallel to the 'dog that rides the spear' killed at the end of a marriage negotiation.

The final funeral feast is held that evening, when kin and affines assemble again to spear a large pig and share a meal of cooked rice. The male 'counterpart to bury the dead' and female mourner go down to the grave, and open up the covering of coconut leaves. The singer may repeat some lines from the dirge to call the soul of the dead, expressing her shock and sorrow at the news of death. The burying counterpart places a serving of rice, pork and liver on top of the grave, and pours coconut water over it all. He receives another share of the pig's thigh, and returns to the origin village with the following gifts: the dead person's betel pouch, the two plates of rice used to feed him, the earthenware dish and spoon used to dish out the meat, the chickens (to be used in the divination later that evening), and the second coconut. These have now become ritual objects which he will use in the rites to remove the pollution of death from the house. As he leaves, he makes certain that the grave has been closed over with a covering of green bark so that it will not be disturbed by wild animals.

That evening a divination is held to 'mend the gaps in the floorboards and close the tears in the walls' – to restore the house after the trauma of death, and the departure of one of its members. Chickens are killed as augury, to determine the correctness of the responses received from the ancestral spirits through spear divination. The divination is conducted by male ritual specialists, and it marks the return of men to centre stage in the ritual arena. They are the only ones able to converse directly with the spirits concerned and determine which of them was angry enough to relax his normal protection, 'letting the human soul slip from under the wing, allowing the birth-fate to fall from the armpit'. The interactions conducted in the course of this divination follow the strict etiquette of spirit communication which I have described elsewhere (Hoskins in press). The official mourner is then able to come out of her seclusion and bathe. She will usually wash her hair with coconut cream to 'cool her head', and wrap herself in fine textiles gathered at the funeral. Other textiles are divided among those wife-takers who have brought livestock to the sacrifice, and additional gifts of horses or gold may be made to the wife-givers, especially those two individuals designated as the counterparts to bury the dead person. At this point, the round of mortuary exchanges is finished, and people may go home.

When the mourning is ended, it is assumed that the soul of the deceased has been officially separated from the community, and should travel uneventfully to the land of the dead. Occasionally, the ghosts of dead persons may return to their living descendants in dreams to make additional demands: movement to a better stone grave, the return of a family heirloom, the staging of a feast which had been promised to the ancestors but never carried out. The immediate duty of ushering the dead ceremoniously into the other world has, however, been fulfilled. The dead have been transformed into generally passive, benevolent spirits (*ndewa tou mate*). The only exceptions to this rule are those individuals who cannot be completely transformed on this occasion because of the suddenness of their detachment from life (those who have died a 'bad death'), or those individuals who will be re-integrated into the community after their deaths as named ancestors (*marapu*). To these problematic cases we now turn.

The undetached dead: ghosts and named ancestors

It has been my argument thus far that gender inequality is expressed in Kodi in terms of notions of complementary agency: male and female are distinguished by different modes of acting on the world. The friendly mixing observed in everyday life, where male and female spheres seem only hazily distinguished, rests nevertheless on a more complex underpinning of notions about the appropriateness of male activity and female passivity. This division of powers and of agency has perhaps its strongest expression in the transformations of the soul which occur after death. I have said that the souls of most dead persons are 'feminised' when they are transferred from the world of the living to that of the dead. They become, like brides, sources of life and nurturance with a diminished power to act on the world. A few, however, retain the male-identified mode of action, and continue to play an active role in community affairs as disembodied ghosts or ancestors. Although both men and women may become named ancestors, most are men; the category *marapu* seems to be conceptually male even when applied to women actors. This may also be true, to a lesser extent, of the ghosts of those who have died a sudden, violent death.

The category of 'bad death' in Kodi is linked to two specific circumstances: dying outside the home (and thus, by definition, the protective walls guarded by local spirits), and being attacked by a sharp weapon or precipitous accident. Falling from a tree, being struck by lightning, drowning, being attacked by a wild animal or being murdered are all classified as bad deaths. The category is also labelled *mate moro*, referring to the colours we would call blue or green. A sudden death is 'green' in the sense that it cuts down a young plant which is still green, not yet golden, on the stalk. It cuts short life in an unexpected way, yet (unlike childhood illnesses, which also cut off young life) does not waste away the vital energies but instead claims them whole. *Mate moro* could also be translated as 'raw death', since *moro* has the sense of raw, and thus incompletely processed. The souls of those who die a violent death are 'startled' and do not wait around the corpse for mortuary ceremonies to gradually usher them into another world. In their surprise at the sudden assault on their bodies, they fly off into the sky and are held captive by the sun and the moon, 'held by the feet of the moon, gripped by the teeth of the sun' (*ela ngape witti wyula, ela ngandu mata lodo*). They remain suspended in this condition, part of neither the world of the living nor that of the dead, for a period of at least four years. Then, their living descendants must perform a singing ceremony followed by a pig sacrifice to 'call down the dead person' and bring him or her back into the community. A small bamboo pole is erected at the front corner of the house, and sometime in the early hours of the morning, the soul's return can be discerned through a loud noise, a flash of light, or the traces of footprints in ashes scattered at the base of the pole.

The process of mourning for such a death is similar to that for someone who has died of natural causes, except that it is much longer and more protracted. Death songs are sung both at the initial funeral (when the body is given a provisional earthen burial outside the village gates) and at the later ceremony to disinter the bones and move them into the village where they can be reburied, usually in a stone tomb. But the stages of grief presented and the sentiments expressed can be quite different, as this brief song sung for a young girl killed by a truck demonstrates (full text in appendix).

The song begins with familiar denials of the death, and assertions that the living have no choice but to comply with often inexplicable events ('There is no way to turn away one's nose/ The horse must stretch out its neck willingly/ There is no way to shake one's tail/ The buffalo must follow along'). Then, the mother–child bond is evoked directly as a sharing of substance produced in the womb (the child is seen as 'twisted entrails' or a 'stomach filled with rotten rice'), along with specific praise for her beauty and finely formed young body ('Child of the straight river reeds/ ... Child of the carved spear handle').

The horror expressed at her death stems partially from its suddenness, and from the fact that it occurred outside the protective walls of the house. Many Kodi listeners found references to the *setting* of the accident extremely moving because they reflected the exposed, unmediated nature of her death. The suffering and humiliation of the family is much greater for having lost a daughter to outside disruptive forces, having her rest 'at the banyan tree near the dry stream ..., [pillow] her head on the raised earth'. The death is 'green' and inappropriate because of her youth (dead with blue-black hair, dead with white teeth undarkened by betel) and unmarried state ('before she had a betel post to cling to ... before she reached the top of the tall tree').

Since no one had ever died in a traffic accident before, the singer had to invent several new lines to describe the manner of her death, while staying within the traditional canons of ritual speech. She created a new couplet ('Dead because of the speeding car/Deceased because of the returning truck') to fit these needs, but also added a more original reflection on the absolute destructiveness of Western consumer objects. While an earthen dish could be re-assembled and re-baked, and a wooden plate be re-planted, there is no way to renew the powers of a modern porcelain dish or green bottle. The young girl struck by the truck was the first Kodi victim of an outside force which does not allow regeneration or re-assemblage from previous materials. Like the disposable items of consumer production, she was left to waste beside the road, her soul also wandering and errant throughout the skies. In this way, a single metaphor sheds light on the arresting similarity between the wastefulness of a world of easily separable objects, and the directionless separation of the souls of those dying bad deaths. A more extreme loss is experienced in these cases, because the deceased cannot be immediately 'feminised' and re-integrated into the nurturant community of the dead souls.

The singer could not follow the trajectory of grief just outlined for the earlier dirge, since mourning which culminates in a catharsis of feelings of grief and helplessness cannot be finished at this stage. The souls of those who have died violent deaths remain unhappy and capricious presences, which linger beside the roof thatch and the ceiling drain, awaiting a ritual resolution of their fate. They fly off into the skies, where they are hidden in the lontar leaves, by Tila 'who rides astride the sun, [grasped in] the teeth of the moon', by Pati 'who guards the moon'. Incompletely detached from the human community, they must continue to remind their descendants of obligations to hold the proper rites on their behalf. Not part of the living world nor yet integrated into the community of dead souls and ancestors, they are portrayed as literally 'dangling' from various celestial bodies, which will not release them until another singer has called down the soul and fed these deities with pig flesh.

The tone of the dirge for a girl who died violently does not finish with the same resolution as the earlier one quoted, for a relapse into the inevitability of death is not an option when such a relapse would visit years of illness and misfortune on the village. It ends on a much more uneasy note of unresolved tensions and uncertain efforts to rectify such an extreme violation of the protective boundaries around the human community.

The ghosts of people who die bad deaths are, then, incompletely detached, and (until rites have been held to call down the soul) incompletely incorporated into the spirits of the dead. They remain uneasy and invisible presences within the village, not yet 'feminised' by the rites which produce the *ndewa* and thus capricious and individualistic rather than appropriately nurturant towards their living relatives. Their mode of agency remains male and active, as their personalities have yet to be dissolved into the vast, anonymous sea where the spirits of the dead wait for requests from the living.

While the undetached nature of such ghosts leaves them dangerously dangling, the named ancestors (*marapu*) are re-attached to the community after death through prestige feasts which raise them to the status of active guardians and arbiters of public morality. Their names are repeated at important sacrifices and, through the actions of their descendants, may eventually be incorporated as a part of the ritual designation of their clan and village. The detached spirits of the dead attain immortality only at the price of anonymity, and thus disappear from memory in much the same way that women disappear from genealogies. Only a few particularly active and influential persons – usually, although not exclusively, men – continue to exert an active role on the community after death, through the roles given to them by their descendants in the self-validating process of creating important ancestors to assure the continuity of one's own status. Thus, the 'processing' which a dead person undergoes after the loss of the *hamaghu* or life breath leads first to the production of passive 'feminine' souls, and later only occasionally into a male active guardianship.

The first stage of re-attaching the named ancestor to the community begins at the divination. Persons who have in their lifetimes performed the full series of feasts which qualify them for the traditional title *rato* need only be confirmed in this status through the examination of the livers of pigs and buffalo killed at the funeral. Unless there are counterindications in the auguries which signal strong opposition from the deities (or, more likely, human fellows), their names are incorporated into a litany of ancestors invoked at important clan gatherings and given the role of enforcing traditional law. The personal characteristics of these ancestors are remembered, and usually rather elliptical reference is made to their exploits in the couplet name that they are given. Thus, the ancestor who founded the village of Rangga Baki four generations ago is known as *Rangga nja pa talo, Ngundu njapa ela*, or 'Rangga who cannot be beaten, Ngundu who cannot be equalled', a name which extolls his wealth and bravery. The praise names assure a certain continuity of reputation, and are often subject to later interpretation and exegesis.

Other important persons who not have been addressed as *rato* during their own lifetimes may attain this status after death, if their descendants are prepared to sponsor large feasts to consecrate their graves, or name new houses after them. Sometimes, a specific request will come from a dead person to perform these ceremonies or construct a new lineage house in order to assure such immortality. Within our own system of social interpretation we would tend to see many such requests as devices for their descendants to legitimate the group's current status and provide an ancestral justification for claims to ceremonial importance. In all cases, however, some mention of this goal must be made at the rite which closes the funeral. The divination which 'closes the gaps and mends the floorboards' normally re-erects boundaries around the house and closes it off from dangerous incursions. The men who question the deities at this stage to determine the cause of death finish off the complex mortuary exchanges and finalise the status of the deceased. In exceptional cases, a door is left open to the dead to attain the status of 'masculine' *marapu* with a continuing power to act in the house and village.

While women have moved uncertainly over boundaries and turned the once dangerous ghost into a passively benevolent spirit of the dead, men re-erect the dividing lines and recite genealogies which make temporary social leaders into enduring ancestral figures. The female form of agency is identified with passive acquiescence in the regeneration of life, stressing the universal and unchanging attributes of humanness. The male form, by contrast, differentiates and particularises social roles, allowing a select few to make a more enduring mark upon the world.

Complementarity and inequality

In the earlier discussion of Kodi social organisation and concepts which relate to male and female parts of the person, I noted that female transmission of *walla* identity is generalised and inalienable, while male patriline position signals membership in social groups which can be manipulated by social actors. Similarly, the transformation of the dead person into an *ndewa* or spirit of the dead is, like its *walla* identity, a generalised human process, in which the dead (like women) are alienated from their natal villages and incorporated into another group. Since no person can escape the inevitability of human mortality, this status is an attribute of humanity and cannot be modified. On the other hand, only a very few of the dead become named ancestors who are invoked at religious ceremonies. In order to achieve this position, a person must have been someone of great social prominence, active in the ceremonial feasting system and most probably the progenitor of many descendants. His/her passage into the special category of named ancestors is not certain, however, until the divination which follows the death, where a dialogue with the spirits concerning the cause of the death must contain this last request for renown beyond the grave.   The songs and mourning procedures carried out by women are concerned with the inevitable experience of death and the sorrow felt at the loss of the child or husband, only rarely with the personal characteristics of the deceased. In fact, women say that the best way for them to 'cool their hearts' and learn to accept this death is by seeing it as part of a universal progression that we are all subject to, a necessary stage in the renewal of the generations and the replacement of one person by another within the patriclan. Women's actions in death ceremonies serve to negate individual personhood, while helping to mend the emotional turmoil suffered by the house and village. In contrast, male actors are concerned with differentiating out the causes for the death, repairing those social ruptures which it has caused, and assuring the social reproduction of the clan. In order to do this, the personhood of specific individuals is maintained across the generations and their names are given a special status.

My argument about inequality and agency in relation to this process of cosmological renewal is that 'male' and 'female' distinguish for the Kodi two different modes of acting upon the world. Although there are few clearly defined spheres for men or women in public life (where ideas of general appropriateness rather than pollution or exclusion are found), women are often placed in the role of 'sources' and 'delegators' of authority, while men are the 'executors' and the actors in social life. This division of powers has perhaps its strongest expression in the transformations of the soul which occur after death, and which determine the kind of impact that is left after a person's life force has left him or her. It is here that, despite the great importance of women's mortuary roles, their unequal status is demonstrated. The souls which are alienated from the community and sent off to an existence of passive acquiescence are seen as conceptually female; those which remain as active personalities in the community and whose names are invoked at ceremonies are conceptually male. Thus, the often cited complementarity of male and female in this case is yet another language for expressing a mode of granting access and then distancing the real ability to control and manipulate power.

The inequality between men and women that we observe in Kodi relates to different forms of agency. Eastern Indonesian notions of complementarity present an ambiguous and complex picture of male/ female relations: they do not simply delineate male supremacy. This is clearly a society organised more by gender 'difference' than by 'domination'. But we must also ask which of these often cited gender differences is 'the difference that makes a difference'. How truly do notions of balance and harmony affect the balance of power between the sexes? And where are they related to the perpetuation of gender asymmetries, even when these asymmetries are not part of wider systems of clear-cut antagonism?

In mythological terms, the Kodi division of power between the sexes conforms to the classic form of diarchy, defined as 'a rigorous division between spiritual authority and temporal power predicated on a conceptual opposition between female and male' (Fox 1982:11). In the Kodi version of this division, spiritual authority is retained by female actors, but delegated to male executors. Women retreat into a sort of passive acquiescence. Although they (like the dead) are seen as sources of life and nourishment, they are denied a number of options which would permit them to act effectively in the house or village. While ritual couplets praise women as both the source and embodiment of life, particular women may be forced to stay with husbands that they do not like or face the loss of their children to the husband's patriclan at divorce. While mothers are honoured as nurturers and instructors of their sons, they will eventually have to defer to their judgement on the distribution of family properties. While they share even more closely in the lives of their daughters, daughters will be separated from them and sent off to another village in marriages negotiated by men. Men are seen as the owners of the village and the house, and they control exchange paths which channel female 'life' in various directions. Women provide the flow of life-blood which allows the village to reproduce itself, but have little chance to direct that flow themselves.

I have argued here that Kodi gender complementarity involves an exchange between modes of action, based on a contrast in kinds of agency. Male and female, as abstract categories, provide a language for talking about ways of effective action. When thus applied to human action, these gender identifications take on a very different significance from their usual role in dual classifications. At the level of most ritual oppositions, male and female are simply used to express contrasts which may be applied recursively. As Fox has noted: 'A great deal of the symbolic elaboration of dualistic structures in eastern Indonesia involves playing with this principle of recursive complementarity: Male contains Female, Female contains Male; Inside contains the Outside, the Outside the Inside; Black, White, White, Black' (Fox 1983:19). The apparently contrived and playful use of male/female categories as classifiers in other contexts takes on weight and signification, however, when applied to persons, or when relations between categories are compared to relations between men and women. It is precisely because the Kodi insist on *personifying* the dead, on seeing them as similar to brides, that dead souls in their feminine aspect can be said to have a different aspect from the conceptually masculine named ancestors. Personification in this instance creates an asymmetry among the living as well as between the living and the dead, which cannot be reduced simply to two neutral halves of a paired couple.

The femininity of the dead is socially constituted as a matter of their detachability and transferability, just as the female-created part of the person (*hamaghu*, vitality) is that which is lost at death, while the male-created part (*ndewa*, destiny) remains. Yet, the dead are no longer able to act in this world (with the important exception of the few who become named ancestors). So their loss of an active agency is signalled by the process which transforms the active potentiality of the fate or destiny into a passive source of nurturance and blessings. Women, as brides, are transformed from natal members of a given clan into the sources of life who will bring their offspring to 'bloom' and bear 'fruit' (descendants) in another clan. The transformation of their personhood at marriage is paralleled by the transformation of the soul in the final stages of mortuary ritual. Thus, women feel particularly close to the dead and can identify with the process of transition in a way in which men cannot. They grieve not only the loss of the deceased, but also the loss of their own capacity for independent action and self-determination. The dead in their transformed state are like women, robbed of an individuated agency.[5] They are seen instead as a great spiritual resource, offering cool nourishment and support to the hotter battles of male agents among the living.

The Kodi use of gender metaphors to describe relations between the living and the dead connects notions of 'male' and 'female' to a whole system of cosmological balances. Through mortuary ceremonies and the death songs sung at them, a world of the ancestors is created where some of the dead remain active overseers of the world of the living, and others retire into the background. Society is reproduced through a conjunction of unequal forces, women offering life in its generalised, undifferentiated form, while men divide up this life through public transactions and exchanges into clearly established social categories. The female 'source' cannot usually veto the actions of her male 'executor'; the nurturant mother cannot later scold her errant son. Thus women, although seen as conceptually crucial to the diarchic balancing of powers, may feel themselves to be detached and discarded by their own kin. Thus their songs of mourning, although crucial to the processing of ghosts into dead souls and ancestors, may also be seen as reflections on their social powerlessness.

Notes

1. Death songs are composed in the ritual language, a particular style used for various sorts of formal speech and referred to by the Kodi as *panggecango* (an abbreviated version of *paneghe pa panggapango* or 'language which is arranged in pairs'). Characterised by a strict canonical parallelism with both lines of a couplet used to express a common meaning, this speech style is similar to other Eastern Indonesian ritual languages whose stylistic conventions have been outlined by Fox (1971, 1974, 1975) and Kuipers (1982). *Panggecango* is used mainly by male diviners and priests to address the spirits, to negotiate marriages, to take oaths, and to conduct public oratorical confrontations. Most women have a passive rather than active command of the full vocabulary of ritual couplets, as there are few occasions where it is considered appropriate for them to speak. The death songs provide a notable exception to women's usual ritual silence, but there were also a few women able to sing the celebratory songs which accompany dancing at buffalo feasts (*lodo nataro*), stone-dragging (*benyo*) and the telling of epic narratives (*ngara kedoko*). None were however able to communicate directly with the spirits through the question-and-answer format of spear divination. The etiquette of Kodi spirit communication, and different rules applied to the spirits of the inside and outside are described in Hoskins (in press).

   It should be stressed that the coupling of male and female elements in ritual speech is

often conceptually neutral: either element of the pair could come first or second, and the coupling serves as a kind of balanced reinforcement. A statement is 'closed' by being said from both directions, and the same meaning is conveyed by two slightly different, but paired, metaphors. The 'speaking in pairs' which occurs in ritual language is only one aspect of a general cultural preoccupation with order, balance and complementarity, but the terms of this interdependence are not always the same. Thus, when applied to persons such couplets may also be ordered according to some criterion of asymmetry. The specific 'weighting' of male and female terms is not, however, intrinsic to the speech style. As Fox has noted, 'extra linguistic criterion are required to transform parallel elements into the elements of a dual organization or cosmology' (1983:15). Notions of agency in this paper are part of this extra-linguistic weighting.
2. Onvlee (1980) has also written about the division of persons and objects into categories coded in terms of male and female for various parts of West and East Sumba. He classifies *ndewa* as feminine, but opposes it to *pahomba*, and provides no further gloss for the second term. Since it is not widely used in Kodi, it is difficult for me to understand the nature of this opposition. Forth defines it in Rindi as 'the complementary term of *ndewa*', and notes that the clan shrine is designated as the *ndewa pahomba* (Forth 1981:496). In another context, the couplet *ndewa ranja*, *pahomba ranja* is translated as referring to the immortal aspect of the soul (1981:188). It would seem that *pahomba* is related in some way to clan ancestors, although perhaps not in exactly the same way as the named *marapu* invoked at all clan functions in Kodi.
3. The rules for who can serve as the official mourner are the following: a dead man can be mourned by his wife, mother, a co-resident brother's wife or daughter-in-law. In no case may his daughters, sisters or grandchildren fill the position, but if no closely related woman is resident within the house, a son, brother or father could take the role. A dead woman can be mourned by her mother, married daughters or sisters, and her daughter-in-law, with her husband also a possibility if there are no properly related women in the house. She cannot be mourned by her brothers, father, sons or grandchildren. It is important that the mourner be a woman who has been brought into the house by marriage, or a man (if necessary) who has enduring rights there. Married sisters or daughters can serve as mourners only if they have already returned to the home to help the mother during her period of illness, and they are still officially 'guests' in the house of their birth. The association of the dead with the affines is linked to a general perception of them as the givers and takers of life, although the cyclicity of this formulation is not as evident as it seems to be in other societies with asymmetric prescriptive alliance (Traube 1981; Forth 1981).
4. Forth's detailed analysis of mortuary ceremonies in Rindi does not mention the institutionalisation of a single mourner like the Kodi *kalalu* figure, but somewhat similar behaviour is expected of funeral attendants (often slaves) who go into trance beside the grave. They are referred to as the *papanggangu*, which Forth translates as 'those who are made to cross over, transferred', and he adds: 'the *papanggangu* are thought to enter the world of the dead while they are unconscious; and when they awake they are often able to report their experiences in the afterworld and to communicate the wishes of the deceased – which must be fulfilled – to the living. During the period of their ritual employment, the *papanggangu* are thus in a transitional state analogous to the mortuary condition of the dead man himself, hence they must be treated with great respect' (1981:198).

Significantly, Kodinese told me that in the past (when slaves were still kept by important families) slave women were used to *kalalu*, particularly if the period of mourning was to be extended because of efforts made to refurbish a stone grave or move the corpse over great distances. These women were also used to bear the heaviest burdens of other ritual transitions (the period of four days after planting the rice seeds, restrictions which follow repairs on a tombstone) which are said to resemble mourning. Nowadays, occasionally a female object (such as a spindle or cotton rolling board) is wrapped in an old rag and stored in the back of the house to take the place of the slave during these periods.

It should be noted that, if women are appropriate mediators in rites of transition because they are alienated from their natal homes to join their husband's home, slaves are even more appropriate: natally alienated from full membership in any clan or house, they are perpetual resident outsiders who must bear the most dangerous burdens. Some of the most sacred cult houses in Kodi are inhabited only by persons of slave descent, whose duty it is to guard certain sacred objects heavily shrouded in prohibitions. In these houses, it may be strictly forbidden to spit, to eat particular foods, to wear patterned textiles, or to excrete or urinate. The owners of these houses fear the supernatural sanctions of death or disease which would strike violators of these rules, and so prefer to live in their garden huts. By transferring the observance of these prohibitions to those members of society considered most easily expendable, they are perpetuating another form of inequality which combines an important spiritual role with diminished temporal power.

5. The passivity of Kodi women is mandated by their cosmological role, and thus differs quite markedly from the specific magical procedures which allow Tubetube women to empower their men (see the next chapter). While Kodi men acknowledge the dark, silent authority of the female term, they are not bound to seek the support of women in ways that would move them into the same arena of action.

Appendix: Death song texts

1. The Song of a Daughter for her Dead Mother;

Sung by Mbora Loghe, Kalembu Laghughu, Kodi, West Sumba, Indonesia

Aaa ... oooo ...
Ah, tibiyaka inya tana wemu
Ha wawi nja pa ate tana wemu inya
Tana ba tomango nola ndeka rate inya

Ha buku nja pa koko tana wemu
Bu dukingo la hekyoro rendi wyatu

Nola hendi hondi
Ngge inya ... ngge inya
Di douka njapa hali wyangge di
La wei wira njamu nggu
Aaa ... oooo ...
Di douka njapa woti wyanggihi
La weiyo myate mbyoghi nggu
Aaa ... oooo ...
Lawiri ngandi ngingo
Ngge inya...ngge inya
Nja pa kole wadanda
A mate la taloro hudo bokolo

La karangga tuda tola
Ngge inya ... ngge inya
Nja pandidi wyandana

Aaa ... oooo ...
Oh, go ahead now mother you say
The pig without a liver you say
When you go into the land broken up into graves, mother
The snail without a throat you say
When you arrive at the room formed of stones[1]
Under the great burial slab
Where are you, mother, where
This is why we cannot wipe away
The mucus flowing on the corpse
Aaa ... oooo ...
This is why we cannot set aside
The tears falling on the body
Aaa ... oooo ...
The ceiling beams supporting thatch
Where are you mother, where
They did not shake with the impact
When you died in the middle of the great night
The boughs supporting the sides
Where are you mother, where
They did not shift with the sound

A heda la tilu lodo dinjaro	When you passed away at the edge of high noon[2]
Bu dukingo kalunikya la katonga njaingo touna	When you finally came to the veranda with no people on it
La Manjeke rada manu	Home of Manjeke who watches chickens
Njaingo pakode helu ndende	There was no young goat to stand in your place
Bu toma do kalunikya la uma njaingo ihinya	When you finally arrived at the house with no inhabitants
La Bahadi wulu nggoka	Home of Bahadi with a coloured beard
Njaingo maghailyo helu kuko	There was no rooster to crow with your voice[3]
Ba ku ndara nduni byali	I am the horse that came back
La lete oro mburuna	To the steps that it came down
Ba ku bangga bali oro	I am the dog that retraced its tracks
La binye oro loho	To the door that it went out[4]
Nja ku kalo ma rongo	But I didn't even hear it (the news of her death)
Lolikyo paringi	Carried away by the winds
Nja pa dilu tilu	But my ears did not sense it
La naleko kapote	Swirling in the whirlwinds
Nomo la malagho la wiri	When the mouse in the ceiling beams
Na pa kawico kadoru	Came to pinch at the side
Nomo la likuto la karangga	When the rat at the main bough
Na pa katudiko kambihya	Gave me the warning twitch
Ngge inya ... ngge	Where is the one, mother, where?
Pa bughe weihanya halili ana wawi	Who let the piglet slip from the armpit
La kalimyatu wataro	In the hamlet to store corn
Ngge inya ... ngge	Where is the one, mother, where?
Pa weihya weijanda kapa ana manu	Who let the chick fall from under the wing
La bondo lihu pare	In the settlement to keep rice[5]
Orona nani inya	Was this the cause, mother?
Ba ta kaparico kadada	Our poverty of low-lying shrubs
Ba ta milya nja pa ghipo	Our sufferings which cannot be counted
Orona nani inya	Was this the cause, mother?
Ba ta huhu nani lolo	Our simple life of boil-sucking creepers
Ba ta dara nja ha baghe	Our misfortune which cannot be measured
Orona haduna inya	The cause of our mother's illness
La ndoyo danga-danga	Stretching over many years
Orona kalawaro inya	The cause of our mother's fevers
La wulla rehi-rehi	Through many many months
Henyaka henene a dukingo mate	Until at last death itself arrived
Inje dunggero paneghe	And there was nothing more to say
A luluhi malondo	As we sat all in a row

A tomanghu kambunge

Inja ndaleho patera

A watu ku mandende

Nomomuni a hangaka ndo lende

Li hyudo manga ramba ngguka

Wu inya lero ana

Nomomuni a ikico la mbughu

Li lyodo jeke manu keka ngguka

Wu inya kaka baba ana

Ngge inya ... ngge

Nja pa notonda la kalimbyatu wataro

Nja pa ghenenda la bondo lihu pare

Nggena nja ghenenda pandou ha ghoghi buku moro

Yila kanduru oro monggo

Nggena nja pa ghenanda pandou kalilyongo nggengge rara

Yila kawata oro teba

Bu palene ha loko

A hambule pare mboghi

O inya kaka heda

Bu panggabo ma ha mara

A kaneikya liku njamu

O inya kaka mate

Noni tana wemu

Bu duki la banjoro karindi wyatu

A rou kalama hembo

Parudako pandoku

Noni tana wemu

Bu toma la hanjawa wini cana

Pombo watu hondi

Bandalo panda ramu

Noni tana wemu

Na mangeda kioto nguti

Mbani ole kodi piyo

Na madanga pangga peti

Ba heda ole kodi piyo

Ba teba lale tonda piya

Disappearance came inside

And there was no answer to our words

As we stood at a line of stones

Over there the hawk on the ledge

Came at night to snatch you away for himself

You mother with children at the lap

Over there the falcon on the rooftop

Came in the day to steal you like a chick from the nest

White mother cradling her children[6]

Where is the one mother, where?

Was it some fault in the hamlet to store corn

Was it some sin in the settlement to keep rice?

Where did it strike the place for green snails to assemble?

Here among the chopped down bushes

Where did it strike the place for red spiders to crawl together?

Here among the cut down trees[7]

You left us drifting in the river

Your bellyful of rotting rice

O white mother who passed away

You let us wash away in the tides

Your rings of crushed intestines

O white mother who died

Over there you shall tell them

When you come to the chamber lined with stones

Under the coconut leaves from the grove

Left behind there to cover you

Over there you shall tell them

When you enter the layers of seeds in the land

Surrounded by large gravestones

Stored wrapped in pandanus leaves

Over there you shall tell them

There would be many knives ready to cut

If your murderer had been another Kodinese

There are numerous steps taken in anger

To revenge the death in Kodi

If you were killed with a shield alone

Ba heda panaghulongo nambu piya	If you were stabbed with a spear alone
Na danga a likito kalogho	There are numerous branches of the banana
Na mangeda a ndapi ana wawi	There are many generations of piglets
Ta kalenggu langu mbani	To take up the challenge of the fierce bough [of vengeance]
Ta koko ngale helu	To demand a replacement for the cut throat[8]
Nomomuni a marapu mangu dala	Yet up there it was a *marapu* who cast his lethal nets
Na rambaho karikyata	Wearing out the backs of the knees
Nomomuni a kapore wawi diri	Yet up there it was an epidemic like pig disease
Na mbole wali ngenda	Which beat us from behind
No banikya ha mabilo kalulla waingo	That is what made my skin coated with filth [in mourning]
Na banikya ha wokico kabondi waingo	That is what made me loosen my hair from the bun [as a gesture of sorrow][9]
Di douka nja pa woti waingo dihi	So that we cannot wipe away the
La wei wira njamo nda	Mucus flowing on the corpse
La lawiri ngandi ngingo	Under ceiling beams holding up the thatch
Di douka nja pa hako waingondi	So that is why we cannot set aside
Ha wei myata mboghi nda	The tears which fall on the body
La karangga tuda tola	Under the boughs to support the sides!

Notes on the text

1. The daughter anticipates that others will say that she is not qualified to mourn her mother with the singing of this funeral dirge, as she has neither the wisdom that the pig stores in his liver, nor the eloquence that the snail stores in his throat. This denial of competence is a largely conventional opening which expresses the singer's humility in the face of the larger forces of life and death.

2. Sorrow is intensified when death arrives unexpectedly. The daughter portrays herself as staring up at the high-towered ceiling of a traditional house, trying to search for a reason for her mother's death. She found no clues in the structure of the house itself (metaphorically shifted and torn asunder by such a disruption), and therefore searches for clues in other domains.

3. This passage asserts that there was no one to replace the dead mother within her clan village, no one who shared her talents or abilities. Manjeke and Bahadi are two of the founding ancestors of the clan of Bongu, and while the full meaning of their names is a bit obscure, the couplet is generally filled out with references to exploits or personality characteristics.

4. Here Mbora Loghe refers to the fact that she married a husband from her mother's village, a classificatory cross-cousin (MBS). But despite this re-enforcement of the alliance tie with Parona Baroro, she was not aware of the dangers to her mother's life (often seen as coming from her 'origin clan') and did not respond to initial signs ('pinches and twitches') that something was amiss.

5. She wonders what caused the ancestral deities to withdraw their protection from the inhabitants of the garden hamlet, thus allowing death and disease to enter. Was there

some unknown infraction which opened the house to danger, or just the usual burden of hardships and poverty?

6 The spirit which caused the death is here compared to a wild bird preying on the domestic animals in the hamlet. The hawk and the falcon couplet is also used to refer to persons in a position of authority, who may swoop down unexpectedly to protect or punish.

7 These are more elaborate ritual names for the garden hamlet, site of the mother's death. The daughter mourns the fact that her mother has left her children behind unintended (although they are in fact already grown). The children are portrayed as parts of her body ('your bellyful of rotting rice ... your rings of crushed intestines') which are allowed to wash away in the waters.

8 Anger is expressed by telling the dead mother to inform the higher deities that there are many friends and family who would be ready to avenge her death, if it had been caused by another human being ('another Kodinese') rather than a spirit. But, when the agent was a supernatural one, such feelings of anger and vengeance are futile.

9 The skin becomes caked with filth during the four-day period of mourning seclusion, and the hair is worn loose around the face, rather than bound up in a bun. Here, the clearest identification of the singer and the mourner or *tou kalalu* is established, as the daughter portrays herself as undergoing these restrictions, when in fact they must be taken on by a woman who resides within the house. Since all of the woman's daughters were married, the task in this case was assumed by the daughter-in-law.

2. The Song of an Observer for a Girl Killed by a Truck;

Sung by Ndengi Wallu, Bondokodi

Pemuni a hengeti lawo harinya	Alas the fated falling of the sarung
Myori mandi lama	The Lord whose tongue is true
Pemuni a oro bei marakana	Alas the traces of the gold earrings
Myori bihya wiwi	The Lord of the sacred lips[1]
Njaingoka na pei byohongo ngorana	There is no way to turn away one's nose
Ha wu ndara dola kokona	The horse must stretch out its neck willingly
Njaingoka na warahongo kikuna	There is no way to shake one's tail
Ha wu karimbyo manunduka	The buffalo must follow along
Wuu! Tanekya liku njamo	Wuu! The twisted entrails are now gone
Nona Ria na heda la kambu tilu lara	Nona Ria dead like cotton blossoms along the road
Wuu! Hambule pare mboghi	Wuu! The stomach filled with rotten rice
Nona Ria na mate la mata wei marada	Nona Ria dead at the source in the meadow
Wuu! Ana timbu nini	Wuu! Child of the straight river reeds
Nona Ria nopongo kandoki loko tana	Nona Ria rests at the banyan tree near the dry stream
Wuu! Ana kapuda hapadi	Wuu! Child of the carved spear handle

Nona Ria na lunango kalimbyo lali myone
Nona Ria pillows her head on the raised earth

Wuu! Ana nona Ria na mate moro longge
Wuu! Nona Ria who died with blue-black hair

Nona Ria na heda kaka ngandu
Nona Ria who died a child with white teeth

Mate inde kodelo la ando
Dead before she had a betel post to cling to

Heda inde tonggolo kapaka
Deceased before she reached the top of the tall tree[2]

Mbera ghuro tana pighu
If you had broken like an earthen dish

Ku konda helu pepe
I would dig you up again and bake you

Mbera tobo lolo pighu
If you had broken like a gourd plate

Ku tondo helu pupu
I would plant you again and pick your fruit

Pemuni a mbera pengga kaka
Alas you broke like a porcelain dish

Nja pa helu buri
Cannot be formed anew

Pemuni a mbera nggori myoro
Alas you broke like a green bottle

Njapa helu lala
Cannot be stuck together again

Yingga tiku njana wena
I was staying quietly alone

Ku kanduko wudi ryongo
When I heard the commotion in the kapok tree

Nonikya a ana timbu nini
My child of the straight river reeds

Na katongango a tana mete
Was resting on the black earth

Yingga baha njana wena
I was not making any noise

Na kabanda wudi jeta
When I was startled by the clamour at the top of the tree

Nonikya a ana kapuda hapadimu
My child of the carved spear handle

Na nopongo a rumba rara
Was sleeping on a mat of yellow grass

Ku kambura lendu ngamba
I ran blindly to the cliff's edge

Ku dukinikya a ana ngguna hario
I came to the child whose games used to lift our hearts

Na mate oro motoro manamalo
Dead because of the speeding car

Ku palaiyo karodo rame
I rushed into the wild branches

Ku toma nikya a ana ghanggo lelu
I arrived at the child of the cotton playthings

Na heda oro mbemo bali mema
Deceased because of the returning truck

A ndewa tomu, ta na noni la turu ndende
Your personal fate, let it stand again by the upright post

A ura dadimu, ta na noni la nggallu kole
Your cowlick of birth, let it go back to the enclosed corral

Ba na hamanggango la lete pamba uma
As you wait beside the ceiling drain of the house

Ba na engana la wanggeho-kawendo	As you linger beside the roof thatch
Tana bali wani la rengge rou karu di	So you will come back from the concealing lontar leaves
Ela Tila horo lodo	Of Tila who rides astride the sun
Tana mbiku wani la ngape ngandu wulla	So you will be released from the teeth of the moon
Ela Pati njera wulla	Of Pati who guards the moon
Ela lombo alipo rara	From the end of the yellow rainbow
Ela kere awango eada	From the edge of the colourful sky[3]

Notes on the text

1 The mention of a single 'Lord' here is a reflection of the somewhat ambiguous mixture of traditional and Christian influences in this text. The girl who was killed and her family were in fact Christians, but the song was sung by an older, pagan woman who shared their sorrow. She does not explicitly refer to any of the *marapu* in the text, but is emphatic in bemoaning a violent death as particularly disruptive of the house and community.

2 Marriage is here presented as the pinnacle of a girl's adulthood, so her failure to reach this is a clear marker of the tragic incompleteness of her life. She was about nineteen, and several suitors were negotiating possible matches.

3 The wanderings of the soul are described, along with the wish that the dead person can later be called back from the skies and moved into the village of the spirits of the dead. Perhaps some of the sorrow and sense of irresolution in this ending stems from the fact that it is unlikely that a Christian family will hold the appropriate ceremonies to call back the soul and end its ghostly existence.

CHAPTER 8

Flying witches and leaping warriors: supernatural origins of power and matrilineal authority in Tubetube society

MARTHA MACINTYRE

This essay examines ideologies of power and political authority in a southern Massim society. The material on which it is based was collected during fieldwork on Tubetube, a small island in Milne Bay Province, Papua New Guinea. I am concerned mainly with indigenous ideas about sources of power and the supernatural aspects of male and female power as they are elaborated in ideas about sorcery and witchcraft. Tubetube people believe that both men and women have supernatural resources which they can use to further their own interests or to sanction actions which they perceive to be contrary to these interests.

The population of Tubetube is a mere 140 and people live in scattered hamlets of one, two or three households. Prior to colonial intrusion in the region, the population was higher and hamlets were clustered together, forming small villages. At contact in the 1890s there were approximately 400 people who gained their livelihood from trading activities. The people of Tubetube and neighbouring islands remain notorious in legend: as fearless sailors, ferocious enemies and cannibals. While their reputation with the people of Duau and Dobu, neighbours to the northwest, characterises them as uniquely bellicose and maleficent, they are culturally very similar to these two societies. Rituals associated with mortuary exchanges and marriage in all these communities tend to elaborate ideologies of lineage integrity and self-sufficiency. On Tubetube, as on Dobu, post-marital residence alternates between spouses' hamlets so that a balance between groups is preserved. Affinal indebtedness enmeshes people as lineage members and creates tensions expressed in beliefs about witches and sorcerers as agents of their lineages.

In the past, when warfare was a constant element in inter-island political relations, the powers of witchcraft and sorcery were crucial components of lineage authority. Senior men and women who were leaders were held to be such not simply by virtue of their age but because of their magic. Many of the qualities of leadership that a modern observer might interpret as personal attributes were seen to be magically induced and transmitted from one generation to another as secret knowledge. Oratorical skills, the ability to persuade others, commanding physical presence and fighting prowess were all believed to be magical in origin rather than inherent aspects of personality. The people who knew the magic and imparted it to specific members of their own lineage were therefore the controllers of power.

There are interpretative problems with the concepts of power and interest in our own language. These are compounded when we are examining indigenous political ideologies in languages that do not make some of the abstract distinctions fundamental to discussions about political relations in English. Thus Tubetube people make no fine distinctions between capacities and actualities when they are speaking about their own polity. The idea that all women share a supernatural potency, for example, is therefore offered as sufficient explanation for all instances of female authority. Such a view corresponds with the pervasive ideas about egalitarianism. Most normative statements about political participation and activity assume a high degree of commitment, and while autonomy is rejected as a reason for political ambition, individual choice is invoked as an explanation for political passivity or submission. Tubetube people do not have a concept of personhood that embodies an ideal, individual autonomy. Social identity and personhood are initially and ultimately conceptualised within the ideology of matrilineal integrity. Consequently, individual and lineage interests are assumed to be identical. If a person decides to act in a way that others within the lineage find incomprehensible then this means that they cannot attribute his or her decision to an identifiable outside influence, such as magic performed by an outsider. Whimsical or entirely idiosyncratic behaviour is described as *nuabwagabwaga* (lit. 'wayward mind') and not scrutinised. This mode of explanation is in many respects similar to that of the Kawelka (Hagen) people, where individual motivations are ascribed to the *noman*, which is both will and social consciousness (M. Strathern 1968; A. Strathern 1972:143-4). The *nua*, like *noman*, is thought to be physically located in the body and capable of dislocation for a variety of reasons. A person in a state of *nuabwagabwaga* is in a state regarded as asocial and apolitical – this is construed as an abnormal condition and not the result of rational, individual thought. The capacity to think rationally and in a socially responsible fashion is called *nuadudulai* (lit. 'straight mind') and is an attribute that all adults share. Lapses into *nuabwagabwaga* occur because of anger, illness or grief. If a person were to remain in this state for a prolonged time, then he or she would be judged insane – a concept expressed by the mind or *nua* having moved *outside* the body rather than being temporarily dislocated from its normal place in the heart.

While there is an intrinsically interesting aspect to discussions about indigenous categories of thought and explanations of the nature of human intention or action, I have introduced the idea of *nua* simply to stress the normative ideal of interest as lineage-based and collectively determined. In discussions about specific intra-lineage conflicts, people would not admit to the possibility of antagonism rooted in individual hostility, although I had seen them as such. Rather, conflict within a lineage is attributed to the magical imposition of ideas from some extra-lineage source, or to mental derangement. In this fashion almost all disputes are construed as inter-lineage conflicts. This view of socially constituted interests has implications for any analysis of male and female power since it precludes the possibility of opposed interests on the simple basis of sex.

In a society where people perceive primary bonds as those established through women, the ideals of social good, mutuality and lineage interest are ultimately delimited by the same principle. Ideas of harmony, unity and equilibrium are analogically expressed as things being *meduna* ('cross-sex siblings together'). Irreducible difference is also expressed in gender terms but the male and female are then husband and wife. In keeping with the principle of lineage exogamy, the concept of antagonism assumes a lineage-based definition of interest. In practice, all this means is that if a person argues with his or her siblings then they dismiss that person as having been magically influenced by his or her spouse. This is not to say that marriage is characteristically conflict-ridden, but that this relationship epitomises difference, for each spouse is designated 'stranger' in the other's lineage (cf. Fortune 1932:278). Cultural constructions of political and social organisation are thus expressed in terms of gender distinctions derived from a dogma of 'matrilineality'. A. Weiner described a similar ideology for Trobriand Islanders and concluded that:

> The fact of matrilineality gives women a domain of control that men can neither emulate successfully nor infiltrate with any degree of lasting power. (1976:234)

The power to create human life and thereby regenerate the lineage are valorised as female, and in the Trobriands provide a sphere of control which is quite distinct from men's world of economic manipulation and political struggle. There, as in most Melanesian societies, political power is associated with the exchange of prestige goods and control over garden land. Weiner delineates the cosmology of power in terms of blood and land. Women, as reproducers of *dala* or lineage identity, are intrinsically powerful. Men, as controllers of *dala* land, can expand and extend their economic and political powers – but they remain inherently temporal and fragile.

On Tubetube, about one hundred and sixty kilometres south of the Trobriands, women are also perceived as the reproducers of lineage identity, but it is precisely this capacity which is viewed as the basis for their control over land. People explained that as rights to land are determined matrilineally, decisions about land are deemed the province of women. Furthermore on Tubetube, as elsewhere in the Massim, land transactions involve transfers of other forms of material wealth: pigs, shell valuables and axeblades. Women are therefore able to participate in exchanges using the same wealth in the same ways as men.[1] Women participate in *kune* (*kula*) and in public debates about land use, property rights and inter-lineage disputes.

When women enter the political arena it is exclusively as representatives of their own lineages, that is as mothers or sisters, and not as wives. People who presume to speak on behalf of affines (including spouses) are considered meddlesome and disrespectful and their interventions are therefore viewed as counterproductive in a dispute (cf. Nash, this volume). Women who take part in public political activities are skilled orators and their manner of self-presentation is substantially similar to that of articulate men. Here, as elsewhere, political leadership is not simply a matter of prestige or wealth, but has to be demonstrated in forceful talk and the capacity to convince or persuade others with words. Only some men and women have the qualities which, when combined with wealth and prestige, enable them to be leaders of their lineages. As these conceptions of leadership are constructed within a generational hierarchy it usually happens that women who are leaders are the senior members of their lineages. This reflects ideals of lineage integrity which locate power of every kind within a group defined by their shared substance, breastmilk.

The word for lineage, *susu*, is that for breastmilk and nurturance. Each successive generation of a *susu* consists of all men and women who have been nurtured by women of the lineage. The progression of generations is described as the cyclical regeneration of a group of siblings through the middle generation of mothers. People make distinctions within an extended matrilineage on the basis of 'wombs'. When referring to the largest lineage unit, a group of people who share a common ancestress three or more generations distant, a person says 'We are part of the same womb'. Those who share a common grandmother say 'We are of the same womb'. All these ways of expressing social unity ignore the sex of descendants while stressing the female progenitor. People explain that there is no necessary antagonism between men and women of a lineage as they are both related to their mother in the same way. In the event of siblings arguing, the image of a mother's body being rent by her squabbling offspring is rhetorically invoked by mediators in the quarrel.

Women's bodies provide the metaphorical idioms for relatedness and identity. The location of generative powers in women's bodies is symbolised in various ways in myth and in mortuary rituals. In its most extreme expression, there is the idea that women while avoiding incest might yet be able to reproduce the lineage without having to marry exogamously. This mythic vision of the parthenogenic reproduction of the lineage must be seen as the most fantastical extreme of a strongly matrilineal ideology. Often implicit in mortuary rituals, where lineage members are isolated from all affinal relatives, the ideal of lineage self-sufficiency is explicit in many Tubetube myths where the primal social unit is a pair of cross-sex siblings (see Young's account in the next chapter). Before European intervention in the form of Christian missions, colonial administrators and health services, people on Tubetube held beliefs about procreation essentially similar to those described for Trobriand Islanders (Malinowski 1929:179ff.). They thought that the perpetuation of the lineage was dependent upon the ancestors' conferral of viability or spirit to a foetus and not simply the result of sexual intercourse. In a society where sexual activity was not confined to those of reproductive age the question of 'virgin birth' did not arise. (While there is a Tubetube word for hymen, there is none for virginity and the terms denoting early adolescence invoke associations of sexual promiscuity rather than innocence.)

An individual woman's power to give birth, to nurture and regenerate the lineage, is one facet of her body's potency. But it is not an unequivocal instrument for the transmission of life and identity. As witches, women also mediate the supernatural forces of death. Both powers are located in their sexual organs so that female sexuality is the metaphorical source of both life and death, and women as persons are thought to have some control over these forces.

Concepts of power

Tubetube language has only one word for 'power' and that is *kaiwe*. It is the word for physical strength, force, fortitude in the moral and physical senses and for magical and political power. *Kaiwe* is used therefore to mean power derived from natural or physical sources; power which is supernatural in origin but controlled by a person so that he or she is 'powerful'; and power socially and institutionally reified as authority –

such as the power of elders over young people. The word which I would translate as 'control', *loi*, refers to the legitimate exercise of power and means 'rule', 'judge' and in some instances, 'enforce'. Since Tubetube people do not believe that a decision which affects oneself and not others constitutes a judgement, the word *loi* is most commonly used to mean 'decide' and contextually implies that the decision is one which affects others. In this common usage it might be best translated to 'to decide for'.

Kaiwe as energy can be increased or decreased by external magical forces. The devolution of authority and power from one generation to the next is described as a gift from one group to another: '*Tomo lalakili siwolena kaiwe kolili.*' 'Their big people, they give power to them.' There are also degrees of power. A person can be *kaikaiwe*: powerful, fervent or energetic. A very strong person is *kaiwesosi*, whereas one who dominates others is *kaiwegabaieni* – he or she has power that surpasses or goes beyond all others. *Kaiwe* is spoken of positively, as a quality that is morally good. When I elicited antonyms, people sometimes offered long explanatory sentences that revealed the underlying view of *kaiwe* as a socially valued and virtuous quality. They suggested opposition not only in physical terms – *belu*, meaning weak, tired or frail – but stressed the moral implications by given words such as *nua-ibiga*, meaning submissive or easily influenced, or *obiga*, meaning meek or yielding. The condition of *nua bwagabwaga* was also described as being opposite to *kaiwe* for the selfishness of arbitrary or inexplicably idiosyncratic decisions is seen as a moral weakness, or a retreat to a narrow, asocial value system.

Both men and women have *kaiwe* and both men and women can make decisions which effect or enforce changes in the lives of others. Gender distinctions about power are few, but there are some of importance for the anthropological debate about female political power. So far as I could determine, Tubetube people thought that men were generally physically stronger than women. They say that women have more physical stamina than men and that they are only marginally weaker. People with whom I discussed the issue pointed out women's strength as carriers and their regular endurance of childbirth as proof of their physical strength. Few thought that an unarmed man could overpower a woman, and both men and women held that in the event of a man being unavailable, there was no biological basis for a woman being incapable of performing any of the tasks defined as conventionally 'male'.

Like the Nagovisi (described in the previous chapter), Tubetube people were sceptical about rape as a form of assault on women. Male informants claimed that love magic would usually persuade an otherwise unwilling woman to have sexual intercourse. Female informants scoffed at the idea of an assailant succeeding in having sexual intercourse with a protesting, struggling victim. Both men and women were astonished by the idea of rape as a punitive act and incredulous when I suggested terror or injury as the reason why a woman might submit to a rapist. For while they could imagine the idea of physical force being used to make a person do something, they maintained that it would be done reluctantly and without enjoyment. Such a state of mind would not matter if the act was not meant to be mutually pleasurable, but it was incomprehensible that a person could enjoy sex with a frightened, passive or resisting partner.

Sexuality is rarely spoken of in terms of dominance and submission. Sexual intercourse epitomises equal, balanced exchange and is one metaphor used when alluding to a perfectly matched transaction where valuables of equal rank are exchanged between partners of equal renown. Seduction is the art of persuasion and agreement, not conquest and surrender. Love magic, like all forms of magic aimed at influencing others, is meant to obviate conflict or opposition by making the person believe that he or she desires the enchanter. It is perhaps of some interest that female informants thought that men usually had stronger love magic than women, whereas men were convinced that women surpassed men in the diversity and strength of their spells.

But by the time of my fieldwork there was one domain of male power which no longer existed, the power to fight and vanquish enemies. Pacification of the region was effected early this century and the men of Tubetube, who were famous over a wide area as warriors and cannibals, no longer define themselves as powerful fighters. Yet in so far as ideas about male power invoke the capacity to fight and to take the lives of enemies, the ideal of the warrior remains essential to ideologies of male and female sources of power. These ideas are constructed within an historical reality but they also draw on a complex cosmology which locates the origins of life and death in women as mothers.

The Tubetube term that I translate as 'magic' is *kukula* and refers to a body of knowledge and not to a distinct form of knowledge that is supernatural. A male practitioner is called a *balau*, a female *kalawe*. The major difference between the two is that women are believed to be born with an innate propensity to be a *kalawe* whereas men have no natural or inherent proclivity towards being a *balau*. Both sexes have to learn *kukula* from their elders, but women already possess latent powers that simply need to be developed. In a strictly limited sense then, it can be said that men have to be more active in their pursuit of knowledge and power. They have to seek, grasp and assimilate *balau* attributes. Women on the other hand can become powerful *kalawe* by the more passive and naturalistic process of growth and maturation. Both the terms evoke ideas of malevolence. In all initial discussions, Tubetube people provided me with uniformly negative interpretations of the activities of both *balau* and *kalawe*. However, as I learned more about the range of magical practices, it became apparent that *balau* and *kalawe* do not confine themselves to the black art. An essential part of their knowledge is concerned with beneficial magic – healing, protecting people from illness, promoting the fertility of land and lineage and ensuring the safety of seafarers. In fact they have a vast array of magical spells and potions that are unequivocally beneficial. These spells and medicines are all called *kukula* and are only contextually differentiated – when magic is effecting death or evil it is said to *kabiianai*, when it is working to effect good, then it is said to *kabinamwanamwa*. Regardless of the ends, practitioners are called *balau* and *kalawe*.

It is inconceivable that a *balau* or *kalawe* could only learn beneficial magic. Indeed, people who were publicly acknowledged as healers or owners of love and beauty magic were secretly feared for their capacities to inflict illness or death. None of the people who were reputedly capable of dealing in death were socially inadequate or considered deviant by the rest of the community. On the contrary, the two women whose magical knowledge was most feared were those who were invariably consulted about illness and childbirth. All the alleged *balau* and *kalawe* I knew were physically handsome men and women, prominent in community affairs. When I commented upon this, and the way the image of a wizened crone or ugly hermit seemed not to fit Tubetube reality, old people simply affirmed that *balau* and *kalawe* were able to make themselves beautiful – this was a characteristic of their public presentation. Indeed, the further I went with my questions and observations, the more contradictory or paradoxical the information about magic became. While it constitutes a departure from technical anthropological definitions, I have decided to refer consistently to *balau* and *kalawe* as sorcerers and witches, as these terms have in English those connotations of evil also found in the indigenous concepts. Moreover, a more neutral term such as 'practitioner' of magic would obscure their basis of power: people believe that *balau* and *kalawe* can kill. It is the capacity to kill that is fundamental as a sanction, both within and without the community. The capacity to employ magical powers is the central defining characteristic, not the moral assessment of intention or outcome. But the mystery that surrounds magical knowledge and those who practise magic is born of the fear of death.

The following section explores the nature of supernatural power as it is manifest in human beings, and formulated in beliefs about magic, witchcraft and sorcery. I then examine the ways in which the supernatural powers of witches and sorcerers were called upon and manifest in the warrior himself.

Witches, sorcerers and warriors

The cosmology of supernatural power includes beings who are not human but who embody the powers of witchcraft and sorcery. These are archetypes for their human counterparts and mortal practitioners are believed to communicate with them. The male is unique and is called Taumudulele. There are many myths about him and in some respects he constitutes a 'culture-hero'. His heroic enterprises are instances of his use of sorcery and provide images of the duality of power, for his mythic role as *guyau* (leader) is contingent upon his supreme command as *balau* (sorcerer). All myths of Taumudulele refer to his magical conquests of enemies and his capacities to invent, create and transform people and things. His name itself reveals his close links with female sources of power for it means 'He-who-tattoos-female pudenda'. He is attributed with the invention of tattooing which, until missionaries banned the practice, formed part of the female puberty rituals. The tattoos that profusely decorated the area of a woman's body normally covered by a skirt were signs of her sexuality and fecundity. Tattooing was but one of his cultural inventions, but its significance as the representation of marriageability, or the transformation of women into potential wives, constitutes one of his most potent mythical acts.

Taumudulele was born human but became immortal. In his *balau* state he often appears as a handsome man. Indeed, his carnality is crucial to his relations with mortal women. He steals into their houses at night and has sexual intercourse with them. The gift exchanges which ensue from these sexual relationships require that the women feed him the lives of their witchcraft victims in exchange for his instruction in garden magic. They consolidate their pact in macabre feasts on uninhabited islands. Not all witches 'marry' Taumudulele, but those who do are considered to be the most powerful.

Witchcraft

The female archetypal witch is called *kalawetonega* and these beings are immortal. The term itself is made up of the morphemes for 'witch' and 'pure' or 'essential'.[2] Witchcraft has many forms, all of them bearing different names. *Kalawetonega* are spirit-witches who can transform themselves so that they look like particular women and thus deceive people. Image-stealing is one way that they operate, but more commonly they work at night in the form of bats, night-birds, flies or shooting stars. Sometimes they are simply invisible. Human witches can also take on these forms but both *kalawe* and *kalawetonega* are most feared in their form as *gelaboi* or flying witches. *Gelaboi* fly from island to island in pursuit of human spirit-lives. Their sport and special delight is found in shipwrecking large sailing canoes so that they reap the spirits of the drowned and take them off to devour on uninhabited islands. *Gelaboi* and *kalawetonega* represent all negative forces in ways that Taumudulele does not. His sexuality and his capacity to make gardens flourish, fishnets full to bursting point and pigs fat render him ambiguously awesome, whereas *gelaboi* or *kalawetonega* are quite simply terrifying harbingers of death and destruction.

Life and regeneration are metaphorically conceptualised as fire. Tube-tube people distinguish between life as consciousness and signs of life such as breathing. If a person is comatose then his 'life' or spirit has gone and his eyes are said to have become dark or to have lost their fire. Myths on the origin of fire describe the theft of fire by grandchildren who, in stealing from their hitherto bountiful, immortal grandmother, gain control over their own sustenance but are condemned to mortality. The grandmother's resentful flight to the spirit world established an equity between people, for then they could grow, cook and exchange their own food. But the children stole only a burning stick and the grandmother retained control over fire itself which she carried in her vagina. This source confers vitality and the fire of life on mortals. As mothers, women had privileged access to the source of life and its mysteries. As witches they had powers to steal life from people. Female power over reproduction and regeneration entailed complementary powers of death and annihilation. Both were inherent capacities of all women and just as all women were ideally reproducers, all were potentially witches.

Witchcraft is a potentiality that has to be developed in secret. In many respects, the secrecy surrounding knowledge of witchcraft is the basis of its potency and the fear it generates. Like most other things that can be inherited, witchcraft and its mysteries were transmitted matrilineally. Women who chose to develop their bewitching powers – and some did not – taught their daughters the art. People believe that witches worked cooperatively and their accounts of witches' activities represent them as the antithesis of all the normal, nurturant activities of mothers. Mothers give birth, nourish and sustain their children. Witches make women barren, steal the lives of children and destroy crops. Unlike mothers, who cannot eat meat and strong food, witches have feasts of raw meat where they devour the flesh of pigs and human victims. Mothers keep their children warm and light fires which they stoke during the night. Witches' houses are cold for they keep their fire inside their bodies. The presence of a witch is signalled by flashes of fiery light emanating from her armpits and vulva as she flies in the night. Barren women or those beyond childbearing age were particularly powerful for their bodies were no longer committed to the regeneration of life. They could fly from island to island, stealing the lives of people and consuming them, sinking boats, destroying crops or killing pigs.

Although unpredictable, their malice was not arbitrary or capricious. Witches were assumed to act in the interests of their lineages. Their destructive forces were usually unleashed against enemies and affines who had offended them. Fortune, in his study of Dobuan society, stressed the mutual distrust which he believed characterised affinal relationships. His view of Massim marriage focuses on the tensions which exist in a community where the integrity of each matrilineage is more important than the marriage bond. The kinship and marriage systems of Tubetube people are essentially the same as the Dobuan system described by Fortune. And whilst I did not observe or detect the degrees of mistrust and veiled hostility within marriage to which Fortune attested, Tubetube cases of witchcraft against affines tended to fall into patterns similar to his Dobuan examples (1932:133ff.). In-marrying spouses and the children of the men of a lineage were the most common victims of witchcraft within the hamlet.

But witches could also fly. They could travel over land and sea to hamlets on other islands. There they did their deadliest work and met their sisters for flesh feasts, whereas within a hamlet a witch was thought to work individualistically in order to avenge some offence against her or one of her lineage. The two types of witch behaviour – mass destruction off the island, particular victims within the community – must be seen as ideological constructs which reinforce the view of a witch as a conscious, selective and highly political operator. Indeed, people believed that if a senior woman were insulted or offended she would vindictively destroy garden crops or kill her own grandchildren. Witchcraft was a mighty sanction available only to women and women with such powers at their disposal were not to be trifled with.

Sorcery

Women were not alone in their mastery of supernatural powers. Men could acquire the esoteric knowledge of sorcery, *balau*, that enabled them to kill, inflict disease and invisibly move from place to place. Sorcery was not an inherent ability but had to be learned. If a man wanted to learn sorcery he had to pay his teacher, usually but not necessarily a man of his lineage, in shell valuables or pigs. Sorcerers' spells and concoctions were carefully guarded and the accoutrements of his trade – stones, shells and carved wooden sticks were believed to be the repositories of dangerous magic.

Sorcery was not necessarily malevolent. Sorcerers had spells to control weather, sailing conditions and to enhance the speed and buoyancy of canoes. They could heal and divine causes of illness or death. War magic, love magic, beauty and oratory magic as well as magic for *kune* (exchanges of shell valuables, canoes and pigs) were essential areas of knowledge that they used for the benefit of their lineages. Spells and contingent curses for the infliction of disease or death constituted their most powerful sanction against those who offended them. Like witches, sorcerers reputedly used their powers individualistically and against their own kin.

Within a lineage, sorcery and witchcraft were complementary. Sorcerers and witches could cooperate as senior men and women of a *susu* so that their combined forces would wreak havoc in enemy groups. If several members of a particular lineage died over a relatively short period or canoes were lost at sea or drought struck, then people attributed their misfortunes to the witches and sorcerers of an enemy group. Inter-lineage vendettas were often perceived as conflicts managed by sorcerers and witches, so part of their supernatural armoury consisted of spells to avert or nullify the magical forces of enemy counterparts. In the past their cooperation was essential in warfare and in the creation of invulnerable, fearless defenders of the lineage. Warriors were made, not born, and the processes whereby they were transformed from boys to fighters illumin- ate the political role of women in this pre-colonial martial society.

Warriors

Seligman maintained that there were no male initiation ceremonies on Tubetube (1910:494). Certainly the rituals lacked the drama ethnog- raphers of other Melanesian societies have found when groups of boys are made men, but they did exist and were reported by missionaries as late as 1920 (Guy 1920, 1970) some years after fighting had ceased. A boy's mother or grandmother and maternal uncle decided when to perform the rite which then involved only the initiate and his senior female relative. Only men who had been initiated thus were able to carry spears and fighting axes. The following account, one of three I collected from elderly men and women, was offered serendipitously when I enquired about the so-called war deity Yaboaine (Macintyre 1983:24; Ròheim 1946).

Oh no, you have made a mistake. Yaboaine is not like our god. She is our grandmother. You know about that, if that woman is dead then you cannot speak her name. You call on the spirit of the woman who made you a warrior, a spear carrier. How can you call her? [a reference to the taboo on naming the dead]. Only 'a woman' [*Yabo wahine*]. This is about *mesinana* [lit. 'with the mother']. Now, if a person is *mesinana*, we called it that, with his mother. If they, his mother's brother and his senior woman, wanted their child to be filled with the power to fight so that he could go on war raids and nobody could harm him or spear him, then they'd call him and they'd go and *mesinana*. So, one night as it grows dark she goes inside the house. It's dark. She opens her mouth wide and tells him to come inside and into her mouth. He is frightened and he calls out and there is no reply. 'Grandmother, grandmother!'[3] No reply. He is bewitched there and he believes he is inside her belly. He is then pushed out of the little door at the back of the house and he is tranformed. Our people believed that their mother or grandmother swallowed them and then they came out of her anus. Very well, he gets up and the woman leads him inside. They sleep until dawn. She tricks him again saying 'Come, we'll go to the garden'. As they are going she points out a tall coconut tree and says 'Oh my child, you climb and get us a coconut'. When he is halfway up then she gets many spears that she and her brother have prepared and sticks them, point upwards around the base of the tree. When he looks down he is filled with fear. This part is called *suwo*. She says 'Jump, jump'. He pleads 'Oh grandmother I'll be speared!' She remonstrates, explaining that his initiation means no spear can touch him. He leaps and she parts the spears so that he lands between them. She has made him wild and fearless and she explains 'Now, if you fight you will be filled with power. No spear can pierce you. You are now a powerful man'. Then they go down and bathe in the sea then she washes him in magical substances. All those things are for him. That is what it means to be with his mother. Then if they go to battle he calls on her, 'O that woman! You, that particular woman! Look down on me, take care of me as we go to fight!' In Dobu and Logea they say the same, but in their language '*Ebweu waine*!' Like that. 'You guide us! You lead us! We'll burn their village! Your fire!' That was how it went. Now if you've heard that Yaboaine was like our God – well that's not quite true. We, our people in the past put their trust elsewhere, in the great witchcraft powers of our senior women, our mothers. If they said go to war then we fought. If we disobeyed we'd be hurt. Don't make mistakes about our beliefs. Remember about witchcraft.

The initiation by the woman effected a permanent transformation and all spear carriers were entitled *tomalele* [lit. 'person transformed or reshaped']. As warriors, men were referred to as *mesinana* when they were in the state of preparedness for battle after ritual fasting and cleansing. They were ferocious, tireless and belligerent, with their minds set on battle. This state, called *munamunai* or *iauiaule*, corresponds in most respects to the amok or berserk states described by Fortune (1932:163) and Chowning (1961:79) for the neighbouring D'Entrecasteaux islands of Dobu and Fergusson. In this state, the only people who could calm or stop them were the senior women of their lineages. They managed this in two ways. The formal role of women in battle preparation was as diviners and this enabled them to call for delay or abandonment of an intended raid by the simple expedient of interpreting omens as inauspicious. The second method was more personally inspired and occurred most often when women intervened in fights within the hamlet. A woman would remonstrate or argue with the combatants, and if these tactics failed she would take off one of her skirts and throw it over one of the men.

Should for any reason, a woman not want one of her menfolk to fight, she would remove him from the assembled group of warriors by placing her skirt on him. The same action ensured the life of any captive brought back from a raid. If a woman took pity on the person, she would put her skirt over the captive and from that time onwards he or she would be an adoptive member of her lineage. Missionaries and government officers in the early part of this century attributed the efficacy of this action to the sacredness of the skirt (see Romilly 1887:37-8; Seligman 1910:554). My own Tubetube informants offered several explanations. First, that the skirt itself was a powerful object and conveyed magical forces so that the person became 'like the woman'. Second, that it was a symbolic threat of witchcraft and any person who touched the skirt would suffer dire consequences. Third, that touching the skirt of a woman of one's own lineage was an act of gross disrespect, tantamount to incest, which would make the offender ill and constitute an act of self-alienation from the lineage. These explanations are multiple and all locate women as central figures in lineage authority and integrity. The image of power invoked in the ideology of women as diviners and preventers of fighting is structur-ally similar to that of men in politics: namely, that their power is manifest in argument, in actions and rituals of group unity (for the augury reading was done in ritual songs and dances with all lineage women participat-ing). But most important, that all a woman's social intervention was undertaken in the firm belief that she had available to her supernatural powers in the event of non-compliance with her will. My informant's concluding statement: 'If they said go to war then we fought. If we disobeyed we'd be hurt', preserves the underlying ambiguity which marks all Tubetube discussions about female power. For it is unclear whether he is referring to the positive view of lineage women as infallible diviners of war omens or the negative sanctions they might vindictively enforce were these disregarded. The same duality exists in conceptions of the nature of male political leadership which depicts leaders simul-taneously as beneficent guardians and dangerous sorcerers.

If witches made men warriors, sorcerers made them invincible.

Sorcerers had magic which enhanced martial performance and protected warriors from injury. In 1918, the missionary Alfred Guy collected lists of sorcerers' magical powers. More than half were associated with fighting. While it is unlikely that any single sorcerer had magic for every aspect of warfare, the range of spells collected by Guy indicates that sorcerers had important functions in every stage of a battle. When a lineage wanted to gather allies for a raid, the leader consulted sorcerers and used their magic of persuasion and influence. The canoes had to be recaulked and decorated with bespelled substances that ensured speed, buoyancy and invisibility to flying witches. Sorcerers made potions which enhanced strength, stamina, agility and alertness. In fighting, the ability to dodge stones and spears was essential, so that even today people recalled stories which told of magic placed on a warrior's eyelids so that he did not blink and was acutely aware of any movement. There were potions and spells for weaponry and fighting regalia, and magical preparations which produced a state of frenzied anger towards the enemy. Finally, in the event of enemy sorcerers having superior magic, the sorcerer acted as healer. He knew herbs to staunch bleeding and alleviate pain and spells to counteract the sorcery of others both before and after battle.

All male leaders of renown were assumed to be knowledgeable sorcerers. As all women were believed capable of witchcraft, female leaders were thought to be those who had special powers at their disposal. The ability to influence or hold sway over others was held to be supernatural in origin and acquired by the ingestion of certain types of magic called *bwayawe*. People who could orate, debate or dominate others were assumed to have been fed *bwayawe* from childhood, usually by their grandmother and her brothers. This perception of the transmission of power and authority from one generation to another derives from the view of generational progression or regeneration that is fundamental to the Tubetube ideology of a matrilineally ordered world. The senior members of a lineage are constantly reconstructing their descendants in their own image, thereby perpetuating the system of social order which locates power in the supernatural. Elders mediate the relationship, gradually imparting their knowledge in their offspring.

Matrilineal authority

Both men and women have access to magical powers of various sorts but there is a matrilineal bias in the system. For witches are born with an innate potency while sorcerers have to be made. Furthermore, male fighting leaders had to be transformed into armigers before they could even begin to build their sphere of influence, and that transformation could only be effected by women. Young men could only make the initial leap into warriorhood with the aid of their mothers. Male leadership was contingent upon female supernatural powers.

However, this ideology did not sustain an authority structure in which women dominated men. The minimal political unit was the lineage. Given that lineage continuity depended not only on the fertility of women but the martial prowess of men, the creation of warriors through the bodies of witches is a further dimension of the dogma of matrilineality. Just as identity is established through female links, so the warrior role is intimately linked to the lineage's interests and has to be mediated by those who define the lineage. Warriors are not the agents of their mothers or sisters, but of their lineage, and given the prominence of sorcery in war their relationship to senior men is at least as important as their bonds to women.

Tubetube people are not given to scholastic musings over comparisons between male and female power, nor do they present arguments about separate and complementary domains. The powers of witches and sorcerers are in fact viewed as over-lapping rather than distinct because of the assumed unity of interest between men and women as siblings. Many of their spells are similar and have the same ends. Both men and women have spells for fertility and to induce barrenness or abortion. They can cause illness and can heal. Beauty and oratory magic, garden and fishing magic and spells to confer invisibility are not the province of people on the grounds of sex. The opposition of witches and sorcerers at the level of ideological rhetoric breaks down in practice when both are seen to be concerned with killing enemies, growing gardens and furthering the interests of the lineage. Furthermore, spells from one source can be used to counteract spells from another, and many of the most valued spells were protective.

Gender differentiation in terms of the wielding of power within a lineage was, and remains, minimal when compared with patrilineally organised Melanesian societies. As owners of gardens and wealth items, women are able to participate in all forms of prestigious exchange. They can organise large mortuary feasts, rear pigs for exchange and form partnerships in order to circulate and exchange wealth items. Such enterprises are rarely embarked on individually but women often initiate or take charge of major exchanges. As leaders or 'managers' of these events they are called *tanuwaga* – the same term applied to men in charge of such ceremonies. Unlike Trobriand women, who transact with skirts and whose participation is circumscribed to the distribution of women's wealth (A. Weiner 1976), or Nagovisi women who do not transact on behalf of men (Nash, this volume, Chapter 6), Tubetube women at once make exchanges on behalf of both men and women and are not restricted to special forms of wealth. There are no major rituals where wealth, pigs and food are exchanged, exclusive to lineage members of one sex. The participation of women depends on such things as the birth order of elders in a lineage; whether or not women have pigs to give; the relationships pertaining in any specific exchange relationship and the food available to a woman. Thus, a woman who is either the eldest or the eldest female member of a lineage is more likely to lead or manage a feast than either a man or a woman who is youngest of a generation of siblings. One with a large number of adolescent or adult children has a larger pool of labour than a mother of small children, and so is more likely to have produced garden harvests of a magnitude that makes her the acknowledged organiser of a mortuary feast. A woman with many inter-island partnerships for the exchange of pigs and valuables is more likely to give a feast than a man or woman who does not have many *kune* (*kula*) relationships. Age, prestige as a transactor and the capacity to call on the labour of younger people are far more important factors than sex when decisions about *tanuwaga* are made.

Feast-giving and wealth exchanges are public displays of political and economic power. Senior men and women who are *tanuwaga* for memorial mortuary feasts proclaim their prestige and political influence in displays of shell valuables. Rows of slaughtered pigs and piles of yams testify to the *tanuwaga*'s control over material and labour resources of the lineage. Women who could demonstrate such powers were formerly called *kalavata*, an archaic term which like the male term, *guyau*, meant 'leader'. As nobody can earn renown as a feast-giver without being able to organise production and the accumulation of pigs, yams and wealth items, it is clear that the institutionalised role of senior women as *kalavata* attests to their powers in pragmatic as well as supernatural terms.

In the event, power and authority are not simply ideas – they are manifest in social relations, institutions, sanctions and restrictions. Many Melanesian societies, 'patrilineal' or 'matrilineal', acknowledge female access to supernatural power but do not incorporate this into systematic ideologies of legitimate political authority. Men can see their political power as inclusive to the point where, in a crisis, women's interests are subsumed in the male political sphere; or even in the case of the Foi (J. Weiner, this volume, Chapter 10), where women become passive representations of male interests to the point that they actually stand for variations in agnatically defined male politics. In patrilineal kinship systems where institutions such as bridewealth and virilocal residence prevail women's interests may be viewed as divisive and divergent. Once she is married, she is the daughter of one lineage and the wife of another. On Tubetube, in becoming a wife, a woman is not incorporated into her husband's lineage in any significant way. The rules of alternating residence and affinal gift exchanges of food ensure that even when she is not residing on lineage land at least half of the household's produce comes from that source. Exchanges continue throughout a marriage and the emphasis is on balance, equity and the self-sufficiency of each lineage. In the years when she resides in her husband's hamlet, a Tubetube woman's independence of her husband's lineage is publicly proclaimed in the gifts of yams, pigs and pots brought by her brothers and sisters.

Identity and personhood are thus constructed within a dogmatic matrilineal cosmology. The nurturant process is also exclusively matrilineal. As all contributions from outside the lineage are received as gifts which must be repaid exactly and in kind, even gifts of food from a father's garden are counterbalanced by affinal exchange so as to preserve lineage integrity. The language of kinship and terms of address constantly reiterate constructed social relationships. So, for example, children of a lineage are collectively referred to as 'our children' (*natunao*) when they are residing in their maternal hamlet, but as 'outsider's children' (*natunatuliea*) when they live in their father's hamlet. Affinal kin terms preserve the alien status of in-marrying men and women, for they are used with pronominal prefixes denoting their alienability, whereas kin terms for consanguineals all bear the prefixes used for inalienability. Membership of the lineage is never attenuated by marriage and the primacy of the brother/sister relationship is never threatened.

In patrilineal systems where the majority of adult women are permanently resident on their husbands' land, the project of lineage or group cohesion emerges as men's business, with ideologies of power that are mirror images of Tubetube, for they stress the transmission of identity, authority and power through men. Male initiation rites frequently involve rituals which symbolically render men, as warriors, the exclusive products of senior men (see Herdt 1981; Kelly 1976). These reproductive processes often imitatively represent men as the legitimate appropriators of female reproductive capacities. Fictions of clans as male-derived groups can be interpreted as expressions of the politics of contempt, or of subconscious fear and envy, as Young argues (Chapter 9). It is a mistake to assume however that fear and/or envy of a particular category of persons involves the *acknowledgement* of that category's power or superiority at any material or practical level. If those who are allegedly fearful have physical or political forces that can be used against the feared group, the result is more often suppression than concession. An analysis that looks only at ideological constructions of inequality is bound to present subtleties and possibilities that are rarely made manifest. In Papuan Plateau societies such as Foi, a logic of agnatically constructed identity excludes women and therefore becomes a doctrine of male self-sufficiency as well as male dominance. Western doctrines can also conflate modes of 'descent'-reckoning with ideologies of privileged access to super-natural sources of power. Thus people who have no doubts about the procreative capacities of women can dismiss women from any public or representative role on the grounds that woman was 'Adam's rib' or that 'the man is not of the woman, but the woman of the man'. Identity and authority converge so as to validate political structures.

The cyclical regeneration of the Tubetube lineage through women is reiterated in the ritual which transforms boys into armigers. But the development of warrior skills and the achievements of warriors are also contingent upon the contributions of senior sorcerers. So the transmission of secret knowledge and power from mother's brother to sister's son forms an integral part of male identity. In this fashion, each successive generation of men is transformed by the joint efforts of brothers and sisters so that they embody the convergent powers of male and female leaders and become proper matrilineal heirs. The warrior role was thus expressive of an ideal of social and political unity between siblings, and complemented the role of mothers as agents of continuity. Women could instigate and veto conflict, but only through men and only in co-operation with men. Ideally, in the sphere of public political action the interests of men and women are inseparable rather than complementary.

Yet political ideals are universally functionalist and teleological. The neat fit between male and female powers that exists in ideological statements about order and unity cannot be accepted as social fact. While antagonism between men and women is not fundamental to the Tubetube view of gender distinctions, it does happen that specific men and women argue and that some conflicts have to be publicly resolved. Such cases provide the basis for an understanding of the relationship between ideology and political practice.

In 1980 I observed a public debate about a sorcery accusation. The man and woman involved had been divorced for several years and both were reputedly knowledgeable in sorcery and witchcraft respectively. The woman accused her former husband of making her ill because she had alienated the affections of their daughter. The woman presented her own case and the man defended himself.[4] Senior men and women in the community debated the issues and, after several hours of discussion, a consensus was reached whereby the man was held to be innocent. The woman did not emerge as the 'loser' however, because the real point at issue – her exclusive rights to her daughter – was resolved in her favour.

The debate focused on the three issues which illuminate ideas about gender distinction and relative power. First, the man acknowledged his strong attachment to his daughter and his desire to see more of her. Nobody who spoke defended his claims. In fact all speakers dismissed them as inappropriate and unfounded. One speaker after another insisted that the father was socially irresponsible in his fondness for a child outside his lineage and that given this fact, he had no rights over her at all. Second, the accusation of sorcery was treated seriously but eventually discounted – not because they believed him incapable, but because in this instance they believed that the woman's own magic was the cause of her illness. She had reputedly induced sterility in herself in order to take many lovers. By thwarting her own procreative powers she had inadvertently caused her body to accumulate blood which had become malignant and was debilitating her. Finally the public meeting became a forum for debate about the ways in which magical powers were dangerous and destroyed social order when they were used to advance individualistic interests.

In their evaluations of sorcery and witchcraft speakers stressed that neither was the greater form of magical power but that variations occurred on the basis of individual knowledge. The relative potency of specific spells could only be assessed in terms of actual cases. As the woman had been sterile for many years, it was clear to all that she had very powerful magic. The conclusion that her illness was self-induced was virtually a communal condemnation of her social irresponsibility in using her magical knowledge against the interests of her lineage.

From this case emerge discrepancies and contradictions between cosmological structures and pragmatic politics. Clearly a conflict between a witch and a sorcerer is not necessarily a contest between witchcraft and sorcery. Adepts vary in their mastery of the arts and communally determined morality establishes criteria for judgement outside the realm of supernatural power. The use of magical knowledge for private and anti-social ends is considered reprehensible but remains a publicly acknowledged aspect of the power and authority of individual men and women who are leaders. Both men and women use their reputations as possessors of secret knowledge to intimidate, and to sanction the actions of people within and outside the lineage. Fear of their capacities to destroy crops, or to induce illness, death or sterility reinforce hierarchical power structures that are otherwise viewed as the natural and moral order. In the past, initiators of warriors or as sorcerers, men and women cooperated to defend and uphold lineage integrity. But these same forces could be used maliciously and for individual ends. In discussions about the roles of witch and sorcerer in warfare the positive aspects of supernatural powers are stressed. Yet it is these powers which enable men and women to manipulate and coerce personal opponents.

It is apparent that Tubetube women maintained their prominent political role not simply because they were valorised as reproducers of the lineage but because they were feared as witches. My informant's statement: 'If they said go to war, we fought. If we disobeyed we'd be hurt', reveals the extent and basis of the political power of female leaders. They made decisions about war and peace and commanded obedience.

The capacity to coerce or invoke fear of retribution is an essential component of public political authority in most societies. Where warfare is an exclusively male preserve, the power to coerce and publicly intimidate is usually denied women. I have argued that the rigidly defined matrilineal polity ordering Tubetube society before pacification required that warriors be produced by women. The capacities to create life and to mediate forces of destruction were conceptualised as lineage characteristics: dual attributes of female sexuality and male action. Women on Tubetube participated in inter-lineage politics on the basis of their sex. The ideologies of lineage cohesion and self-sufficiency that informed martial political activity provided women with institutionalised authority and sanctions that they have not relinquished in the years following pacification. The conjunction of this political role with their economic control over land means that women on Tubetube are not confined to a separate sphere – as holders of wealth, feast-givers, orators and leaders of their lineages they operate in much the same way as their male counterparts. The gender distinction between sorcery and witchcraft provided a balance of power which is the foundation of lineage leadership by brothers and sisters, together.

Notes

1. It is impossible to state with any certainty that women had *equal* access to wealth in the pre-contact period. On the available evidence I would hazard a guess that they did not. During the period when warfare was endemic, all information indicates that men transacted wealth in circumstances where women were excluded. As payments for homicide, as inducements for vengeance raiding and as payments for magical spells, shell valuables went to men and became their personal possessions. Oral testimony suggests that female participation in inter-island *kune* is a post-pacification phenomenon.

2. *Nega* usually refers to qualities of purity in substances such as water, but is used metaphorically to mean an essential element or state of being such as that induced by the ritual fasting before battle or *kune* (*kula*) exchanges. The language of sorcery and witchcraft abounds in esoteric terms which present problems of translation. The

quality which I interpret as 'pure' seems in some usages to include connotations of sacred or supernatural.

3. The term for grandmother, *tubugu*, indicates that the woman was a senior member of the lineage and is being addressed honorifically.

4. Only women of the woman's lineage attended. Although the woman had one older brother, he did not take any part in the debate. Her eldest sister defended her in one short speech. I suspect that her brothers stayed away because they feared that they would be subjected to the 'shameful' revelations of their sister's sexual life. Avoidance behaviour and the etiquette of respect require that men must never publicly acknowledge their sisters' sexuality. One of the most heinous insults is to refer to a person's cross-sex sibling as the sexual partner of anyone – even a spouse!

CHAPTER 9

The tusk, the flute and the serpent: disguise and revelation in Goodenough mythology[1]

MICHAEL W. YOUNG

'Power is successful to the degree that it disguises itself.'

Michel Foucault

There is a tongue-in-cheek saying in Kalauna to the effect that, long ago, men used to have the breasts for suckling babies and women the whiskers for tickling them. One day the breasts jumped to the women and the whiskers to the men, and it has been that way ever since. This tale demonstrates that Kalauna people do not necessarily perceive sex attributes – and gender roles – as immutable. It points to a lively concern with what the sexes have to transact with one another. Yet the sexual division of labour in Kalauna on Goodenough Island is as formal in its delineation of domestic and political spheres as may be found anywhere else in Melanesia. As sisters, wives and daughters, women are structurally subordinate to men. They find it difficult to 'author' themselves other than in terms of their menfolk's projects, and may find it impossible to define their own value except in its use for men (Young 1983b). This is not to say that men deny women agency, and indeed, despite women's structural subordination, men suspect that they are in some sense ontologically inferior to women. To put it crudely, Kalauna men appear to view their own personhood, their individuated value, as something to be achieved. Their power is incremental, something extrinsic to be appropriated. Women on the other hand, have innate or intrinsic value; their personhood is consequently more stable, and they possess powers which cannot be taken from them (cf. Wagner 1977b; J. Weiner 1983). The precariousness of male value opposed to the givenness of female value is good reason for men to be wary of women, for the latter can subvert male power (by shaming for instance) to the detriment of male value. In this respect men are vulnerable to women's power.

Men's unease is expressed in a diversity of ways, most notably in fear of *doke* pollution. *Doke* ('skirt') is a disease of the belly believed to afflict cuckolds, and is the most blatant evidence of a husband's failure to manage his wife's sexuality. I have suggested elsewhere that Kalauna's

229

repertoire of ribald and obscene stories, in its focus on misplaced and misused genitals, reflects men's anxiety concerning their uncertain ability to contain and manage female sexuality (Young 1977). In these stories (about infibulated or mislaid vaginas, about armpits used for copulation and vulvas used as lime-pots, about women who punish their husband's lust by spiking their vaginas with sago-thorns) one finds the persistent theme of female revenge on male ignorance and sexual folly. Like the migratory breasts and whiskers, sexual attributes are imaginatively re-negotiated in such stories, as if to say: 'Things could be far worse than they really are!'

Goodenough Island, and part of neighbouring Fergusson, are anomalous in that patrilineal descent, succession and inheritance prevail in an enclave within a culture area (the Massim of southeast Papua) notorious for its uncompromising matrilineal ideology. Matriliny casts its shadow on Goodenough, and well-travelled as they are, men are aware that women are more influential, more powerful agents, elsewhere in the islands. To commit the fallacy of reified intentionality for a moment, let us view patriliny as a male conspiracy and indicate how it disadvantages women. Patriliny and its concomitants – including the rule of patrivirilocal residence which separates women from their natal kin – are means to ensure male solidarity and generational continuity. Men attempt to appropriate the value of women – their reproductive capacities – and convert it into value-for-themselves. They succeed to the extent that in controlling the material and spiritual resources of the society, they impose their own meanings on women's activities. Women do not have a self-sufficient realm of meanings by which they might know themselves as independent of men in the way that men perceive themselves to be independent of women. Divided by marriage, women have no other recourse than to define their own activities in terms of men's projects. They are muted and their agency is circumscribed. This amounts to a picture of gender inequality, aptly expressed by the fact that while the word for women (*vavine*) is also the word for wife, the word for man (*kaliva*) does not mean husband, for which there is a different lexeme (*moyane*).

As a strategy of male control, however, patriliny is less than perfect. It sets up relations of identity between men of a lineage but simultaneously opposes them to other such lineages; men need women to reproduce, but they are dependent upon other men to provide them. This fact ultimately protects the value of women. Bridewealth and other marriage payments only partially detach a woman from her natal group (M. Strathern in press b), and her worth is such that her brothers never entirely relinquish her. From a husband's point of view, marriage payments are an attempt to countermand the given maternal identity of his children; they are payments for his right to ensure the continuity of his line. A woman uses the pronoun 'we' after she has borne a child; others refer to her as 'they' or 'them' even if her children should die and she becomes barren. The fact of having given birth confers on her an inalienable plurality of identity. Men, on the other hand, remain 'singular' and ostensibly unchanged by fatherhood. That is why fathers must work hard to make their children by feeding them (Young 1971:40-1). The 'work' of patriliny is to overcome what men see as a kind of entropy: a tendency for children to be reabsorbed by their mothers.

Mythology

My main task in this chapter is to illustrate this configuration of gender relations by examining constructed images of gender difference. Such images are to be found in mythology, of which Goodenough (like most if not all Massim societies) has a particularly rich heritage. Myth is many things, and part of its fascination lies in its protean potential; as Lévi-Strauss puts it, myth is 'interminable'. We can make only limited claims for the ideological content of a myth, for it can mean different things to different people at different times and places. Indeed, there are so many caveats to be made that one could be forgiven for setting myth aside as at once too refractory and too complaisant, too generative of tautologies to yield anything that we do not already know. Myth analysis cannot be a discovery procedure, unless its discoveries lie outside the realm of myth itself: for example, that myth does *not* reflect the structural subordination of women, or that it does *not* engage men's preoccupation with patriliny. But myth analysis can also be a re-discovery procedure, its virtue to explicate what is already known in a manner that finds unexpected connections, thereby yielding new understanding. It is in this spirit of exploration that I examine several myths – from Goodenough and beyond. Reading a myth for its messages is a way of reflecting upon a culture's understanding of itself. Inspecting myths for meanings judged to be significant for the subject of one's discourse is like the trick of looking slightly to one side of a distant clock tower to tell the time. The displacement of vision that myth allows brings blurred images into focus.

The stories I examine are all directly or indirectly about marriage, though I do not claim that gender relations or sexual identities are their essential or even principal subject matter. Indeed, they may be said to be 'about' a great many things: the origin and loss of wealth, the generation and loss of power, the partibility and transactability of persons and valuables. It might be useful at this point to state what I expect these myths to yield, given the configuration of gender relations sketched (and somewhat overdrawn) in my introduction. First, male wealth should appear as portable, detachable, transactable, and susceptible to loss or appropriation by others. Female value, in contrast, will appear as intrinsic, innate or embodied, neither detachable nor alienable. Second, the myths should reflect some of the mystifications surrounding wealth and power; in particular they will depict the duplicity needed by men to protect their power and maintain their wealth. Third, it is predictable that where the loss of wealth or power is a thematic issue, an exposure has occurred, a deception has been uncovered.

For the purposes of this essay I do not distinguish between myth and folktale, though there are some important social and political reasons for the people of Goodenough to do so (see Young 1983a:11-12). As I adduce them here, some of the stories are pared to their essentials. This treatment does scant justice to their oral-literary quality, which in many narrative instances is remarkable for its colour and detail. Even so, Massim myths are characteristically spare in the depiction of event and the delineation of character. A principle of condensation allows basic kin types to evoke society at large.

Matabawe's tusks

Among the valuables that used to circulate around the Kula ring were boar's tusks pendants (*doga* in the northern Massim, *dona* in the south, *matabile* or *maiyala* in Goodenough dialects). According to Malinowski they were 'almost as important as the *mwali* [armshells]' with which they travelled in an anticlockwise direction (1922:357). By Malinowski's time (1914-18) *doga* had all but disappeared from the Kula, and for reasons he was unable to discover they had been withdrawn by communities lying outside the Kula, which presumably valued them more highly. He noted, pertinently, that *doga* were more difficult to reproduce than other Kula valuables since they 'are connected with a rare freak of nature – a boar with a circular tusk' (1922:357). The source of these valuables remains something of a mystery. Malinowski seems to have been unaware of the fact that to produce a circular tusk the upper incisors of the animal have to be evulsed, so that the lower canines can grow – painfully over several years – into a perfect circle. Such practices of tusk-cultivation were known on the northern coast of New Guinea, in parts of New Britain, and in the northern islands of Vanuatu. The peoples of the Massim, however, appear to have been ignorant of this practice and many of them, Goodenough Islanders included, deny that *doga* are boar's tusks at all. They insist that they are the tusks of a giant python, a patent mystification which solves to their satisfaction the question of their origin. As to the problem of their drainage from the Kula, I surmise that they were channelled from the Amphlett Islands to Goodenough, where nowadays they exist in great numbers. What might explain their high value and their gradual accumulation on the island is their use in bridewealth payments, and I shall suggest that the doctrine of their mythical origin equips them (more so than any other local valuable) to symbolise marriage itself; marriage, that is, as a transfer of female reproductive potential from one agnatic group to another.[2]

The myth of Matabawe is known throughout the island, and the cave that was his home is claimed (by several different village communities) to be in widely separate locations. Numerous versions of the myth have been recorded and the one I summarise here is from the west coast.[3]

A woman gardened alone, for her husband was abroad. She lamented to herself, 'There is no fish or meat to eat, only vegetables.' A large snake of the bush overheard her. He cut up his own body into pieces and roasted them, leaving them to smoke on a platform. The woman went to her gardens next day and smelled the meat. She found it and wondered where the owner was. It was still there next day so she took a piece home and ate it. Every day she went back, and finding the meat still unattended, took another piece until she had finished it. When she had eaten the head her stomach grew large in pregnancy and she gave birth to a snake. She hid it in a small cave near her house and fed it daily. Matabawe grew bigger and asked his mother to find him a larger cave. Every night she brought him a pot of food and he gave her one of his tusks. 'You can take my tusks and make *matabile* to wear on your neck. It is your wealth. But I ask you not to let your child, my elder brother, come with you when you bring my food. He must stay behind. I will give you my tusks for your wealth, and when they are finished. I will turn over and give you other things. Your house will overflow with wealth.' And so night after night she took him a pot of food and Matabawe gave her a tusk. Her human child saw his mother take the food and asked to see his younger brother, but she refused saying, 'He is not a good person. He is mottled and ugly. You would cry out in fright.' The child said, 'No, he is my real brother, so how could I be frightened?' He begged to be taken to see Matabawe. She refused. Eventually he nagged so much she agreed to take him providing he stayed well behind and kept silent. They went together. She put the food in the entrance to Matabawe's cave and called him. His face appeared. His elder brother saw him and screamed and fled. Matabawe withdrew into his cave. His mother pleaded in vain with him to come and take his food. 'What did I tell you?' he said. 'You should have heeded my words. Did you want me to be your child? Did you want your wealth? Time after time you took tusks from me. But you should not have let my brother come. He saw me and screamed and I am resentful, so I must leave.' That night there were portents as Matabawe burrowed through the ground to the sea, and there made a passage through the reef. His mother heard and rushed to his empty cave and then to the beach. She saw him beyond the reef and pleaded with him to return. But Matabawe said, 'You should have listened to me. You should have respected and loved me. But you and your child rejected me. I am no longer your son. I will go far away to Sudest and Rossel with their *matabile* and other wealth.' And he dived down and went forever.

The majority of Goodenough men and women would have no hesitation in declaring the central meaning of this myth to lie in the hero's resentful departure. The myth of Matabawe explains why islanders are condemned to poverty, just as the equally important myth of Honoyeta explains why they are cursed with recurrent drought and famine. In 1976, cargo-cult leaders prophesied the imminent return of Matabawe and other heroes, a return that would restore to believing islanders their lost birthright (Young 1983a:251-3). Matabawe, then, is more than a fantastic monster in a folktale; he exemplifies a principle of deprivation. His resentment was the wrath of a god, and the possibility of his return is a misty golden hope. Indeed, there are some on the island who believe that he never left, but remains underground, his head beneath the splendid peak of Mt Madawa'a (where tablets of gold are nowadays said to be hidden), and his tail beneath the volcanic crater of Dobu Island. The discovery of petroleum oil off the eastern coast of Goodenough in 1973 confirmed these beliefs that Matabawe was waiting, comatose, beneath the islands. The oil so avidly sought by white men was thought to be his urine.

Let us examine the myth more closely. The latter half centres upon the relationship of human mother and her snake son, but this is built upon a relationship established in the first half between human wife and surrogate snake 'husband'. Initially, the woman is only half of a married pair: her diet lacks meat as her nights lack sex. The python replaces her husband as provider of both meat and sex (in one version of the myth the woman is vaginally penetrated by the snake). Her oral pregnancy eventually yields oral wealth in the form of Matabawe's circular teeth, just as her initial loss (of absent husband as a source of meat) is brought full circle to final loss (of absent son as a source of wealth).

The narrator of this version makes every excuse for her. We are invited to sympathise with her plight as a grass widow, with the temptation she suffered once she smelled roasting meat. She scrupulously asks time and again whose meat it is before she succumbs and takes a piece home; it is a gradual and blameless seduction. The image is of a good woman, passively seduced by a trick, guiltily swallowing the head of the snake in the darkness. Then Matabawe is born and she secludes her anomalous child; she is ashamed, but maternal enough to care for him. She feeds her fast-growing son with food from her gardens, to receive in return her son's valuable tusks. He instructs her to keep his secret, but alas, her first-born insists on seeing his 'brother'. She warns him but he persists, and on seeing the monster the terrified child cries out. Matabawe is angry and resentful (*unuwewe*). He refuses his mother's entreaties to eat and he withdraws, repudiating their relationship. He dives for distant islands, taking his wealth with him.

Turning to the serpent's role in the myth, it is evident that it embodies a principle of paternity. He recycles himself through the woman, who is both vehicle of his regeneration and provider of his nurture. Marriage exchanges on Goodenough are characterised by gifts of game, fish, pigs and shell valuables (nowadays cash also) made to the wife-givers, who typically reciprocate with pots of cooked food. In the myth, the python offers himself as game, and there is another simulated marriage exchange between the mother and her son: tusk valuables for pots of food. It is not uncommon in reality for a son to make such payments to his mother's kin if his father had died young or been otherwise deficient in his duty.[4] In some versions of the story it is men of the woman's village (her 'brothers') who appropriate Matabawe's tusks and other body-part valuables. But the crux of the myth is that a disjunction eventually occurs, and the exchange breaks down irrevocably when the son, insulted by his half-brother, abandons his mother. What can be the meaning of the insult to which Matabawe responds with such grossly inordinate resentment (*unuwewe*)?

In some versions Matabawe is offended by the broth splashed into his eyes by the terrified child. According to Jenness and Ballantyne's version from Bwaidoka (1920:158), the hot water causes the snake 'to writhe in agony', implying that physical pain was the cause of his *unuwewe*. But there is perhaps no need to seek a plausible sufficient cause for the hero's action since the very point about such mythical heroes is that they are amoral, and therefore cannot be controlled by exchange like ordinary mortals. Their heroic resentment reflects what Goodenough people perceive to be at once a cosmic principle, a social starting mechanism, and the expected behavioural response of any adult to damaged or devalued identity (Young 1983a:72-4; 267-8). However, in the episode of Matabawe's *unuwewe* it is possible to see a deeper principle, one that addresses conceptions of power.

Matabawe and other mythical monsters – particularly those of man-eating propensities - are generically called Itaita, literally 'Seeing One' (*ita*, 'to look, to see'). Lexically, Matabawe is a double pun: *mata* - 'eye', *mwata* – 'snake'; *bawe* – 'pig', *bawa* – 'to smoke over a fire'. In the well-known Honoyeta myth there is an explicit connection between the snake-man hero (whose skin is destroyed by his wife) and the all-seeing sun. He hangs his discarded skin on a 'plant of the sun', and after his search for death he transforms into the sun itself, whence he regulates drought and famine as a 'serpent of time', a cosmic fertility principle (Young 1983a:Ch.3). What I am suggesting is that the fateful act of the child in the Matabawe myth, partly condoned by the mother, is motivated by the meanings implicit in 'seeing'. Matabawe strenuously warns his mother against his being 'seen'. Apart from the idiomatic connotations of 'challenge' and 'confront', seeing means revelation: Matabawe's secret is revealed. His resentful withdrawal is analogous to Honoyeta's suicidal quest following the destruction of his skin by the wife who 'spied' on him and discovered his secret. Matabawe abandons Goodenough to poverty just as Honoyeta abandons it to periodic famine. 'Seeing' the source of the hero's power is thus tantamount to an 'original sin' in these myths. This prompts the formulation of a socio-political principle for Goodenough Islanders: sources of power must remain concealed, for great loss is attendant upon their revelation. If we ask what kind of power is at issue in these two myths there are numerous hints – to be amplified below – that the power of the heroes is the power of regeneration and the control of wealth to that end.

Serpents and the origin of wealth

Matabawe is radically transformed in a cognate myth from northeastern Normanby Island (Duau). Róheim (1950:202) gives a truncated version, which he states to be a 'kune [i.e. Kula] origin myth', but a far more detailed version is given by Thune (1980:411-13), of which the following is a brief but faithful summary.

Mwatakeiwa is a female python who gives birth to a human daughter. The woman grows up and steals food from a man's gardens. He spies and catches her, taking her for his wife. She bears a daughter. While the parents are gardening, the serpent grandmother comes and secretly nurses the child. One day the husband comes upon them, and thinking that the snake is about to crush his daughter, he kills his mother-in-law and chops her into pieces. Her daughter is distraught and sheds tears of *chama* shell [*sapisapi*, used for necklaces]. She reconstitutes and magically revives her mother who retreats resentfully to her cave. There Mwatakeiwa assigns her other 'children' [armshells, necklaces, tusk pendants, and other valuables] to different places in the Massim. Then she leaves for Rossel Island, abandoning her human daughter and her son-in-law.

Mwatakeiwa the snake-mother is a source of wealth like Matabawe the snake-son. In the rigorously matrilineal society of Duau females provide continuity, as represented by the lineal sequence of women in the myth. They constitute one *susu* ('breast milk'). The only male is an affine, whose role it is to perpetrate the 'original sin' by acting on appearances, thereby denying himself of the wealth she commanded. In Róheim's version the daughter also leaves with her mother; in fact Róheim takes them to be 'really one person' (1950:203), just as I have suggested that Matabawe is father to himself. Whether or not Mwatakeiwa's daughter is to be literally identified with her mother, the loss of the wife is the common resolution of a number of Massim myths of this genre in which a man marries the daughter of a monster. The marriage is doomed once the husband has unwittingly killed his mother-in-law, for his wife returns to her element (usually the sea) to be symbolically reunited with her mother.[5] This outcome is one variant of the 'matrilineal solution', for such myths articulate the problem of affines (usually in the form of an intrusive husband) in face of an ideal of matrilineal solidarity and self-sufficiency. Their implicit message is: 'If only brothers and sisters could marry one another, then there would be no need of wealth'.

Affines are a necessary evil, however, and in the societies of the Massim a principal function of traditional wealth is to facilitate social reproduction by 'buying' the reproductive capacities of persons and standing for them symbolically in exchange. What then of 'marriage payments' in the Mwatakeiwa myth, such as we found in Matabawe's exchange with his mother? The answer is that there are none, for the myth is marked by a sequence of negative or non-reciprocal transactions. The serpent's daughter steals food from the man; the man abducts and marries her without brideprice; the serpent nurses her granddaughter without her son-in-law's knowledge; her son-in-law perceives her as a threat and not as a benefactor. Finally, the revived snake disperses her wealth-children to deny her son-in-law any future benefit ('He wanted to kill us', she says, 'Let us go'). It is a punishment identical to Matabawe's resentful departure. The only reciprocal transaction in the myth is a matrilineal one: the image of self-sufficiency evoked by the daughter's regeneration of her mother. Of the girl's own father (and the father of the wealth-children) there is no mention.

At this point we need to become more familiar with the concept of wealth as it appears in these and other myths. It has a great many significations, of course, for it is not an undifferentiated category. There is, for example, food-wealth, pig-wealth and shell-wealth. We are particularly concerned here, however, with 'valuables' such as those used in Kula and mythically produced and dispersed by the likes of Matabawe and Mwatakeiwa. Why should such wealth be represented so often as the product of serpents? Can unequivocal gender identification be given to wealth objects? Do valuables stand in any precise metaphorical or metonymical relationship to persons?

Let us begin with the persistent and Massim-wide association between serpents and valuables. Besides Matabawe and Mwatakeiwa there is the Sudest and Rossel Island serpent – said by Lepowsky's informants (1983:490-1) to be the very one which left Goodenough – who gave, in exchange for an old woman's pots of food, its excrement of *daveri* shell currency. On nearby Misima there is reputedly a giant snake who guards a cave full of gold, most precious valuable of whites (Hess 1982:49). Throughout the Massim, *sapisapi* shells are variously said to be snake's scales, excrement or its 'insides', and I noted above that Mwatakeiwa's daughter cried tears of *sapisapi*. These 'tears' were said to be the very shells with which the skin-shedding hero Kasabwaibwaileta began the Kula (Thune 1980:412). Another skin-shedding culture hero of the Massim, Tauhau, committed incest with his sister, and the belly of the pig he killed in her honour yielded armshells and necklaces instead of faeces. Róheim argues that the pig 'is' Tauhau's sister-wife, and it is in her insides that he finds 'shining shells, primitive equivalents of money or valuables' that are both 'excremental symbols' and the 'good body contents' of the child in her womb (1950:201).

If valuables are 'excrements' such as urine, faeces, tears and teeth, then menstrual blood, semen and even babies might also qualify. The following myth from Duau suggests that they do so, again by mediation of a snake-man.

Kusimamalawe [Long Penis] had intercourse with a woman who was weeding in her garden. His penis was so long he could wind it around his waist like a belt. Her brothers saw them and were angry; they chopped his penis into pieces and took their sister back to the village. She gave birth to twins: an armshell and a necklace. Her husband [who had re-joined his penis] followed their footprints back to the village. He took the armshell and sent it to Kiriwina, and the necklace he sent to Muyuwa. That is why men must go and search for them.[6]

Here the children – shell valuables destined for the Kula – are the issue of a human female and a snake-man. The fate of his penis is the fate of many serpents in Massim mythology: to be chopped up by envious rivals. Whether or not there is regeneration, it is an image which suggests another ubiquitous political principle of Massim society: those with outstandingly powerful attributes must be cut down to size. Mythologically, however, the chopping up of serpents leads to a dispersal of wealth (necessitating men's interminable quest for it in trade and Kula), or to a release of fertility (expressed in some myths by abundant gardens, in others by the incestuous union of brother and sister, and in yet others by the origin of sugar cane, a symbol of sexual pleasure).

The association between serpents and cannibalism is also widespread in the Massim, though to explore this connection would take us too far astray. It is pertinent, however, in that two images of the serpent are counterposed yet indissolubly linked: as a source of wealth the serpent presents a benign, generative aspect; as a destructive power it presents a malign, devouring aspect. The Papuan python does indeed grow to an impressive size; it is carnivorous and swallows its prey whole. It can also regurgitate, and the sticky gorge with which the prey is covered resembles the membrane of a neonate. It eats infrequently and sheds its skin periodically, hence it appears to be self-sufficient, self-renewing, and immortal. The python is sexually ambiguous; it can be perceived as either 'all penis' or 'all womb' (cf. Lévi-Strauss 1973:411). Small wonder, then, that it provides a potent natural image of birth and creation, death and destruction, and of androgynous self-sufficiency and self-regeneration. The serpent's association with wealth, therefore, is motivated by its perceived status as a supreme reproducer, an epitome of self-contained generative power.

The foregoing also suggests an answer to the problem of the sex ascription of wealth objects. If the mythical python is essentially androgynous its body products have correspondingly indeterminate gender. This means that Matabawe's tusks are not unequivocally 'male' any more than Mwatakeiwa's wealth-children were all 'female'. Malinowski reported that Kiriwinans regarded armshells as female and necklaces as male; when exchanged in Kula they were said to have 'married' (1922:356). More recently, anthropologists have found in Kiriwina and in other islands of the Kula circuit that armshells are identified as male and necklaces as female, if only because armshells (like men) are more 'mobile' than necklaces which (like women) are more 'sedentary' and harder to solicit (e.g. Campbell 1983:247; J. Leach 1983:24; Munn 1983:290-1). Munn also notes that when tusk pendants were exchanged for necklaces on Gawa, the tusk was said to go 'to meet its wife', clearly implying that the tusk was male to the necklace's female (Munn 1983:306). Such gender ascriptions appear to be contextual and contingent, however, and it is probably the case that valuables do not and cannot have fixed or unambiguous gender associations. Like the Sabarl shell necklace described by Battaglia, the various kinds of Massim valuables are likely to have 'hidden mixtures of masculine and feminine referents' (1983:299). This does not mean, however, that certain valuables may not be owned, transacted, or worn exclusively by one sex.[7]

What is important for my analysis here is the use of valuables in marriage exchange. While other forms of wealth are transacted at marriage (vegetable foodstuffs, pigs, game, fish, pots, mats), there is a sense in which shell wealth, including tusk pendants on Goodenough, are the most vital items of brideprice. Not being self-sufficient like the serpent, kin groups (whether matrilineally or patrilineally constituted) are obliged to enter into exchange for reproductive purposes. These valuables, like pigs, facilitate exchange by 'standing for' persons. Their symbolic potential is enhanced by their durability. Game, pigs, food-stuffs, and so forth are consumables and their use in long term investments is limited. Valuables, on the other hand, can increase in value with age and exchange history; they often bear names and acquire in time something like a personality, as the 'children' they are sometimes said to be (see Campbell 1983 for an example of Kula shell-valuation). Typical-ly, it is tusk pendants, armshells, nosebones, necklaces, shell belts and decorated limesticks that are given by the groom's group to the bride's group on Goodenough. In cases of divorce or premature death these items are given back to the husband or his kin: a return suggestive of their metonymical significance in symbolising the reproductive value of women.

It is possible to be more precise concerning the generative symbolism of the tusk pendant? Let us consider with the aid of an illustration the iconography of a *maiyala* from Kalauna.[8] The ornament consists of several named parts: the tusk itself (*ala*, canine or tusk; or *nigona*, tooth); the pandanus string or twine (*kwayo*) on which the tusk is suspended; the white egg-cowrie (*fue*) which serves as a 'clasp' for the strings, threaded through it and knotted; the decorative cluster (*bole*) of pink *sapisapi* shells which hangs from the root of the tusk; and finally, the neat rows of *sapisapi* shells, stitched on to the woven backing that forms the two side pieces. Goodenough people do not spontaneously offer symbolic read-ings of these named parts, nor of the object, in part or whole – unless to insist that the tusk is Matabawe's. (Kalauna is one of the places that can claim his home, a disappointingly small cave in a cliff above the village.)

It takes little imagination, however, to see in the tusk pendant a conjunction of reproductive symbols, fitting for an object given at marriage. Thus, the tusk (Matabawe's extracted tooth) is in this context suggestive of the penis, while the egg-cowrie is a symbol of female genitalia. Joining them is a twine collar decorated to resemble coarse snakeskin (recalling also that *sapisapi* shells are said to be the excrement of serpents). When seen from the front, the pendant and its scaly decoration is indeed an icon of Matabawe. In view of the skin-shedding myths we shall consider below it is pertinent to note that the string of the pendant is renewed every generation or so as it ages and the shells loosen and fall off. The tusk and the less valuable cowrie endure, while the 'snakeskin' is shed and replaced. These observations may seem fanciful. I cannot claim that modern Goodenough Islanders 'see' their *matabile* or *maiyala* in precisely this way – though once I had suggested the male/female signification of the tusk/cowrie, and remarked the likeness of the side-bands to snakeskin, my informants were enthusiastic in their endorsement! I take the myth of Matabawe to be objectified in the decorative elaborations of the tusks he bequeathed.

This interpretation provides a clue to the mystification of the origin of the tusks and the islanders' stubborn denial that they are pigs' tusks. If they are valued so highly as marriage gifts, then it would scarcely do to admit that they are the 'excrement' of pigs, especially since a whole pig normally constitutes part of the bridewealth. Since the islanders did not cultivate boars for their tusks, they can in innocence claim that *maiyala*, *doga* and such cannot possibly grow on pigs, and they can affect to be shocked at any such suggestion which devalues them. Only mythical serpents are capable of producing tusks of such value that they can, without disrespect, be offered in part exchange for the most precious gift of all.

The affective, overdetermined value of the tusk pendant is nicely illustrated in the sentiment *nuadoya*, which means unstinting generosity, gifts of love made repeatedly and without thought of return. It is a compound of *nua* (heart) and *doga*; literally, 'heart-tusk'. As one informant explained, 'The old men used to wear their *maiyala* close to their hearts all the time, taking them off only to wash'. It is as an emblem of generosity that a *kaiwabu*, a 'chief of the feast', wears a tusk pendant at his sumptuary food distributions (see Young 1971:248-53).

Dogalivina's inalienable 'child'

Nuadoya introduces another myth and another turn to my analysis. One of the properties of any tooth is that it can be extracted; unlike many body parts it is detachable, and of those that are detachable it is the most durable. On these attributes is the myth of Matabawe predicated. The following story – itself predicated on the Matabawe myth – takes the detachability of the tusk (or pendant) as its problematic: as if a local mythologer had also worried over the problem of the metonymical relationship of valuable to person. It is a Bwaidoka story, recorded from a woman.[9]

A woman called Dogalivina [*doga* – tusk, *livina* – uncertain, but possibly a contraction of *lilivana*, meaning something near or close] was born with a *matabile* stuck to her chest. It was her birthmark [literally, 'birth-child']. Her husband pestered her time and again to take it off and give it to him so that he could hang it on his own neck. She refused, explaining that it was fused to her skin, her birthmark. Again he asked, and again she replied, 'I cannot take it off, it is stuck to me.' He continued to ask, until finally she asked her mother to fetch

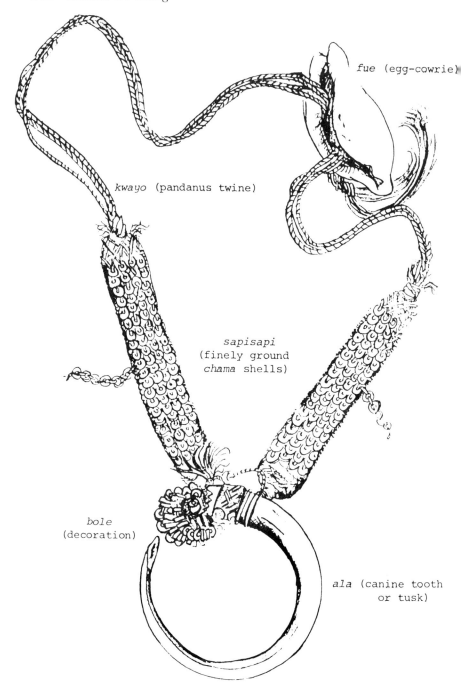

fue (egg-cowrie)

kwayo (pandanus twine)

sapisapi
(finely ground
chama shells)

bole
(decoration)

ala (canine tooth
or tusk)

Figure 1 A Kalauna *maiyala*. Original drawing by Julian Young.

food from the garden and cook for her. While they were eating Dogalivina told her about her husband's impossible demand. 'How can I give it to him?' Her mother warned her son-in-law that the *matabile* he coveted was 'born together with' her daughter, that they grew together in her womb, and that if he were to try to cut it off her breast she would die. That night the husband began imploring again. At dawn she told him, 'Go and break a piece of sharp obsidian.' His wife lay down saying, 'Go on, slit it.' He slit up one side of the *matabile*, then down the other. He finished, and took the *matabile* and hung it around his neck. His wife had already died. They sent for her mother. 'Dogalivina has died.' 'Why?' 'Because her husband cut the *matabile* and took it.' 'Oh, I warned that man but I thought he was joking. Now he has killed my child.' Everyone came and cried, then they carried her home and buried her. But her husband's brothers-in-law came and avenged their sister by killing him.

This poignant tale turns on the fact that Dogalivina's tusk pendant is not detachable, something her covetous husband does not seem to acknowledge. Lacking 'heart tusk' himself he surgically, and fatally, removes hers. Structurally, the story resembles many of the 'matrilineal' myths in which the intrusive affine commits an atrocity and is disposed of by male members of the matrilineage. In the first place, we have a woman born with a *matabile* 'close to her heart', a natural appendage to her body. Having married her, the man believes it to be his right to possess the valuable and wear it himself; this makes sense only if tusk pendants are exclusively 'male wealth'. But in light of my argument that Matabawe's tusks are androgynous symbols of generativity, the husband's attempts to acquire his wife's *matabile* appears as a violent appropriation of her fertility.

We can go further. The self-sufficiency of the python, announced by Matabawe when he repudiated his mother, is also symbolised in the aspiring circle of the tusk (the closer the tip to the root, the more valuable the tusk is said to be). The common symbol of self-generation and cyclical time is the circle formed by the serpent with its tail in its mouth, a motif that occurs on the rims of pots and wooden bowls. Among its significations, then, Matabawe's tusk is an icon of androgyny and reproductive self-sufficiency. Might not this be a clue to Dogalivina's predicament?

Born with a tusk fused to her breast, the heroine is self-sufficient. With the mark of the serpent on her what need does she have of a husband? The narrator refers to her in the plural, the pronominal form used for women once they have borne children, though Dogalivina and her husband appear as a childless couple in the tale. The term translated as 'birthmark' may be significant here: *tubukwamana* is a compound of *tubu* ('born', 'grow', but also the reciprocal kin-term for grandparent/ grandchild), and *kwamana* ('adopted child'). Thus *tubukwamana* can be construed to mean 'adopted grandchild'. Following this hint, could it be that Dogalivina's tusk pendant is her own 'child', and therefore 'grand-child' of her mother? This granted as a possible reading, the myth takes on new meaning as a matrilineal parable, in which the mother (herself ostensibly without a husband) bears a daughter and her daughter's child at the same time. The hapless husband is simply trying to claim his 'child', as he would have every right to in patrilineal Bwaidoka. But the child is inseparable from its mother and the latter dies when, in exasperation, she gives in to her husband's demands to surrender it. Whether the *matabile* is a child or a valuable, however, it is the husband's disappointed assumption that he can detach it from his wife that seeds the tragedy. (I should make it clear that along with other valuables *matabile* are normally inherited from father to son. In default of a son, a daughter may 'look after' them for a generation, but she cannot transmit them to her own children and they should revert to her own patriline.)

The Kusimamalawe myth from Duau provides indirect confirmation for this reading of Dogalivina's story, for they are structural inversions of one another. Kusimamalawe, whose penis was chopped up by his brothers-in-law after he had fathered valuables, asserts paternal control of his 'children' despite the matrilineal norm. Dogalivina, whose breast is cut open by her husband in his attempt to assert control of her valuable, retains maternal control of her 'child' despite the patrilineal norm. Thus both myths are concerned with the 'intrusive affine' and both cleverly invert the normative rules of succession and inheritance.

A skin-changing trader

The myths I have discussed so far have an unmistakable moral. Those deceived by appearances are losers: they forfeit access to wealth and power.[10] The myths which follow introduce the notion of deliberate duplicity in the image of the skin-changer. They too deal with deceptive appearances and duped losers, but commensurate with the protagonist's alternating identity, there is room for winners also.

Molima is a language group on the south coast of Fergusson Island (Chowning 1962; 1983). Its cognatically based communities are cultural-ly intermediate between Dobuan and other matrilineal peoples of the eastern D'Entrecasteaux, and the patrilineal peoples of western Fergus-son and Goodenough. The following story from Molima, therefore, provides an apt transition to the remaining Goodenough myths I wish to explore. It concerns a snake-man more actively human than Matabawe, but one less serpentine in his self-sufficiency. In fact his double identity poses something of a problem for him in keeping a wife.

To'une'une [Trader] was a man by night and a snake by day. He never gardened and did nothing but trade, going from place to place and getting valuables. He had married five times, but each wife had recoiled when they saw him as a snake, and he quickly divorced them. One day while he slept in a tree on an isolated island, a beautiful woman appeared and made a shelter underneath. She had been marooned by her cross-cousin, a witch who was jealous of her success in attracting suitors. The witch returned at night to eat her, but each time she appeared To'une'une, secluded in his tree, frightened her away. Having thus rescued the beautiful woman he took her to his village. He told her to decorate herself and then presented her to his mother who welcomed her as a new daughter-in-law. While To'une'une slept, his mother warned the woman, 'Tomorrow you will climb up with his food. He will deceive you, but do not recoil.' She took his food to him next morning. He awoke, and his snake's tongue vibrated. The woman just laughed. People went to fetch guests for the marriage feast. To'une'une's divorced wives came and were remorseful: 'We had meant to stay with him,' they said. That night To'une'une decorated himself and descended a handsome man. He said to his mother: 'Look after this woman. The women of our village, their way is not like hers.'[11]

'Beauty and the Beast' is a popular genre in the Massim and this version conflates a number of stock themes: a skin-shedding hero, the marooning of a successful rival, the testing of a woman who shows compassion rather than disgust and who thereby wins the handsome (and wealthy) hero. The ending is not always so happy, for the witch sometimes succeeds in killing her good rival. The hero is a great trader, by definition a man of considerable wealth and persuasive charm. The wives he spurned because they failed the test of 'seeing' him in his guise of a serpent are remorseful at having lost him. They recall the remorseful mother of Matabawe who failed to keep her son when his half-sibling recoiled at his ugly appearance. The rejected wives of To'une'une are in a similar position of being deprived, for only his new wife will enjoy his wealth and beauty.

To'une'une recalls also those heroes of the Kula, Kasabwaibwaileta and Tokosikuna (see Malinowski 1922:308-9; Fortune 1963:216-20; Róheim 1950:184-91; Young 1983c). The secret of these men's success is their ability to slough their old and ugly skin to reveal an irresistibly beautiful one beneath. To'une'une is presumably a successful trader for the same reason, though the Molima did not traditionally conduct Kula and this hero's trading activities appear to have been haphazard. What all these myths illustrate is the compelling power of physical beauty – a supreme asset, apparently, in the quest for wealth and fame (or 'name'). Such beauty is 'normally' kept hidden beneath an old or diseased skin. But ugliness, to reverse the common axiom, is only skin-deep; appearances are deceptive, and true value lies within – as the rejected wives of To'une'une learn to their cost.

Why do they hide their supreme asset, these beauteous heroes? The simple answer is that to flaunt it would bring retribution, for the egalitarian spirit of Massim society abhors the display of naked power. Everyone must defer to this principle, on the surface at least. The beautiful, the talented and the wealthy are continually at risk from witches or the sorcery of the envious. A particular perception of power is at issue here, one I shall return to below. But beauty itself is not always enough, and other symbolic instruments of persuasion may be brought into play.

Deceptive flutes

Nose or mouth flutes of reed or bamboo are sometimes to be found in the Massim. Nowadays they are far from common, and even traditionally appear only to have been played by youths or girls during courtship. They are solitary rather than social musical instruments, and their sweet, somewhat mournful sounds are for beguiling lovers.[12] Two stories about a character called Flute (Kulele) are known on Goodenough. Since one of them is male and the other female, a comparison of their respective captivating powers is instructive for an understanding of perceptions of gender difference.

Kulele lived on a mountain on the mainland. His mother hid him because he was covered in sores. But at night he played a flute and its sound went far and wide. On Goodenough there was a wealthy man with two lovely daughters. The elder lay awake night after night listening to Kulele's music until she was enchanted. She asked her father to find the man who made this sound. He sent out canoes, and men searched the mountainside. They found Kulele's mother. 'I'm all alone,' she said, 'except for my son who is full of sores.' They insisted on taking him and carried him to the coast on a stretcher. They returned waving flags and blowing conch shells, and the wealthy man and his daughters met them on the beach. When she saw the young man lying in the canoe, his body crawling with maggots, the elder daughter told them to throw him in the sea. The younger daughter protested: 'He is human. I will look after him.' So she fed and sheltered him and dressed his sores. Later the family went to a drum festival on Fergusson Island, but the girl told Kulele he must remain behind ('Otherwise people will spit when they see you, and I will be embarrassed'). So he remained, while the others went to dance. When they had gone he stood up and shook off his sores. He decorated himself, took a canoe, and appeared at the festival. His dancing and his beauty charmed everyone. When the feast-givers began to distribute food Kulele hurried home. He put on his stinking skin and lay down in the ashes again. The girl returned and told him about the handsome man who had appeared at the dance. 'If only I could have been there,' he said. Night after night the family went to the festival, and Kulele secretly too. Finally, the girl decided to find out where the handsome stranger came from, so she told her father she was sick the next evening and stayed behind in her house. She watched, and later saw Kulele shake off his ugly skin and depart for the dance. 'Ah, he has been hiding who he really is!' She burned his slough, then prepared food and spread out a new mat. Meanwhile, Kulele felt something was wrong with his skin. He saw that the younger daughter was not at the dance. He returned to the village quickly, and saw the smoke of the fire. 'Oh, she hid and saw me!' 'Welcome my friend,' she said, 'I have found you out. Come and eat this food I have cooked.' So they sat and ate together. When the others returned she told them she had eaten and would stay in her house, but eventually her father looked inside and saw her sitting with the handsome man. 'This is the man with sores who lay in the ashes,' she said. 'Our daughter has married Kulele,' he told her mother. The elder daughter was angry and began to quarrel with her sister. 'No,' said Kulele, 'before you rejected me. I wanted you but you would have thrown me in the sea. Now your younger sister has got me, and we shall stay together.' Then her father gave his valuables and his wealth to Kulele. 'Look after them,' he said, 'for now I am retired'.[13]

This charming romance – reminiscent of European folk tales in which a poor, despised hero comes to win a king's daughter and a royal inheritance – has to be completely recast to accommodate a heroine in the principal role.

Kulele lived alone with her mother. She was very beautiful and had a flute like a bone in her upper arm. Every night she would play it by drawing out the bone and pushing it in again. It was melodious like the rising and falling of waves, or the sweet songs of birds. Yaloaiwau, a big-man, held a drum festival in his village. Kulele donned an old and wrinkled skin and went to the feast. People were disgusted and spat at her. But Yaloaiwau told them, 'She has come because of our name; you must not spit at her.' And he gave her betel nut and pepper leaf. When Kulele went home her mother asked if anyone had been kind to her. 'The big-man', she said. 'Then he will be your husband.' Kulele went to the feast several times in the guise of a disgusting old woman. People always spat at her but Yaloaiwau was always solicitous. On the night the festival was to finish, Kulele's mother told her to go and marry the big-man. She decorated herself and did not don the old skin. She was beautiful and her body shone. When she walked into the village everyone exclaimed, and all the men wanted to marry her. Yaloaiwau and his first wife made room for her on the sitting platform above the crowd, and Kulele sat between them. Then she played her flute and people were entranced and came close to listen. Later they slept. Yaloaiwau's son [his namesake] was curious about his step-mother's flute. While she slept he uncovered it and tried to play it by pulling and pushing. He broke it and she died. The boy woke his father and all the people. They were dismayed, and buried her. The old woman refused to come, saying she would mourn in her house, but asked only that they cut off Kulele's hair and send it to her for her remembrance. This was done after they buried Kulele. The old woman put her daughter's hair in a bowl, poured water on it, and stirred until the girl came to life again. Then she sent for Yaloaiwau to bring her firewood and coconuts. He was very ashamed and refused to come, for widowers do not venture into their dead wives' hamlets.

The old woman was insistent. She finally persuaded him to enter the house, though he wept with shame. Then he saw Kulele and they wept and embraced. The old woman warned her son-in-law to look after her daughter, and never touch her flute, for if she died again it would be forever. They returned to live in Yaloaiwau's village.[14]

Kulele's 'flute' is a rather puzzling appendage, and it may help to note the narrator's exegetical comments. He referred to her flute as *yawai*, 'breath' or 'life'. The life of any flute is breath, so the life of Kulele is in her flute; hence also her instant death when it was 'broken'. Her 'flute' was normally concealed beneath an armband on her left upper arm (left, because flutes are played with the left nostril or left side of the mouth), and she made her beautiful music every morning and evening. She had secretly entertained people at the festival, and only on the final night did she reveal her instrument and the source of her beguiling power.

To facilitate comparison of the two Kulele myths I shall tabulate their most obvious parallels and contrasts:

1. A captivating flute-player is secluded with his/her mother: Kulele (m) is an ugly son; Kulele (f) is a beautiful daughter.
2. Kulele (m) secretly shed his diseased skin to attend a drum festival; Kulele (f) secretly dons her diseased skin to attend a drum festival.
3. Kulele (m) disgusts all except the chief's younger daughter; Kulele (f) disgusts all except the chief (and his wife?).
4. The younger daughter destroys Kulele's skin; The chief's son (his namesake) destroys Kulele's flute/life.
5. Kulele (m) returns, marries the younger daughter, and inherits the chief's wealth; Kulele (f) is revived by her mother, and reunited with her husband, the chief.

Perhaps the most interesting contrast between the two protagonists is in the nature of their flutes. Male Kulele's instrument is extra-somatic and nothing is heard of it after he has been brought to Goodenough. He switches codes, as it were, from aural beauty to visual beauty. Female Kulele's flute is integral to her body: it is her inalienable 'life'. Associated with these differences are their respective skin-changing tactics. To attend the festival Kulele (m) sheds his 'normal' ugly disguise, whereas Kulele (f) disguises her 'normal' beautiful appearance. However, they both use their revolting skins to disguise 'true' identities in order to test the sympathies of prospective marriage partners.

There is the curious incident of Kulele (f) being 'played' by her step-son while she sleeps, an event whose structural parallel in the first version is the burning of the hero's skin (in other snake-man myths the destruction of his skin causes him to die or to seek death in *unuwewe-*

driven resentment). Given that Kulele puns on *kelele*, 'to copulate', (as also upon *aku lele*, 'my search'), there may be incestuous overtones in the boy's attempt to play with his step-mother, though we should note that Yaloaiwau's son is his namesake, indicating their identity. Indeed, it would make little difference to the structure of the tale if the father/chief had himself killed his new wife (compare Dogalivina's death at the hands of her covetous husband). Whether or not it is a euphemism for sexual intercourse, the attempt by a male to play her flute can be interpreted as an attempt to discover the secret of the mysteriously seductive power which inflames the passions of all men who hear her. Like the attempt to separate Dogalivina's *matabile* from her breast, it is expressive of a tragic male assumption that women are separable from their value, which can be appropriated as 'wealth'. Because her value is embodied, the flute-girl is more at risk than her male namesake, who not only lays his flute aside but survives the destruction of his skin.[15]

Disguise and revelation

Skin-shedding is more than a plot device; it engages conceptions of personhood and social action, and evokes those impossible cultural ideals of self-sufficiency and self-regeneration. In a general sense, the dual-skinned, duplicitous hero (or heroine in the single instance of Kulele) exemplifies a principle of power and metaphorises an attribute of value. When power is disguised and value is concealed dissimulation becomes a way of life. That one does not know another's mind is a Melanesian axiom; that Papuans have white skins beneath their brown ones is common belief. The inside of a fruit, a tuber, a person, a house, a basket, a tree, a mountain or a stone is where the true value of these things is to be found. Humanity itself came from inside the earth, emerging from a hole at the top of a mountain. Sorcerers and magicians contain their secret powers in bundles kept in baskets hung in dark recesses of their roofs. Everyone keeps their valuables in boxes or baskets likewise hidden away in their houses. To be 'showy' is a prerogative of rank – a transient attribute at best, temporarily accorded to feast-givers – or the privilege of marriageable youth. Display (of self, of wealth, of beauty) has its place, but the normal state of affairs is concealment, a studied modesty, and a cultivated shabbiness. There is a disregard for appearances, an indifference to aesthetics. But this belies the inward state. The diffidence is a cultural affectation, a display of non-display. That it is motivated is evident from the occasions when display is enjoined: at feasts, distributions, marriages, mortuary ceremonies, canoe-launchings and other inaugural occasions. Then men and women paint their faces, rub their skins with coconut oil, decorate their hair with the brightest flowers and feathers, adorn their limbs with scented leaves and shell valuables. To an outsider, the effect is dry land blooming after rain; the visual shock of the sudden flowering is all the greater for the unpromising aridity of the usual condition. People are revealed as aesthetes after all, beautiful beneath the skin.

So Kulele is Everyman and Everywoman, shedding their drab skins for the occasion of the festival, revealing their best (and 'true') selves in an orgy of competitive display. The skin-shedding protagonists of myth, then, are exemplars of normal social conduct with its dissimulations and periodic revelations. But there is more to them than this, for the exemplification of a cultural theme is insufficient to account for the mythological saliency of these snake-men with their exaggerated powers. They wilfully disguise themselves in disgusting skins; they cunningly reveal themselves to win adulation; then they redisguise themselves as if they preferred duplicity as a way of life. Kulele (m) would presumably have kept his double identity indefinitely had not the girl caught him out. Only the female Kulele seemed voluntarily to renounce her duplicity, for she made herself singular in order to marry. There is an implicit comment on gender differences here, one consonant with the notion that whereas men's power (and value) is largely achieved, women's power (and value) is essentially innate. In their competition with one another, men seek to retain the advantage of duplicity, but women must surrender theirs when they marry. Once married, women's value is revealed: bearing children confers on them a public duality, a 'we-ness' that assures them of confident status.

The imposter wife

By way of conclusion I draw upon one more Kalauna myth, one that makes the point about the inalienability of women's value in another way. Instead of non-detachable appendages, it exploits the idea of the imposter. Whereas the theme of skin-sloughing involves one person claiming two identities, the theme of the imposter involves two persons claiming one identity. The imposter is thus complementary and opposite to the skin-changer, for one represents the diminution of power while the other represents its increment.

A man and his wife returned from visiting kinsmen. They brought back gifts of sago, pots, and bananas on their canoe. The man told his wife to cook some bananas while he goes to fish. They would climb up to their village after eating. While the husband was fishing, a *balauma* [spirit] woman appeared and sat by the wife. 'Perhaps you will eat me,' said the spirit woman. 'No, maybe you will eat me,' replied the wife, 'I'm a woman and don't eat people.' They sat while the wife began to cook. 'Your nosebone, give it to me,' said the spirit woman. The wife refused: 'No, I cannot give you this or my mother will be angry with me.' The *balauma* begged and pleaded until the wife finally gave it to her. She placed it in her nose. [This routine is repeated with various ornaments; each time the spirit woman pleads until the exasperated wife yields the valuable. Finally, the woman surrendered her skirt. When the husband returned the spirit woman looked like his wife, and the wife looked like the naked *balauma*.] 'Husband come and sit here by me, this *balauma* woman is bothering me,' said the disguised *balauma*. 'She wants to steal my things.' The man hit his wife. She wept and protested that she is his wife and the other woman is a *balauma* who has tricked them. He refused to believe her. He ate the fish and bananas, and the poor wife was left to pick the bones out of the fire and chew on the discarded banana skins. Before they lay down to sleep the spirit woman told him to hit his wife again. He beat her with a stick till she was bruised and bloody. Later they climbed up to their village, while the real wife went to her mother's house and wept outside. 'Where is your skirt and where are your valuables?' her mother demanded. The woman explained how the *balauma* tricked her and took her place. Her mother went to see her son-in-law. 'Where is my daughter?' 'Here!' 'No, that is not my daughter. Give me back my things, my valuables.' The husband realised his mistake and was very ashamed. He beat the *balauma* and drove her off. Then he killed a pig for his mother-in-law and asked for his real wife back. She refused him. 'I've already got a pig.' So he took her an armshell. She accepted it: 'Ah, a stand for my pot.' But she would not let her daughter return. He took her a tusk pendant. 'Ah, thank you,' she said, 'To hang firewood from my roof.' He took her a shell necklace. She accepted it saying, 'Ah, I can tie my firewood with it.' Her daughter stayed. He took her a decorated limestick. 'Ah, my paddle [for stirring food].' The man got angry and thought, 'I am wasting all my things!' He took her shell earrings. 'Ah, thank you my son-in-law for my pigs' earmarks.' Finally he took her a white pig. 'Ah, that is what I really want. Now my daughter can return.'[16]

A Bwaidoka version of this tale (Maribelle Young 1979) dispenses with the role of the mother, and it is the wife who exercises her power to humiliate her husband. The woman is tricked by a *balauma* into allowing herself to be tied up in a mat, and when the husband returns the *balauma* persuades him to throw her into the river. The woman (who is pregnant) drifts downstream, sets up house in isolation, and gives birth to twin sons. Meanwhile the husband discovers his *balauma* wife is an imposter and banishes her. One day he comes upon his sons playing in the river and they take him to their mother. His wife rejects him, however, and incarcerates him (and the children) in a pig-pen. She keeps them there until they are wretched and starving, then she releases them and they are reunited as a family.

Both tales concern the loss of a wife whose husband is tricked by an imposter into rejecting her. In both tales the husband has to undergo humiliation before regaining his wife. In the Kalauna version he is obliged by his mother-in-law to pay a second, more massive brideprice; she further humiliates him by devaluing it, piece by piece, until the final gift of a white pig (a rare phenomenon more highly valued than the ordinary brindled animal). By affecting to see them as household items of functional use only the valuables are diminished by being denied exchange value. 'My daughter is worth more than your paltry gifts,' in effect, says the mother-in-law.

There is a structural parallel between the *balauma*'s stripping of the wife's identity by taking her valuables one by one, and the husband's attempt to reclaim his wife by incremental payment of valuables. Could this be a hint that women like men can be diminished through depleting their wealth, subtracting from their value, and then reconstituting their identity again by restoring wealth? If so, it is illusory, for the woman 'in reality' retains her essential value – hence the husband's determination to get her back. The wife only 'appears' to lose her value, and it is her husband's error to suppose that she has indeed lost it by confounding appearance with reality. By implication, the *balauma* woman is of no value whatever. It could be that she was motivated to become the man's wife in order to have a bogus value conferred upon her. The *balauma* woman is 'empty', as Goodenough people would say, meaning that she is infertile or barren. (Being immortal, *balauma* and other spirits do not reproduce; by definition there can be no spirit children, no spirit families or clans. *Balauma* are solitary and vengeful, believed to envy humans their reproductive powers.) So the husband disposes of the spirit wife once he realises his error; besides the fact that she tricked him out of a 'good' woman, she can be of no use to him. In assuming the wife's identity and role, then, the *balauma* does not thereby appropriate the wife's real value (which is hidden and inalienable), and she is therefore an inadequate replacement. That the wife retains her value after being denuded of her ornaments is evident from the huge price her mother exacts for her return. Or in the Bwaidoka version, the wife's uncompromised value is evident in her bearing of children, her establishment of a new home in the bush complete with gardens and pigs, and not least in her power to reduce her husband to a 'pig' on his rediscovery of her.

The moral of these tales, then, is that the rejected wife retains her essential value, though she is stripped of her wealth and deprived by banishment of her power to influence her husband. With the transference of ostensible identity to the *balauma*, the imposter wife achieves some power as an agent in that she is able to persuade the husband to beat his wife or cast her in the river. But it is a power wholly contingent upon deception.

The wider moral, perhaps, is that women *can* be separated from their wealth objects only when these metonymically represent them. The appendages of Dogalivina and Kulele (f) are more properly metaphoric expressions of their value, the one an emblem of fertility 'born' onto her chest, the other a seductive instrument which is her very 'life'. For men, the serpent's tusk and the magic flute are metonymical expressions of their power: they can be lost or discarded without forfeiture of life. As symbols of generative power and potent agency, the tusk and the flute have an instrumental valency for men, but an essential and non-instrumental valency for women.   This configuration is consistent with my earlier contention that male identity in Goodenough is achieved, contingent and precarious; it must be sought and maintained through competitive enterprise. Female identity, on the other hand, is given, essential and inherently stable; it need not be sought (beyond assumption of the roles that men define) and requires no special enterprise to maintain. This definition of Goodenough gender differences is conver-gent with those of other 'patrilineal' ideologies and historical male chauvinisms, whose central tenet is ever that 'women are born but men are made'. The flexibility – and fragility – of the Goodenough construc-tion, however, betrays the position of this island of patriliny in a sea of matriliny. The men of Goodenough, one fancies, are forever glancing over their shoulders, wondering about the stories they hear from other islands. Theirs is not a secure patriliny, nor a confident chauvinism.

Notes

1. Fieldwork on Goodenough Island, conducted in 1966-8, 1973, 1977, and 1980, was generously supported by The Australian National University. I gratefully acknowledge all those narrators whose texts I have used in this essay; my wife Maribelle de Vera for recording and transcribing some of them; Ann Chowning for permission to use a Molima myth she collected; Carl Thune, for permission to cite a Duau myth from his unpublished thesis; Martha Macintyre for sharing her ideas on the symbolism of wealth in the Massim; and not least, my son Julian for his drawing of the tusk pendant reproduced here. For their helpful comments on my first draft I thank Terry Hays, Jill Nash, Marie Reay and Jimmy Weiner.
2. I have dealt with these issues concerning the tusk pendant in greater detail in Young 1984.
3. Recorded by Maribelle Young in 1973; the narrator, a man, was Aluwageya of Augana.
4. See the case of Didiala of Kalauna, described in Young 1983a:151-2.
5. See Montague 1983 for a published version from Kaduwaga in the Trobriands. Martha Macintyre collected several such myths on Tubetube Island in the southern Massim.
6. Based on a version collected by the Revd. A. Guy and made available by Martha Macintyre. Róheim gives a similar version from the same region of Duau, though he believes that the girl was the sister of 'Long Penis', and the wealth-children his 'brothers'. Hence, for Róheim, the myth is about incest and the mastery of castration anxiety! (1950:194).
7. With respect to the tusk pendant on Goodenough, for example, Jenness and Ballantyne state that it is 'worn only by men' (1928:249). While I never saw women wear tusk pendants, the version of the Matabawe myth given here has the hero tell his mother that his tusks are for her to wear. Again, a Summer Institute of Linguistics booklet of vernacular texts by Goodenough authors (Huckett 1976a) describes *matabile* under

the general heading 'Women's Personal Adornment'. Clearly, there is room for doubt that these valuables are associated exclusively with one sex.

8. This particular item (in my own possession until I next return to Kalauna), is called *Awana Bolibolimanina* (His-Mouth-Blows-Like-the-Southeast-Wind). It belonged to the notorious cannibal tyrant Malaveyoyo, who was killed and eaten just before the advent of Europeans (see Young 1971:186-7; 1983a: Ch.4). His enemies appropriated the ornament (he was apparently wearing it when they ambushed him) and kept it until several of them died from his curse. The survivors handed it back to his lineage in Kalauna. During the next three generations it circulated in restricted fashion in marriage and death payments, until it came to be inherited by Kawanaba, one of Malaveyoyo's agnatic descendants. Kawanaba gave it to me in exchange for financial assistance in establishing a trade store (Young 1983d:93).

9. See Maribelle Young 1979:3-6. As one of the homes of Matabawe, Bwaidoka or Bwaidoga yields the suggestive etymology *bwai + doga*; *bwai* is vegetable broth, which in local versions of the myth is what the child spilled in the snake's eyes.

10. I am grateful to Terry Hays for sharpening my appreciation of this point.

11. This is a considerably shortened version of a myth recorded from a Molima man by Ann Chowning in 1957.

12. The introduction of European jew's harps brought a rapid decline in the popularity of the flute on Goodenough at least.

13. This version of Kulele is a summary of one recorded by Lawrence Yaubihi, a man of Yafa'olo, eastern Goodenough. It is published in Huckett 1976b.

14. Recorded from Kawanaba, a Kalauna man, in 1980.

15. One senses that the happy ending of Kulele (f) is optional if not gratuitous, and there are probably versions to be found which end with her death. Notwithstanding her magical revival in this version, it is her mother who delivers a sombre warning concerning the inseparability of her value from her life: 'You must not damage her flute again or she will die properly.'

16. Recorded from Manawadi, a Kalauna man, in 1968.

CHAPTER 10

Diseases of the soul: sickness, agency and the men's cult among the Foi of New Guinea

JAMES F. WEINER

In 1940, F.E. Williams summarised his description of the people of Lake Kutubu, located in the Southern Highlands of New Guinea, as follows:

> One could write almost endlessly on Kutubu belief and practice in relation to disease ... Indeed, had I made a fuller study of the people, sufficient to justify it, I think the best method of expounding the culture of Kutubu would be to write a book on this subject in particular, bringing all the rest ... into relation with it. It would be quite feasible, and would do no injustice to the culture at large, to present the beliefs and practices connected with disease as its leading motive. (1977:272)

This insight, so neglected for years by ethnographers of interior Papua New Guinea and yet so illustrative of Williams' grasp of Papuan culture, is the starting point for this discussion. The Foi, as the people of the Lake Kutubu and Mubi River Valley call themselves today, number approximately 4 200 and subsist on the products of sago processing, gardening, hunting and fishing. I have described aspects of their social structure, mythology and cosmology elsewhere (1984; 1985; 1986). Here, expanding on Williams' observation, I wish to interpret illness as a central theme of Foi culture and explain why the elaboration of illness and its etiology embodies the Foi's constitution of social and individual identity, including the distinction between the sexes.

There are two senses in which the concept of affliction can be interpreted as an analytical entry point to a cultural system. From one point of view, illness is always an interior state which the afflicted individual must assimilate. Hence, notions of illness everywhere embody ideas concerning vitality, animation and individual variation, both physical and emotional. In speaking of the manner in which sickness affects an individual, people must elaborate their ideas concerning the strengths and vulnerabilities of their bodies, the variable relations between the physical and psychical components of their identity, and so forth. But even if it is 'self-evident' that illness affects the individual, the cause of illness itself is not necessarily restricted to the processes of individuation, which are sociogenic in nature. The etiology of illness can be ascribed to any number of agents, and it is in etiology that we must locate fundamental ideas concerning agency, responsibility and cause, as opposed to their effects. To use an analogy, the nature of female gestation is an individual state; pregnancy, however, can be the result of factors not necessarily restricted to individual action and responsibility.

Illness is therefore both an aspect of individual identity and a theory about how such identity is constituted. Like any other aspect of identity, both individual and collective, its significances are constructed semiotically, by way of the symbolic operations with which people apprehend their cultural realities. And so this chapter must first of all examine the way in which such cultural realities are formulated.

As Westerners, we view our collective institutions as artifice, the concrete manifestations of human rationality and evolution. Our more individual selves and urges are opposed to it and must be controlled and brought into line in accordance with it. We draw a sharp distinction between natural predispositions and drives and the 'cultured' roles that must be adhered to in a functioning sociality. For people like the Foi, however, such collectively defined conventions as, for example, language itself, are 'natural', a part of each individual's innate constitution. Their moral or cultural imperative, in direct contrast to the Western view, is one of maintaining proper distinctions and segregations within a world of self-evident continuity.

The Foi situate this realm of human action and moral initiative within an innate flow of vital energies, forces and distinctions (cf. J. Weiner 1984). The flow of water from west to east, the cyclical alternation of the sun and moon, and the seasons, the rhythmic cycle of women's fertility as signalled by the onset of their menstrual periods, the constant movement of wealth objects between men, the growth, maturation and death of animals, plants and human beings, all evince a movement, and orient the Foi themselves within a set of cardinal points linked by these movements. Opposing this constant flow of moral and cosmological energy are the actions and purposes of men who cut, channel, halt and redirect such energies to their own culturally construed ends: they manipulate the flow of wealth objects so as to allocate women as wives among patrilineally organised groups of men; they dam rivers so as to catch edible fish; they segregate women from male society so as to channel the potency of menstrual blood itself into child-bearing, and so forth.

Such channelling and control is the essential responsibility of men.

Their primary moral goal can be summarised as the necessity to maintain three main categorical separations: 1) between men and women; 2) between the living and the dead; and 3) between certain categories of in-laws. These three oppositions are by no means as conceptually separate as they are normatively, and indeed the content of most traditional Foi religious life can be neatly summarised as the attempt to establish the homological equivalence of these oppositions. The subject of this chapter is how the maintenance of these distinctions precipitates Foi individual and collective identities. Furthermore, it does so from a male point of view since these three oppositions also form the conceptual armature for the most important of the traditional Foi secret male cults.

This chapter is thus necessarily concerned with the problem of male initiation, for initiation ritual is most commonly seen by ethnographers as the crucible of male identity in the societies of interior Papua New Guinea. If the Foi ritualise the achievement of male status, or differentially mark male as opposed to female responsibility, we might be justified in classifying such marking as a form of initiation, a *rite de passage* in Van Gennep's sense. But, as A. Strathern (1970) has cogently pointed out, most interpretations of initiation carry unacceptable functional implications concerning, for example, the strength of male solidarity, the amount of male–female antagonism, and the jural and political status of women in these societies. They imply, in other words, that initiation *necessarily* has to do with male–female relations, and, moreover, concerns such relations on a number of analytic levels (political, behavioural, psychological). What training of young men existed among the Foi in traditional times, however, concerned none of this but rather, quite simply, instruction in healing techniques. In so far as healing is a responsibility of men, I will not demur if one wishes to label the ritualisation of such instruction among the Foi as boys' initiation.

But such 'initiation' for the Foi was therefore strictly speaking neither an overt depiction and segregation of male and female domains, a purification of men, nor the psychologistically motivated inculcation of male values (as most interpretations of initiation in Papua New Guinea can be categorised). It seemed rather to be men's attainment of esoteric lore revolving primarily around a set of responsibilities to combat illness and maintain fertility, the definition of Foi agency in its marked form. In this latter sense, it can, as Poole (1982) notes, be said to involve the definition of the male self. I wish to side-step, in other words, problems inherent in interpreting male cults in New Guinea from the functional perspective of the necessity to maintain the solidarity of men.[1] Such assumptions cannot help but impinge upon our further understanding of the content of gender relations in these societies, for then the reflexive definition of femaleness becomes a provocative issue. But Foi men define agency, responsibility and the locus of important differentiating activity as essentially male. For them, the problem of female identity is not an issue.

In what follows, I first contrast Western and Foi notions of illness and etiology and how they serve to highlight distinctions in the semiotic foundation of identity and agency. I then describe the parameters of Foi sexual segregation and investigate their theories which underlie the notions of male responsibility, contingency and assertiveness. These ideas are generalised in relation to broader theories of the constitution of the soul and person, and the nature of the soul's detachability. Detachability is in fact the key concept in understanding the ethical dimorphism of the sexes, for men and women are differentially categorised in terms of their relationship to wealth objects. Men's perceived responsibility to control the allocation of women among patrilineally composed groups of men parallels that of 'allocating' souls of the dead to the afterworld. Both were, in specific instances, the focus of the *Bi'a'a Guabora* men's fertility rites. The breakdown in the segregation of these realms precipitated illness, however, and curing illness involved the male members of the *Usi Nobora* healing cult. I thus describe some of the details of these cult activities and relate their symbolism to the problem of intersexual mediation among the Foi. Finally, my conclusions offer a criticism of current approaches to male cult activity in Papua New Guinea and comment on the implications of such approaches for our understanding of gender differentiation in general.

Individual and social affliction

Westerners characteristically view the individual as a unique and inimitable bundle of integrated personality traits. Drives, desires, emotions, intelligence, physique and physical health are all particular and individual, while social lives, that is, public and productive lives, by contrast are described in terms of the roles, functions, jobs, kin statuses (such as husband, mother, child, employee and so forth) to which are attached conventional rather than individual significances.

Common ideas concerning illness regard it as something which results when an individual is careless or abusive of one's health: when one eats wrongly, smokes too much, does not wear proper clothing in cold weather, is insufficiently hygienic, one becomes ill (of course there are those other diseases whose causes are still mysterious, such as cancer, and whose contraction we attribute to luck or fate, which is also individual and specific). In her remarkable interpretation of Western ideas of illness,

Sontag precisely notes the point at which people ceased 'to consider disease as a punishment which fits the objective moral character [and made] it an expression of the inner self' (1977:50). Tuberculosis, in particular, was characteristically viewed as a condition which lent romance and mystery to an individual personality, and 'It is with TB that the idea of individual illness was articulated ... and in the images that collected around the disease one can see emerging a modern idea of individuality' (1977:35).

Western cures, by contrast, deploy the conventional artifice of medical science. Doctors prescribe medicines and more importantly 'correct' ways of taking them, daily regimens and diets. They in fact stipulate in great detail a conventional role that an afflicted person must assume (sometimes only temporarily, sometimes for longer periods) if he or she is to become well again. Medicine must assimilate an individuating somatic dysfunction to a conventionally understood symptomology.[2] This is the semiotic foundation of diagnosis.

The Foi also speak of illness as being the result of 'not being careful', but they are referring to lapses in social protocol rather than to individual states. When men are careless concerning food restrictions, avoiding their wives when the latter are menstruating, or in discharging their material obligations towards their affines, they render themselves and their children liable to illness. Illness is, as Sørum describes for the culturally related Bedamini, 'connected with abnormality of social relations' (1980:294) as it must be among people who characteristically internalise their collective conventions. For the Foi too it is symptomatic of a flaw in a social arrangement, most commonly intersexual segregation or affinal solicitude. And so instead of deliberately collectivising their identity as we do in response to illness, the Foi deliberately differentiate, firstly by isolating the afflicted person from the other members of his domicile and secondly by men's assuming (in traditional times) ritual curing roles which placed a number of sexual, residential and consumptive restrictions on them not usually enjoined otherwise. But whether the source of illness is the detached soul itself (that is, a ghost), or the detachable functions of male action (wives and affines), it is the soul which constitutes the afflicted part of the person. The soul *is* collective convention for the Foi, and ghosts are but the detached and objectified agents of an incompletely articulated human morality.

The Foi word for illness in general is *ma'amegara*, sometimes shortened to *ma'agari*. Semantically, it consists of two words: *ma'ame*, 'thing, something' and also 'pearlshell', and *gara*, which in this case means 'belongings, property'. Thus like the word for pearlshell itself (*ma'ame*), the semantic basis of *ma'amegara* relates the general with the specific, the diffuse basis of Foi convention and its particularisation by individual human beings. It is, quite generally, that 'something' which belongs to an individual, that part of shared convention which manifests itself only when it has been impaired or disturbed. In short, illness is but a special manifestation of the soul itself, a disease of the soul if you will, an affliction of one's moral, rather than physical, identity. The semiotics of illness always locate it within the realm of the innate and as opposed to the contrasting domain of human intention. For Westerners, this centres around individual distinctiveness, while for the Foi, it focusses on the soul, the collectively shared part of each person.

It is this social identity which Foi etiology elucidates, and it amounts to nothing less than a description of those contexts in which the three categorical contrasts outlined above characteristically become unfocused or ambiguous. If the Foi consciously 'do' differentiation, if their locus of human deliberation and action is the maintenance of boundaries, then similarity, the erosion of contrast, is what 'happens' to such contrasts in the counter-invented world of incident and innate event. When they fail to differentiate properly between the living and the dead (if, for example, the men fail to find game for the Fifth and Nineteenth Day mortuary feasts, or if mortuary payments are not sufficiently and properly made), then the deceased's soul will stay in the world of the living, causing illness and death. The ghost has not been properly 'invented' *as a ghost*:

> The ghost is an individualized and particular spirit-being, a part of the innate, whose relation to the living is controlled and 'set up' by collective acts of mourning and ritual. It is projected and counter-invented by a collective response to the sense of relativization (ambiguity and confusion between the realms of living and dead, between human action and the innate) brought on by the occurrence of death. Since death, as a part of the innate, is compelled by human action, people feel compromised in their ability to prevent it, and so resort to collective ('ritual') action. (Wagner 1981:93)

As the ghost in this state is responsible for sickness, so is sickness also the result of improperly drawn contrasts between men and women (often labelled as 'pollution' by Highlands anthropologists) and between affines. Symbolically illness is the manifestation of an incomplete or incorrect referential differentiation between these realms, a breakdown in the protocol that maintains their separateness. It is important to understand that I derive the moral force behind maintaining these distinctions not from some transcendent functional imperative to avoid unintentional liminality (cf. Douglas 1980; Turner 1969) but from Foi men's statements on the distinction between their own and women's responsibilities, and the cosmological dimensions of these contrasts that comprise the foundation of my own analysis. The maintenance of these contrasts and the correction of any ambiguation in them in semiotic terms comprises the fundamental *métier* of male definition and action among the Foi. I wish to make it clear that Foi men perceive an analogy between their responsibility to despatch souls to the afterworld and their obligation to despatch their women to other patrilineal groups. Men who are particularly adept at these roles – those men who take the responsibility for raising other men's bridewealth, who have special rapport with ghosts, and who have special knowledge of curing ritual – Foi call 'head men'. They are in every sense of the phrase, the artificers of Foi society. Male identity in its unmarked form for the Foi is, precisely, head-manship. There is no opposing category of 'ordinary' men to which it is compared, except as a contrived explanation to anthropologists. The only other type of men are *dibumena*, 'poor men', whose social status has been retarded or insufficiently formed.

Social organisation

The residential unit of Foi collectivity is the longhouse community and centres around the men's house (*a hua*, literally 'house mother'). The men's house is the communal residence of up to 50 adult men representing between 3 and 13 different patrilineally composed exogamous, totemically named clans. Flanking the longhouse on either side are the women's houses in which reside the men's wives and unmarried female agnates.

Three or four longhouse communities occupying contiguous territories and whose longhouses are close to each constitute what I have called an extended community (which Williams referred to as a 'tribe' [1977:171]). In pre-contact times, such extended communities comprised units in warfare and today they still represent the political units involved in competitive large-scale pig-feasting. In addition, each can be described as a marriage community: 89 per cent of all marriages recorded in the genealogies I collected took place within one extended community of four longhouses. Further, over 50 per cent of all marriages took place between men and women of the same longhouse.

Each local clan represents a segment of a larger totemically designated dispersed clan which has representative segments in several villages. But men of the same clan of different villages assume that they have a common ancestor, and that the dispersal of the clan resulted from conflict within an originally localised patrilineal group. Men characteristically attribute the resulting fragmentation of the local patriline to internal strife following such events as murder, sorcery or adultery accusations. An immigrant group thus most commonly consists of an accused man and his close kinsmen, affines and followers (cf. Langlas 1974). A group migrating to a new longhouse in search of refuge is characteristically 'adopted' (*garani*, literally, 'to eat together') by a head-man of the host longhouse. This man and his clansmen through him extend political and economic asylum to the refugees as well as providing them with access to land and other resources, all of which are considered inalienable. Because all men of a single longhouse 'live together' and share food and land (the Foi word for this type of commensality, *garanobora*, 'eating together', includes all of these connotations), they consider themselves 'brothers' in the widest sense of the term.

'Relationship' or 'kinship' in this sense is an automatic consequence of long-term coresidence and the sharing it implies for the Foi. Sociality therefore begins not with the conscious effort to relate the members of different clans within a longhouse or extended community but rather with the deliberate attempt to *differentiate* them sufficiently so that they may establish opposed affinal relationships. The idioms by which the Foi describe their affinal arrangements thus all involve the idea of 'cutting' or 'severing' an already implicit relationship of kinship before such arrangements can be made.

The units of marriage negotiation and exchange are the local clan segment, all of whose male members are obligated to contribute and share in bridewealth, and the smaller subdivisions consisting of a man and his sons, which represent the units of affinal relationship and beyond which the protocol of affinal avoidance is unnecessary. Every marriage involves the clan segments of the groom and his mother and the bride and her mother, although it is the male representatives of the immediate families of the bride and groom who take charge of the negotiations. These are the individuals constrained by the *yumu* relationship, which entails the prohibition on seeing the face, uttering the name, or eating from the plate of one's wife's elder female relatives. *Yumu* affinal avoidance is thus the Foi conceptual opposite of *garanobora* commensality, and the intersection of the two modes of relationship effectively defines the universe of Foi social relationship. But before such affinal arrangements are described in more detail, it is necessary to briefly introduce Foi theories concerning conception.

Male responsibility

Foi men radically contrast their role in procreation with that of women. They say that a man's semen merely blocks the flow of menstrual blood from a woman's uterus, allowing it to coagulate within her body and so form the foetus. Semen itself only accounts for the white, hard parts of a gestating foetus, the nails, bones and teeth. The rest of the body's tissues are derived from women's menstrual blood. Despite the fact that semen has this limited role in the formation of foetal tissue, it is clear that men consider menstrual blood as the fertilising substance in its unmarked sense. Furthermore, women are not weakened or enervated by their continual and spontaneous production of menstrual blood. Men, on the other hand, are ultimately debilitated by repeated ejaculations and by contact with menstrual blood itself which has a deleterious effect on the health of adult men. They must therefore avoid sexual contact with women while engaged in those pursuits that demand a maximum of male vigour: primarily hunting and curing ritual.

Femininity is associated with the flow of vital fluids and directions which forms the substrate of Foi sociality, while masculinity accords to itself the complementary function of halting, channelling or interdicting this flow. Such associations inflect the Foi's perception of appropriate male and female productive roles. Men cut down trees, carve canoes, build houses and clear the bush for gardens. They fish with long pronged spears, build and set traps, tap tree oil, engage in ceremonial trade and make tools of war and work. Women process sago, tend and harvest gardens, care for pigs and children, make string bags and most items of apparel and fish with nets. While it is beyond the scope of this chapter to examine the symbolism of male and female work in detail, it should be noted that most of men's work consists of cutting, carving, collecting, damming, and trapping, all of which are activities that halt continuity or movement while that of women chiefly concerns growing, rearing and caretaking and making the various containers that men and women use. Foi ideas about procreation are thus congruent with this contrastive allocation of male and female activity.

These ideas concerning the differential properties of men's and women's procreative substances form the basis of the ideology that I have described elsewhere, following Wagner, as the contingency of males versus the self-sufficiency of females (J. Weiner 1987:Ch.3) Men lack the power of menstruation and hence of childbirth. The continual regeneration of female procreative substance and of birth itself is an aspect of the innate flow of vital energies that comprises the Foi realm of 'nature'. In order to control and channel this innate female power, men control wealth items in the form of bridewealth, which transforms female birth into the artifice of male patrilineal continuity and social cohesion. The unmarked form of sociality for the Foi consists of the resulting male groupings: men's house communities (*amena a fore*, 'men house large'), clans (*amenadoba*, 'men line'), lineages (*amena ira*, 'men tree').

Social identity thus begins when men give wealth to their wives' male relatives in order to secure the patrilineal affiliation of their wives' children. A solidary group of men view themselves as comprising a pool of wealth items upon which its members draw to make such payments. These wealth items, primarily pearlshells and ropes of cowrie shell, are the tangible, partible tokens of male continuity and solidarity. Men detach these tokens of male productivity and assertiveness in exchange for rights to its female counterpart, childbearing and female domestic productivity.

The socially recognised continuity between a man and his children, what an observer might label a 'rule' of patrilineal recruitment, is an artifice of men's manipulation of wealth items. Men maintain a flow of pearlshells that runs counter to what they perceive as an innate flow of female procreative substances, replacing a 'factual' continuity between a woman and her children with a more socially appropriate one between fathers and children. Men view this as necessary since they control productive resources, including women themselves. But since the flow of female procreative substance, is, like the other movements that orient their cosmos, a ceaseless one, then the flow of pearlshells set up to channel it must likewise be continuous. Thus, Foi men feel that their obligation to compensate their wives' male relatives is a continuing one, a life-long obligation that must not lapse if one's children are to remain healthy and vigorous.

In common with other Papuan societies of this area such as Wiru (A. Strathern 1968, 1982), Daribi (Wagner 1967, 1972, 1977b) and Polopa (Brown 1980), Foi say that men have the ability to induce illness in their sisters' children if they are dissatisfied with the amount or quality of shells they have received as bridewealth. If a man feels that the bridewealth he has received for his sister or other close female relative is not satisfactory, his heart will become 'hot' with anger and frustration. This heat is sensed by the ghosts of his maternal and paternal clans, who then take it upon themselves to cause illness in that woman's children. The father of a sick child perceives the maternal cause of the illness in a dream, during which he sees his wife's clan's totemic bird or animal biting or attacking his child. He thereby identifies the child's affliction as *hua busiremo hubora*, 'mother's side striking'. At this point, he gives between one and five medium-sized pearlshells and several ropes of cowrie shells to the sick child. The child then takes them and presents them to his mother's brother: although Foi say that any maternal relative can cause *hua busiremo hubora*, it is usually the mother's true brother who is responsible. The maternal relative's heart then ceases to be 'hot' with anger and the ghost desists.

The manner in which Foi men conceptualise the origin of this illness neatly encapsulates the notions of agency and male responsibility that I have described so far. The 'cause' of this illness lies not in the ghost's immediate attack, nor in the heat of an angered maternal relative, but rather in the failure of a man to properly compensate his wife's close male relatives. He is the agent of his child's illness just as he is the sole agent of its health, for it is men's responsibility to maintain the artifice of patriliny as a constant flow of wealth items between affinally related men.

A man's power to induce illness in his sister's children is akin to the ability of women themselves to adversely affect men's health through contact with their menstrual and sexual secretions – these are permanent, immanent and innate facilities. They are analogues of one another in so far as they constitute the impetus to maintain sexual and affinal segregation. Thus, the control of shell valuables in bridewealth and mortuary payments is men's analogic appropriation of women's reproductivity, and their sorcery techniques imitate female powers of menstrual illness and debilitation. The conceptual definition of bridewealth and menstruation, of maternal illness, menstrual pollution and sorcery, are not dissimilar. They all stem from the categorical nature of substances and ghostly intrusion themselves, the fundamental analogy between female, matrilateral and ghostly influence (cf. Wagner 1967). What differentiates them is their normative or institutional differentiation, the agents responsible in each case, and the social goals towards which they are separately deployed.

Souls and ghosts: Foi male cult activity

The Foi define the body's spiritual aspect as that which animates the body and leaves it after death. In this form it is known as the *amena ho̧*. A person's facial expression is his *i̧ ho̧* or 'eye ghost'. The *i̧ ho̧* leaves the body during sleep and experiences the actions apprehended in dreams.

If men pay bridewealth to secure the attachment of children to their patrilineally composed groups, they gave mortuary payments in the past for precisely opposite reasons: to ensure the departure of a dead person's soul from the world of the living. The associated ritual is in all respects an inversion of bridewealth and marriage ceremony. As the women accompanied the bride to her new home, detaching her from her natal group, so do the men accompany the recently detached ghost of the deceased into the bush, hoping to reconcile the ghost to its permanent separation from the world of the living. In this respect, the men's interpretation of the ghost's intention is of utmost importance, for it forms the motivation for their own action. By contrast, the marriage ceremony emphasises at every point the passivity of the bride, her non-action.

The journey of the souls of the recently dead to the afterworld, which the Foi call *haisureri*, is downstream, or from west to east, paralleling the direction of flowing water in the Mubi Valley. *Haisureri* itself is a counter-invented world of ghosts, a caricature of human society, as are innumerable Christian conceptualisations of heaven, hell and all after-worlds bridging them. There, the ghosts are thought to subsist on special varieties of vegetables only found in *haisureri*, and they also speak to each other in the language of ghosts rather than the Foi tongue. The dilemma that a Foi community faces when there is a death is that of re-establishing its identity as a living society. The traditional sequence of mortuary exchanges and feasts was intended to sever the ties of affinal and maternal relationship that linked the clans of the dead person's spouse, father, mother, father's mother and mother's mother. Here I focus on the final and most important mortuary ceremony, the *Kigiye Habora*.

On the fifth and nineteenth day after death, the male relatives of the deceased made payments of shell wealth, pork and forest game to the maternal and grandmaternal clans of the deceased. The last feast, held on the thirty-seventh day after death (thirty-seven is the 'last' number in the Foi counting system), was called *Kigiye Habora*, literally, the 'bone-making' and was associated with the *Bi'a'a Guabora* cult, the 'black palm splitting' or 'Arrow-Head' cult as Williams translated it (1977:283). The latter was concerned with ensuring general fertility and in particular success in the hunt. If an inauspicious intrusion of ghostly identity made itself felt in the form of illness for the Foi, then a proper contrast between human and spiritual agency manifested itself as the promotion and maintenance of fertility and health in its most general form. Both conditions, therefore, are a function of the strength, efficacy and skill of a community of men. I consider the Arrow-Head cult in more detail shortly.

Men prepared secretly for the thirty-seventh day hunt and left the village at night, so women and children would not see them. They would stay in the bush between five and six days, collecting and smoking game they caught in a small bush house, the *Bi'a'a a*, which they had built beforehand. The deceased's brother or other close agnatic relatives would secretly take the jaw bone of the corpse (accessible at this point due to the advanced state of decomposition). This, according to my informants, was to force the ghost to accompany the hunters and ensure their success. It represented the first step in the ghost's reconciliation to human society. The men would periodically call out the deceased's name and the ghost supposedly answered by making whistling sounds. The ghost was also thought to be responsible for any of the portents of good fortune that Foi men characteristically seek when in the bush – the cries of certain birds which are thought to signal the future acquisition of shell wealth, pigs, long life and success in hunting.[3]

The men returned to the village the night before the thirty-seventh day after death. Before they left the *Bi'a'a a*, they would gather the leaves of the *Piper methysticum* and spitting on them, rub them on the dead man's jaw bone and on their string bags of meat. They then returned to the village and placed the jaw bone above the door of the longhouse. On the thirty-seventh day they decorated themselves and brought the meat into the longhouse. There they distributed it to all the men present. My informants told me that, at this time, women and children were not allowed to see the hunters return nor participate in the feast. They were constrained to stay in the women's houses with the doors securely fastened.

The next day, the deceased's brother or other close agnate returned the jaw bone to the coffin and gathered it with all the remaining bones of the corpse and placed them in a string bag. He and the other men returned to the village where they hung the string bag from the verandah of the longhouse. At this point the widow was permitted to leave the woman's house and view the bones of her dead husband. Previously, she had been kept in seclusion in the exact same manner as women are secluded during childbirth and menstrual periods, because she was thought to be a dangerous focus of her dead husband's anger and frustration.[4]

The traditional Foi sequence of mortuary ceremonies represented the gradual replacement of an affinal opposition with a more inclusive one between men and women. The sequence began when the widow's agnates presented her dead husband's agnates with the shell wealth or pigs of the death payment known as *ka yaro bana'anu*, reversing the direction of and 'closing' the initial bridewealth transaction. The ensuing payments that the deceased's agnates made to the maternal and grand-maternal clans of the deceased in turn severed these kinsmen's claims and forestalled the sickness they could be liable to induce if they did not receive it.

The items exchanged in these transactions were shell wealth and pigs, 'the things of marriage' as the Foi say. The Nineteenth Day feast, however, called for male hunting, and the game which the men brought back was shared by all male and female members of the deceased's community. These men and women represented themselves as sharers of meat who in turn offered the bones to the ghosts, thus replacing the exchange between affines and maternal relatives with that between the living and the dead (or between the village and the bush, the spatial dimension of that opposition). Finally, the men themselves held their own Thirty-Seventh Day feast from which as we have seen women were excluded, returning the community to its more secular dichotomy of male and female.

Although the successful completion of these mortuary rites effected the proper segregation of ghosts and their living relatives, such segregation was not permanent. Foi men and women were always alert to the possibility of ghosts intruding upon the world of the living. The maintenance of this separation constituted the primary rationale of the secret cult activities of men. Both Williams and I were told that the hunting ritual of the male *Bi'a'a Guabora* cult was an integral part of the Foi mortuary ceremonies, and indeed, it is difficult to separate the two conceptually: it would be just as accurate to view the mortuary rituals themselves as male cult activity for the Foi, since it is only in terms of received anthropological conventions that we insist upon its functional distinctiveness. The remainder of this essay is thus devoted to a consideration of the theoretical problems in interpreting male initiation and other cult activity in interior New Guinea and a description and analysis of the most important of the Foi male cults. Like A. Strathern (1970) and M. Strathern (1978), I am concerned with questioning the status of men's cult activity as an index of male solidarity, or of the tension and opposition between the sexes.

It is significant that Foi did not possess a single men's cult but many. The implication is that selective membership in various healing and propitiatory cults served to differentiate men as much as they differentiated men from women generally. Williams reported that in 1938 approximately half of all men and adolescent boys were members of Usi, the most widely practised healing cult in the Foi area. My own estimates made in 1979-80 for the non-lacustrine Foi villages where I was situated were slightly higher; other male cults about which I have less information apparently had smaller memberships.

The mortuary hunting expeditions and the *Bi'a'a Guabora* fertility ritual that attended them in the last stage were not restricted to cult members. Thus the *Bi'a'a Guabora* was not, strictly speaking, a cult, as were Usi or another called Hisare, for the latter were defined by their particular concern with a specific group of ghost patrons. Foi mortuary rituals involved the differentiation of the living and the dead in general, with the attributes of ghostliness in general. They were the responsibility of those men directly involved in the funerary ceremonies by virtue of their relatedness to the deceased. The cults, by contrast, were concerned with the appropriation of a more individual power by men through their differential relationship to various powerful spirits. Let us briefly explore the details of these different men–ghost relations.

Bi'a'a Guabora: the tools of life

The Arrow-Head ritual was indeed, as Williams first reported it (1977:283-9), designed to ensure general fertility and in particular, the abundance of game animals and the success of the men's community in obtaining them. It was associated with at least these occasions: the Fifth and Thirty-Seventh Day mortuary feasts, the completion of a new longhouse and the performance of widow purification rites.

The rites connected with *Bi'a'a Guabora* were not elaborate. Participation in the ritual itself was not restricted but was considered the duty of every able adult man in the longhouse. Young boys were informally admitted to the hunting expeditions that constituted the most important part of the ceremony as they reached adolescence. There were no special preparations prior to the expedition. Men simply left for the hunting preserves north of the Mubi River and stayed in their own bush houses between ten and twelve days collecting as much game as possible. They then gathered in a small house built previously a short distance from the longhouse and called the *Bi'a'a a*, the 'Arrow-Head house'. There they smoked the meat they had brought and filled their string bags with it. Half of the men then returned to the longhouse to prepare sago, bamboo and vegetables for the impending feast. The rest remained in the *Bi'a'a a* and decorated themselves with fronds of the light-coloured *ka'ase* and *a'oa* cordyline varieties. During this period, women and children were forbidden from seeing the meat the men had caught, and for this reason the men readied their bags of game in the Arrow-Head house.

When all was finished, the men from the bush returned to the longhouse. They walked in single file, carrying the bags of meat. They silently marched up and down the central corridor of the longhouse several times while the other men looked on. Then the man leading the procession took a branch of *Piper betel* and as the other men stood still, went from one to the next, striking the bags of meat with the branch and saying 'Heh! This man has killed animals!'. The last man handed him a branch of *Piper* from which he took a bite. Then, one by one, the remaining men each took a bite of the branch. Those men who had brought the meat to the longhouse were then each given a tiny morsel of meat to eat. When they had finished this, they cooked sago and vegetables and ate the rest of the meat along with it. This ended the ceremony, according to my informants.

Williams, who witnessed the *Bi'a'a Guabora* ceremony, offers more information than my elderly informants did in 1979. He noted that the 'extra rites' of the *hibu yiyi* cult (which he rendered as *Gagebo-ninyi*) were often carried out in conjunction with *Bi'a'a Guabora*.⁵ Simply, the rites consisted of a symbolic offering of meat to the ghosts associated with the Arrow-Head cult, through the medium of the *hibu yiyi*, or 'stone axe handle' (*hibu* or *gagebo* = stone axe; *yiyi* = handle or branch [the handles of stone tools are made from forked tree branches found growing at the proper angle]). Upon the completion of the *Bi'a'a Guabora* feast, the men tied a tiny replica of an axe handle around the entrails of one of the animals and threw it on the fire, invoking his ancestor's ghost to partake of the offering (Williams 1977:287). Williams definitely aligned the symbolism of the axe handle with the associated focus of the *Bi'a'a Guabora*, the arrowhead itself. This black palm arrowhead was tied to the *Bi'a'a* after the men's feast and it was upon this occasion that the spell designed to ensure future success in hunting was recited (1977:288). The spell he recorded is a standard one for hunting which several men taught me during my time in Hegeso Village, and which they employed on a number of occasions.

These archetypal Foi men's tools – the arrow and axe – are, like the pearlshells with which they are purchased and compared, metonyms of male productivity and identity. They are as detachable and self-contained as pearlshells – or souls – and indeed, Foi men tell a myth about a society of living axes (J. Weiner 1983). In traditional times, stone axes were considered a valuable (like steel axes are today) and could be used in any kind of payment for which other wealth items were appropriate.

In the *hibu yiyi* rite, men represented themselves metonymically to the ghosts through the medium of the axe, detaching a part of their individual productive identity to ensure a collective prosperity. At each step of the *Bi'a'a Guabora* and *hibu yiyi* ceremonies men represent themselves as a *community* of men. These rites thus stand in direct contrast to those of the *Usi Nobora* healing cult in which men appropriated ghostly identity for the purpose of fostering their individual powers of curing and sorcery. I therefore conclude by examining some of the symbolism of the *Usi* initiation procedures.

Usi Nobora: the seeds of the ghosts

Although the Foi did not practise any explicit form of boys' initiation, the important Usi cult fulfilled this function, since Foi men told me that over half of all boys were admitted to the cult. Thus, unlike most of the initiation rituals described elsewhere in interior New Guinea (see Herdt 1982), the acquisition of male social identity was precisely the acquisition of healing skills. A Foi man's identity is thus first and foremost defined by his ability to treat illness. His responsibility to maintain a proper segregation between men and women, and between the living and the dead also includes the knowledge to correct the results of any breakdown in such separation.

What set the Usi procedures apart from those of the other ghost appeasement cults was the ingestion by the novices of the 'fruit' or 'seeds' of the Usi ghosts. These consisted of the white exudation of insects found on tree branches and called *denane kosega*, 'ghosts' saliva'; the shoots of the red *yu'uri* cordyline; red *Bixa orellana* pods; male human molars painted with red *Bixa* dye; the juice of the red *foreyabe* cordyline; and red *ka'i* leaves.[6] It was the successful internal assimilation of these items that gave the initiate a permanent and substantial rapport with the spirit familiars of the Usi cult. After the initiates had eaten these items, they were each given a man's small finger bone, red birds' feathers, the roots of the *waro* tree. They were expected to keep these items concealed permanently in a tiny woven basket which could be hidden under their armpit. These items would henceforth be referred to as the Usi fruit but actually represented the fruit that the initiates had eaten previously. They would be displayed by an Usi practitioner when, during a curing ceremony, he sucked a fragment of bone or feather from a sick person's body and revealed the proof of ghostly intrusion.

The second thing that set the Usi cult members apart from other men was the special and additional powers of sorcery they gained by their ingestion of the Usi seeds. For if they were able to remove such items from a sick person's body, they were equally capable of acting like ghosts themselves and using the fruit to induce illness and death in their enemies. To the extent that the Usi men had control over sickness and health through this medium, they had become like ghosts themselves, and the Foi men who explained the meaning of the cult to me used this phrasing.

Former members of the Usi cult explained quite succinctly that 'When we ate the Usi fruit, the ghosts came inside us'. Although men and women are physically and productively differentiated, it is this special responsibility of men, the responsibility to assimilate ghostly personae that distinguishes their particularly masculine contribution to the maintenance of a moral collectivity. Their control of healing and its converse, sorcery, is tantamount to their control over the conceptual and spatial separation of the living and the dead.

※   ※   ※

Two cults complexes, each with opposed semiotic functions: in the *Bi'a'a Guabora*, men maintain an innate distinction between the living and the dead (this is no contradiction: the realm of the 'innate' is as much a semiotic construct as its opposed realm of artifice), and do so by means of eminently detachable parts of their male identity. In this respect, the funeral rites have the same semiotic function as bridewealth where men detach pearlshells so as to maintain the flow of women which defines the distinction between wife-givers and wife-takers – it is significant that Foi men time and time again explained that death payments and marriage payments were identical. In the Usi cult, however, an opposed semiotic function is apparent: men attempt to render stationary within their own bodies the representation of this flow, the Usi fruit, whose objects are overtly equated with pearlshells and with the two major components of conception.

The first complex focuses on the collective identity of men, backgrounding men's individual identity in the interests of maintaining a cosmological convention. The second does the opposite: it takes the commonality of male existence and definition as a background against which the individual capacities of men can be articulated. Thus, some men became known as great Usi healers, while others were less efficacious practitioners. When the young men ingested the Usi fruit, it was assumed that some would assimilate the ghostly personae more easily than others, and it was up to the leaders of the cult to determine the specific accommodation that each initiate had made. Skill in performing Usi cures and facility in controlling one's ghostly familiar was a path to 'head-man' status. The point to make is that we cannot view cult and initiation activity as axiomatically 'social' or 'socialising' activities, since, in the case of the Usi cult, they have as their overt goal the creation of individual differences among men rather than their collective commonality.

Collectivising and individuating symbolism

I have asserted that illness is a central metaphor of Foi society – but such an assertion is dependent upon clarifying the manner in which I am using the concept of metaphor. In one sense, I am asserting that metaphor *is* culture, and in this chapter, I locate Foi culture primarily in the ideologies that men use to define their domain of responsibility and action. But in another sense, I also define culture as the intersection of collectivising and individuating modes of symbolisation, itself a metaphor, and it is this more general theory of culture that now deserves detailed explication.

There is a fundamental contrast in the way individual and collective identities are construed in Western and non-Western societies such as that of the Foi. Wagner (1981: Chs.3-4) suggests that cultural meaning lies in the mutually defining relationship between semantic reference, which draws a sharp distinction between signified element and signifying vehicle, and figurative or metaphoric reference, in which the symbol assimilates its referent within a self-signifying construction. Both are necessarily aspects of all symbolic operations though their semiotic functions are in direct contrast. Semantic or conventional symbolisations

generalise or collectivize through their capacity to link commonly held signs together into a single pattern ... All conventional symbolizations, to the degree that they are conventional, have the property of 'standing for', or denoting, something other than themselves (1981:42).

Metaphoric or figurative symbolisations, on the other hand, contrast with literal ones because they juxtapose symbolic elements in non-conventional or innovative ways. 'By exempting themselves from conventional denominative orders, they pre-empt the representational facility and become self-representing' (Wagner 1977a:391). Such constructs differentiate themselves from conventional semantic orders even as they provide the contexts for further syntagmatic reference.

Within any given cultural system, one of these modes of symbolisation is recognised as comprising the domain of human action and intention, the realm of human artifice, while the other is viewed as 'innate' or 'given', or prior to human intervention.

We might call this collective orientation the 'conventional masking' of a particular culture. In the modern American middle-class Culture of science and collective enterprise, with its emphasis on the progressive and artificial building up of collective forms, conventional masking amounts to an understanding that the world of natural incident (the sum of all nonconventionalized contexts) is innate and given. (1981:49)

In contrast to this Western cultural orientation, in the world of tribal peoples such as the Foi, 'with its stress on the priority of human relationships, it is the incidental realm of nonconventionalized controls that involves human action, whereas the articulation of the collective is the subject of ... conventional masking' (1981:49-50). Foi men are confronted with a universe of cosmic and moral energy, embodied in such things as the flow of women's menstrual blood for procreative purposes; the movement of water from west to east; the path of souls of the dead to the afterworld; the seasonal variation of their political economy. It is their responsibility to harness such ceaseless and innate movements for socially appropriate ends, and to channel them into the contrasts that comprise the principles of their sociality.

The collective realms that an anthropologist might identify for the Foi – their men's house communities and patrilineal clans, the afterworld and the domain of the living, wife-givers and wife-takers, male and female – are all the result of successive and repetitive acts of individual differentiation on the part of Foi men: the giving and receiving of bridewealth, which though collectively gathered and distributed, is nevertheless an affair of individual men; the despatching of souls to the afterworld and the consequent attempt to gain the power of ghosts for individual ends; the remarriage of widows and the restructuring of bridewealth networks it implies; and so forth. Illness, I have argued, occupies the boundaries of these individually drawn distinctions: between men and women; between maternally related kin; between ghosts and the living. When illness occurs, it signals an improperly drawn contrast, a failure of an individual man's agency.

Those authors writing about Eastern Highlands societies, the *locus classicus* of debate concerning male initiation in the Papua New Guinea Highlands (see esp. Herdt 1982), have used as their starting point the idea of male vulnerability to female influences. Such approaches lack any consideration of what constitutes sickness and debilitation; most authors are unwilling to see that it is the ideas of illness and vulnerability that are of cosmological importance, rather than male identity *per se*.

The prevention of sickness and its implicit converse, the promotion of general fertility, is a theme of male definition throughout the southern fringe area of the highlands of New Guinea as Williams maintained it was for the Foi after his fieldwork at Lake Kutubu in 1938. Both Schieffelin (1982) and Sørum (1980) have recently examined the ritual and conceptual foundations of this ideology for societies of the Mt Bosavi area to the west of Lake Kutubu. Sørum (1980:273) notes that Bedamini religious belief primarily centres on sickness and death and the relationship between living society and that of the ancestral spirits. Furthermore, the implicit relations of individual and collective identity he refers to by this idiom are the focus of male definition: 'Males are involved in the cure [of sickness], while abnormality of social relations is blamed on women through the identification of female witchcraft' (1980:294).

The assumption of male vulnerability forms the functional core of most interpretations of boys' initiation in Papua New Guinea. I have tried to demonstrate that such a functional connection may be largely unfounded. Thus, although the rituals of Usi resemble at many points an initiation programme for adolescent boys, this is not its intent or primary goal in Foi male thinking. It is more a competitive appropriation of ghostly power by men, deployed for both collective and individual benefit.

Schieffelin comes closest to suggesting a more viable approach to male cult activity in viewing the Kaluli *bau a* or 'boys' house' as concerned with mediation between the realm of the living and that of the *memul* spirits. He then adds that 'it is a matter of becoming known, or being taken seriously, through the assertion of personal dynamism and the appeal of engaging personality and appearance' (1982:192-3), suggesting that such assertion and the necessity for action is also for the Kaluli a particularly male trait. The necessity for males to mediate between the living and the dead is underlined by phrasing the *bau a* ritual in the language of marriage alliance, with its implied focus on relationship rather than status.

For the Foi, it is men's metonymic relationship with detachable items (wealth objects), substances (meat and semen), and 'vital forces' (the soul) that is problematic. Because they are detachable, their control by men is always in question. The eating of Usi 'fruit' gave men a permanent and substantial link with efficacious ghosts; the inherent detachability of wealth items, 'male fruit', by contrast gives them a permanent and substantial link with living human beings (the children of men).

But detachability itself, as a concept, is a function of the manner in which the Foi characteristically focus on differentiation as the primary mode of human action. This is what grounds the extended analogy between men's dealings with ghosts and with women. In other words, ghosts and women are equated not in some semantically defined structuralist sense, for example, because both are spoken of as being 'downstream', because both can make men ill, and so forth. To formulate such semantic parallels is not the same thing as explicating the ideology that makes their comparison meaningful for the Foi. They are equated because the identity they represent is one exogenous to men's actional and intentional constitution, and their control is therefore an overt problem to Foi men. It is this ideology which Schieffelin invokes when he notes that the mediation between men and the *memul* spirits during the Kaluli *bau a* is phrased in terms of marriage alliance (1982:193).

There are two senses in which I have located agency among the Foi. One is the specific agency of men, which has formed the subject of this chapter, defined here as their moral responsibility to maintain the artifice of human sociality. The other is a characteristic of all human beings and detached human spirits, the quality of volition itself. Foi locate this capacity in the heart, the seat of understanding, thought, deliberation and intention, and in this respect it is characteristic of women also. In other words, it is not that women are not ascribed any agency; it is merely that their volitional capacity is confined to actional spheres which have no consequences for the definition of the parameters of Foi sociality. They cannot mediate between the living and the dead (unlike most other Papuan societies of this region, the Foi lack the institution of the female spirit medium); they cannot manipulate wealth objects to affiliate children (though they may at times own and control both wealth objects and pigs); they cannot cure illness, though they are in fact the specific and metaphorical sources of a great proportion of men's illness. Women as widows (cf. J. Weiner 1984) embody the very ambiguities against which men oppose their collective actions. In other words, women's intentions have idiosyncratic rather than sociocentric properties, though their collective identity becomes precipitated as a by-product of certain collective male contexts, such as the distribution of bridewealth.

That the maintenance of identity is a male and not a female prerogative is further underlined in the widow's purification rites, in which the woman is the passive recipient of the new husband's ministrations. Her identity is problematic, in other words, only in so far as she is a danger to men, for she is not a danger to herself or to other women. But this is male responsibility, and not the functional imperative of maintaining control over women. Men are protecting themselves, not appropriating women's power, although part of the nature of this responsibility is maintaining the patrilineal credentials of a woman's children.

I thus speak of intersexual *mediation*, rather than the creation of gender roles. This is not mere hair-splitting, for the latter implies that the relationship between male or female roles is 'assumed' or self-evident, while the former takes the relationship itself as the focus of definition and entailment. The contrast between men and women is not at issue for the Foi, for such a contrast is, in the strictest possible sense, part of the nature of things. As Lévi-Strauss (1962) once defined the nature of totemism, their mediation, or accommodation is the focus of human concern, not the statuses themselves. This is where the content of 'pollution' lies, in the problematic mediation between contrastive male and female capacities. To merely end one's definition of pollution as the capacity of women to debilitate men thus only restates the problem of what constitutes pollution.

Finally, Foi ideology has implications for our understanding of the nature of 'big-man' identity. It is universally assumed that big-men in highlands societies are atypical and that they are contrasted with so-called 'ordinary' men. Although in Foi society head-men are few and 'ordinary' men numerous, it might be more profitable to see the head-man as the 'normal' Foi male identity. Ordinary status implies a failure to control ghostly power, wealth items and curing ritual. A Foi man would not aspire to such status any more than he would wish himself sick. The Usi cult involved most men, and by Foi standards they were all 'big-men' – some were merely bigger men than others. But as is abundantly clear from many other examples from Highlands New Guinea, big-men do not always act in the interests of men collectively – they may or may not promote the interests of their local group and it would be injudicious to assert that they are promoting the interests of all men as against women, or against men of other groups. In other words, while big-men display all of the collectively agreed upon male values, their individual actions are only congruent with this collective ideology when there is an implied functional necessity to maintain male solidarity. This is emphatically not the case in Foi society; the individual actions of men and the collective image of male assertiveness that encompasses them are two separate analytic phenomena and it is only in the didactic interests of a functionalist methodology that the congruence between them becomes problematic.

Notes

1. This is a characteristic assumption of the studies to which I have alluded.
2. Just as advertising achieves its semiotic force by allowing the individual to particularise the conventional attributes of a product and associated life styles.
3. I describe the metaphorical basis of the interpretation of such portents elsewhere (J. Weiner 1987).
4. I describe customs pertaining to the treatment of widows among the Foi in J. Weiner 1986.
5. My informants of Hegeso and Barutage Villages knew of *hibu yiyi*, but did not offer any information about it and maintained that it was not traditionally practised by the men of that area.
6. The nature of these items varied from longhouse to longhouse apparently, and even between different initiations held in the same longhouse village, depending on the man who was designated the leader of the initiation.

Conclusion

MARILYN STRATHERN

These are conclusions of a rather personal kind. I excise a specific item of value for myself from the rich material presented by the contributors to this volume.

Much of it would seem to bear out Rosaldo's observation on the universal role of men in 'the organisation of collective life' (1980a:394). Certainly for many of the cases reported here, men appear to be the principal public transactors of values embodied in women, and thus the 'difference' between the sexes appears to be that of transactor and transacted (Rubin 1975). They recall Rosaldo's (1974) and Ortner's (1974) earlier formulations that men are everywhere constituted as a distinctive social category by their authoritative responsibility for public and cultural activity. Moreover, at first blush it might also appear that whatever the endeavours of either sex, whatever the range of actions or effectiveness they demonstrate, femaleness remains essentially associated with powers and forces we conventionally know as 'reproductive'. Females consequently emerge as passive vehicles, in so far as these powers lie in the nature of things. Men's prominence in public life and women's value as reproducers of children once again seem to fall into a familiar pattern of differentiation. In fact such a conclusion rests on a false conflation (between women and procreativity) and a false antithesis (between male and female agency), at least as far as the various systems presented in these chapters are concerned.

Before the point can be substantiated, however, it is necessary to be more precise about the concept of difference. I therefore preface my comments with an excursus into one set of ideas which lie behind much social science thinking on the question of domination and inequality in gender relations.

The problem of difference

In popular Western thinking, the world is divided into active subjects and the context and objects of their action. Objects may be seen as inert, as constructed by subjects, while the context for action may be forces beyond human construction which present themselves as constraining 'facts of life'. Inherent differences in the environment are seen to be overcome by common human drives towards a viable cultural existence. In an equally tenable view, the constructed variation of human social life, created by active subjects, operates against the uniform laws of a given nature. From either vantage point, mechanisms of human reproduction in being particular to the species also constitute a substratum of biological fact members of the species necessarily share in common. In this vein anthropologists may conclude that observed inter-societal differences – as in the varying themes apparently presented here of how men in one way and another 'control' female sexual or reproductive powers – are simply the workings of social differentiation itself, evidence of how societies differently deal with the facts of nature.[1]

As a concept, difference itself turns on notions of uniformity and variability. The procedure of deducing generalisations from particulars rests on such a scheme. I draw attention to this conceptual phenomenon through relating an analytical problem (how does one generalise from a range of particulars?) to a social one (how does one achieve unity in the face of diverse individual experience?). This will not only give an entry into some of the findings to be drawn from these various case studies, but also provide a little evidence for the assertion made in the Introduction, that the diversity of intellectual positions replicates the diversity of social ones.

An editorial in the Winter 1982 issue of *Signs* confronts the relationship between 'the urge felt by some of us to seek commonality among women' and 'the creativity that lies in recognizing differences between and among women' (1982:193-4). The Editor points out the danger of ignoring individual variety in women's lives and of making generalisations that 'can so easily become the imposition of self and erasure of other'. Similar dangers arise when generalisations drawn from particular cultures erase other cultural selves. And this lesson, the journal claims, is something anthropology can teach: 'feminist scholars are becoming increasingly aware that they may have been using (to quote Atkinson) "Ideological constructs that have their history in Western European society and misrepresent the thought and experience of people in other times and places"' (1982:238).

Here we glimpse the view that in simultaneously encompassing other systems and its own, anthropology attains transcendence. Yet an equally strong argument can be made that its descriptions of others merely reproduce knowledge of its own world. Hence Sahlins's aphorism: he asks whether anthropology is any more than a 'grand intellectual distraction, bourgeois society scratching its head' (1976:2), and Bourdieu's (1977) point about codifying procedures which render other systems of knowledge as themselves codes. These parallel views of the discipline, on the one hand encountering worlds outside itself and on the other assimilating those worlds to cultural concerns of its own society of origin, comprise a model for its approach to difference. Anthropology is certainly very interested in the manner in which Western concepts are contextualised, but is not itself exempt from contextualisation. Its frames do not transcend but constitute the kinds of relationships perceived between 'Western society' and others. They obviously have consequences for the way in which we think about social and cultural differences in the lives of men and women, and of the difference between the sexes itself.

Attempts to resolve the antinomy between unity and diversity are instructive. We see an acute antithesis between the grounds on which one would like to make common issue out of common interests, and appreciation of personal, cultural and social distinctions which challenge unity. Augé (1982:14-15) spells this out for anthropology's relation with 'the other'. The antinomy is also at the heart of opening up women's concerns to cross-cultural scrutiny. Thus the Editor of *Signs* remarks of the 1982 National (United States) Women's Studies Association conference, that part of Angela Davis's presentation dwelt on 'the recognition that different experience can nonetheless serve as a source of union'. The semantic paradox can be resolved if one allows the terms to refer to separate levels. 'Union' can refer to common aims which override or underlie 'different experience'. The one is encompassed by the other (common aims embrace different origins) or else forms a base for the other (a fundamental unity underlies different manifestations). This kind of propositional hierarchy holds its own clue to how we often approach the concept of difference as such. What interests me is the extent to which this approach takes its form from Western understandings of a material world mediated by industrialisation. Where agency is linked to subjectivity, it implies a self-evident relationship between persons and what they do, and the kinds of control persons exercise over the natural world and over one another. That such relations constantly reduce to a hierarchical form makes it difficult to conceptualise 'difference' in a non-hierarchical manner. For example, in the circumstances just quoted, to make a common cause we point to characteristics which unify, since we hold that to concentrate on differences between persons is to put some at an advantage or disadvantage in respect of others.

Not all relations are structured as encompassing ones, nor is difference experienced only as hierarchy. It would be absurd to imagine that. The point is rather that contemporary Western culture possesses one exceptionally powerful *model* of human enterprise based on certain perceptions of industrial experience. The fashioning of natural materials to cultural ends equates enterprise with productivity, and productivity, as Sahlins (1976) has reminded us, with utility. Thus it is possible to ask of any item differentiated from another, what use the one has in respect of the other. In the same way the question may be asked of any social relationship predicated on a difference between individual persons whether one gets more productivity out of their interaction than the others.

Dumont's view (1971) is that the individual in this normative sense belongs to 'modern ideology'. One might add that such an ideology necessarily brings into relation the normative (moral, cultural) and the biological. For the individuated person so constructed receives its definition from being both of nature and in acting as a conscious agent apart from nature. Encompassment by nature is reversed in the image of the individual subordinating nature to its own ends. This means that the individual person in turn becomes hierarchised. That is, its actions appear separable from its subjectivity – because these actions also become joined with the natural world as an object in relation to the agent as subject (Ollman 1976). I cite below a contemporary rendition of this view of the individual (in the words of MacKinnon). The location of agency thus shifts. A person may be seen to control nature/nature may be seen to control the person. Any activity or behaviour can be expressed by this model of encompassing agency, including the agency of natural 'laws' or 'forces'. In respect of other persons, subjectivity becomes defined by the extent to which what he or she does or makes is seen to remain under the individual agent's control. Such an interest in the relationship between a person and his or her actions corresponds to perceptions of industrial process as an encompassing conversion of less useful things into more useful things. The conversion itself creates a significant difference (the manufactured item is different from the raw material), differentiated items thus standing in an encompassing or hierarchical relation to one another. This kind of difference becomes a function of encompassment, (cf. Dumont 1982:224-5), which in social terms leads to difference being synonymous with inequality.

Let me briefly develop the industrial location of these ideas. Although a post-industrial culture may well mark their obsolescence, they still inform widespread contemporary Western views of personhood. By referring to the way in which 'we' handle such ideas, in the following passages, I mean to suggest one possible base for some of the assumptions prevalent in anthropological theorising on the subject of person and agency.

The industrial model of agency entails a vision of personal creativity and of relationships between persons based on the transformation of labour into products (including activity into actions). This is simultaneously a creative and a domesticating process. At the same time as subduing something outside, one is also domesticating oneself. Domestication 'brings under control', a matter of subordinating objects to *ends* of one's own and thus to one's subjectivity.[2] Almost any exercise of agency can be seen as a productive transformation in so far as the agent's ends define things as relatively useful or useless *in reference to itself*. Conversion can be repeated endlessly: (useless) labour is converted into (useful) labour power, that is converted into (usable) products, and so on. Input of agency at each stage is encompassed rather than negated by further processing. Previous (relatively useless) input becomes part of the object's 'natural' properties to be domesticated. I see a parallel here with certain analytic choices open to social scientists. Given evident differences in the social placement of persons, an underlying cause may be sought in the conversion of one individual's (natural) ends to the interests of another, in the actor's ability to subdue others to fulfil ends of his or her own devising.

This particular industrial model of human activity as production and domestication creates a means by which to think about male–female differentiation, including differences in physiology. Where the model allocates creative differentiation to individual or collective (societal, cultural) human authorship, it establishes nature as uniform. Yet it is also possible to account for differences in nature by reference to special events. Natural selection, speciation, adaptation – these processes can be thought of as the outcome of events which have themselves created diversity out of unity. Evolutionary process is thus in this regard analogous to cultural process, essentially a matter of transformation and encompassment. Traces of primary sources are retained, modified, in the new version. 'Nature' in the popular evolutionary view is not a composite of forces different in kind, but becomes differentiated through the sequencing of events. Consequently, the model creates a problem for absolute difference, in that most differences are ultimately explicable in terms of transformative process. (Self-generating change is no problem, since the same structure of event and encompassment which characterises an organism's relations with the outside world can also hierarchise its internal composition.) Differences may be located in the nature of things, but such things are also the products of selective or historical forces.

As far as the sexes are concerned, these notions prompt us in two directions. First, we take differences in reproductive function as a result of selective evolutionary forces, analogous to cultural differentiation but occurring outside culture. In so far as these processes occur outside culture, of course, they can be perceived of as innate in relation to culture. Second, we take the different social circumstances which surround women and men as a direct product of societal or cultural differentiation. Cultural differentiation is distinguished from natural differentiation by its element of subjective agency, and in terms of our model typically perceived as a matter of one sex having control over the other.

This leads to the question of measurement. 'In a commodity economy, because of the operation of the law of value, two heterogeneous things [exchanged against one another] are treated as equivalent and the problem is to find the common measure' (Gregory 1982:47). 'Human beings' can be seen to have a common measure. 'Men' and 'women' pose a problem here. The view of cultural differentiation between men and women which regards the activities of one encompassed by (the intentions and acts of) the other is underlined in the further proposition that what they have in common is always altered by the quality of their interaction. Attempts to find a measure between women and men, and hence compare them, must draw on apparently non-gendered and thus 'universal' human attributes. When it is asked, what is it that differentiated commodities have in common, it is possible to answer, the socially necessary labour time they represent. In the same way, to ask of persons what is it they have in common invites the answers of the order of (say) a capacity to work. When persons are socially unequal, therefore, the one must be doing something with (say) the labour of the other. Although we also know that individual concrete labours cannot be measured against one another (Harris and Young 1981; Smith 1978), at the same time these ideas prompt the question whether the social divide between the sexes is the very mystification which prevents their mutual evaluation as human beings.

If such concepts do contribute to Western notions of difference, they also incorporate the eighteenth-century view that it is through work that human beings find themselves and consequently that the products of labour are the objects through which people relate to the natural world. In the words of MacKinnon (1982:27):

Objectification [in marxist materialism] is thought to be the foundation of human freedom, the work process whereby a subject becomes embodied in products and relationships.

She goes on to observe:

Alienation is the socially contingent distortion of that process, a reification of products and relations which prevents them from being, and being seen as, dependent on human agency.

Where human agency is located in other than the worker, the worker suffers a diminution of humanity.

From the point of view of the object, objectification *is* alienation. For women, there is no distinction between objectification and alienation because women have not authored objectifications ... Women have been the nature, the matter acted upon [original italics]

In this view women have not 'authored' objectifications; that is, they are objects for the use of the other for ends only the other can create. In dealing with the sexes, then, a dichotomy is forced upon us. We tend to allocate creativity to the one *at the expense of* the other. MacKinnon's critique grapples with the entailments of reification, since in this scheme women are rendered, as they were for de Beauvoir, into passive objects. Her reflections on women as men's 'otherness' elaborate a Western metaphor which draws on gender to talk about subject–object difference.

Male power is real; it is just not what it claims to be, namely, the only reality. Male power is a myth that makes itself true. What it is to raise consciousness is to confront male power in this duality: as a total on one hand and a delusion on the other. In consciousness raising, women learn they have *learned* that men are everything, women their negation, but that the sexes are equal. The context of the message is revealed as true and false at the same time: in fact, each part reflects the other transvalued ... The moment it is seen that ... the sexes are not socially equal, womanhood can no longer be defined in terms of lack of maleness. (1982:28; original italics)

Agency has become that of authorship – who persuades whom they have power. Furthermore, this authorship is conceived as individual and singular in so far as it is the activity of a singular agent. (The singular agent may be a collectivity of persons, but that does not alter the nature of interaction with the other.) The productions of the active person also turn on a singular relationship. There is a taken for granted identity between the agent as a subject and his or her actions upon the world in so far as a person's acts and work are held to belong to that person. To take them away or control them is to dominate and diminish that person's exercise of agency.

Such a model[3] of human enterprise influences the manner in which 'we' conceptualise persons and relations between persons. It makes anthropologists ask questions about inequality wherever they encounter instituted social difference. I have suggested its counterpart, source even, in a model of industrial process as turning upon constant conversion and encompassment, so that everything can be measured by its relative use. Agency is similarly construed in a hierarchical manner: a subject constantly making objects, through subordinating other things to the agent's own ends. This activity also differentiates the agents themselves, whose successes may be compared.

Annette Weiner (1982:52) comments on the need to understand the constitution of value hierarchies. The chapters in this volume force us to the same conclusion. My patchy excursus into certain Western industrial structurings of difference cannot possibly be offered on serious comparative grounds; it will do, however, as a reminder that the idea of hierarchy is not to be taken for granted. It has also touched on the extent to which certain Western constructs utilise gender, meaning here a set of ideas about the difference between the sexes. If gender is also an organising metaphor in the non-industrial societies of the Southwestern Pacific, the focus of the anthropological comparison between 'us' and 'them' must shift from considering the gender concepts themselves to what they stand for – from considering the particular values to which they may refer to considering the structuring of value as such. Are comparisons between entities made according to a common scale, yielding the possibility of converting one order of events into another, or are they set up as antithesis or opposition? It occasions no surprise that 'we' and 'they' both utilise gender as a source of symbolism. Investigation is required, Bloch and Parry (1982:9) argue apropos mortuary symbolism, as to what that symbolism might refer. And this must include the very form of the comparison between male and female, and thus how values are structured.

Creating value

'Value' can of course mean as much or as little as one chooses. Anthropological accounts frequently entail assumptions about value without having any real theory of value to offer (Schneider 1983:395).[4] However, value always turns on comparisons such as those encountered in the constructions of difference discussed in the preceding section. By analogy with my emphasis on industrial productivity, the widespread character of gift exchange among the Melanesian and eastern Indonesian cases from the Southwestern Pacific suggests that value created through such exchange will bear on ideas about agency.

An initial definition is in order. As Gregory (1982) notes, the economic concept of value implies a comparison of entities, either as a ratio (the one expressed as a proportion of the other) or in terms of rank equivalence. Both like and unlike items may be so compared. In addition, however, this part of the world (the Southwestern Pacific) is dominated by a third relation of comparison: between an entity and its source of origin. Value is thus constructed in the identity of a thing or person with various sets of social relations in which it is embedded, and its simultaneous detachability from them. Here lies much of the significance of gift exchange.

I have drawn inspiration specifically from the Chambri material presented in Chapter 2. Before the general point is developed, some remarks may be made about all the societies represented in this volume. An initial caution is also in order. The following comments, it must be made clear, have the same limitations as the preceding set: they do not comprise a historically grounded appraisal of these various societies, but sketchily indicate some conceptual obstacles in the way of an easy translation from Western notions of difference as they apply to gender relations. How values are created is essential to this exercise. In concentrating on the obstacles, however, I objectify the difference between 'us' and 'them' in my account, and do so deliberately. This is partly a product of the material presented in this book. None of the accounts is ahistorical, but with one or two exceptions (Keesing, Bell, Devereaux) the colonial and post-colonial context is not given explanatory power in the exegesis of indigenous concepts. It is also a product of trying to understand the specificity of the concepts which underwrite analytical endeavour. Rather than turning to critiques which also exist within Western social science, my own critique is based on what can be grasped as 'different' about other societies such as those which have been described here.

Ideas about industrial production and cultural productivity as involving conversions of a kind prompt us, I have suggested, to think about agency as the subject in subject/object relations. This is true whether the subject is a person acting 'subjectively' or whether 'causes' lie in systems or social forces. Errington and Gewertz have drawn attention to the particular Western connotations of such cause–effect relations, in the subduing of another to the subject's will or effectiveness. Acts, events, products, culture all display the effects of an agent on some thing, person, situation which is altered by the application of that agency. The altered form thus registers alteration as a process. Consequently we are able to construe personal identity in terms of the difference which gender or ethnicity or status or whatever makes to the (non-gendered, pre-ethnic, neutral) person.[5] From the point of view of persons, the capacity to alter the world becomes one of the prerequisites of the self-validating agent, and is evinced as a moment of domination.

If other societies do not draw on ideas of conversion in the industrial sense, then we are unlikely to be dealing with a conceptualisation of agency that registers itself as dominance over an altered nature. Yet this is one major source for general anthropological theorising about control, evident when anthropologists categorise persons in terms of their controlling what others have to offer. The suggestion that men seek to control female fecundity, for example, was central to a whole generation of theories about marriage exchange and the arrangements men make to obtain and dispose of women and their innate attributes of fertility and sexuality. However the material presented here does not at once suggest that the ideational association between women and their fecundity is of a unitary kind, such that control of women is to be equated with control of their fecundity.[6] Apart from whether or not fecundity is a woman's principal attribute, it would have to be shown step by step that agency is held to be evinced in works which alter a passive nature. Certainly as far as the Melanesian and Indonesian cases are concerned, their cosmologies point in other ways. Fecundity is not an innate value of females to be subdued by a transcendent agent, to be converted and modified, for the 'uses' of (male) society. These people hold that persons engage in perpetual transactions with parts of themselves. This is true of both sexes. The difference between them lies in the symbolic process of personification (cf. Gregory 1982:41), or via a Massim idiom, the animation (Battaglia 1983:301), of the values of specific relationships.

One implication is that what women personify is not to be taken as having inert object status. In so far as women embody values, men's deployment of these values involves their constructing and entering into concrete relations with women themselves. To use an analogy with domestic labour, when relationships turn on the flow of fertility we are not dealing with a commoditised 'social' fertility but with a 'concrete' fertility inseparable from relations between men and women.[7]

Where men's agency appears to be of a collective kind, it may rest less on their interests in controlling resources which lie outside them than in creating among themselves a context of action in which as men they also embody, and themselves personify, value. In gift exchange systems, they personify the transactability of things. Actions can thus carry their 'names'. This does not necessarily entail the encompassment of one-way conversion, turning things to use. Yet the collective life they make –

ceremonial exchange, politics, male cults – we tend to construe as an exaggerated agency. The Western equation between personal subjectivity (and its exercise on others inert in respect of it) and the creation of society/culture tends to regard the public realm/political life as an exercise of an enlarged subjectivity. Women's frequent exclusion from the domain of public affairs continues to bother us for this reason. The larger the sphere within which persons can be seen to expand their subjective selves' the more they appear persons. The very idea that being a person can be a matter of degree (greater or less so) is of course based on an evolutionary, developmental model of society unlikely to be shared by exegetes in the traditional systems under study here.

In two recent works, Allen (1981, 1984) examines the development of male public life through a contrast between 'matrilineal' and 'patrilineal' kinship systems in island Melanesia. He is interested in the kinship-free forms of male political association as are found in secret societies and public grades. Such organisations appear kinship-free in being based on principles other than descent. One might remark, however, that they are certainly not gender-free (cf. Shapiro 1983). On the contrary they appear to signify the specific activities of men rather than women. Female rank-taking, where it occurs, does not affect this distinction, which is underwritten in terms of the sexual division of labour and the manner in which wealth is created (Jolly 1981). Rodman (1981) specifically analyses, for one case, a separation between men's and women's sphere of exchanges which on occasion are integrated but not merged. The arguments are relevant to the concerns of many of the contributors here.

However Allen also introduces a secondary argument about the self-evident nature of female value. 'The dramatic visibility of female reproductivity universally provides a prominent natural model for the conceptualization of social interrelatedness' (1984:37). At the same time these concepts are of limited flexibility for the development of political organisations; agnation, based on paternity, he suggests, provides a more adaptable kinship ideology of association. Autonomous (kinship-free) political institutions are therefore more likely to develop under matriliny because the kinship idiom of maternity is not itself suitable. This interesting argument leads into two difficulties. First, it is a mistake, still being made in spite of Leach (1961), to see paternity as a simple analogue of maternity: if within one system they interlock as parts of a single conceptual device, they cannot be excised and compared as discrete elements across systems. Second, referring to early theorists, with whom he seems to concur, Allen repeats that 'Everything to do with female reproductivity ... is visibly grounded in nature' (1984:27). He ambiguously notes that no effective critique has ever been made of this argument.

What Allen does not add is that in the contexts in which he is dealing with female reproductivity, he in fact encounters a valorised power, an instituted social value. An analogy between reproductivity and other embedded human values would be fruitful. For exactly the same point applies to the ideology of labour power, that work thereby appears 'visibly grounded' in nature. But the observer generally recognises in the idea of work (as a particular human activity) the form of a social value. The crucial issue, then, is how female reproductivity acquires value, how it comes indeed to incorporate a notion of interrelatedness. Innateness may well be one of its cultural attributes. But the 'incontrovertibility of maternity' (1984:37)[8] is a social artefact, and must be understood by the observer as part of, rather than the cause of, the way gender relations are construed.

It is often assumed that female reproductivity, like female labour, acquires value because it is appropriatable. The Mexican material analysed by Devereaux (Chapter 3) is pertinent. In Zinacanteco gender ideology, the value which one sex enjoys is clearly construed as its value *for* the other, in reference to the joint household. This yields a model of sexual complementarity. The very structure of this model forces the ethnographer to go beyond it in seeking explanation for the experienced inequalities of everyday life. Consequently, the values which the sexes are seen to have for each other cannot themselves be taken as the single cause of the tenor of relations between them. Far from a property-based peasant system, Bell (Chapter 4) elucidates a comparable complementarity in Aboriginal relations. But the complementarity is based on a perceived separation of agencies rather than their combination. By inference from her other writings, it is apparent that men's and women's reproductive powers are exercised for the 'country', and are efficacious precisely because they are separately enacted. It is in part to protect that efficacy that contemporary Aboriginal women seek an arena which promises a separate existence of the kind guaranteed in the past by a discrete pattern of daily and ritual life.

These two chapters point up the bias of analyses which suppose that gender relations are to be understood as ultimately a matter of one sex appropriating the powers of the other. I turn directly to the specific constructions encountered in the Melanesian and eastern Indonesian material, and especially to the significance of gift exchange in this part of the world. In doing so, I take up the argument offered by Bloch and Parry (1982) about 'male' control of 'female' powers, since they deliberately address systems in which exchange relations are of organisational consequence. Contrary to appearance, it will be seen that these Pacific societies do not sustain a unitary conflation between women and reproductive power, nor a simple antithesis between public male activity and passive female value. Their cosmologies do not rest on the Western notion of utility, with its connotation of conversion and thus of the subordination of perceived reproductive powers *to ends beyond* reproduction itself. These ends are commonly defined in anthropological analysis as a male interest in solidarity or in power itself assumed to have a self-evident value. But female reproductivity cannot in the cases considered in this volume be conceived as simply put to male use.

Brides and corpses

Many of the issues raised in the earlier chapters bear on Bloch and Parry's specific investigation, noted by Hoskins (Chapter 7), into the relationship between the presentation of death and of fertility and rebirth in funeral rituals. They observe that female sexuality is frequently associated with the idea of death, as for instance in a recurrent 'affinity between women and rotting corpses' (1982:22). Ritual is thus provided with an object to overcome: birth, sex and death must be controlled. This is not an essentialist view. Their argument is that the 'world of biology is elaborately constructed as something to be got rid of so as to make way for the generation of the ideal order' (1982:27).

The view that Bloch and Parry are putting forward, then, does not rest on any simple equation between women and a value (fertility and sexuality as reproductive power) which men try to appropriate. On the contrary, they argue that societies represent themselves as life-forces in contradistinction to death, and in doing so deploy a split between fertility and sexuality. By fertility they mean general productive and regenerative powers which are valorised as working on behalf of society at large, in antithesis to the biological processes of decay which afflict individual persons and for which sexuality comes to stand. If sexuality is associated with death, it is to separate off such depleting processes from productive fertility. Mortuary rituals often re-present this opposition as one of female and male attributes.

In this attempt to master the world of biology, gender symbolism often provides ... the crucial mechanism. Fertility is separated from and made superior to the biological processes of sex and birth by analogy with the taken-for-granted difference between the sexes. (1982:24)

A distinction between male and female powers thus becomes a vehicle to concretise, by analogy, other distinctions. This is an important advance for our understanding of the operations of gender symbolism. However Bloch and Parry also have some suggestions about the place of exchange in societies such as those we have described, and here one must raise an objection against their analysis.[9]

The implication of their argument is that in so far as women are associated with death and its dangers, men emerge as the ritual controllers. If they could, men would create a society without exchange. Speaking of Melanesian material, from the Massim and the New Guinea Highlands, they point to a connection between the reluctant dependence of groups on outside women and the painful necessity to enter into exchanges with others, which men yearn to abandon in favour of an 'ideal order' without exchange. The need to rely on women thus fuels the contradictory desire to be rid of women. This (male) fantasy, they suggest, is also inscribed in the equation between women and polluting, deathly powers.

I wonder what they would do with some of the present discussion. Kodi (Chapter 7) make a precise identification between the deceased and femininity: the departed soul is treated like a bride, and funeral ceremonies replicate marriage ceremonies. Foi (Chapter 10) construct a similar analogy between the departed soul and the new bride, in the passage of mortuary and bridewealth payments. Men's exchanges create the affinal relationship just as their rites separate living from dead. Keesing (Chapter 1) suggests a Kwaio analogue between women's care of their bodies and men's care of ancestral power. However, Tubetube people do not deal in analogues: women draw directly on ancestral matrilineage power, as mothers and as life-stealing witches. Rather more indirectly, Nagovisi (Chapter 6) death payments feed into the nexus obligations between affines, but like affinal exchanges in Kove (Chapter 5) refer primarily to payments for labour and nurture. Kalauna (Chapter 9) present specific equations between male wealth and the products of fertility, as in Chambri (Chapter 2), where valuables denote women and a mortuary service leads to sexual claims. The kinds of connections which exist between regeneration and death are thus objectified in the general circulation of wealth items which move against persons and the loss of persons. At the same time, as Errington and Gewertz observe, persons are not to be confused with what stands for them.

Material exchanges in these examples are evidence of transactions between persons and thus of the transactability of the values persons have for one another. Foi wealth simultaneously stands for the innate value of women and the flow of life, and for men's 'artificial' manipulation and channelling of it. These transactions affect bodily states and social relationships. The flow of valuables thus registers loss and detachment, as well as the connections created between donor and recipient. Gender is employed to discriminate between the whole and the detachable part. But the cases discussed here make it clear that it is *not* only value conceptualised as 'female' which is detachable. Detachability may also be construed as male. Now this observation does not rest on the grounds that Nagovisi women can also be leaders or that Tubetube women organise public lineage life and give feasts. Nor on the grounds that in Kalauna wealth valuables turn out to be androgynous symbols of generative power, and that for Foi and Kodi in the same way as women are detached as brides, men or men and women are detached as ghosts from the living clan. Nor, for that matter, that in their generative responsibilities, Kwaio men and women are equally separated from the central life of the settlement. I shall return to some of these points briefly. But the immediate question can be approached directly through the evidence about the values for which female-ness does seem to stand.

Bloch and Parry observe that the 'ideal social order' (as constructed in ritual) is a representation of the world which transcends what it devalues, but thereby always perpetuates what it devalues. Thus time and again ritual is brought to bear on recalcitrant biology. This dialectic – between the biological world which must be mastered and those acts of mastery – appears to imply an equation between society so created and those who necessarily defeat women (1982:21) because of what women are associated with. Society is unwittingly gendered in this account. One might suggest that such gendering, as has Rosaldo (1974) apropos male domination in general, and as has Biersack (1984) for a New Guinea Highlands case, becomes an indigenous vehicle for a self-reflective and abstract conceptualisation of society as such. This certainly matches the Western analytic investment in the notion of society as encompassing the relationships and institutions people create. The domain of creative ritual activity appears social par excellence to this kind of scheme.[10]

Two points can be noted. First, the imagery of transcendence: Bloch and Parry deploy an analytical vocabulary which resonates with the hierarchical process of conversion I suggested is characteristic of certain Western constructions of difference and value. This does not mean it is restricted to such constructions of course (see n.14). But it does postulate that people are searching for symbols for an order they regard as ideally encompassing of their lives. Second, while I am sure Bloch and Parry would not wish one to jump from a symbolic equation between femaleness and death or sexuality to the actions of women as social actors, they fail to make one aspect of this gendering activity explicit: namely, the relationship between men as agents in the ritual process and the apparently social invisibility of women. The ideal order is understood as the specific responsibility of men who act against biology on its behalf.[11] Thus women's participation as actors at funerals – and women invariably seem to have special mortuary roles – becomes in their introductory account merged with a general 'association' with death, either because of its danger and pollution, or because it is like birth.

In so far as the authors of the chapters here have been dealing with agency, they focus on the question of responsibility. If being a socially responsible cause is attributed to certain gender-specific positions, we should consult our ethnographic sources as to how people construct the need to control or master what they imagine they are controlling or mastering and who is effective enough to do it. Bloch and Parry would agree with this. But what is problematic in their account is the analytical necessity to conceive of a 'social order' (for which one sex rather than the other assumes responsibility). An indigenous concept of an ideal social order cannot be assumed in the present context.

It is clear from our accounts that if women are equated with wealth objects, then that is a primary part of the action which 'causes' others to act. They are not inert artefacts for an action taking place elsewhere, but are intrinsic to the definition of the relationships so established. Macintyre, for instance, has noted apropos recent studies of Massim mortuary rituals that women certainly participate as agents of regeneration, but in doing so transact with items which are specific symbols of their own work and capacities. A woman is not an anonymous producer or representative of female powers: the participants act as wives, daughters, mothers, sisters, each prestation denoting a specific relationship. Often this is a relationship with a man or between women through men. In giving mortuary gifts across lineages women are dealing with differences (between lineages) which require men as mediators. These exchanges allow a continuity of interest to be formulated in the persons of lineage women as agents.

The chapters show women taking 'active' parts in a direct sense. In Kwaio (Chapter 1) they organise wealth exchanges and give mortuary feasts, even if they are not often named as the sponsor. Nagovisi women (Chapter 6) manage certain life-cycle feasts. If on Tubetube (Chapter 8) potency for life and death is combined in women, so it is with men, with the difference that men individually acquire an art which is a potential of all women through innate lineage membership; Tubetube women as well as men act as leaders. Where women take an active organising role in feast giving, in certain capacities they also make speeches or control talk. For Kove (Chapter 5), as for Chambri (2), Foi (10) and Kalauna (9), in so far as organising activity is largely in the hands of men, the question is the extent to which women's value is transactable. Yet Kove women are responsible for the success of the exchanges, and participate directly with valuables themselves. Chambri, Foi and Kalauna women are more remote causes. In Chambri, we might note, mothering is as much the cause of women's as of men's obligations, but the sexes are differently placed in their capacity to discharge the debts so created. Again, Kodi (Chapter 7) women become socially prominent at funerals, and carry the responsibility for the mourning which makes the dead one of them. None of these interactions requires us to suppose that one sex or the other acts in reference to an imagined social order. Each is 'active' in reference to the powers seen to be located in the other. They together construct the grounds for interaction – for 'sociality' rather than for 'society', one might say.

Yet what do we do with the differences in these cases? If women are in one context associated with wealth, in another with corpses, we can certainly suggest common metaphors of detachability or transactability. However the wholes from which parts may be detached may be quite differently construed. Possibly it seems odd that not all the authors place equal weight on the institutional forms which differentiate 'matrilineal' (Nagovisi, Tubetube) from 'patrilineal' (Kove, Chambri, Foi, Kalauna) systems or combine in the 'double descent' of Kodi (with both matriclans and patriclans). Chowning voices important reservations about thus classifying entire systems. Nevertheless, the contributors who make most use of the terms (Nash, Macintyre, Young) deliberately go beyond the delineation of modes of kin reckoning and take the 'lineal' bias to stand for a whole ideological constellation of values about collective and individual action. When Young talks of matriliny and patriliny he deploys a shorthand for entire cultural orders. Lineality cannot be taken therefore as an autonomous variable. Nor in terms of the material presented here can lineal systems be simply compared with non-lineal, if we were to consider the 'cognatic' Kwaio as an example or look further afield to central Australia and Zinacantan. Understanding how people represent sociality to themselves, to follow James Weiner – how they structure the common interests on which particular people can act together, how they fashion the collective values in relation to which individual action becomes necessary – is part of the phenomenon we are describing, and cannot be treated independently of it. And if the structuring of sociality (including the nature of kinship systems) is to be part of our data, then we should look to the relationship between responsibility for action on the one hand and the causes or ends of action on the other.

The extent to which agents act for themselves or themselves cause others to act depends on what these selves are. English language conventions make the reflexive 'for the self' a matter of subjectivity. Yet we are frequently dealing here with categorical positions and with persons defined by relations. And where the English language definition of agency implies a congruence between the active subject (responsible for actions) and an interest also located in the subject (so that the self is both cause and end of actions, even when 'interacting' with another), here we encounter a split. Another person may be the cause of action, not as one mind overriding another's, but in terms of the requirement of a relationship in which the presence of one party is necessary to and created by the other, and the necessity is construed as a matter of the difference between them.

In the Melanesian cases the split is frequently registered through gender. Depending on the contexts in which men and women are responsible for their actions, *qua* men and women, the source of their action and their aims may be matched in same-sex idioms (the power of the matrilineage transacting its own products; men in ceremonial exchange transacting with male wealth), but they may also be contrasted in cross-sex ones (assisting a spouse to prestige; prestations owed to maternal or paternal kin). Thus being a cause can either entail self-responsibility (as for Tubetube, Nagovisi and Kwaio women) or make others responsible for acknowledging this (as in Foi, Chambri). These positions are by no means mutually exclusive: a married woman in Kove is at once a crucial support for men's wealth exchanges and the reason for them. It remains to draw attention to the fact that the material we have presented gives instances both of 'men' transacting with values conceptualised as 'female' in relation to themselves, and of 'women' being the cause of men's masculine definition, to the point of an identification between objects and a capacity conceptualised as 'male'.

It is true that for many of the systems being described people use images of innateness to refer to female powers of procreativity. This is as marked among the 'matrilineal' Tubetube as for the 'patrilineal' Foi. Yet the kind of action which they compel people to take is specific to the structuring of collective relations. For Tubetube and Kodi, for instance, innate female power is construed as a source of collective (matriclan) regeneration, whereas it is set against collective male action in both Kwaio and Foi. The gender of this collectivity, so to speak, is a function in turn of the manner in which such powers are feminised or masculinised. In so far as 'men' and 'women' embody male and female attributes, either sex may emerge at specific junctures as the crucial agent of the other's actions.

When the innate 'flow' of life is specifically feminised, it may be detachable under proper conditions to be circulated by men as evidence of male productivity and exertion (Foi, Kalauna, and Kodi mortuary ritual cast in terms of relations created by men between wife-givers and wife-takers). James Weiner argues that the very capacity to differentiate is regarded by Foi men as a male one; the image of men exchanging feminised values can also be rendered as men exchanging parts of themselves (for instance, female agnates). What they objectify as detached values to be exchanged can become masculinised in the process, an observation which Gillison (1980) originally made for the Eastern Highlands Gimi. Thus in Chapter 10 Weiner refers to wives as 'the detachable functions of male action'. Detachable values may consequently have a male aspect, as things men create by the very action of detachment. In this sense the powers of procreation are 'female' parts of a 'male' identity.

However in others of the societies we have discussed, the masculinisation of items for transaction is brought about by female agency. A capacity which is otherwise innate, such as matrilineage strength, may be detached as a 'male' quality in respect of a feminised collectivity, evinced for instance in men's work as formerly constructed by Nagovisi groomprice; women's work cannot be so detached from the vitality of the matrilineage. Kodi detachment of the masculinised soul could also be interpreted in this way. And one may note how on Tubetube men become objects of women's creativity – the armiger is actually masculinised in being given the strength to engage in inter-lineage combat. The senior woman who acts on behalf of the lineage produces an object of matrilineal strength but in masculine (warrior) form; when a warrior is drawn back, he is placed again under a woman's skirt. The military strength of the matrilineage is innate in the substance which its members share, as are the powers of procreation. But whereas procreation is a largely internal process, for such strength to be effective externally, in relation with other lineages, and thus an instrument of transaction, it has to be detached and objectified in persons who must stand in a distinct relation to matrilineal bonds, as 'male' warriors rather than 'female' mothers. Thus men's capacity to embody and transact with such strength is not conceived as innate, because the capacity to transact – be effective in external relations – is itself in antithesis to internal regeneration.

A further caution must be recorded here. When the meanings and references of symbolism turn so much on context, there is something too simple about the kinds of equations selected for mention here. The only justification is that they are being pressed into the service of a simple comparison. One difference between these Melanesian and Indonesian notions of innateness and Western essentialism lies in the limits on convertibility. For instance, the Foi concept of the innate in relation to which action is necessary would seem very different from the dual Western model, on the one hand of irreducible nature, on the other of nature modified and transformed. The 'ideal worlds' imagined under these latter conditions frequently suggest totalitarian possibilities of infinite control, of complete possession. Indeed, property idioms come to mind in Bloch and Parry's analysis, as of course framed the remark from Lévi-Strauss to which they refer, that mankind has always dreamed of gaining without losing and (prompted by an Andaman myth) of a heaven where women will no longer be exchanged, a world one might keep to oneself.[12] The systems we have been describing conceive of all sorts of relations between men and women, but I do not think that we can really postulate that men dream about a genderless, exchangeless society (Bloch and Parry 1982:31).[13] One of the points of the mythic matrilineal solution on Duau to which Young refers (Chapter 9) is surely that without wealth and exchange *there would be no men*. Indeed the very notion of a single truth (ideal order) from which present society has lapsed must derive from cosmologies of a kind alien to these Pacific systems (cf. Errington 1984:162-3).[14] However, Bloch and Parry's argument about the contradictions generated by collective representations is still important. One particular contradiction which affects those whom we are talking about arises, I conjecture, from the way people invest their acts with value. For items, acts or relations to be compared with their source, value must be established both in reference to the quality of what is being transacted (what it stands for) and in reference to its capacity to be transacted (as identified with but not identical to what it stands for).

This primary differentiation is crucial to the conceptualisation of 'value' in gift exchange. There are indeed dangers to be imagined in a state of non-exchange (as A. Strathern 1982 argues), for it would obliterate evidence of differentiation. We may put this in abstract terms, that agency is visible in the manner in which items are caused to move in differentiated contexts. There is no notion of transcendent authorship which can also comprehend agency as the final mastering of a (unitary) universe (cf. Lloyd 1983). If these people conceive of undifferentiated entities such as the internally homogeneous matrilineage or men's house, it is because the identity of things exchanged or transacted must be separated from the activity of exchanging. Things exchanged are thus conceptualised as detached or excised from pre-existing entities (such as the lineage). The pre-existing entities are presented as having innate or intrinsic qualities, standing only for themselves(Wagner 1986). They take the social form of 'persons' not things (Gregory 1982).

Buchbinder and Rappaport (1976:32) point to the process of nominalisation in symbolic constructions. The idea of a wealth object also involves a symbolic consciousness which allows that things both are and are not what they seem to be. I would argue that the capacity to create transactable wealth which stands for aspects of persons and relations simultaneously produces the capacity to conceptualise persons and relationships as of innate value.[15] This includes a value on procreation. It is in the context of 'wealth' moving in transactions, then, that people also construct their 'persons' as having value. The process creates the dualism of a whole:part relation. Value can inhere in the whole person (the clansman or clanswoman)[16] or adhere to detachable parts (the products of work, fecundity), in terms of the comparison between them. Thus work or procreativity appears as at once intrinsic and detachable attributes of the person.

Agency is made visible, then, through the transactability of items. An item (a wealth object, a bride, a warrior) may indicate value both in reference to its source and in reference to its own transactability. Consequently the (detached) items appear to refer to things other than themselves. Male wealth may be said to 'stand for' female fertility – flowing against it, evincing a counter source in male efficacy (Foi). Or a female source will empower male action (Kodi, Tubetube). The 'difference' between the sexes as it is employed in such constructs, creates the conceptual conditions for the disjunction between an entity and its source on which a comparison and thus the relation between them must rest. Inasmuch as these societies deal in difference, this inevitably implies that they also deal in the creative combination of discrete labour/ procreative powers, to use Damon's (1983) phrase. Biersack proposed that moral discrimination through gender categories results in asymmetric evaluations of what becomes associated with one or other sex. We can now see that there is one reason for asymmetry which lies beyond the self-reflection to which she and Rosaldo referred. In systems where people define relationships through the circulation of wealth objects, those objects must always be both more than and less than the relations and attributes to which they refer. Collective life also appears as both more than and less than the parts which it organises. If they were isomorphic, and there were no comparison between actions and their cause, between entities and their source, transactions would not hold the 'value' they have.

A caveat rather than a conclusion. To compare the societies of the Southwestern Pacific with those from elsewhere in the world might lead one to generalise about men's involvement in exchange and warfare, and to point to women's general association with procreation. But we must know how such a description relates to Western interests in the question of equality between the sexes. People do not everywhere reach the same conclusion about the naturalness of female fecundity, neither that it is natural nor that what women evince is an exclusively female power. Men and women are differently compelled to act 'as men' and 'as women' in relation to different collective interests. No blanket classification of 'the relationship' between the sexes, and thus no summary conclusion about equality, can be offered. Hence none of the single terms – complementarity, dominance, separation – will in the end do, because there is no single relationship. We may wish to measure the dimensions of a single relationship for analytic ends, such as relations of exploitation, participation in public life or whatever; but we cannot then draw for evidence on people's symbolisation of men and women, for the simple reason that they are unlikely to be constructing such measurements. Coming to grips with indigenous notions of agency has instead followed an indigenous separation between the cause and exercise of power. Situations where persons act for themselves or are compelled to act by others have been considered not in terms of interpersonal relations of dominance but in terms of how gender is conceived. In taking account of the comparisons they do make, we arrive at an absolute difference. This absolute difference is constructed not in the nature of persons as the end-products of processes of differentiation (the 'Western' conversions referred to earlier). Rather, it is instantiated each time a difference between the sexes signifies the relation of an active agent to the source of or reason for his or her actions.

A person, categorically speaking, who is the cause of another acting becomes thereby inactive. It follows that the actions of these different agents cannot be measured against each other. This is not quite the same as the Western asymmetry of subject and object, or of one set of persons passive in the face of another's domination; there, cause and action can be conflated in a single social person who acts in relation to others as his or her instruments, constituted as objects of his or her regard. In many of the contexts described here, these elements are separated out. Indeed, what links several of these societies is the fact that exertions of a spectacular, public kind are classified as 'male', while their cause, like the triumphant and humiliated mother's brother in *Naven* (Bateson 1958; also Clay 1977:ch.7), or the debased all-powerful wives of Gimi men (Gillison 1980), is reciprocally 'female'.

Let me indicate one difference between the Western idea of inequality and those representations which have little interest in measuring the sexes according to a common scale. If we think of the subject–object relation in general Western parlance, we can take it both as transitive (one person acting on another), and as reflexive (each receives its definition from the other), a conflation which Simone de Beauvoir put at the heart of gender relations. The two can be realised simultaneously in

the hierarchical Western model of human enterprise as at once production and domestication, in so far as one person's ends can be conceived as
encompassed by another's. For the cases considered here, the relation
between the person who is cause and the person who is caused to act also
appears transitive and reflexive. Yet what is made an object, so to speak,
is not the constituted 'other' but efficacy, the very ability to take action,
to engage in transactions, even to procreate. I have pointed to the way in
which gender difference concretises, in Bloch and Parry's word, the
comparison of a product or action with its source. What the construction
does not admit is that image of domestication particular to Western
industrial culture whereby subjects create objects only in relation to
themselves, so that efficacy resides within the one who takes action.

This is important for the interpretation of male–female interaction. In
these Pacific societies neither sex stands for the idea of an exclusively
defined value (the agent which causes itself to act, society which
encompasses). Consequently there can be no gender-free domains of
action – the male world of politics or a female world of matrilineage
affairs does not incidentally exclude or acknowledge the opposite sex: it
is constituted in deliberate antithesis or combination. By the same token
there can be no ultimate encompassment: the ends of one sex are not
subsumed under those of the other.

Notes

1. The point is made in Wagner 1975, but needs stressing again. The oppositional (even
   contradictory) nature of the propositions about unity and diversity are precipitated by
   the Western nature–culture dichotomy (cf. M. Strathern 1980). I regard such ideas as
   underpinning much scholarly endeavour, including in the social sciences, yet 'popular'
   in so far as whatever their origins in seventeenth- or eighteenth-century European
   philosophy and science they now have a general cosmological status.
2. And is thus also self-domestication: in bringing things under one's control one also
   becomes dependent upon them for one's definition – this is the sense in which we
   equate domestication with culture or civilisation.
3. The model draws both on capitalist commodity relations and on humanist critiques of
   them. Identification of worker and product under capitalism makes them both into
   objects (commodities); yet the humanistic critique *also* constructs an identification here
   in supposing the opposite, that under other conditions human creativity is realised
   through labour (conceived as part of the subjective self). In so far as we accept that
   social representations work to evaluate or transform 'the relationship' between a
   worker and his other product, or that labour is appropriated because it is productive,
   such critiques uphold the same suppositions about the constitution of persons as
   inform the dominant ideologies themselves. They are based on a pervasive notion of
   society's industry in relation to the natural world, a cosmology that sees transformative
   process at the heart of the individual: society or nature: culture relationship. Yeatman
   (1984a) dubs a cognate constellation of ideas as the modern 'ruling paradigm' in social
   science.
4. But see Dumont, e.g., 1982. Other honourable exceptions are Gregory 1982;
   Schwimmer 1979. I am grateful for Christopher Gregory's comments on this section,
   and to general discussions with Deborah Gewertz. I have since read Stanner 1985. His

expansion of Radcliffe-Brown's concept of social value makes several of these points much more clearly than I do. Indeed his provocative market metaphor of the ratio of interests in an 'object' which thus produces its 'value', applied to the analysis of certain kinship relations, might have proved a more satisfactory approach than the one adopted here. I note that he argues that all conceptions of value necessarily involve the idea of hierarchy or order – but by this he means I think that the entities so valued are ranked with an inequality in the different interests focused on the entity. In the exchange-based systems described here, however, I think that we are dealing not simply with the comparison of interests in a third entity but with a comparison between an entity and what is simultaneously constructed as its source.

5. This is the context in which Illich's (1982) 'economic' sex makes sense.

6. I would suggest that an image of non-partibility, of an entire or unitary asset, derives from certain types of property relations. The manner in which objects are used in ceremonial exchange systems, on the other hand, rest on attributes of partibility. In this world, objects simultaneously stand for parts of persons and can be transferred between persons. Women's part in social reproduction is defined less as requiring control over an asset of self-evident value (as in property-based systems) – but rather in its relation to the value put on all the bits and pieces of persons that circulate between and constitute social categories. Ceremonial exchange celebrates the circulation of 'men' as well as the circulation of 'women and children'. I might add that it is not of course gifts but values which are personified, and the gift is their form. Hence their intrinsic connection with the 'human values' of kinship (Modjeska 1982; cf. Gregory 1982:45,67).

7. This is close to A. Weiner's (1976) discussion of female 'power' in the Trobriands, as it is objectified into wealth objects. In many of the societies of this region, such concrete location of value results in the abuse as much as the glorification of women's (as well as men's) persons (cf. Buchbinder and Rappaport 1976:33). The observation about 'concrete' fertility is a technical description of a type of value system, not a description of the way people experience worth.

8. He is referring to the fact that childbirth is a visible event, so the resultant mother–child tie is not open to adjustment and re-definition. There is no space here to engage in an argument about who is seen to cause the birth, and what the tie therefore means. Collier and Rosaldo (1981) effectively describe a range of societies where maternity fails to provide a model for interrelatedness.

9. Their argument is worth spelling out in more detail with respect to the Melanesian systems with which they deal. These include a Massim society (Dobu), where images of propagation deny to affines any ultimate role in the perpetuation of the descent group (1982:29). (Only sisters reproduce the matrilineage.) A similar point is made of Hagen, from the New Guinea Highlands, where they emphasise 'the dangers attendant on the necessity of exchange with others exemplified by a reliance on outsider women' (1982:31). Hageners, they suggest, entertain a fantasy of an enviable order without exchange – one created in rituals but which their institutions based on exchange makes impossible to realise. Thus they argue that Hageners simultaneously elaborate exchange as an institution and 'entertain the countervailing vision of an ideal order without exchange' (1982:31). Dobuans suppress affinity; Hageners wish to deny exogenous sources of nurture. As will become clear, I dispute such an interpretation. The hint of annihilation is not necessarily that of a return to an absence of exchange secretly coveted. Such a vision would have to rest on a cosmology that defined a single 'universal' world order, with an ideal of self-sufficiency. Underlying their account of both Dobu and Hagen is the assumption that it is the reproduction of descent groups that is at issue and that these groups deploy women as assets ('the objective is ... to appropriate what belongs to others while hanging on to your own'; 1982:29): Dobuans elaborate the equation between endogenous yams and their sisters; Hageners suppress the exogenous status of in-coming wives in replacing women by clan territory as the crucial source of food. So this view in the end also incorporates an assumption about the self-evident nature of women's reproductive contributions as something to be contained or controlled. (People imagine to themselves 'ideal worlds', utilising for their representations bits and pieces of their own contradictory real social worlds to do

so; faced with death and sexuality they envisage life and asexual replenishment; and among the objects of contemplation, women present themselves to men as creatures of sexual reproduction.)

10. Bloch and Parry carefully argue, 'with Hertz we share a concern with the social implications of mortuary practices, though not his view of society as an entity acting for itself. If we can speak of a reassertion of the social order at the time of death, this social order is a *product* of rituals ... rather than their cause ... the mortuary rituals themselves being an occasion for *creating* that "society" as an apparently external force' (their italics).

11. 'Sexuality is set in opposition to fertility as women are opposed to men' (Bloch and Parry 1982:19).

12. It is notable that they proceed to de-universalise these yearnings in comparing Melanesian exchange with the practice of Hindu asceticism which reverses the fantasy. A. Weiner refers to the 'fundamental societal problem' in the same property idiom: 'how can one draw on the resources and substances of others while maintaining and regenerating one's own resources and substances' (1982:61). For a critique of such implicit economism see Whitehead 1984.

13. Chowning (pers. comm.) indicates that as spouses Kove men might dream of a society free from endless affinal exchange. The point of Bloch and Parry's account is not of course individual fantasy, but a cultural fantasy that moves peoples' representations of themselves. In this sense I do not think men so 'dream'.

14. With all respect, I think that the ideal world which Bloch and Parry posit has been borrowed from rather different social bases, as are found in systems where endogamous status groups have property to protect. Here may be envisaged 'natural' values to which women are assigned on a categorical basis. Idioms of control of the natural world mirror the manner in which assets are manipulated and appropriated. For an ideal world without external dependence is a property-based conceptualisation, I would argue, that serves to construct property as self-perpetuating. In crudest terms, a denial of dependence on exchange is denial of exploitation of others and appropriation to self of the natural regeneration of assets. The very notion of an ideal order is thus to be contextualised. The suppression of difference Bloch and Parry encounter in their respective ethnographic situations emerges in the interests of a (unitary) 'social' order; whereas in the Melanesian system they address, the perpetual re-creation of difference is the basis for a 'sociality' which 'deals' in the difference, rather than overcoming it. Damon (1983) gives a lucid exposition of a system where the return to stasis is not a desire to negate exchange but to terminate one cycle in order to start afresh.

15. Without labouring the point, I put it like this to get away from the naturalistic model which supposes that value could be perceived in a human activity (such as bearing children) before it becomes an object of people's relations with one another, and is thus somehow the sole cause of objectification. The argument here is developed with the analogy of the mutual constitution of the use value and exchange value of commodities in mind.

16. The Foi 'soul' is a whole construct of this kind: wives and affines emerge as detachable products of male activity.

Bibliography

Aberle, David. 1963. 'Matrilineal descent in cross-cultural perspective', in *Matrilineal Kinship*, D.M. Schneider and K. Gough (eds.). Berkeley: University of California Press

Allen, Michael. 1981. 'Rethinking old problems: matriliny, secret societies and political evolution', in *Vanuatu: Politics, Economics and Ritual in Island Melanesia*, M.R. Allen (eds). Sydney: Academic Press

1984. 'Elders, chiefs, and big men: authority legitimation and political evolution in Melanesia', *American Ethnologist*, 11:20-41

Anderson, Robert J. and William W. Sharrock. 1982. 'Sociological work: some procedures sociologists use for organising phenomena', *Social Analysis*, 11:79-93

Atkinson, Jane Monnig. 1982. 'Anthropology' (Review Essay). *Signs: Journal of Women in Culture and Society*, 8:236-58

1983. 'Identity, complementarity, and difference in Wana constructions of gender.' Paper prepared for the Social Science Research Council Conference on the Construction of Gender in Island Southeast Asia, Princeton, New Jersey

Augé, Marc. 1982. *The Anthropological Circle: Symbol, Function, History* (trans. by M. Thom). Cambridge: Cambridge University Press

Australian Law Reform Commission. 1982. Aboriginal Customary Law Reference, Field Trip No. 7, Central Australia

Bachofen, Johann. 1861. *Das Mutterrecht*. Basel: Benno Schwabe

Bateson, Gregory. 1958. *Naven*. Stanford: Stanford University Press

Battaglia, Debbora. 1983. 'Projecting personhood in Melanesia: the dialectics of artefact symbolism on Sabarl Island', *Man*(n.s.), 18:289-304

Beckett, N.T. 1915. 'Report on Aborigines to the Chief Protector of Aborigines, Darwin', *Report of the Northern Territory*. The Parliament of the Commonwealth of Australia, 26-8

Bell, Diane. 1980.'Desert politics: choices in the "marriage market"', in *Women and Colonization*, M. Etienne and E. Leacock (eds.). New York: Praeger

1982. 'Outstations: Reflections from the Centre', *Service Delivery to Outstations, Darwin*. The Australian National University, North Australia Research Unit Monograph, 85-92

1983. *Daughters of the Dreaming*. Melbourne/Sydney: McPhee Gribble/George Allen and Unwin

Bell, Diane and Pam Ditton. 1984 [1980]. *Law: The Old and the New.*, Canberra: Aboriginal History [2nd ed.]

Berndt, Ronald M. 1962. *Excess and Restraint*. Chicago: University of Chicago Press

Biersack, Aletta. 1982. 'Ginger gardens for the ginger woman: rites and passages in a Melanesian society', *Man*(n.s.), 17:239-58

1984. 'Paiela "women-men": the reflexive foundations of gender ideology', *American Ethnologist*, 10:118-38

Bloch, Maurice. 1975. 'Introduction', in *Political Language and Oratory in Traditional Society*, Maurice Bloch (ed.). London: Academic Press.

1977 'The past and the present in the present'. *Man*(n.s.),12:278-292

1982. 'Death, women and power', in *Death and the Regeneration of Life*, M. Bloch and J. Parry (eds.). Cambridge: Cambridge University Press

Bloch, Maurice and Jean H. Bloch. 1980. 'Women and the dialectics of nature in eighteenth-century French thought', in *Nature, Culture and Gender*, C.P. MacCormack and M. Strathern (eds). Cambridge: Cambridge University Press

Bloch, Maurice and Jonathan Parry. 1982. 'Introduction', in *Death and the Regeneration of Life*, M. Bloch and J. Parry (eds.). Cambridge: Cambridge University Press

Bourdieu, Pierre. 1977. *Outline of a Theory of Practice* (translated by Richard Nice). Cambridge: Cambridge University Press

Bourque, Susan C. and Kay Barbara Warren. 1981. *Women of the Andes: Patriarchy and Social Change in Two Peruvian Towns*. Ann Arbor: University of Michigan Press

Braverman, Harry. 1975. *Labor and Monopoly Capital: The Degradation of Work in the 20th Century*. New York: Monthly Review Press

Bricker, Victoria Reifler. 1973. *Ritual Humor in Highland Chiapas*. Austin: University of Texas Press

Brown, D.J.J. 1980. 'The structuring of Polopa kinship and affinity', *Oceania*, 50:297-331

Brown, Paula and Georgeda Buchbinder. 1976. *Man and Woman in the New Guinea Highlands*. Washington, D.C.: American Anthropological Association (special publication no. 8)

Buchbinder, Georgeda and Roy Rappaport. 1976. 'Fertility and death among the Maring', in *Man and Woman in the New Guinea Highlands*, P. Brown and G. Buchbinder (eds.). Washington, D.C.: American Anthropological Association (special publication no. 8)

Burridge, Kenelm. 1973. *Encountering Aborigines: A Case Study: Anthropology and the Australian Aboriginal*. New York: Pergamon Press

Campbell, Shirley. 1983. 'Attaining rank: a classification of shell valuables', in Leach and Leach 1983

Cancian, Frank. 1965. *Economics and Prestige in a Maya Community: The Religious Cargo System in Zinacantan*. Palo Alto: Stanford University Press

Chinnery, E.W. Pearson. 1924. *Notes on the Natives of South Bougainville and Mortlocks (Taku)* (Territory of New Guinea Anthropological Report no.5:69-121). Canberra: Government Printer

Chowning, Ann. 1961. 'Amok and aggression in the D'Entrecasteaux', in *Proceedings of the Annual Spring Meeting of the American Ethnological Society*:78-83

    1962. 'Cognatic kin groups among the Molima of Fergusson Island', *Ethnology*, 1:92-101

    1973. 'The recognition and treatment of abnormal mental states in several New Guinea societies', in *Psychology in Papua New Guinea: 1972*, M.A. Hutton, R.E. Hicks and C.J.S. Brammal (eds.). Port Moresby: Australian Psychological Society (Papua New Guinea Branch) and Society for Papua New Guinea Psychological Research and Publications

    1974. 'Disputing in two West New Britain societies: similarities and differences', in *Contention and Dispute: Aspects of Law and Social Control in Melanesia*, A.L. Epstein (ed.). Canberra: Australian National University Press

    1977. *An introduction to the peoples and cultures of Melanesia*. Menlo Park: Cummings Pub. Co. [2nd ed.]

    1978a 'Changes in West New Britain trading systems in the twentieth century', *Mankind*, 11:296-307

    1978b. 'First-child ceremonies and male prestige in the changing Kove society', in *The Changing Pacific: Essays in Honour of H.E. Maude*, N. Gunson (ed.). Melbourne: Oxford University Press

    1979. 'Leadership in Melanesia', *Journal of Pacific History*, 14:66-84

    1983. 'Wealth and exchange among the Molima of Fergusson Island', in Leach and Leach 1983

    1987. 'Sorcery and the social order in Kove', in *Sorcerer and Witch in Melanesia*, M. Stephen (ed.). Melbourne: University of Melbourne Press

Clark, Gracia. 1975. 'The Beguines: a medieval women's community', *Quest*, 1:73-80

Clay, Brenda Johnson. 1977. *Pinikindu: Maternal Nurture, Paternal Substance*. Chicago: University of Chicago Press

Collier, Jane F. 1973. *Law and Social Change in Zinacantan*. Palo Alto: Stanford University Press

Collier, Jane F. and Michelle Z. Rosaldo. 1981. 'Politics and gender in simple societies', in *Sexual Meanings*, S.B. Ortner and H. Whitehead (eds). New York: Cambridge University Press

Connell, John. 1977. 'The economics of big-men: reflections on a Siwai paradigm.' Paper presented at a work-in-progress seminar, Department of Economics, Research School of Pacific Studies, The Australian National University, Canberra

Damon, Frederick H. 1980. 'The Kula and generalised exchange: considering some unconsidered aspects of *The Elementary Structures of Kinship*', *Man*(n.s.), 15:267-92

    1983 'Muyuw kinship and the metamorphoses of gender labour', *Man*(n.s.), 18:305-26

Dominy, Michele D. 1986. 'Lesbian-feminist gender conceptions: separation in Christchurch, New Zealand', *Signs*, II:274-89

Douglas, Bronwen. 1979. 'Rank, power, authority: a reassessment of traditional leadership in South Pacific societies', *Journal of Pacific History*, 14:2-27

Douglas, Mary. 1969. 'Is matriliny doomed in Africa?', in *Man in Africa*, M. Douglas and P. Kaberry (eds.). London: Tavistock
1980. *Purity and Danger*. London: Routledge and Kegan Paul

Dumont, Louis. 1971. *From Mandeville to Marx: The Genesis and Triumph of Economic Ideology*. Chicago: University of Chicago Press
1982. *On Value*. The British Academy: Oxford University Press

Dwyer, Daisy Hilse. 1978. 'Ideologies of sexual inequality and strategies for change in male–female relations', *American Ethnologist*, 5:227-40

Errington, Frederick K. 1974. *Karavar: Masks and Power in a Melanesian Ritual*. Ithaca: Cornell University Press
1984. *Manners and Meaning in West Sumatra: The Social Context of Consciousness*. New Haven: Yale University Press

Errington, Frederick and Deborah Gewertz. 1985. 'The chief of the Chambri: social change and cultural permeability among a New Guinea people'. *American Ethnologist*, 12:442-54

Faithorn, Elizabeth. 1975. 'The concept of pollution among the Kafe of the Papua New Guinea Highlands', in *Toward an Anthropology of Women*, R. R. Reiter (ed.). New York: Monthly Review Press
1976. 'Women as persons: aspects of female life and male–female relations among the Kafe', in *Man and Woman in the New Guinea Highlands*, P. Brown and G. Buchbinder (eds.). Washington, D.C.: American Anthropological Association (special publication no. 8)

Fardon, Richard. 1985. 'Sociability and secrecy: two problems of Chamba knowledge', in *Power and Knowledge: Anthropological and Sociological Approaches*, R. Fardon (ed.) Edinburgh: Scottish Academic Press

Feil, Daryl. 1978. 'Women and men in the Enga tee', *American Ethnologist*, 5:263-79

Forge, Anthony. 1972. 'The golden fleece', *Man*(n.s.), 7:527-40

Forth, Gregory L. 1981. *Rindi: An Ethnographic Study of a Traditional Domain in Eastern Sumba*. The Hague: Martinus Nijhoff

Fortune, Reo. 1932. *Sorcerers of Dobu*. London: Routledge and Kegan Paul
1963. *Sorcerers of Dobu*. London: Routledge and Kegan Paul. [Revised ed.]
n.d. 'Field notes'. Unpublished document. University of Auckland

Fox, James J. 1971. 'Semantic parallelism in Rotinese ritual language', in *Bijdragen tot de Taal-, Land- en Volkenkunde* 127:215-55
1974. 'Our ancestors spoke in pairs: Rotinese views of language, dialect and code', in *The Ethnography of Speaking*, R. Bauman and J. Sherzer (eds). London: Academic Press
1975.'On binary categories and primary symbols: some Rotinese perspectives', in *The Interpretation of Symbolism*, R. Willis (ed.). London: Malaby Press
1982. 'The Great Lord rests at the centre: the paradox of powerlessness in European–Timorese relations', *Canberra Anthropology*, 5:7-20

1983. 'Category and complement: binary ideologies and the organisation of dualism in Eastern Indonesia'. Draft paper for the Conference on Dual Organisation

Freud, Sigmund. 1925. 'Mourning and melancholia', in *Collected Papers*, vol. IV. London: Hogarth

Fried, Morton. 1967. *The Evolution of Political Society*. New York: Random House

Friedl, Ernestine. 1975. *Women and Men: an Anthropologist's View*. New York: Holt, Rinehart and Winston

Geertz, Clifford. 1973. *The Interpretation of Cultures*. New York: Basic Books

Gewertz, Deborah. 1977. 'The politics of affinal exchange: Chambri as a client market', *Ethnology*, 16:285-98

1981. 'A historical reconsideration of female dominance among the Chambri', *American Ethnologist*, 8:94-106

1982. 'The father who bore me: the role of the Tsambunwuro during Chambri initiation ceremonies', in *Rituals of Manhood: Male Initiation in Papua New Guinea*, G.H. Herdt (ed.). Berkeley: University of California Press

1983. *Sepik River Societies: A Historical Ethnography of the Chambri and their Neighbors*. New Haven: Yale University Press

1984. 'The Tchambuli view of persons: a critique of individualism within the works of Mead and Chodorow', *American Anthropologist*, 86:615-29

Giddens, Anthony. 1984. *The Constitution of Society: Outline of the Theory of Structuration*. Cambridge: Polity Press, with Basil Blackwell, Oxford

Gillen, Frances James. 1968. *Gillen's Diary: the camp jottings of F.J. Gillen on the expedition across Australia 1901-2*. Adelaide: Libraries Board of South Australia

Gillison, Gillian S. 1980. 'Images of nature in Gimi thought', in *Nature, Culture and Gender*, C. MacCormack and M. Strathern (eds). Cambridge: Cambridge University Press

Godelier, Maurice. 1982. 'Social hierarchies among the Baruya of New Guinea', in *Inequality in New Guinea Highlands Societies*, A.J. Strathern (ed.). Cambridge: Cambridge University Press

Goody, J. 1969. 'A comparative approach to incest and adultery', in *Comparative Studies in Kinship*, J. Goody. London: Routledge and Kegan Paul

Gough, Kathleen. 1963. 'Variation in matrilineal systems', in *Matrilineal Kinship*, D. M. Schneider and K. Gough (eds.). Berkeley: University of California Press

Gregory, Christopher A. 1982. *Gifts and Commodities*. London: Academic Press

Guy, Alfred. 1918-71. Unpublished diaries and papers

Hamnett, Michael. 1977 *Households on the Move: Settlement Patterns among a Group of Eivo and Simeku Speakers in Central Bougainville*. Ph.D. dissertation, University of Hawaii

Harris, Olivia and Kate Young. 1981. 'Engendered structures: some problems in the analysis of reproduction', in *The Anthropology of Pre-Capitalist Societies*, J.S. Kahn and J.R. Llobera (eds.). London: Macmillan

Harrison, Simon. 1982. *Stealing People's Names: Social Structure, Cosmology and Politics in a Sepik River Village*. Ph.D. dissertation, The Australian National University

Hartmann, Heidi. 1981. 'The unhappy marriage of Marxism and feminism: towards a more progressive union', in *Women and Revolution*, L. Sargent (ed.). Boston: Southend Press

Hartwig, M.C. 1965. *The progress of white settlement in the Alice Springs District and its effects upon the Aboriginal inhabitants, 1860-1894.*, Ph.D. dissertation, University of Adelaide

Hau'ofa, Epeli. 1981. *Mekeo: Inequality and Ambivalence in a Village Society*. Canberra: Australian National University Press

Haviland, John. 1977. *Gossip, Reputation and Knowledge in Zinacantan*. Chicago: Chicago University Press

Haviland, Leslie and John Haviland. 1983. 'Privacy in a Mexican Indian village', in *Public and Private in Social Life*, S.I. Benn, and G.F. Gaus, (eds). London: Croom Helm

Heppell, Michael and Julian J. Wigley. 1981. *Black Out in Alice: A History of the Establishment and Development of Town Camps in Alice Springs* (Development Studies Centre Monograph No. 26). Canberra: The Australian National University

Herdt, Gilbert H. 1981. *Guardians of the Flutes*. New York: McGraw-Hill

Herdt, Gilbert H. (ed.) 1982. *Rituals of Manhood: Male Initiation in Papua New Guinea*. Berkeley: University of California Press

1984. *Ritualized Homosexuality in Melanesia*. Los Angeles and Berkeley: University of California Press

Herdt, Gilbert H. and Fitz John Porter Poole. 1982.' "Sexual antagonism": the intellectual history of a concept in New Guinea anthropology', in *Sexual Antagonism, Gender and Social Change in Papua New Guinea*, F.J.P. Poole and G.H. Herdt (eds.). *Social Analysis* (special issue), 12

Hertz, Robert. 1973. 'The pre-eminence of the right hand: a study in religious polarity', in *Right and Left: Essays on Dual Symbolic Classification*, R. Needham (ed.). Chicago: University of Chicago Press

Hess, Michael. 1982. 'Misima – 1942: an anti-colonial religious movement', *Bikmaus*, 3 (1):48-56

Hogbin, I. 1964. *A Guadalcanal Society: The Kaoka Speakers*. New York: Holt, Rinehart and Winston

Hoskins, Janet Alison, in press. 'Etiquette in Kodi spirit communication: the lips told to pronounce, the mouths told to speak', in *To Speak in Pairs: Essays on the Ritual Languages of Eastern Indonesia*, J.J. Fox (ed.). (Pacific Linguistics C-82). Canberra: Department of Linguistics, Research School of Pacific Studies, The Australian National University

Hotchkiss, John C. 1967. 'Children and conduct in a Ladino community of Chiapas, Mexico', *American Anthropologist*, 68:711-18

Huckett, Joyce. (ed.) 1976a. *Dewa Kahihina*. Ukarumpa, PNG: Summer Institute of Linguistics

1976b. *Hida Nainaiya*. Ukarumpa, PNG: Summer Institute of Linguistics

Huntington, Richard and Peter Metcalf. 1979. *Celebrations of Death: The Anthropology of Mortuary Ritual*. Cambridge: Cambridge University Press

Illich, Ivan. 1982. *Gender*. New York: Pantheon Books

James, Kerry. 1983. 'Gender relations in Tonga, 1780-1984', *Journal of Polynesian Society*, 92:233-43

Jenness, Diamond and Andrew Ballantyne. 1920. *The Northern D'Entrecasteaux*. Oxford: Clarendon
    1928. *Language, Mythology, and Songs of Bwaidoga*. New Plymouth: Avery and Sons

Jolly, Margaret. 1981. 'People and their products in South Pentecost', in *Vanuatu. Politics, Economics and Ritual in Island Melanesia*, M.R. Allen (ed.). Sydney: Academic Press

Josephides, Lisette. 1982. *Suppressed and Overt Antagonism: A Study in Aspects of Power and Reciprocity among the Northern Melpa* (Research in Melanesia, Occasional Paper 2). Port Moresby: University of Papua New Guinea
    1984. 'Big men, great men, producers and women: exploring dimensions of power and inequality in the New Guinea Highlands'. (Review of *Inequality in New Guinea Highlands Societies*, A.J. Strathern (ed.).) *Bikmaus*, 5:41-6

Keesing, Roger M. 1967. 'Statistical models and decision models of social structure: a Kwaio case', *Ethnology*, 6:1-16
    1968. 'Chiefs in a chiefless society: the ideology of modern Kwaio politics', *Oceania*, 38:276-80
    1970a. 'Shrines, ancestors and cognatic descent: the Kwaio and Tallensi', *American Anthropologist*, 72:755-75
    1970b. 'Kwaio fosterage', *American Anthropologist*, 72:991-1019
    1971. 'Descent, residence and cultural codes', in *Anthropology in Oceania*, L. Hiatt and C. Jayawardena (eds.). Sydney: Angus and Robertson
    1978a. *'Elota's Story: The Life and Times of a Kwaio Big Man*. St. Lucia: University of Queensland Press (page references to 1973 edition, New York: Holt, Rinehart and Winston)
    1978b. 'Politico-religious movements and anti-colonialism on Malaita: Maasina Rule in historical perspective', *Oceania*, 48:241-61; 49:46-73
    1981. *Cultural Anthropology: A Contemporary Perspective*, 2nd ed. New York: Holt, Rinehart and Winston
    1982a. *Kwaio Religion: The Living and the Dead in a Solomon Island Society*. New York: Columbia University Press
    1982b. 'Kastom and anticolonialism on Malaita: culture as political symbol', in *Reinventing Traditional Culture: The Politics of Kastom in Island Melanesia*, R.M. Keesing and R. Tonkinson (eds). *Mankind* (special issue), 13:357-73
    1985. 'Kwaio women speak: the micropolitics of autobiography in a Solomon Island society', *American Anthropologist* 87:27-39
    in press 'Sins of a mission: Christian life as pagan ideology', forthcoming in *Christianity and Colonialism*, M. Jolly and M. Macintyre (eds.)
    n.d. 'Big man, killer, priest: reflections on a Melanesian troika'. Paper presented at seminar, Department of Anthropology, Research School of Pacific Studies, The Australian National University, Canberra

Keesing, Roger M. and P. Corris. 1980. *Lightning Meets the West Wind: The Malaita Massacre*. Melbourne: Oxford University Press

Keil, Jared Tao. 1975. *Local Group Composition and Leadership in Buin*. Ph.D. dissertation, Harvard University

   1979. 'Women in Buin'. Paper presented at 8th Annual Meeting of the Association for Social Anthropology in Oceania, Clearwater, Florida

Kelly, Raymond C. 1976. 'Witchcraft and sexual relations: an exploration in the social and semantic implications of the structure of belief', in *Man and Woman in the New Guinea Highlands*, P. Brown and G. Buchbinder (eds.). Washington, D.C.: American Anthropological Association (special publication no. 8)

Kruyt, A.C. 1919. 'De Soembaneezen, *Bijdragen tot de Taal-, Land- en Volkenkunde* 78; 466-608

Kuipers, Joel C. 1982. *Weyewa Ritual Speech: A Study of Language and Ceremonial Interaction in an Eastern Indonesian Community*. Ph.D. dissertation, Yale University

Lamphere, Louise. 1977. 'Review essay, anthropology', *Signs: Journal of Women in Culture and Society*, 2:612-27

Lancy, David and Andrew J. Strathern. 1981. '"Making twos": pairing as an alternative to the taxonomic mode of representation', *American Anthropologist*, 83:773-95

Langlas, C.M. 1974. *Foi Land Use, Prestige Economics and Residence: A Processual Analysis*. Ph.D. dissertation, University of Hawaii

Langton, Marcia. 1982. 'The Black Gin Syndrome'. Unpublished manuscript

   1983. 'Medicine square: for the recognition of Aboriginal swearing and fighting as customary law'. BA (Hons) thesis, The Australian National University

Lawrence, Peter. 1984. *The Garia: An Ethnography of a Traditional Cosmic System in Papua New Guinea*. Melbourne: Melbourne University Press

Leach, Edmund R. 1961. *Rethinking Anthropology*. London: The Athlone Press

Leach, Jerry W. 1983. 'Introduction', in Leach and Leach 1983

Leach, Jerry W. and Edmund R. Leach. (eds.). 1983. *The Kula: New Perspectives on Massim Exchange*. Cambridge: Cambridge University Press

Leacock, Eleanor Burke. 1981. *Myths of Male Dominance*. New York: Monthly Review Press

Lederman, Rena. 1983. 'The cultural is political: cultural construction of gender and female status in Mendi.' Paper presented at American Anthropological Association meetings, Chicago

Leeds Revolutionary Feminist Group. 1981. 'Political lesbianism: the case against heterosexuality', in *Love Your Enemy?* London: Only Woman Press

Lepowsky, Maria. 1983. 'Sudest Island and the Louisiade Archipelago in Massim exchange', in Leach and Leach 1983

Lévi-Strauss, Claude. 1962. *Totemism*. Boston: Beacon Press

   1973. *From Honey to Ashes*. New York: Harper and Row

Lindenbaum, Shirley. 1982. 'The mystification of female labours'. Paper presented at Feminism and Kinship Theory Conference, Bellagio

Lloyd, Genevieve. 1983. 'Reason, gender and morality in the history of philosophy', *Social Research*, 50:490-513

Losche, Diane. 1984. 'Utopian visions and the division of labour in Abelam society'. Paper presented at Symposium, Sepik Research Today, Basel

n.d. 'Through the glass darkly: the construction of gender and sexuality by anthropologists in Melanesia'. Unpublished manuscript

Lukes, Stephen. 1974. *Power: A Radical View*. London: Macmillan

Lutkehaus, Nancy. 1982. 'Ambivalence, ambiguity and the reproduction of gender hierarchy in Manam society: 1933-1979', in *Sexual Antagonism, Gender and Social Change in Papua New Guinea*, F. J. P. Poole and G. H. Herdt (eds.), *Social Analysis* (special issue), 12:36-51

Macintyre, M. 1983. 'Warfare and the changing context of kune on Tubetube.' *Journal of Pacific History*, 18:11-34

MacKinnon, Catharine A. 1982. 'Feminism, Marxism, method, and the state: an agenda for theory', in *Feminist Theory: A Critique of Ideology*, N.O. Keohane, M.Z. Rosaldo and B.C. Gelpi (eds.). Sussex: Harvester Press

Malinowski, Bronislaw. 1922. *Argonauts of the Western Pacific*. London: Routledge and Kegan Paul

1929. *The Sexual Life of Savages*. G. Routledge and Sons Ltd. London

Marshall, Mac. 1983. 'Introduction', in *Siblingship in Oceania: Studies in the Meaning of Kin Relations*, Mac Marshall (ed.) (ASAO Monograph no.8). Lanham MD: University Press of America

Martin, M.K. and B. Voorhies. 1975. *Female of the Species*. New York: Columbia University Press

McLennan, John. 1865. *Primitive Marriage*. Edinburgh: Adam and Charles Black

Mead, Margaret. 1935. *Sex and Temperament*. New York: William Morrow and Company

n.d. 'Field notes'. Unpublished document. Washington, Library of Congress

Meggitt, M.J.

1964a. 'Indigenous forms of government among the Australian Aborigines', *Bijdragen tot de Taal-, Land- en Volkenkunde*, Pt 120:163-78

1964b. 'Male–female relationships in the Highlands of Australian New Guinea', in *New Guinea: The Central Highlands*, J.B. Watson (ed.), *American Anthropologist* (special publication), 66:204-24

Millar, Susan Bolyard. 1983. 'On interpreting gender in Bugis society', *American Ethnologist*, 10:477-93

Mitchell, Donald D. 1976. 'Land and agriculture in Nagovisi, Papua New Guinea'. Boroko: Institute of Applied Social and Economic Research (Monograph no. 3)

Modjeska, Nicholas. 1982. 'Production and inequality: perspectives from central New Guinea', in *Inequality in New Guinea Highlands Societies*, A.J. Strathern (ed.). Cambridge: Cambridge University Press

Montague, Susan. 1983. 'Trobriand gender identity', *Mankind*, 14:33-45

Morgan, Lewis Henry. 1887. *Ancient Society*. New York: Henry Holt and Co.

Munn, Nancy D. 1977. 'The spatiotemporal transformations of Gawa canoes', *Journal de la Société des Océanistes*, 33 (54-55):39-54

1983. 'Gawan kula: spatiotemporal control and the symbolism of influence', in Leach and Leach 1983

Murdock, George P. 1949. *Social Structure*. New York: Macmillan

Nash, Jill. 1974. *Matriliny and Modernisation: The Nagovisi of South Bougainville* (New Guinea Research Bulletin no. 55). Canberra: Australian National University Press.

    1978a 'A note on groomprice', *American Anthropologist*, 80:106-8

    1978b. 'Women and power in Nagovisi society', *Journal de la Société des Océanistes*, 58(34):119-26

    1981. 'Sex, money and the status of women in Aboriginal South Bougainville', *American Ethnologist*, 8:107-26

Needham, Rodney. 1973. *Right and Left: Essays on Dual Symbolic Classification*. Chicago: University of Chicago Press

    1980. 'Principles and variations in the structure of Sumbanese Society', in J. Fox (ed.) *The Flow Of Life:Essays on Eastern Indonesia*, Cambridge: Harvard University Press.

New South Wales Anti Discrimination Board. 1982. *Study of Street Offences by Aborigines*

Ogan, Eugene. 1972. *Business and Cargo: Socio-Economic Change among the Nasioi of Bougainville* (New Guinea Research Bulletin, no. 44). Canberra: Australian National University Press

Ogan, Eugene, Jill Nash and Donald D. Mitchell. 1976. 'Culture change and fertility in two Bougainville populations', in *Measures of Man*, E. Giles and J.S. Friedlaender (eds.). Cambridge, Mass.: Peabody Museum Press

O'Laughlin, B. 1974. 'Mediation of contradiction: why Mbum women do not eat chicken', in *Woman, Culture and Society*, M.Z. Rosaldo and L. Lamphere (eds). Palo Alto: Stanford University Press

Oliver, Douglas L. 1943. *The Horomorun Concepts of South Bougainville*. *Papers of the Peabody Museum of American Archaeology and Ethnology*, Harvard University, 20

    1949a. 'The Peabody Museum expedition to Bougainville, Solomon Islands 1938-9', in *Studies in the Anthropology of Bougainville, Solomon Islands*. *Papers of the Peabody Museum of American Archaeology and Ethnology*, Harvard University, 29

    1949b. 'Economic and social uses of domestic pigs in Siuai, Southern Bougainville, Solomon Islands', in *Studies in the Anthropology of Bougainville, Solomon Islands. Papers of the Peabody Museum of American Archaeology and Ethnology*, Harvard University, 29

    1955. *A Solomon Island Society: Kinship and Leadership among the Siuai of Bougainville*. Cambridge, Mass.: Harvard University Press

Ollman, Bertell. 1976. (1971). *Alienation: Marx's Conception of Man in Capitalist Society*. Cambridge: Cambridge University Press, 2nd ed.

Onvlee, L. 1980. 'The significance of livestock on Sumba' (trans. by James Fox and Henny Fokker-Bakker) in J. Fox, (ed.) *The Flow of Life: Essays on Eastern Indonesia*. Cambridge: Harvard University Press

Ortner, Sherry B. 1974. 'Is female to male as nature is to culture?', in *Woman, Culture and Society*, M.Z. Rosaldo and L. Lamphere (eds.). Palo Alto: Stanford University Press

1981. 'Gender and sexuality in hierarchical societies: the case of Polynesia and some comparative implications', in *Sexual Meanings*, S.B. Ortner and H. Whitehead (eds.). New York: Cambridge University Press

1984. 'Theory in anthropology since the sixties', *Comparative Studies of Society and History*, 26:126-66.

Ortner, Sherry B. and Harriet Whitehead. 1981. 'Introduction: accounting for sexual meaning', in *Sexual Meanings*, S.B. Ortner and H. Whitehead (eds.). New York: Cambridge University Press

O'Shane, Pat. 1976. 'Is there any relevance in the women's movement for Aboriginal women?', *Refractory Girl*, 12:31-4

Peterson, Nicolas. 1970. 'The importance of women in determining the composition of residential groups in Aboriginal Australia', in *Woman's Role in Aboriginal Society*, F. Gale (ed.). Canberra: Australian Institute of Aboriginal Studies

Poole, Fitz J.P. 1982 'The ritual forging of identity: aspects of person and self in Bimin-Kuskusmin male initiation', in *Rituals of Manhood: Male Initiation in Papua New Guinea*, G. Herdt (ed.). Berkeley: University of California Press

Powdermaker, Hortense. 1933. *Life in Lesu*. New York: Norton

Rapp, Rayna. 1979. 'Anthropology' (Review Essay). *Signs, Journal of Women in Culture and Society*, 4:497-513

Reiter, Rayna R. 1975. *Toward an Anthropology of Women*. New York: Monthly Review Press

Richards, A.I. 1950. 'Some types of family structure among the Central Bantu', in *African Systems of Kinship and Marriage*, A.R. Radcliffe-Brown and D. Forde (eds.). London: Oxford University Press

Rodman, Margaret. 1981. 'A boundary and a bridge: women's pig killing as a border-crossing between spheres of exchange in East Aoba', in *Vanuatu. Politics, Economics and Ritual in Island Melanesia*, M.R. Allen (ed.). Sydney: Academic Press

Rogers, Susan C. 1975. 'Female forms of power and the myth of male dominance: a model of female/male interaction in peasant society', *American Ethnologist*, 2:727-56

Róheim, Geza. 1946. 'Yaboaine, a war god of Normanby Island', *Oceania*, 16:210-33; 319-36

1950 *Psychoanalysis and Anthropology*. New York: International University Press

Romilly, H.H. 1887. *The Western Pacific and New Guinea. Notes on the Natives, Christian and Cannibal, with some Account of the Old Labour Trade*. London: John Murray

Rosaldo, Michelle Z. 1974. 'Woman, culture, and society: a theoretical overview', in *Woman, Culture, and Society*, M.Z. Rosaldo and L. Lamphere (eds). Palo Alto: Stanford University Press

1980a. 'The use and abuse of anthropology: reflections on feminism and cross-cultural understanding', *Signs, Journal of Women in Culture and Society*, 5:389-417

1980b. *Knowledge and Passion: Ilongot Notions of Self and Society.* Cambridge: Cambridge University Press

Rosaldo, Michelle Z. and Louise Lamphere (eds.). 1974. *Woman, Culture, and Society.* Palo Alto: Stanford University Press

Rowley, Charles D. 1970. *Outcasts in White Australia.* Ringwood, Victoria: Penguin

Rubin, Gayle. 1975. 'The traffic in women: notes on the "political economy" of sex', in *Toward an Anthropology of Women*, R. Reiter (ed.). New York: Monthly Review Press

Rubinstein, Robert L. 1981. 'Knowledge and political process in Malo', in *Vanuatu. Politics, Economics and Ritual in Island Melanesia*, M.R. Allen (ed.). Sydney: Academic Press

Sacks, Karen. 1979. *Sisters and Wives: The Past and Future of Sexual Equality.* London: Greenwood Press

Sahlins, Marshall. 1972. *Stone Age Economics.* Chicago: Aldine-Atherton
   1976. *Culture and Practical Reason.* Chicago: Chicago University Press
   1981. *Historical Metaphors and Mythical Realities: Structure in the Early History of the Sandwich Islands Kingdom.* Ann Arbor: University of Michigan Press

Sanday, Peggy R. 1981. *Female Power and Male Dominance: On the Origins of Sexual Inequality.* Cambridge: Cambridge University Press

Schieffelin, Edward L. 1980. 'Reciprocity and the construction of reality', *Man*(n.s.), 15:502-17
   1982. 'The *Bau A* ceremonial hunting lodge: an alternative to initiation', in *Rituals of Manhood: Male Initiation in Papua New Guinea*, G. Herdt (ed.). Berkeley: University of California Press

Schlegel, Alice (ed.) 1977. *Sexual Stratification: A Cross-Cultural View.* New York: Columbia University Press
   1978a. 'Male and female in Hopi thought and action', in *Sexual Stratification*, A. Schlegel (ed.). New York: Columbia University Press
   1978b. 'An overview', in *Sexual Stratification*, A. Schlegel (ed.). New York: Columbia University Press

Schneider, David M. 1983. Conclusions to *Siblingship in Oceania*, M. Marshall (ed.) (ASAO Monograph no. 8). Ann Arbor: University of Michigan Press

Schwimmer, Erik. 1979. 'The self and the product: concepts of work in comparative perspective', in *Social Anthropology of Work*, S. Wallman (ed.). London: Academic Press

Seligman, C. 1910. *The Melanesians of British New Guinea.* Cambridge: Cambridge University Press

Shapiro, Judith. 1983. 'Anthropology and the study of gender', in *A Feminist Perspective in the Academy*, E. Langland and W. Gove (eds.). Chicago: Chicago University Press

Signs. 1982. Editorial. *Signs: Journal of women in culture and society*, 8:193-4

Smith, Paul. 1978. 'Domestic labour and Marx's theory of value', in *Feminism and Materialism*, A. Kuhn and A. Wolpe (eds.). London: Routledge and Kegan Paul

Sontag, Susan. 1977. *Illness as Metaphor.* Harmondsworth: Penguin Books

Sørum, Arve. 1980. 'In search of the lost soul: Bedamini spirit seances and curing rites', *Oceania*, 50:273-96

Southwold, Martin. 1978. 'Definition and its problems in social anthropology', in *The Yearbook of Symbolic Anthropology, I*, E. Schwimmer (ed.). London: C. Hurst and Co

Stanner, W.E.H. 1985. Radcliffe-Brown's ideas on 'social value'. *Social Analysis*, 17:113-25

Strathern, Andrew J. 1968. 'Sickness and frustration: variations in two New Guinea societies', *Mankind*, 6:545-51

   1970. 'Male initiation in New Guinea Highlands societies', *Ethnology*, 9:373-9

   1971. *The Rope of Moka*. Cambridge: Cambridge University Press

   1972. *One Father, One Blood*. Canberra: Australian National University Press

   1979. 'Gender, ideology and money in Mount Hagen', *Man*(n.s.), 14:530-48

   1982. 'Death as exchange: two Melanesian cases', in *Mortality and Immortality: The Archaeology and Anthropology of Death*, S.C. Humphreys and H. King (eds.). London: Academic Press

Strathern, Andrew J. (ed.). 1982. *Inequality in New Guinea Highlands Societies*. Cambridge: Cambridge University Press

Strathern, Marilyn. 1968. 'Popokl: the question of morality', *Mankind*, 6:553-62

   1972. *Women in Between*. London: (Seminar) Academic Press

   1978. 'The achievement of sex: paradoxes in Hagen gender-thinking'. *Yearbook of Symbolic Anthropology, I*, E. Schwimmer (ed.) London: Hurst

   1980. 'No nature, no culture: the Hagen case', in *Nature, Culture and Gender*, C. MacCormack and M. Strathern (eds). Cambridge: Cambridge University Press

   1981. 'Culture in a netbag: the manufacture of a subdiscipline in anthropology', *Man*(n.s.), 16:665-88

   1984a. 'Discovering "social control"', *Journal of Law and Society*, 12:111-34

   1984b. 'Domesticity and the denigration of women', in *Rethinking Women's Roles: Perspectives from the Pacific*, D. O'Brien and S. Tiffany (eds.). Berkeley and Los Angeles: University of California Press

   1985. 'Dislodging a world view: challenge and counter-challenge in the relationship between feminism and anthropology', *Australian Feminist Studies Journal*, 1:1-25

   in press a. *The Gender of the Gift*. Berkeley and Los Angeles: University of California Press

   in press b. 'Producing difference: connections and disconnections in two New Guinea Highlands kinship systems', in *Gender and kinship*, J. Collier and S. Yanagisako (eds.). Palo Alto: Stanford University Press

Strehlow, T.G.H. 1971. *Songs of Central Australia*. Sydney: Angus and Robertson

Sykes, R. (Bobbi). 1975. 'Black women in Australia: a history', in *The Other Half*, J. Mercer (ed.). Ringwood, Victoria: Pelican

Taussig, Michael. 1980. *The Devil and Commodity Fetishism in South America*. Chapel Hill: University of North Carolina Press

Thornton, Frieda. 1979. 'Situation report: Aboriginal communities in Alice Springs and fringe camps', Appendix 1 in D. Bell and P. Ditton, 1984

Thune, Carl. 1980. *The Rhetoric of Remembrance: Collective Life and Personal Tragedy in Loboda Village*. Ph.D. dissertation, Princeton University

Thurnwald, Hilde. 1934. 'Women's status in Buin society', *Oceania*, 5:142-70
1938. 'Ehe und Mutterschaft in Buin', *Archiv für Anthropologie*, 24 (n.s.):214-46

Thurnwald, Richard. 1934. 'Pigs and currency in Buin', *Oceania*, 5:119-41

Toohey, John. 1984. *Seven Years On: Report by Mr Justice Toohey to the Minister for Aboriginal Affairs on the Aboriginal Land Rights (Northern Territory) Act 1976 and Related Matters*. Canberra: Australian Government Publishing Service

Traube, Elizabeth. 1981. 'Affines and the dead', *Bijdragen tot de Taal-, Land- en Volkenkunde* 136: 90-115

Tsing, Anna Lowenhaupt and Sylvia Junko Yanagisako. 1983. 'Feminism and kinship theory', *Current Anthropology*, 24:511-16

Turner, V.W. 1969. *The Ritual Process*. Chicago: Aldine

Tuzin, Donald F. 1982. 'Ritual violence among the Ilahita Arapesh: the dynamics of moral and religious uncertainty', in *Rituals of Manhood: Male Initiation in Papua New Guinea*, G.H. Herdt (ed.). Berkeley: University of California Press

Vogt, Evon Z. 1969. *Zinacantan*. Cambridge, Mass.: Belknap Press

Wagner, Roy. 1967. *The Curse of Souw*. Chicago: University of Chicago Press
1972. *Habu*. Chicago: University of Chicago Press
1975. *The Invention of Culture*. Englewood Cliffs, New Jersey: Prentice-Hall
1977a. 'Scientific and indigenous Papuan conceptualizations of the innate: a semiotic critique of the ecological perspective', in *Subsistence and Survival: Rural Ecology in the Pacific*, T. Bayliss-Smith and R. Feachem (eds). London: Academic Press
1977b. 'Analogic kinship: a Daribi example', *American Ethnologist*, 4:623-42
1978. *Lethal Speech: Daribi Myth as Symbolic Obviation*. Ithaca: Cornell University Press
1981. *The Invention of Culture*. Chicago: University of Chicago Press [2nd ed.]
1986. *Symbols that Stand for Themselves*. Chicago: University of Chicago Press

Wasserstrom, Robert. 1983. *Class and Society in Central Chiapas*. Berkeley: University of California Press

Watson, Graham. 1984. 'The social construction of boundaries between social and cultural anthropology in Britain and North America'. *Journal of Anthropological Research*, 40:351-66

Weiner, Annette B. 1976. *Women of Value, Men of Renown: New Perspectives in Trobriand Exchange*. Austin: University of Texas Press
1982. 'Sexuality among the anthropologists: reproduction among the informants', in *Sexual Antagonism, Gender, and Social Change in Papua New Guinea*, F.J.P. Poole and G.H. Herdt (eds.), *Social Analysis* (special issue), 12:52-65

Weiner, James F. 1983. *The Heart of the Pearlshell: The Mythological Dimension of Foi Sociality*. Ph.D dissertation, The Australian National University

1984. 'Sunset and flowers: the sexual dimension of Foi spatial orientation', *Journal of Anthropological Research*, 40:577-88

1985. 'Affinity and cross-cousin terminology among the Foi', *Social Analysis*, 17:93-112

1986. 'Blood and skin: the structural implications of sorcery and procreation beliefs among the Foi of Papua New Guinea'. *Ethnos*, 51:71-87

1987. *The Heart of the Pearl-Shell: The Mythological Dimension of Foi Sociality*. Berkeley: University of California Press

Wheeler, G.C. 1912. 'Sketch of the totemism and religion of the people of the islands in the Bougainville Straits', *Archiv für Religionswissenschaft*, 15:24-58

Whitehead, Ann. 1984. 'Men and women, kinship and property: some general issues, in *Women and Property: Women as Property*, R. Hirschon (ed). London: Croom Helm

Williams, Drid. 1975. 'The brides of Christ' in *Perceiving Women*, S. Ardener (ed.). London: Malaby Press

Williams, F.E. 1977. 'Natives of Lake Kutubu, Papua', in *The Vailala Madness and Other Essays*, E. Schwimmer (ed.). Honolulu: University of Hawaii Press

Wouden, F.A.E. van 1935. *Social structuurtypen in de Groote Oost*. Leiden: Ginsburg. (Published in English translation by Rodney Needham as *Types of Social Structure in Eastern Indonesia* in 1968. The Hague: Martinus Nijhoff)

1956. 'Locale groepen en dubbele afstamming in Kodi, West Sumba', *Bijdragen tot de Taal-, Land- en Volkenkunde*. (Republished in an English translation in 1977 in P.E. de Josselin de Jong, ed. *Structural Anthropology in the Netherlands*. The Hague: Martinus Nijhoff)

Yeatman, Anna. 1984a. 'Gender and the differentiation of social life into public and domestic domains', *Social Analysis*, 15:32-49 (Spec. issue, *Gender and social life*, ed. A. Yeatman)

1984b. 'A Rejoinder' (to comments on Anna Yeatman's 'The Procreative Model'), *Social Analysis*, 16:26-43

Young, Maribelle. 1979. *Bwaidoka Tales* (Pacific Linguistics D-16). Canberra: Department of Linguistics, Research School of Pacific Studies, The Australian National University

Young, Michael W. 1971. *Fighting with Food*. Cambridge: Cambridge University Press

1977. 'Bursting with laughter: obscenity, values and sexual control in a Massim society', *Canberra Anthropology*, 1:75-87

1983a. *Magicians of Manumanua: Living Myth in Kalauna*. Berkeley: University of California Press

1983b. '"Our name is women: we are bought with limesticks and limepots": an analysis of the autobiographical narrative of a Kalauna woman', *Man*(n.s.), 18:478-501

1983c. 'The theme of the resentful hero: stasis and mobility in Goodenough mythology', in *The Kula: New perspective on Massim Exchange*, J.W. Leach and E.R. Leach (eds). Cambridge: Cambridge University Press
1983d. 'The art of giving good advice', *Bikmaus*, 4:92-8
1984. 'The hunting of the Snark in Nidula: ruminations on pig love', *Canberra Anthropology*, 7:123-44

Index

Aberle, D., 150
Aboriginal Australians, 11, 18, 28-9,
   112-29, 289, 294; Land Rights Act,
   121; Women's Task Force 123; and
   Torres Strait Islander housing panel 121
administrators, 115, 118, 122
adultery, 147, 149n.6, 164
affinal avoidance, 262
affinal exchanges, 291; Kalauna, 235, 237,
   239; Kodi, 186; Kove, 131-9 *passim*,
   146, 148
affinal relations, Chambri, 67, 72-5, 77, 78;
   Kodi, 189
afterbirth, 92
afterworld, 266, 273, 274
age difference, Nagovisi, 167; Zinacantan,
   108
agency, 21-5, 278, 280-2, 287, 294-5,
   298-9; Foi, 257, 258, 265, 274, 276;
   Kodi, 178, 182, 185, 193, 195, 196,
   197, 198; Nagovisi, 150; Zinacantan,
   102, 106
alcohol, 112, 122
Alice Springs, 112-13, 121-2, 123, 126, 127
Alicurang (Warrabri), 112, 114-18, 119
Allen, M., 7, 150, 173n.23, 288-9
alliance, 178
Alyawarra, 113, 114, 118
Amphlett Is., 233
ancestors, Kodi, 176, 178, 179, 180,
   183-84, 191, 193, 206; Kwaio, 75
Andaman Is., 297
antagonism, 3, 209, 225
Aranda, 113, 114
armshells, *see* shells; *see also* wealth
Atkinson, J.M., 1, 4, 14, 31n.11, 150, 156,
   165, 166, 279
Augé, M., 280
autonomy, 115, 131, 144-5, 147-8

Bachofen, J., 173n.23
Ballantyne, A., 235, 253n.7
Banoni, 151
Barrow Creek, 113
Bateson, G., 162, 299
Battaglia, D., 23, 239, 287
beauty, 245-6, 249-50; *see also*
   skin-changing
Beckett, N. T., 114
Bedamini, 259
beguinage, 127; *see also* nunnery
Bell, D., 1, 112-29
Biersack, A., 8, 23, 32n.16, 292, 298
big man, 2; Foi, 276-7; *see also mahoni*
birth, *see* childbirth
Bloch, J., 6
Bloch, M., 6, 159, 189, 285, 289-93
   passim, 297, 300, 301n.9, 302nn.10,
   11, 12, 14
blood, feud, 53-5; as matrilineal substance
   179, 180, 197
boar's tusk pendant, 232, 233, 239-44,
   251, 253n.7, 254n.8; *see also* wealth
Bourdieu, P., 97, 280
Bourque, S., 11, 31n.3
bride, 177, 186, 191
brideservice, 106, 107, 108
bridewealth, Foi, 264, 265, 267, 274;
   Kalauna, 230, 233, 235, 241, 251;
   Kodi, 180, 186; Zinacantan, 106, 108
Bricker, V. R., 100
brother, *see* sibling relations
Brown. P., 163
Buchbinder, G., 156, 163, 297, 301n.7
Buin, 131, 154, 166, 171nn.2, 9, 173n.26
Burridge, K., 6
Bwaidoka (Goodenough Is.), 251, 253,
   254n.9

319